Mods To Rockers

By

COLIN STODDART

Dedication

This book is dedicated to my family – to my wife Pat, for patiently listening to all my group stories over the years and then painstakingly editing my story, when to her surprise, she even discovered some new stories along the way!

To my two sons, Daniel and Thomas, and their encouragement to write the book, suggested after I constantly regaled my stories to their friends, always at the most inappropriate time!

And a very big thank you to my band mates for simply being there at the time to join me on our rock 'n' roll journey and providing me with life-long memories and friendships.

Thanks also to my 'British Invasion' friends at Booknook.biz for doing such a great job.

Finally to Aaron Williams, graphic designer, Daniel's friend and a great vocalist, for designing the book cover – www.electrosetstudio.com

For more group visuals visit our website at –

https://thecandles1960s.wordpress.com

INTRODUCTION

This is the story of Colin, a young man bearing witness to one of the greatest decades Britain ever knew – the 60s. From his last day at school to supporting The Who, this was the time for the Mods to rise and throw off the shackles of previous generations and their grey and dreary music.

Post-war Britain in the early 60s was recovering from the financial pressures of the Second World War, and the death knell had sounded as its once-mighty Empire slowly sank beneath the waves. Britain had reached its own 'crossroads'. Now, with peacetime conscription ending, no uniforms to wear and no regulation 'short back and sides' haircuts to endure, a new civilian army of youths was entering the workplace. Being the most prosperous decade since World War II, the working youth of the day now had a disposable income with money to burn.

This was a new battleground and the electric guitar became the weapon of choice. From the first battle between Mods and Rockers at Cockett Wick in 1961, to the notorious beachfront confrontations with coppers in Brighton in later years, Colin and his generation were sounding the drum for a new style, beat and ethos to take Britain into a brighter and more confident future.

His prevailing love of the guitar and rock 'n' roll music had prompted him to form a group with his friends at school, and so he pursued a parallel career over the next eight years while continuing to work in the bank. In a world consumed with music, his banking career took back seat, but would teach him how to count banknotes at high speed, a useful requisite should the group hit the big time and make it's millions.

Follow the tale of a young man's journey into adulthood as he faces jail for being among a group of Mods who took on the Rockers in the first-ever major altercation near Clacton in 1961 – with the press coverage read by his non too impressed bank bosses – their pursuit of stardom, the opening of a new scene laced with Purple Hearts', and the call of the dingy pubs and clubs, a million miles away from the super groups of the 60s like The Stones and The Beatles.

Learn of their travels during the very early years of the British rock 'n' roll era, sharing a stage with veteran American rock 'n' roll stars and eventually becoming the desired support group for many emerging British acts like The Who, Tom Jones, The Dave Clark Five, The Merseybeats and The Love Affair, plus numerous other popular groups of the time. An unforgettable highlight moment for the author and his pals was to meet and play on the same stage with one of his childhood heroes, the wild man of rock 'n' roll, Jerry Lee Lewis.

The new youth culture of the 60s took on the establishment and helped change the world forever. From a grimy black and white beginning, to a fun loving colourful 'fab' world known as the 'swinging sixties'. And Colin saw it all.

Table of Contents

1

THE BATTLE OF COCKETT WICK – 4 AUGUST 1961

I had walked out of school a year ago straight into permanent work and, now aged 17, I was about to undertake my first holiday without my parents, spending two weeks in a caravan with three close friends.

This is the story of the first major confrontation between the Mods and Rockers ever recorded in the British national press. Most people will have heard of the legendary battles between the Mods and Rockers that took place on the beaches of Brighton in the mid 1960s, made famous by the cult film 'Quadrophenia' (1979) and based on The Who's Mod-nostalgia album of the same name. The Who were a British group formed in 1964, and their early publicity machine billed them as one of the first Mod groups of their generation. A more recent film entitled 'Brighton Rock' (2010) was set in Brighton during the 60s, and one scene contains a very realistic backdrop of Mods and Rockers clashing on the beaches there.

Articles still continue to be written on the subject and the events are re-told again and again on TV and radio to this day. Many books have been published describing the events and one book in particular has become the definitive social science book on the subject. It is called 'Folk Devils and Moral Panics: Creation of Mods and Rockers', written by Professor Stanley Cohen. However, all the books refer to the first violent confrontation between the Mods and the Rockers as taking place over the Easter weekend in April 1964 in Clacton-on-Sea.

Wrong! They all fail to acknowledge that the first actual skirmish between the Mods and Rockers took place nearly three years earlier over the August Bank holiday weekend in 1961 in a country lane close to a sleepy village called St Osyth, located six miles outside of Clacton. Because the terms Mods and Rockers hadn't yet been recognised by the national press at the time, the affray was never acknowledged as the very first clash between these two groups.

Why the sleepy Essex village of St Osyth? Maybe because it had on its outskirts a large, sprawling caravan site and had become a popular holiday destination spot, attracting many families and young people, especially those from deprived inner London areas. The incident might have remained a local story had it not been for a shotgun being fired that day. Within hours of the incident, local police had rounded up 30 perpetrators and confiscated two double-barrelled shotguns, a single barrelled shotgun and a selection of other small weapons, ranging from chains, studded belts, a bayonet and a knuckle-duster. Many discarded broken bottles were found at the scene. The two groups met face to face in Cockett Wick Lane, close to a small caravan site, and one local newspaper reported the conflict with the headline 'The Battle of Cockett Wick'.

The events of the day had been leaked by the Clacton police to local journalists, who in turn reported their version of events to various news agencies. No doubt, if journalists from the local and national press had actually been there, talking directly with the youths when they were released from Clacton police station later that day, they would have picked up on the term Mods and Rockers and established the reason behind this conflict. Also, any astute investigative reporter would have noted that the young people leaving the police station looked and dressed differently to the average young teenager of the day. But the story was big and deadlines had to be met, so the basic story was prone to some 'artistic journalism'.

The following day, 5 August 1961, The Daily Express's front page headline was 'Boys Battle at Camp' and the Daily Herald's front page declared '30 Arrests at Teenage Gang Fight'. Inside the more conservative

Daily Telegraph, the story was reported under a headline 'Gang Fight Youths had Shotguns'. However, the front page of the Daily Mail felt the need to embellish the story by stating in a bold front page headline '30 Campers Held After Wild West Battle'. The article went on to say '30 youths in Wild West outfits fought a pitched battle' and concluded that 'as they left the police station many of the youths still wore their cowboy hats, decorated with silver stars'. Total fabrication!

It wasn't until nearly three years later, over the Easter weekend of 1964, that a similar confrontation between the two rival groups took place in central Clacton, with numerous arrests again made by the police. However, by this time the national press had become aware of the existence of these two sub-cultures and the affray was widely reported. Now the opposing gangs of youths were referred to in the headlines as Mods and Rockers.

By the Whitsun and August Bank holiday weekends of that year, the national press was having a field day. 'Battles' between Mods and Rockers broke out simultaneously in popular seaside resorts in the south of England. The largest gathering by far took place in Brighton, when over one thousand Mods and Rockers clashed on the beaches and on the streets. Further serious outbreaks between these rival groups were reported in Margate, Bournemouth, Hastings, Southend-on-Sea, Broadstairs and Clacton-on-Sea. The Mods and Rockers phenomena had reached its zenith. There were further sporadic clashes during 1965 and 1966, but never with the ferocity of those earlier confrontations of 1964, and by the end of 1966 it was all but over. Youth culture was on the move again. Psychedelic music was coming to the fore and with this new sound, a new look. By the summer, a movement called 'flower power' had exploded into the 'Summer of Love' and the peace-loving hippy had arrived. Time had marched on, music and fashion tastes had changed, and the Mods and the Rockers had been relegated to the history books.

**FRONT PAGE HEADLINE IN THE DAILY MAIL
– SATURDAY 5 AUGUST 1961**

2

HAPPY HOLIDAYS – ST OSYTH CARAVAN SITE

This is my story of what actually happened on that fateful day at Cockett Wick and the events that led up to the confrontation.

St Osyth caravan site is situated just outside the lovely old village of St Osyth and positioned close to a stony beach on the Essex coast. The nearest major town is Clacton-on-Sea, a six-mile bus ride away. Clacton had for many years been a popular holiday destination with the working class families of London, who fled the big city in their droves every summer for their annual holidays beside the sea.

Little did anyone realise at the time that, within a few years, many of these regular annual visitors would be lured away to sunnier climes due to the emergence of High Street travel agents and budget holidays. Why spend two weeks on a caravan holiday in Britain and take a gamble on the weather being good when, for similar money, you could fly out to Spain, spend a fortnight in the sun in a hotel with full board, and drink yourself silly for next to nothing!

During my last year at school, I had formed a group and the four of us had become close friends. This was our first holiday together since leaving school and, more importantly, as working men or, as we liked to think of ourselves, working Mods. In the summer of 1960 we had proudly walked out of St Edward's School for the very last time. John Wilkinson, Martin Palmer and John Rixon (nicknamed JG) had taken up apprenticeships and I had entered the Westminster Bank. Now, a year later, we were going on our first holiday without our parents, with money in our pockets and suitcases filled with the latest Mod gear.

The four of us just stood there as the coach accelerated away in a cloud of dust and exhaust fumes. We continued to watch it as it made its way up the road between the seemingly never-ending rows of caravans. As far as the eye could see, there were hundreds and hundreds of white caravans standing side by side in neat rows, with not a single tree in sight.

The coach had conveniently dropped us outside the site's main office, so in we went to register and pay for our two-week stay. We were subjected to a little preamble about the site's rules and regulations, and where the clubhouse and cafe were situated. Finally, the keys were handed over and the exact position of our caravan was pointed out to us on a large wall chart.

Off we trundled, up the road in the general direction of where we had been shown, but within five minutes we were lost. Everywhere just looked the same. Where the heck was row R? One minute we crossed row P, so we must be getting closer, then it was row T. We had just decided to split up into pairs when suddenly there it was, row R. Now all we had to do was find caravan number 55.

As we continued along row R, the caravans were definitely getting bigger and, having taken on the responsibility of booking up the holiday, I was beginning to feel pretty pleased with myself. It looked like we were going to be spending the next two weeks living in a large luxurious caravan similar to the ones we were passing by. I really thought I'd cracked it.

Suddenly, ahead of us, JG yelled out 'Here it is' and, as we caught up with him, it all went very quiet. The four of us dropped our cases and just stood there aghast. Not a word was said for a moment as we eyed up this small caravan, sandwiched between two much larger, newer models. It was by far the smallest and shabbiest caravan around and was certainly in need of a good coat of paint. From the styling, it looked pre-war and had certainly seen better days. 'Didn't you know when you booked the holiday that it was going to be such a small caravan?' someone asked.

'You ungrateful lot' I replied. 'That's all that was available when I telephoned a few weeks ago.'

Not wishing to be drawn into a further slanging match, I dropped my suitcase and quickly unlocked the door. We all piled in to view our new home for the next two weeks. It was very cramped. To the left of the door was a small table with bench seats either side and opposite was a small cooking range and sink. A small door further along revealed a tiny loo, and at end of the caravan were two single beds. Privacy was provided at each window by net curtains plus blue and white gingham check ones.

Having checked out the interior, JG said 'So what's the sleeping arrangement then?' I suggested 'Let's toss a coin to see who sleeps where.' I didn't want to sleep near Martin, who had already gained a reputation as an early riser and prone at night to making rather loud grunting noises in an effort to clear his throat before falling off to sleep. 'OK' piped up John, 'I'll tell you what. I'll sleep this end of the caravan and Martin the other end. We'll toss a coin to see who sleeps up this end with me.' The coin was tossed, caught, and now lay hidden by John's left hand. 'What'll it be Colin, heads or tails?' called John. 'Tails' I said. I held my breath. 'Tails' he shouted. Thank goodness! Poor old JG was going to spend the next fortnight bedded next to Martin. A very clever move by John. Obviously Martin's reputation had preceded him.

A week into our holiday, we had arrived back at the caravan site, having spent an evening in Clacton town centre just mooching around, and decided to investigate the caravan site's social club before retiring to bed. We were expecting to hear music and a general hum of people enjoying themselves as we approached the club, but it was eerily quiet. However, the lights were still on inside.

As we entered, it was immediately apparent that earlier there had been some sort of trouble. In one corner, tables and chairs were overturned and broken glass was strewn across the floor. As we stood surveying the scene, two young men approached us and the taller one, wearing a navy blue pork pie hat, explained what had happened. Apparently, only half an hour earlier, the club had been packed with holidaymakers enjoying themselves, when some Rockers from another caravan site burst in and started a fight. Now the only people left were just a handful of young men surveying the damage. Bar staff were righting the overturned tables and chairs and sweeping up the broken glass, but still on some tables were the drinks and packets of crisps that had been abandoned in the rush to evacuate the club when the fighting broke out.

'We need your help brothers. We are rounding up as many Mods on the site as possible so we can get our own back.' We were well chuffed at being referred to as 'brothers' and being instantly recognised as Mods simply by the way our hair was cut and the clothing we were wearing. The smaller guy, wearing Levi jeans and a button-down shirt with a tie, cut in. 'We're all meeting at the cafe, the one situated at the entrance to the caravan site, tomorrow morning at nine o'clock. Can we rely on you to be there to help us out?' None of us really wanted to get involved – we were on holiday just having fun. Then, to our disbelief, our unelected spokesman Martin suddenly piped up, 'Sure, happy to help out. We'll be at the cafe at nine o'clock tomorrow.' Now where did that sudden surge of confidence suddenly come from? It wasn't like we had ever been involved in street fighting before! Well that was it – we were now well and truly committed! We said our farewells and filed out of the club. Once outside, I just couldn't contain myself. 'Christ Marty, fancy saying we'd be there! Suppose there's a fight tomorrow, then what?' Heads nodded in agreement, but Martin was obviously elated by the whole affair. 'Oh come on you lot, it'll be fun – I bet you nobody turns up anyway. Look on the bright side – at least we'll get a good breakfast out of it.'

I awoke with a start the next morning. Who the hell was that banging on the side of the caravan? I lay there for a moment trying to gather my thoughts. Oh no! It came to me in a flash – the night before we had promised to help some Mods gang up on some Rockers. For a brief moment I panicked. I just wasn't thinking clearly. Surely the Rockers hadn't tracked us down and were making a pre-emptive strike?

I was aware of John moving next to me and, as I turned over, he was peering out between a crack in the drawn curtains. The banging was getting louder. Suddenly John yelled out 'It's only bloody Palmer' and pulled back the curtains. Seeing John at the window, Martin yelled out 'Come on you lot, we're supposed to be down at the cafe at nine o'clock.' Inside John shouted 'For Christ's sake, we're on holiday, give us a break' and, from the other end of the caravan, JG yelled out, 'Bloody well go back to bed will you!' Martin took no notice and continued his crusade to get us up.

We were now all fully awake and, after a lot of deliberation, I finally stressed the point. 'Of course, if we don't turn up, what are we going to say if we bump into those blokes again. We made a promise and we'll look like cowards if we don't go.' That apparently was the deciding factor. We got up, dressed in our finest Mod garb, and set off to the local cafe.

We entered the cafe to find it packed full of young Mods and stood for a few minutes waiting for a free table, nervously looked around to see if we could spot the two guys from last night who had asked us for our assistance. Suddenly a table became available by the window and we managed to get there before anyone else. Now we were seated, the number one priority was to get some food down us.

We were tucking into a good old fry-up when the door opened and a head appeared. It was one of the guys from last night. 'Hurry up you lot, the Rockers are coming down the road.' The reaction inside was instant. There was a deafening clatter of knives and forks being dropped onto plates, cups hitting saucers and chairs scraping across the floor, as about 15 young men evacuated the small cafe and spilled out onto Jaywick Sands Lane.

Apart from a family of four sitting in the corner, we were the only people left in the cafe still tucking into our food. Suddenly our friend from last night was banging on the window and calling for us to come out and join them. 'Mods to the fore' I thought. Reluctantly we abandoned the remainder of our breakfasts and went outside to see what was going on.

WE HEAD OFF INTO BATTLE

There they were, about ten of them, too far away to identify them by their distinctive clothing, but they had to be the Rockers. Some were standing on the running board of a slow moving black car, while the remainder jogged either side. Suddenly they ground to a halt.

They surveyed us as we surveyed them. They were outnumbered two to one and the odds were on our side, but the four of us had no appetite to head off into battle, odds or no odds. What were we doing here in the first place – remaining loyal to two young men we had met only briefly the night before? This was ridiculous! We hadn't really wanted to get involved in any actual fighting – we weren't the fighting types. What initially was bravado was now turning sour. We hadn't even been able to finish our juicy breakfasts!

The night before, we had all decided that if we kept to the back of the Mod group, it would give us a certain degree of safety, so we surreptitiously worked our way to the rear. We turned and watched with trepidation as both sides stood their ground and just stared at each other. The air was electric. With a bit of luck, both sides would see the futility of it all and call it a day. The Rockers were clearly outnumbered.

It had never occurred to any of us at the time, nor since, or even now, as I write this story some 45-odd years after the event – how come the Rockers knew that the Mods would be waiting for them in the local cafe the next morning? Had the Mods arranged the previous night to meet them face-to-face the next morning at 9am?

Suddenly, the car did a three-point turn and sped off, with the Rockers standing on the running boards hanging on for grim death, while the remainder of the gang took flight across a nearby cornfield. That action immediately triggered the Mods to take up the chase and a mass of bodies suddenly surged forward. Meanwhile, at the back of the throng we kept pace, and felt pretty safe, jogging along behind. As we ran, wisecracks were being made which brought about some nervous laughter. 'Its all your bloody fault Palmer' I heard John shout, and we all agreed. After all, he was the one responsible for getting us involved in this mess.

Little did we realise, as we jogged along the road, what we were letting ourselves in for and that our actions would be replicated a number of years later by future Mods and Rockers, to eventually be recorded as part of Britain's social history.

The Mods were now in hot pursuit. When they reached the spot where the Rockers had separated, they started climbing over a fence and into a cornfield that belonged to Cockett Wick Farm. It must have been at this stage, as we approached the fence and climbed over, that we became separated from each other. As I jumped over a small stream, I suddenly realised I was on my own – where were the others? The corn by now had already been flattened by the advance party of Rockers and now even more so by the advancing Mods. I started to jog behind a couple of guys in front of me. There was no sign of Martin or the two Johns – where were they? At the top of the field was the local caravan site's rubbish dump and standing close by was the guy wearing the pork pie hat. He yelled out 'Grab some bottles mate – arm yourself!'

I don't know why, but I just did as he said. Probably bravado again – or just sheer stupidity. I grabbed a couple of empty bottles, broke them against a nearby log and casually walked through an opening in the bushes into Cockett Wick Lane. Having been one of the last to arrive, I now found myself in this narrow country lane at the front of this 20-odd mob of angry young men, brandishing a broken bottle in each hand! This wasn't the plan at all. We had planned to remain at the back of the gang for relative safety. Now I was on my own, standing next to three strangers. I started to panic – was I really going to use these broken bottles? I wanted to run. I was frightened. Where were the others? For all I knew they were back at the cafe wondering where I was.

Suddenly I froze. About 30 yards ahead, rounding a bend in the lane came the Rockers. They were marching towards us, literally shoulder to shoulder, with the guy in the front swinging a large chain and another had what looked like a long dark brown stick. Upon seeing us they halted. My brain was racing – should I run for it now before it was too late? But still I didn't want to be branded a coward. Only 15 yards separated us and I could now clearly see the faces of our adversaries. Nobody spoke. We just eyed one another up. Who was going to make the first move? Then events happened so quickly. I didn't see anyone move. Bang! A large branch from a tree overhanging the lane fell to the ground in front us followed by falling leaves. An instant decision was made – 'Shit, I'm off!'

I dropped the bottles and darted back through the opening in the bushes, not looking back. It was every man for himself! All I could think about, as I ran over the flattened corn, was a gun had been fired! Had anyone been hurt? Reaching the bottom of the field, I leapt over the stream, clambered over the fence, and ran down the long straight road towards the cafe.

I was one of the first to arrive back at the cafe, which was quickly filling up with the retreating Mods, but there was no sign of Martin or John or JG. The firing of the gun was the main topic of conversation and, as we traded our individual views of events, I had one eye on the door. Where were the others? The door suddenly opened and, to my great relief, there was Martin. He looked around, saw me, and came and sat down. We both laughed nervously as we discussed our narrow escape. Martin had also found himself on his own after we had crossed the fence and since then, he hadn't seen either of the Johns. It turned out that, after the shotgun went off, Martin had also cut through the bushes and fled across the cornfield, unaware at the time that I was just ahead of him.

The door opened again and there stood JG. Were we pleased to see each other! 'Have you seen John?' I asked. 'No' replied JG. 'As soon as the gun went off, we turned and ran down the lane like mad, and that was the last I saw of him.' So, where was John? When it appeared that everyone had made his way back to the cafe, we began to ask around if anyone had seen him.

We were able to piece together from different eyewitness accounts, that after the shotgun had been fired, everyone scattered in various directions. Some went through the gap in the bushes and fled back across the cornfield like Martin and I did, while others had turned and run down the lane away from the Rockers. Two Mods told us that, as they approached the bottom of Cockett Wick Lane, they saw a police car and were sure they had spotted youths getting into the back. As soon as they saw the police car, they had jumped across a ditch, through a hedge and fled across a cornfield. As the car started to head up the lane towards them, other youths had apparently avoided detection by simply throwing themselves into the ditch, hiding until the car passed by.

We sat there, huddled around a table, contemplating our next move. If youths had been seen getting into the back of the police car, perhaps one of them was John. We had no idea how many Mods had joined in the action earlier that morning, and many had already dispersed back to their caravans. Another group of youths sitting at the next table over-heard our conversation and confirmed that a couple of their pals were missing as well. We all agreed to wait it out a bit longer, just in case they had remained in hiding. After half an hour, when nobody had appeared, I volunteered to telephone the main police station in Clacton to establish if they were holding our friend.

So the three of us left the cafe, crossed the road and stood outside a red telephone box, discussing what I was going to say. We all then squeezed into the telephone box. I picked up the directory that was hanging on a chain and looked up the number of Clacton police station. I put money into the machine, picked up the telephone and, after a short wait, gave the operator the telephone number of the police station.

A CUNNING MOVE BY THE POLICE

'Good afternoon, Clacton police station' came the response. 'Oh… er… hello,' I said. 'I believe you may be holding a friend of mine called John Wilkinson at the police station. If that's the case, could I talk to some-body about it please?' 'Yes, one moment.' After about a minute, a voice came back on the line 'Just putting you through.' Suddenly a deep voice broke the silence. 'Hello, may I take your name please?' I gave him my name and explained the situation. 'Yes, we do have a Mr John Wilkinson with us plus two other young men who are currently helping us with our enquiries concerning a confrontation that took place earlier this morning near the Cockett Wick Farm outside of St. Osyth. Were you involved at all?' I had to think quickly. Even if I admitted to being involved, they had no idea where I was calling from. 'Yes I was.' 'Well, would you be prepared to help us with our enquiries? The quicker we have all the facts, the quicker we can release these young men. Also, it would help to speed up the process if any of the other people involved volunteered to give us information as well.' Now what do I do, I thought to myself. I made a quick decision. 'I'll discuss this with my friends and call you back' and, before the officer could utter another word, I hurriedly put the telephone down. I certainly didn't want to be faced with any further questions. Anyway, we needed to talk with the other Mods back at the cafe. Hopefully they would be prepared to help us out and give their version of events to the police as well. Arriving back at the cafe, I recognised Pork Pie Hat sitting at a table in the corner with five other Mods. As I approached, they looked up. I told them I had contacted the Clacton police station and yes, they were holding our friend and two others. I went on to explain that they needed to interview any people who witnessed the event and to take down their statements, which would help in the early release of the three. Immediately Pork Pie Hat stood up saying 'Us Mods must stick together.' I wonder if he sleeps in that bloody hat, I thought to myself. This was the same guy who had asked us for our help the previous night at the social club. 'Don't worry' he said. 'Leave it to me. I'll round up everyone involved. I know where they're staying and we'll meet you outside the telephone box over the road.' I was now totally convinced that this guy had taken on the role as our unofficial leader, but I was well chuffed. A united front meant that we could get John and the other two guys released quickly, and get back to the rest of our holiday – how young and naive we all were! The consequences of what happened next would haunt us for many years to come.

Within ten minutes of leaving the cafe, there was quite a crowd of

Mods milling around the telephone box and I confidently called the police station again. I explained to the same constable that I had rounded up most of the people who had been involved in the skirmish earlier in the day. He sounded very pleased, and then asked exactly where we were and how many of us were there. Once I had explained our whereabouts and numbers, he responded by saying, 'We should be with you in about ten minutes, so don't go away.'

We chatted amongst ourselves as we waited for the police to arrive, everyone in high spirits. This affair would soon be over and our friends released. Eventually a convoy of seven police vehicles, ranging from marked police cars, a Land Rover and some unmarked saloon cars, pulled up by the telephone box. There were two police officers in each vehicle and they greeted us with friendly smiles on their faces. The officer driving the lead vehicle wound down his window and said, 'Hello boys, sorry to keep you waiting.' He switched off the engine and got out of the car, apologising for having to drag us down to the station. He went on to explain that before they could release our friends, we had to accompany them to Clacton police station where statements would be taken from each of us and assured us that they would bring us back to the caravan site when we had finished. The overall mood was still very light-hearted and I just couldn't get over how friendly the police officers were.

The other officers remained in their vehicles, and we were politely asked to get into the back of each of them in threes and fours, where our names and addresses would be recorded. We did as we were told, and when the final name and address had been noted, the convoy headed back to Clacton police station. The atmosphere in our car as we drove along was still friendly, with the odd joke being cracked as we made our way into central Clacton. Not long now and John would be released. I bet he'll be pleased to see us, I thought to myself.

The convoy finally pulled into a walled yard to the rear of the police station and, one by one, the vehicles parked. As the last car entered, two waiting police officers hastily closed the two steel doors, thus sealing the courtyard. It was then that the friendly atmosphere instantly changed. A police officer started shouting at us 'Come on you lot, move it' and we were directed towards a large open steel door. People ahead of me sauntered into the room, and I could hear someone inside yell out 'OK, form a line over there. Come on, quickly now.'

As I walked into the room, the first person I recognised, standing to my immediate right, was the driver who had been so friendly while he drove us here. 'Hello again,' I said. 'How long do you think this is all going to take?' But his persona had completely changed. There was no response at all. He just scowled at me, grabbed my arm, swung me round and pushed me up against the wall. In a loud voice, and to demonstrate his authority, he shouted out, 'Shut up and stand over there.' There was immediate silence in the room. A few moments later, somebody else asked a similar question, but again was told to shut up.

After the last person had entered the room, the steel door was slammed shut and locked. We were all huddled at one end of the room facing four police offers sitting behind desks. A few minutes passed in silent disbelief as the reality of what was happening began to dawn on us. In our stupid naivety, we had all been well and truly conned by the police. Their initial friendly approach from the outset had been well orchestrated in order to lure us to the police station. We had been like lambs to the slaughter.

Suddenly a door opened and a senior officer marched into the room and stood before us. 'You are all under arrest and face a charge of riotous assembly. You will be released on bail pending a future court appearance. My officers will proceed to fill out a charge sheet for each of you and your fingerprints will then be taken. Please form a queue behind each desk.' I looked around, trying to see if I could locate Martin and JG and catch their reaction, but I couldn't see either of them. Where were they? People around me were discussing the implications in hushed tones. Close to me, somebody shouted out, 'We were told we only had to give you a statement. Nobody said anything about being arrested.' The senior officer immediately responded, 'I have explained to you why you have been detained and what the procedures will be so, in the meantime, be quiet and just do as you are told. Start forming queues at each desk so my officers can make a start.' I felt a shiver run through my body. Suddenly I was frightened as I stood in this bleak, dimly lit, cold room, waiting to answer questions and to have my fingerprints taken – fingerprints! I wasn't a criminal! One of my main concerns at that moment was what would my mum and dad say when they found out! It was hard to believe that just over an hour ago, we had voluntarily stood around outside a telephone box, chatting and laughing amongst ourselves, waiting for the police to arrive. Now what lay ahead?

I was beginning to realise that we had utterly failed to comprehend the severity and the implications of a gun being fired in a public place. Perhaps it had been the fact that no physical contact or violence of any kind had taken place, before or after the gun had been fired, which had made this event appear pretty harmless to us.

Something I have thought about over the years was did the Rockers carry the shotguns (three were eventually found by the police) simply to just scare us, but not intending to actually use them? Or had the shotgun been fired deliberately to disperse us or was it to warn us that they intended to use the guns on us if necessary, as they were outnumbered two to one. Fortunately for everyone concerned, that one shot fired over our heads resulted in everyone dispersing in all directions, thus breaking up the confrontation and preventing any further violence. However, if the incident with the shotgun had never occurred on that day, would there have been a lot more physical and bloody violence?

I, for one, was scared out of my mind moments before the gun had been fired. I wasn't a street fighter. Yes, I was out for a laugh that morning, but nothing more sinister. But being involved in physical violence had never entered my head. Why, for some inexplicable reason, had I been coerced into brandishing a broken bottle in each hand, when I had no intention at all of using them?

I was deep in thought when my name was called and, because of my slow reaction, an officer grabbed my arm. 'Move it' he said and yanked me up. The officer behind the desk went through the usual procedure establishing who I was, full name, address, and date of birth. When it came to next of kin, I gave my parents' names and pointed out that I was still living at home. The next question was my worst nightmare. 'Can I have your home telephone number? We will need to contact your parents to arrange bail.'

Oh my God, it suddenly occurred to me – my parents were on a driving holiday in Switzerland with Martin's mother and father. They still had over a week left of their holiday before they returned to England and I had no way of knowing where they were to contact them. When I explained this to the officer, my charge sheet was put in a separate tray and, without looking up, he said 'We'll look into this and let you know the outcome.' I was about to ask the 64,000-dollar question, was I to remain in custody while waiting for my parents' return, when he looked up and yelled 'Next!'

As I turned away, I was directed towards another table where my fingerprints were taken. I was then asked to empty everything out my pockets into a large brown envelope and my name was written on the outside. I was informed the contents would be returned to me after my bail release.

I turned and made my way to the back of the room where everyone was congregating. Martin was standing alone, leaning against the wall and, as I approached, he looked up. I could tell immediately he was as frightened and confused as I was. 'Am I pleased to see you' I said. 'Have you seen JG?' 'Yes, he's over there' pointing him out in one of the queues. Martin's main concern was the same as mine. 'Who's going to bail us out if our parents aren't in the country?' I told him that I had asked the same question and was told they'd get back to me and that we would just have to wait and see. JG finally joined us and we stood there voicing our various concerns in hushed tones.

INCARCERATION

One of the officers who had been filling out the forms stood up and faced us. 'Can I have quiet.' There was an immediate hush. 'You will now be taken to a cell and will remain there until bail release. We will be contacting your next of kin and, as soon as they arrive and bail is settled, you will be released.' My God, I thought, things were going from bad to worse. Now we were going to be put in a cell! We looked at one another in total disbelief. The officer continued, 'Please form a line in front of this door', and everybody started shuffling around forming a line.

We were led in single file down a staircase that opened out into a stone floored quadrangle surrounded by cells. At least five of the cell doors were wide open. The first eight people in the line were told to remove any ties, belts and shoes, and to leave them in a pile on the floor. When that process was completed, they were directed into an empty cell and the door locked behind them. It may be surprising, but many of the Mods on that day had gone into battle wearing ties! The dress code for Mods at the time was Levi jeans or baggy pleated trousers and a lounge shirt with a plain coloured or regimental tie. Some Mods had also been wearing the favoured Fred Perry short-sleeved cotton shirt, a cotton bomber jacket, or long woollen knitted waistcoat with leather buttons, and moccasins or pointed leather shoes. We were Mods to the core, whatever the occasion!

This process continued and, as it came to us, an officer yelled out, 'Two of you over here. Remove your ties, belts and shoes and put them with that lot' pointing to a pile on the floor. The cell door was unlocked, held open and, with a nod of the officer's head, Martin and I walked in and the door slammed behind us.

The cell was already occupied with about six or seven other youths. Some were sprawled over a single bed, while others sat on the floor with their backs against the wall. They talked quietly amongst themselves and hardly gave us a glance as we came in. Martin and I just stood there with our backs against the door. I noticed they all had slicked back greasy hair with long sideboards and wore drainpipe trousers and suddenly realised that we'd only been locked up with some of the Rockers who had been picked up earlier this morning by the police! How ridiculous! Only hours earlier these guys had been the enemy and had fired a shotgun, thankfully over our heads, and now we were sharing a cell with them! One of them looked across at me and spoke. 'Were you involved in that fight outside St Osyth this morning?' I hesitated and, before I could say anything, Martin piped up 'Yes we were.' I held my breath but nothing further was said and they carried on talking amongst themselves.

With such little available space in the cell, Martin and I had no option but to remain standing by the cell door and just kept to ourselves. I peered through the small hatch in the cell door and looked around as much as I could. I saw other faces peering out of the cells, but strangely no police officers were present.

I was just looking at all the shoes, belts and ties piled up on the floor outside, when I spotted a pair of black moccasin shoes with a brass buckle on the side. John Wilkinson had an identical pair. Could they be John's? Was he in one of these cells? I had the identical pair of shoes but in brown. We had bought them together in Saxone shoe shop in Princes Street in Edinburgh, whilst on a holiday in Ayr in Scotland last year with my parents.

The last time I had seen John was when we were running up the road, chasing the Rockers. I'd lost sight of him once we'd climbed over the fence and into the field. I turned to Martin and we both peered out of the hole. I pointed to the pile of clothes outside the cell door opposite. 'See that pair of shoes, the black moccasins with the brass buckles. Well, John has an identical pair. I wonder if he's down here too.' 'Call out his name' Martin suggested. So I did, and a face appeared at the hole in the cell door opposite. 'Is that you Colin?' It was John! 'Am I pleased to see you!' I called out. Then another face appeared in the cell next door. It was JG. He must have recognised our voices. What a relief! Well, at least we were all together again, albeit sharing three separate police cells!

After a couple of hours, footsteps could be heard coming from the concrete staircase and five officers appeared. One announced 'We are going to unlock the cell doors and you will be led upstairs where you will be given some food and drink.' We were pleased just to get out of those claustrophobic cells and stretch our legs. We made our way back to the same room where hours earlier we had had our personal details recorded and in single file went up to a table to collect a mug of tea and a fried egg sandwich. Both were just about warm and it crossed my mind to complain and also to inform them that I preferred my egg to be well done, but I thought better of it! As we were eating, a door burst open and in marched a senior officer. He made his way to the centre of the room, stood there silently for a moment and, when the room was quiet, he announced in a loud voice, 'Your next of kin have now been contacted and informed of your arrest and that bail will be required for your release. As and when your next of kin arrive and the bail release is completed, you will be notified of the date of your pending court appearance. After that you will be free to leave.' Before anybody could ask any questions, he spun round and left the room. Within a few minutes, we were back inside our respective cells and the doors slammed behind us.

The atmosphere inside our cell was now pretty subdued. I think the reality of the mess we had gotten ourselves into was beginning to dawn on us all. It was bad enough spending time in a police cell, but a court case! My parents were going to go mad! And what if the bank finds out! Would I lose my job? If only Martin had slept in this morning. If only we hadn't bothered to meet up with the other Mods at the local cafe this morning. If only John had managed to make his way back to the cafe after the gun had been fired, instead of being picked up by the police. If only I hadn't been so naïve when I'd called the police station, believing that they just wanted to ask us a few questions before releasing John. But if I hadn't called the police station, John would be sharing this whole frightening episode with two strangers.

I was miles away when Martin suddenly said 'Who do you think will stand bail for us? Arty Rixon?' He was JG's father. I thought about it for a moment. 'I guess so. Otherwise there's only Olive and I doubt she'd travel down to Clacton on her own'. Olive was John's mother and single at the time. Martin nodded in agreement. We both then went quiet, thinking about our situation. 'Can you imagine the reaction there's going to be when our parents find out about what has happened when they get back from their holidays!' 'Don't remind me' said Martin. 'I was just thinking the same thing myself.'

RELEASED ON BAIL

Suddenly there was a noise outside our cell. An officer called out 'Stephen Jones, please make yourself known. Your parents have arrived to bail you out.' A face appeared at a cell door opposite. 'I'm in here' came the response, and a policeman went up to the cell window and asked 'Are you Stephen Jones?' 'Yes sir' came the reply. 'Please confirm your home address' and, as the address was called out, the officer looked down a list on his clipboard and made a mark. Another officer unlocked the cell door and out came Stephen Jones who was escorted up the stairs.

Within minutes, the same procedure took place again, and another youth was escorted upstairs to waiting parents. No sooner had they disappeared, than two more officers were taking another person out of a cell. This continued for quite a while and Martin and I surmised that many parents, most probably living east of central London and having received the telephone call from Clacton police station, had caught the same train out of Liverpool Street station. We waited expectantly, and after about 20 minutes we heard footsteps coming down the stairs. Two officers appeared and called out, 'John Wilkinson, John Rixon, Martin Palmer and Colin Stoddart. Please make yourselves known.' At last we were getting out and, as our cell door was opened, the remaining half a dozen Rockers nodded to us as we walked out. How strange, less than 12 hours previously, these guys, given half the chance, would have laid into us causing who knows what injuries.

I was the first to be brought out of our cell, with Martin following directly behind me. We stood together and watched as John and JG emerged from their cells. The odd nod and smile said enough – we were so relieved to be reunited again. We collected our shoes, ties and belts from the pile on the floor and were led up the stairs and out into the station's front office where we came face to face with John's mum, Olive. It looked like she was standing bail for all four of us. The only person to speak was a police officer. 'Here are your personal belongings' and he handed us four large manila envelopes, each marked with our names. 'Please sign here that you have received all of your belongings' and after a quick look in the envelopes, we obediently placed our signatures in the large book.

He continued with a very matter of fact attitude, 'Mrs Jones has agreed to stand bail for all four of you, and you are being bailed to appear at Clacton-on-Sea Magistrates Court on Monday 28 August 1961 at 10.30am on a charge of riotous assembly.' After pausing for breath, he then went on to quote the penalties for breaching the conditions of bail. All I kept thinking was please can we get out of here! Then I heard those magical words. 'Each of you are to sign here and then you are free to go.' Hastily we signed the release papers and next minute we were standing out in the street – free at last! We all gathered round Mrs Jones and thanked her profusely for travelling down to Clacton and bailing us out, and apologised to her for getting into trouble with the police.

By now it was early evening and Mrs Jones pointed out that by law, she was now responsible for all of us, and she wasn't prepared to leave us on our own at St Osyth to finish our holiday. Our hearts sank. We weren't really in a position to try to change her mind – our last hope was John. He promised his mother that we would all be on our best behaviour for the rest of the week, but she wasn't having any of it. By now the last train for London had left Clacton station, so Mrs Jones decided to return with us to St Osyth and to spend the night in our caravan.

In the morning we had to pack up our clothes and generally tidy up before vacating the caravan, and then we handed back the keys. Mrs Jones insisted on seeing us board the coach for Romford. She wasn't taking any chances and, because of a prior engagement, John accompanied his Mum and went home by train.

A week later, our respective parents returned from their joint continental holiday and Martin and I decided that we would confess our sins to our respective parents in the privacy of our own homes. Surprisingly, when I sat my parents down and explained what had happened, there wasn't the almighty explosion I had expected. Of course, they wanted to know all the facts but I have to confess I omitted to tell them that I had, at one stage, stood in Cockett Wick Lane brandishing a broken bottle in each hand. Now that really would have made me out to be a thug! Their greatest concern, and mine also, was how would my employers, the Westminster Bank, react to learning of my criminal activities. It made me smile at the thought. It certainly wouldn't look good for the bank if it ever came out in the press that a bank clerk had been involved in an affray where guns were used. It was amusing to think of thousands of people panicking around the country rushing into their local branches and withdrawing all their money!

The next few days were quite dramatic. My father decided to contact the other parents, suggesting that they hold a crisis meeting at the Stoddart family home, to discuss what they could do to help us. Our parents had briefly met one another over the past few years, but never all together under such circumstances. It was unanimously agreed that a barrister should be employed to handle our case and to represent us in court. Our parents would share the cost.

By now, we had all gone back to work and had about two weeks to go before our appearance at Clacton Magistrates Court. Our parents, quite understandably, were nervous in case we got into any more trouble, so we had to give personal undertakings that we wouldn't go to any dance halls and to generally steer clear of any pubs and cafes. A week before we were due to appear in court, we each received a letter from Essex County Constabulary informing us that the defence solicitors had requested an adjournment and that our court appearance at Clacton had now been postponed. Our bail had been extended and we now had to appear in court on Monday 11 September 1961.

I just wanted to get our appearance over and done with, but now we had to wait a further two weeks, and the social restrictions imposed by our parents remained in place. Banking in 1961 was a very staid and respected profession and it felt strange to be at work in the local branch of the Westminster Bank, knowing that soon I would be making an appearance in court. Could I keep it all under wraps without the bank ever finding out, whatever the outcome? My accomplice in trying to achieve this objective was to be my mother. At first she refused point blank to help me, but after much cajoling and, when I finally explained that I'd probably lose my job if the bank found out, she finally relented.

3

TRIALS AND TRIBULATIONS

Going anywhere with my dad, you always had to leave early to make sure you got there on time and nothing was ever left to the last minute. Always being on time was a way of life for him. This probably stemmed from his job as he was employed as a Time and Motion Study engineer at the Ford Motor Company in Dagenham. He worked in the Ford car seat assembly division and was responsible for improving production times. To achieve this, he would stand next to a production line worker and, using a stopwatch, time how long it took to cut fabric into sections for a seat. Or time a machinist to establish how long it took to sew the sections together. Or how long it took to insert the padding and assemble the finished seat. Once the fastest times were established, these became the guidelines that each worker was expected to achieve. I can only imagine that he was not the most popular person at the Ford plant!

THE TRIAL - CLACTON MAGISTRATES COURT - 11 SEPTEMBER 1961

Finally the big day had arrived and so the four of us, dressed in our best sombre suits and ties and sporting our newly cut hair, were ready to face our accusers. I wasn't surprised when my dad insisted we left early and so we all drove down to Clacton in plenty of time for our 10.30am court appearance. In the meantime, my mother had called the bank to explain

ESSEX COUNTY CONSTABULARY

Telephone No: Clacton 1314-5-6
Telex: 1969

Police Station,

CLACTON-ON-SEA.

In reply, please quote
Ref. No: P.P.11.9/J.B/E.S.

22nd August 1961.

Dear Sir,

With reference to the charge of riotous assembly at St. Osyth on the 4th August 1961, on which you were bailed to appear at Clacton-on-Sea Magistrates' Court at 10.30a.m on Monday, 28th August 1961, I write to inform you that this case will NOT now be proceeded with on this date, but will be adjourned until the same Court on Monday, 11th September 1961.

Your bail is extended accordingly and you are now required to attend Clacton-on-Sea Magistrates' Court at 10.30a.m on Monday, 11th September 1961, instead of 28th August 1961.

The adjournment is being made at the request of defence solicitors.

Yours faithfully,

Superintendent.

Mr. Colin STODDART,
55 Seymour Road,
ROMFORD,
Essex.

THE SUMMONS I RECEIVED FROM ESSEX COUNTY COUNCIL CONSTABULARY TO APPEAR AT CLACTON-ON-SEA MAGISTRATES COURT ON MONDAY 11 SEPTEMBER 1961.

that her son was feeling a bit feverish and wouldn't be going into work that day – good old mum!

Arriving in Clacton, we parked the cars and headed off to the Magistrates Court. As we approached the court, we could make out quite a few people milling around outside the entrance. It was interesting seeing the Mods and the Rockers again. Both groups were virtually unrecognisable, wearing their best suits and ties, and most of the Rockers, who always had the longest hair, had also been to the barbers shop for a good trim. Like us, they were all there with their parents.

The court doors were opened at 10.00am and we filed in, policemen directing the parents to the gallery, and us through swing doors to an area in the court that had been made available for us. It wasn't a very large court and was certainly not built to accommodate 30 suspects. We all sat huddled together on long dark wooden bench seats, which had obviously had been brought in specially to seat us as they didn't match the overall light oak panelling and other furniture in the court.

At 10.30am sharp we were all asked to stand and the judge entered the court by a side door. The charge of riotous assembly applied to 19 of us and our respective names were read out. A further charge of riotous assembly and carrying offensive weapons applied to the remaining 11 youths and their respective names were read out. We had all pleaded not guilty. As the story slowly unfolded, it reached the part where, following my telephone call to Clacton police station to enquire about John, a convoy of police vehicles was dispatched to pick us up outside the only telephone box on the St Osyth caravan site.

The judge ordered the 19 Mods to stand and gave instructions to sit down when their name was read out. It was confirmed that each vehicle contained two policemen, a driver and an accompanying officer. Seven vehicles were involved and each officer had to stand in the dock and state his name, rank and number, confirm his role on the day, and to relate his version of events. The accompanying officer, before leaving the dock, referred to a small notebook and read out the names of the youths who had entered his particular vehicle.

We had already listened to four officers giving the required information to the court and next to take the stand was the policeman who had recorded our names. He opened his notebook and read out three names and three people sat down. It was my turn next. I sat there nervously waiting for my name to be called out, but the officer closed his notebook, turned and left the dock. I couldn't understand it. I was sure I could recall giving my name as I climbed into the car. Eventually, when the last officer had left the dock, my name still hadn't been called out and I was the last remaining person still standing. I looked across at our barrister who had put his head down quickly, shuffling various sheets of paper. Had he spotted the glaring discrepancy?

It soon became apparent that the defence lawyers wanted actual clarification that the names recorded in the police notebooks matched those of the 30 suspects sitting in the court. So the judge stopped the proceedings and demanded that the seven non-driver officers were recalled to the dock to call out the names of the youths who had entered their respective vehicle. However, this time the judge insisted that as each name was called out, the youth in question should stand up, and remain standing, until all of the names had been read out. He reminded the officers that they were still under oath.

When the last policeman had left the dock, I was the only youth still seated. My mind was racing. What was happening here? Our barrister had obviously spotted this error earlier and was quick to point this out to the judge. 'Your Honour, my client, Colin Stoddart, still remains seated, so we must assume that he was not there on the day in question.' This was followed by some muted laughter from the gallery. The prosecution and the defence councils were huddled up together and talking in whispered tones. Confusion reigned for a few minutes.

There was no doubt that I had been there on the day in question. After all, I had been picked up by the police at St Osyth and, with others, driven to Clacton-on-Sea police station where we were arrested and incarcerated awaiting bail. The paperwork and the fingerprints could prove that. But what was embarrassing for the police and the prosecution council today was that it showed a weakness in their evidence. Our barrister used this error to point out to the court that the police were not infallible, asking, 'What other mistakes did the police make on that day?'

When the court reconvened after lunch and the judge was seated, he made an announcement. 'After careful consideration and, taking into account the complexities of this case together with the sheer number of defendants involved, I have decided that this court is not large enough to handle the case.' He then looked down to where we were all seated and continued, 'You will be summoned to appear at the next court of the Quarter Sessions for the County of Essex, to be held at Shire Hall, Chelmsford, Essex on Wednesday 27 September 1961, where you will be tried.' We were instructed to stand, and the judge made his exit from the court.

While we were still standing, the Clerk of the Court walked up to us and announced 'As and when your name is called, please come up to the desk and you will be handed a notice giving details of your next court appearance. In the meantime please remain seated.' I turned to John and whispered 'Bloody hell! My days as a junior bank clerk are definitely numbered!' Within half an hour we had all been handed our notices and we then joined our parents who had been waiting outside the courthouse. As we made our way to the car park it transpired that, while waiting for us, they had spoken earlier with our barrister who apparently didn't appear duly concerned that the case had now been transferred to Chelmsford Quarter Sessions. I remember thinking to myself 'of course he won't be concerned, he'll be earning more money out of it.' A date had been arranged for us to attend the barrister's office to discuss our next court appearance and our drive home was somewhat subdued to say the least.

For the next couple of weeks, all four of us were on our best behaviour. Our promise not to visit dance halls, pubs or cafes continued. We were fully aware that any confrontation with the law at this stage would have dire consequences for us. Then another letter arrived from the court advising us that the case had been adjourned until Monday 9 October at 9.45am. That meant just over another week to behave ourselves but, as you would expect from four young 17 to18-year-olds, we did break the rules slightly, and met up at Sherry's Cafe in Romford's South Street on a couple of occasions to have our Horlicks fix.

Horlicks came in a powered form. It was a malted beverage and the company advertised their product with the slogan 'Unwind for a good night's sleep.' We didn't drink this to make us sleep – we just enjoyed the thick creamy taste! Three to four teaspoons of Horlicks mixed with water into a paste, then hot milk added and stirred – this was how the drink was made at home. But in a cafe, now that was a totally different drinking experience providing they had the all-important Horlicks Mixer. The paste and hot milk, and here comes the secret, was put into an aluminium flask and whisked for two or three minutes in the Horlicks Mixer producing this very smooth drink with at least an inch of thick froth on the top – absolute heaven. In those days, you could buy a small pocket-sized tin of Horlicks tablets, each tablet individually wrapped. Looking back, for a product advertised to aid a good night's sleep, why would you want to eat Horlicks tablets during the day – another one of life's mysteries!

It will seem strange in today's youth culture of binge drinking, to read about four lads going to a café to drink Horlicks, but back in the early 60s, binge drinking by youths was unheard of. A Saturday night visit to a pub would be a round of drinks, with me usually taking a small glass of vodka and lime. One glass would suffice for most of the time, but on occasions it had been known for another round to be called. Even then, asking for a vodka and lime at the bar would produce some strange looks. But I just couldn't stand the taste of beer. Vodka was nearly tasteless and the lime made it acceptable. Eventually I did progress to a more masculine drink, 'half a larger and lime please landlord.'

Under instruction from our parents, and no doubt a suggestion by our barrister, the previous weekend the four of us had paid another visit to our local barber. Outside the shop, and attached to the wall in a vertical position above the door, was the traditional barber's sign – a long red and white revolving pole encased in a plastic tube. It always amazed me, watching this revolving pole, how the red rings worked their way down the pole and disappeared off the end!

We stood outside the barber's shop window staring at the various framed black and white sketches, which were lined up in a row along the inside window ledge. Each sketch showed a man's head with a particular hairstyle. 'I think I'll go for style number three, a 'Perry Como' but not as short as depicted in the sketch' I said to the others. 'I'll join you' said JG. Martin had decided on style number five, which was not dissimilar to a 'Perry Como' but the hair at the front on the forehead was just that bit longer. We egged John on to go for a 'Tony Curtis'. The sketch showed the hair greased back at the sides and falling down on the forehead like a bunch of grapes. 'That'll confuse them in court. They'll think you're a bloody Rocker,' Martin said. We laughed and John responded 'I could go for a DA (duck's arse) as well' pointing to a sketch on the far right, where the greased sides came around the back of the head and met in the middle. It was given a vertical parting, which was made by a deft stroke of the comb. A duck's arse! 'On second thoughts I might as well go for the 'Perry Como' as well' John decided.

As we entered the shop, a bell on the door rang announcing our entry, and we sat down and waited our turn. Within about half an hour we were all done and the regulation puffs of talcum powder were applied to the back of the neck where the hair had been shaved. Then came the discreet question in your ear as the cloth catching the cut hairs was being removed. 'Anything for the weekend, sir?' I happened to be one of the last to get my hair cut and I could see behind me in the mirror, the others sitting sniggering away as I answered 'Not today thank you.' Once we had paid and were out of sight of the shop, we all fell about laughing.

That simple question 'Anything for the weekend, sir?' always made us laugh, just out of sheer embarrassment really. Fancy somebody asking you if you'd like to buy a contraceptive for the weekend – is that the only time you did it in those days? In the early 60s there were no male contra-ceptive machines conveniently located in pub toilets or on full display to buy at garage or supermarket cash desks. Back then contraceptives were only available in appointed family planning clinics or from a chemist or barber's shop and it was unheard of for a young man to walk into a clinic and buy contraceptives if he wasn't married. I just couldn't contemplate strolling into an austere chemist's shop, as they were then, and ask a young female assistant for a packet of contraceptives. My 'just in case' purchase, would be made via a friend who was braver than me. However, our lives as males were soon to be transformed, as in 1961 the female contraceptive pill was just being made available.

THE TRIAL - SHIRE HALL, CHELMSFORD - 27 SEPTEMBER 1961

I had given my mum strict instructions to call the bank first thing in the morning to inform them that I had been sick during the night and that I wouldn't be attending work for a few days. As usual, we set off early and arrived in Chelmsford an hour before the case started. We parked both cars and then strolled into the centre of town to locate the court. As it turned out, it wasn't difficult to find.

Shire Hall was a large imposing Georgian building situated on the High Street in Chelmsford. We all just stood there staring in awe at this very large building. 'So this is Shire Hall, where we are going to be tried for doing absolutely nothing' I said in a slightly bitter voice. Or nearly next to nothing, if I included the two broken bottles I had in my hands, but never used, I thought to myself. My comment received a few nods, but nobody spoke.

The building of Shire Hall had been completed in 1791 and replaced a previous courthouse that had stood on the same site where the trials of some 250 witches had taken place. It is one of Chelmsford's oldest build-ings and still operates as a judicial courthouse to this day.

Legal jargon doesn't seem to have changed much since 1791. An extract from my notice of court appearance reads as follows: 'Wednesday the 27th Day of September 1961 at the hour of 10.45 in the fore noon, and there surrender yourself into custody and take your trial upon any indictment preferred against you.'

IN THE COUNTY OF ESSEX

PETTY SESSIONAL DIVISION OF TENDRING

TAKE NOTICE that you Colin Stoddart,

of 55, Seymer Road, Romford, Essex.

are bound by a recognizance in the sum of ~~TEN~~ TWENTY POUNDS as principal,
~~and you~~
~~of~~
~~in the sum of TEN POUNDS, as surety,~~ that you, the said principal appear before the next Court of Quarter Sessions for the County of Essex to be held at Shire Hall, Chelmsford, Essex, on Wednesday the 27th day of September, 1961, at the hour of 10.45. in the fore noon, and there surrender yourself into custody and take your trial upon any indictment preferred against you, and unless you, the said principal, appear accordingly, payment of the said sum will forthwith be enforced by due process of law ~~severally~~ against you, the said principal, ~~and you, the said surety.~~

DATED the 11th day of September, 1961.

THE SEAL OF THE JUSTICES FOR THE DIVISION OF TENDRING COUNTY OF ESSEX

Clerk of the Magistrates' Court sitting at
Clacton-on-Sea.

Notice to principal
~~and surety.~~

THE SUMMONS I RECEIVED TO APPEAR AT CHELMSFORD COURT OF QUARTER SESSIONS ON 27 SEPTEMBER 1961, FOLLOWING MY EARLIER APPEARANCE AT CLACTON MAGISTRATES COURT.

We joined a small group of people already waiting outside the court entrance, which grew in number as more defendants and their parents arrived. Looking around and seeing all these youths dressed in their suits and ties, and with their newly cut hair, it was hard to believe that nearly seven weeks ago we were two opposing gangs, ready to knock heads.

The doors to the court swung open at 9am sharp and, as we entered the building, all defendants were directed upstairs. This was a large trial with 30 defendants, three magistrates, assorted defence and prosecution lawyers, various court staff, and members of the public. To accommodate such a large influx of people, the original ballroom no less, which was the largest room in Shire Hall, had to be converted into a courtroom.

As we entered the ballroom, we gave our name and address to a clerk who allotted us a number. We were then directed to a large raised wooden platform situated in the middle of the courtroom. It was about a foot high and, from the smell of the untreated wood, it had recently been constructed especially for the trial. On it in rows, stood 30 chairs and attached to the back of each chair was a five-foot high pole with a white card on the top, each card numbered in black from 1 – 30. We were instructed to sit in the chair displaying the same number we had been given by the clerk of court. John, Martin, JG and myself had all been given what appeared to be random numbers. I sat down on seat number 19. The others were all scattered around and it was then obvious that they didn't want us sitting together.

As the empty chairs around me began to be occupied, I had a good look around at this huge elegant ballroom with its towering windows, large crystal chandeliers and oil paintings hanging on every wall. It seemed wrong that all this splendour now housed a temporary courtroom. Slowly the large room began to fill up with members of the defence and prosecution council, all decked out in their black robes and horsehair wigs. An assortment of law clerks and a stenographer took their places and, on the right, the witness stand stood empty. Suddenly, the two large swing doors leading into the courtroom were closed and we were asked to stand. Three magistrates entered through a side door, all wearing their robes. It was very grand, and quite intimidating.

As they took their seats, we were instructed to sit down. One of the magistrates gave a brief account of the proceedings, informing the court that there were 30 defendants on trial, 19 charged with riotous assembly and 11 charged with riotous assembly plus carrying offensive weapons. The prosecution started the proceedings by giving an account of what exactly had happened at St Osyth on Friday 4 August 1961.

We all expected the case being wrapped up by the end of the day, but towards the middle of the afternoon, only a third of the police officers had given their evidence, so it was clear this case was going to drag on.

As we left the court at the end of the first day, to our dismay we noticed several BBC mobile television vans busy filming us as we filed out of the building. We quickly hid our faces as best we could. We arrived home that evening in time to watch the BBC's regional news bulletin, 'Town and Around' which always followed the main BBC 6 o'clock news broadcast. I anxiously watched as the report concluded by showing lots of people spilling out of the Chelmsford courthouse and onto the street. Fortunately you couldn't make out our party or identify any individuals. A thought crossed my mind. Imagine my bank manager, sitting at home relaxing and watching TV, suddenly seeing Stoddart, his junior clerk, walking out of a court when he was supposed to be ill in bed!

Before the case resumed on Thursday morning, one of the magistrates made an apology on behalf of the court. Apparently, a report on the first day of the trial had somehow been leaked to the press and London's Evening Standard had reported that the 30 accused had all pleaded guilty. The judge reprimanded the newspaper and demanded it make a correction and apologise for the mistake it had made.

Further evidence was read out from the witness box during the day by one of the first arresting officers on the scene. It was a comment John had made to the policeman when first apprehended. It went on to make a banner headline in the Evening Standard that evening on Thursday 28 September 1961. It stated in bold letters 'WE DID NOT BARGAIN

FOR SHOTGUNS'. The article went on to say that '11 youths (the Rockers) were further accused of riotously assembling together, and carrying offensive weapons including two double-barrelled shotguns, one single-barrelled shotgun, and other weapons.' In the final paragraph it stated 'ALL HAVE PLEADED NOT GUILTY' and went on to say that in an agency report, published yesterday in the Evening Standard, it had been erroneously reported that the 30 accused had pleaded guilty to the charge of the alleged affray. The plea was, in fact, not guilty. The Evening Standard apologised for the error.

The magistrate went on to say that no further information was to be leaked to the press until the case had reached its final conclusion. The next police officer to take to the witness stand was the second arresting officer who, with his colleague, responded to the telephone call made by a local St Osyth farmer, informing them of a local gang fight, and that a gun had been fired. He went on to say how they were in their patrol car, and just as they were about to drive into Cockett Wick Lane, a couple of youths appeared running towards them. When stopped, one youth told the police a shotgun had been fired, and lifted his top to reveal two red weals on his back. The other youth, and we knew this to be John as he had related the incident to us on a number of occasions since the event, had stated 'We did not mind a fist fight, but we did not bargain for shotguns.'

The last policeman to give evidence before the court adjourned for the day, read his report from a small notebook, and listed the names of the youths who had travelled in his car from the St Osyth caravan site to Clacton police station. When he'd finished giving evidence, he stepped down from the witness box. Immediately our barrister stood up and quickly seized the moment, as he had in the Clacton-on-Sea court, and pointed out that the police had given conflicting stories to the court over the past two days of what had taken place on that day. He went on say 'If we can't rely on the police to give an accurate account of what exactly happened on that day, who can we rely on?' and to labour the point, he then went on to deliver his coup de grace. He pointed out that only 29 names had been read out to the court by the various officers giving evidence, when in fact there were 30 defendants sitting in the court today. 'The missing name is that of my client, Mr Colin Stoddart, who is sitting in this court.' A quiet murmur ran throughout the court.

As before, one of the magistrates demanded a recall of the names. The court clerk and the stenographer worked together and, after a few minutes, handed to the judge a list of all the defendants' names given by the various police officers under oath. After the judge had compared both lists of names, he looked up and requested 'Colin Stoddart. Please stand up and make yourself known to the court.' As I stood up, our barrister continued to berate the police for their inaccuracies, while I still stood there wondering whether I was supposed to remain standing or should I sit down again.

A few minutes passed and I was still standing and now beginning to feel decidedly embarrassed. As our barrister continued with the questioning, I wondered again whether I should sit down. Luckily, our barrister caught sight of me and could see my dilemma, so he motioned to me to sit. What a relief!

Papers were being shuffled around by one of the other defence lawyers and he suddenly stood up and requested to approach the bench. He spoke with the magistrates in hushed tones for some minutes, and then a court official turned to the court and said, 'All rise.' The court rose and the magistrates filed out of the court. None of us had a clue what was going on, but within five minutes they returned and one of them addressed the court to say that four of the defendants, originally charged with possessing offensive weapons in a public place, had changed their plea from not guilty to guilty. So, four of the Rockers had finally admitted to having offensive weapons after all, probably a move by their defence council to try and obtain a lighter sentence for them. Sentencing would have to be delayed while reports were obtained. All 30 of us were told to all report back to the court on Monday 9 October 1961 when the case would resume, and so the court was adjourned.

I was relieved not to have to attend court the next day, but annoyed that we had to return again next month, with more lies being given to the bank. Again, as we left the building, the BBC cameras were waiting outside to film us as we headed back to our cars.

BACK IN COURT - MONDAY - 9 OCTOBER 1961

There was a definite feeling of déjà vu. We drove out of Romford at the same time as before, headed along the same road, parked the car in the identical car park, climbed the steps into the courthouse, and I sat again in seat number 19. We all rose on command as the same three magistrates entered the court and sat down.

By mid-afternoon, the final evidence was read out and the court was informed that the prosecution and the defence teams could carry out their individual summaries in the morning. The court was adjourned for another day. We were now getting close to the end of the trial so, with a bit of luck, tomorrow would be our final day in court. I descended the steps of Shire Hall with head bowed against the prying cameras and walked towards the car park with the others.

Tuesday 10 October 1961 – here we go again. Please let this be our last day, I thought to myself. It was the same routine. Please rise, please be seated, and then we all waited in silence as the magistrates took their seats. The prosecution started by attempting to make a case over all the broken bottles that were found by the police in the road, and referring to them as offensive weapons. But as nobody had admitted to carrying the bottles, and that included me of course, the prosecution lawyer was overruled by a magistrate. Our barrister was the last of the defence council to address the court and, summing up, he made quite a damning statement. 'Speaking generally, as far as the group of 19 youths is concerned, the whole trouble is that the prosecution has sought to level charges of appalling gravity against them. None of these 19 youths should have been brought to this Quarter Session in this formal manner. They should have been dealt with on a much milder charge in the court below', referring to the Chelmsford Magistrates Court on the ground floor of Shire Hall.

After the usual break for lunch, we were finally called to take our seats around 3pm. This surely was going to be the moment of truth. 'Please all stand' the court clerk announced and in filed the magistrates, followed by the instructions 'Please all sit down.'

The magistrate seated in the middle started by pointing out that after careful consideration and due to insufficient evidence, the court had no case to answer. The two counts of Riotous Assembly and Affray, with which 19 defendants had been charged, were dropped upon motion of council. The same applied to the remaining seven defendants who, in addition, were charged with the third count of Possessing Offensive Weapons in a Public Place. All three counts were dropped. The remaining four defendants had already admitted their guilt and for them the case would continue. They were required to attend court on 12 October 1961 for final sentencing. Looking directly at us, the magistrate pointed out that, although we had been found not guilty, our actions had brought us within an Act of Parliament by which the bench could require us to be bound over.

He then went on to announce 'There are 26 of you' and he nodded to the clerk of the court who stood up and read out 26 names to the court. The magistrate then went on to say 'You are each bound over to the sum of £20, to keep the peace and be of good behaviour for a year.' He went on to say 'It is very much in your own interests, as well as your duty, to be a good deal more wise and a good deal more careful about how you conduct yourselves in the future.'

Upon instruction from the court clerk we all stood up. The magistrates rose from their chairs and walked out of the court. It was finally over! As we stood ready to file off the platform, I caught sight of Martin, John and JG and we smiled at each other acknowledging our relief. The double doors of the ballroom were swung open and we marched out passing a hoard of waiting journalists. They were obviously there to obtain the names and addresses of the defendants, which would now be officially released by the court.

Again we came out of the court, bowing our heads and looking away from the BBC cameras. On the walk back to the car, the atmosphere amongst us had changed to a light banter and laughter. Even our fathers appeared happy. We popped into a local cafe, ordered drinks and sat there discussing the events of the day, all agreeing how lucky we'd been to get off so lightly. Although the court had not found us guilty which was the most important issue, we were bound over to keep the peace for a year, so we were going to have to keep our heads down for the next 12 months and not get drawn into any confrontations. We hoped the case wouldn't be covered in tomorrow's newspapers and I, for one, was relieved that hopefully the bank would be none the wiser about my involvement in the affair. The case against the remaining four youths, who had changed their plea to guilty, had been adjourned for two days, so it was back in court for them, where their sentences would finally be read out. We eventually found out that they were to be put on probation for three years, and their weapons confiscated. They also had to contribute to the prosecution costs. The magistrate pointed out to them that the gravity of the case was certainly made the greater by the fact that they had all been in front of a court at least once before.

Since this confrontation was first reported in the papers on 5 August 1961, the list of weapons confiscated at the time has varied. The official court papers listed the weapons seized as follows:

2 Double-Barrelled Shotguns
1 Single-Barrelled Shotgun
1 Starting Pistol with its barrel bored out
3 Studded Belts
1 Combined Spike and Knuckle-Duster

JOB OR NO JOB?

The next morning I walked to work feeling confident that the bank wouldn't find out about my escapade at St Osyth and my job would be safe. On the way, I stopped off at a local newsagent to buy some cigarettes. Outside the shop I froze with disbelief. There, mounted in a newspaper headline board, was a printed poster that read 'Romford Times – Local Boys In Gun Battle'. I was stunned. I went inside, bought a pack of cigarettes and a copy of the Romford Times. I hastily scanned the front page and under a banner heading stating 'Holiday Camp Affray', the article went on to describe the events at St Osyth and how a group of 30 youths had gone into battle that day, armed with shotguns and other weapons. It also stated that among the 19 youths charged with unlawfully fighting and making an affray were… and to my absolute horror, there in bold type it listed our four names together with our full addresses and occupations. My own name immediately sprang out at me – Colin Stoddart 17, bank clerk! We had been found not guilty and the charge of causing an affray was dropped but the bloody newspaper couldn't even report the case accurately. There, directly beneath our names and addresses, was a sub-heading in bold type 'Shotguns and Knuckle Duster'. Anyone quickly reading the article could easily be mistaken in thinking that us four local lads carried the weapons.

I looked at my watch. I had ten minutes to get to work, so I started walking quickly. My head was spinning. What was I going to do and say when I got to the bank? I had naively expected the story to be reported in one or two of the national newspapers, but I hadn't thought that our local newspapers would carry the story, and certainly not print all our names and addresses. I knew the bank had both local papers delivered every week, basically for the manager to check on local court cases and bankruptcies which might involve some of the bank's customers. The only glimmer of hope I had was that the bank manager might not bother to read the front page of the newspaper and simply turn to the Court section. Some hope!

I walked up to the front door, rang the bell and strolled into the small banking hall. Members of staff appeared concerned about my well-being and I assured everyone that I had made a full recovery. As I had left home that morning, I had attempted to put the court case behind me but now, with it splashed all over the front page of the local paper, I'd lost my confidence. Had any of the staff already read the article? However, everything appeared normal that morning. The safe was opened and I was handed yesterday's pile of cheques and credit slips. My job now was to enter these items on each individual customer's statement via a National Burroughs machine. So off I went to my little corner to complete this task.

The last member of staff to arrive as usual was the branch manager, which was his privilege of course. The ring on the doorbell heralded his arrival. He strode straight into his office and closed the door.

I continued quietly with my assigned work, but I couldn't concentrate properly. Within about ten minutes, the manager's internal door opened. 'Stoddart' he barked. I froze. I bet he's read the story, I thought to myself. Obediently I jumped up and made my way up to his office. Knocking on the door, I entered and sat down opposite him. He didn't look up, but I could see he was reading the front page of the Romford Times.

My mind was racing when he looked up and said 'So, what's this all about then?' I feebly mumbled how we'd quite innocently got involved in a dispute, which had led us to be picked up by the police, and that it had taken a court case to prove we were innocent. He looked straight into my eyes and said 'You know I'm going to have to report this to Head Office' and I replied 'Yes sir.' He continued 'To have a member of my staff involved in a fight where guns were used and then to have his name, address and occupation blazoned across the front page of the local paper, is an extremely serious situation.' 'Yes sir, I do realise' was all I could think of saying. He continued 'Well, that's all for now. I'll let you know the outcome once I've spoken with Head Office.'

The first thing I thought of when I returned to my desk was, Head

Office – oh shit, now I'm in big trouble. I continued my work for another ten minutes, then made tea and coffee for everyone except the manager. The door to his office was still closed. I had just sat down at the machine again when the manager's door swung open and he bellowed out 'Stoddart, my office!'

I dutifully knocked on his door again, entered his office and sat down. 'Head Office want to see you today. If you have any personal effects in the branch take them with you. If you leave now, you'll be there with plenty of time for your appointment at 2pm. When you get there, go to reception and tell them you have an appointment to see Mr Abbott in the personnel department.' He stood up, and I did the same. 'Good luck' he said. I certainly hadn't expected that from him! At the same time, he extended his right hand and we shook hands. My parting words were 'Thank you sir.' I felt a twinge of sadness as I walked out of the bank and headed for the station. I could imagine the staff all gossiping away discussing what had happened to me, with somebody probably saying 'He seemed such a nice quiet boy….'

While I sat on the train on my way to Liverpool Street station, I started to think about the bank manager. Having been asked to take any belongings with me, I realised that I probably wouldn't be returning to that branch again and I suppose I was getting a bit nostalgic. Although we'd had a few falling outs over nothing that important, I quite liked the man for some inexplicable reason.

I had worked at this small sub-branch for nearly 14 months and, including myself, only six people were employed there, so we all knew one another quite well. The manager (clerk-in-charge) basically kept to himself. He was not a particularly well man and suffered from extremely bad headaches on a regular basis.

Two years previously, he had worked at the local Westminster Bank in Gidea Park, Romford and, as a key holder, he was required to arrive early at the bank every morning to open up, ready for members of staff to arrive. But unbeknown to him, thieves had earlier broken into the bank and were waiting for him to arrive. As he entered the banking hall they pounced on him, beat him around the head with a lead cosh, and took his keys. Naively, the gang had thought that only one set of keys was required to open the main safe. However, on discovering that two sets were required, they panicked and fled before the second key holder arrived. His head injuries were so severe that it required hours of surgery and reputedly 86 stitches to repair the damage. It took over a year of convalescence before he could return to work.

His compensation from the bank was a promotion to clerk-in-charge of a sub-branch, although we always referred to him as the manager, and he was directly responsible to the manager of the main branch in Romford. But considering what he'd gone through, and what I'd been involved in, I was surprised he was kind enough to wish me good luck.

I stood at the bottom of the steps looking up at a very imposing building, 41 Lothbury, Westminster Bank's Head Office, situated directly behind the Bank of England in Threadneedle Street. Just about 18 months previously, I had attended a number of interviews here before receiving an official letter of appointment on 18 July 1960. I walked up the steps with trepidation. Would I still have a job when I walked back down these steps!

I sat in the Staff Controller's office waiting room and at 2pm on the nail, I was escorted into Mr Abbot's office. We shook hands and I sat down. He wanted to know the full story of what happened. So I related my story of events, omitting the broken bottles and, as he listened, he kept shaking his head. When I'd finished he said 'So, what have learnt from this experience, young man?' 'Just to walk away from any possible trouble, and not to get involved, sir.' He nodded his approval and went on to say 'Now, because of the adverse publicity this court case has received and the fact that your name, address and occupation has been openly revealed in your local newspaper, we have no alternative (here it comes, I said to myself – the big chop) but to transfer you to a branch well away from the Romford area, where nobody knows you. As from tomorrow you are to report for work at the Westminster Bank on Stratford Broadway at 9am sharp. The manager there has been notified accordingly of your immediate transfer.'

'I understand you have already picked up your personal effects from the Victoria Road branch before you left.' 'Yes, sir' I replied in a croaky voice. A huge sense of relief had washed over me – so I hadn't lost my job after all! Mr Abbot finalised the meeting by saying 'The bank will turn a blind eye on this one occasion. This matter will not be held against you and the affair will not be entered on your records. However, the court has bound you over to keep the peace for 12 months, and the bank will do the same. You are now on a 12-month probationary period.' He stood up and we shook hands. 'Just steer clear of any trouble and keep your nose clean, young man.' 'Yes sir, and thank you very much.' We said our farewells and I left the building somewhat elated, jumping down the steps two at a time and out onto the busy street of Lothbury.

As I walked to the tube station, I turned things over in my mind. The personnel department must have pulled out all the stops on this particular occasion as within a few hours of receiving the initial telephone call from my manager, I was sitting opposite Mr Abbot in the City of London being told my fate. Deciding what to do with me must have given a very staid organisation like the Westminster Bank a massive headache. To this day I'm still very surprised I wasn't dismissed. A bank clerk involved in a gun battle! Whatever next, old chap!

The Romford Times' main competitor was the Romford Recorder, which was published every Friday. My father was a part-time journalist and had been writing for the Romford Times for many years. He was their football and boxing correspondent and wrote weekly articles on both subjects under the pseudonym 'Ross Ferguson'. These are old family names from Scotland – my brother's middle name is Ross and my middle name is Ferguson.

That middle name 'Ferguson' was to haunt me for many years, before I became quite proud of it. Having failed the 11-plus examination, much to my parents' disappointment, I followed in my brother's footsteps and attended St Edward's Church of England Secondary School in Romford.

This charity foundation school was established in 1728 and was supposedly a 'cut above' the other local secondary schools in the area.

On the first day of term at the new school, our teacher compiled a class register and pupils were asked to call out their names in alphabetical order. All was going well until we reached Melvyn Crutchley. When asked for his middle name Melvyn called out Clement, and the class fell about laughing. Names continued to be called out. As we were getting nearer to my name and had reached John Smith whose middle name was Peter, I realised everyone had a normal middle name, apart from Melvyn Crutchley and myself. It was now my turn. Stoddart, Colin – no middle name I called out. No way did I want the class laughing at me, and possibly giving me a nickname.

After the register had been prepared, our teacher then requested that we all brought our christening certificates in to school. Looking back I wonder why. Was it because the school wanted to know how many pupils in attendance were not Church of England?

My mother handed me my christening certificate and I knew what I would read. There, for everybody to see, was my middle name – Ferguson. I had read, in one of my craft books, that ink could be removed with bleach, so I deviously removed my middle name with a matchstick dipped in bleach. I was now simply Colin Stoddart, and remained that way throughout my school life.

My father always had a free copy of The Romford Times posted through our letterbox every Wednesday evening by a member of the newspaper's staff making his way home and so he wasn't aware of the article until he arrived home. When he read it he was furious with the newspaper, his part-time employer for over ten years. Why hadn't the editor, a friend, contacted him when he'd read the story and saw the surname Stoddart. He knew our address and, had he got in touch with my father, could have perhaps been persuaded to bury the article in the middle of the paper, not blatantly displaying the story in the centre of the front page. What angered my father even more was the fact that the article had been written ambiguously implying that four local lads had gone into battle carrying dangerous weapons, just to give greater impact to the story.

The following morning, he walked unannounced into the editor's office of the Romford Times and put his case forward. Knowing my father, I suspect it was told in a somewhat aggressive manner. An argument ensued and he resigned on the spot. Fortunately no blood was spilt! He then walked down Romford South Street and into the Western Road offices of the Romford Recorder, the rival newspaper, and offered his journalistic services. He was hired on the spot and became their boxing correspondent for the next 24 years, writing under the pseudonym of 'The Ringman'.

OUR MOMENT OF NOTORIETY

My mother and father were over the moon and very relieved I still had a job. All social bans were now lifted so to celebrate, the following evening myself and my three 'partners in crime' set off for our favourite Saturday evening haunt, the Wykeham Hall, which was situated in Romford's marketplace. We needed to listen to some groups playing good old live rock 'n' roll music!

We paid our money and entered the crowded dimly lit hall. As we stood at the back for a while just taking everything in, we started to notice people were whispering and turning around to look at us. We always liked to get close to the front of the stage to study and watch the groups when they came on to play and, under normal circumstances, this would mean slowly weaving our way between the crowds of people. But tonight our reputation as 'gunslingers' had obviously preceded us! A group was about to start and, as we started to make our way towards the stage, people just voluntarily moved aside ahead of us – the parting of the Red Sea came to mind! Even when we'd found our usual spot, near the stage, we were given a wide berth all evening.

Let's face it, who would want to tangle with four shotgun toting, knuckle-duster and studded belt wielding Mods? We just loved our moment of notoriety!

The four of us never offended again – well, not in the public sense that is. In 1970, during my time working there, the Westminster Bank and the National Provincial Bank merged and the annual staff assessment procedures changed in favour of the National Provincial Bank's method of grading individuals. On paper I lost out and took a step backwards and I realised it was time to get out and move on. Was that court case still on my records when the re-assessment took place? I'll never know. But ten years later I left the bank forever.

Being bound over to keep the peace for 12 months meant that, providing we didn't re-offend, at the end of that time our individual police records including fingerprints, would all be destroyed. I wonder, did that ever happen?

However, we weren't finished with Shire Hall, Chelmsford yet as a couple of years later we were back, but thankfully not attending another court case. By then we had formed a group called Johnny Lonesome and The Travellers and had been booked to play at an up-market wedding reception there following a marriage ceremony held in Chelmsford Cathedral on Saturday 28 March 1964. By the time we came to perform late afternoon, the wedding feast had already taken place and most people by then were very intoxicated. The tables and chairs had been moved earlier to the side to reveal the original ballroom floor and, as soon as we started into our first song, everyone was up dancing.

As I played away, I looked around the ballroom from my elevated position and, in my mind's eye, I could envisage where the large, newly built wooden stage for our trial had once stood, and where all 30 youths had sat awaiting their fate. For a brief second I caught a glimpse of myself sitting there on chair number 19, surrounded by 29 others.

4

THE INSPIRATION

My first introduction to rock 'n' roll music came via a large brown paper carrier bag full of 78 rpm records, which my brother had borrowed from a friend. I must have been about 14 years old at the time and nursing a rather large carbuncle on the back of my neck. According to my doctor, this rather painful abscess, much larger than your average boil, was brought about by a lack of nutritious food, and necessitated a week or so off from school plus an immediate course of vital vitamins.

Unbeknown to my parents, and with me being totally naive to good eating habits at that age, I used my weekly school dinner money to indulge in a daily diet of wonderful sticky Swiss buns, rather than suffer eating a school dinner. My mother, thinking I had eaten a full 'square' meal at school every day, was quite happy to feed my sweet tooth in the evenings with a bread and jam tea. Wonderful as this newfound diet was at the time, after a couple of months a very painful Mount Vesuvius erupted on the back of my neck in the form of a carbuncle!

Now, with plenty of time on my hands and feeling very sorry for myself, I started to read through a pile of old comics and, at the same time, decided to play the 78 records I'd discovered in that paper carrier bag. Stretched out on a settee, I read one comic after another, and one by one a record was plucked from the carrier bag and placed on the turntable. Most of the artists were unknown to me, but I was young and curious and if my brother, five years older than me, liked them, then I should as well. By mid-afternoon I had made two piles of records – the ones I liked and the ones I didn't. The latter was the bigger pile.

Engrossed in a Dan Dare adventure in one of the Eagle comics, without thinking I leaned across and put another a record on the turntable. Suddenly the sound that jumped out from the small speaker on the Dansette record player made the hair on the back of my poisoned neck stand up. Wow! What was that! As soon as it had finished, I played it again. I could barely make out what this man was singing about, but that didn't matter. It was a mixture of singing, mumbling and hiccupping to a driving rhythm with plenty of electric guitar and lots of echo. I took the record off the turntable and studied the label. 'Baby Let's Play House' by Elvis Presley – a name I had vaguely heard of but at the time meant nothing to me. That would rapidly change! It introduced me to rock 'n' roll music and the love of the guitar, ultimately adding a new dimension to my life in a few years' time.

The 78 rpm record had derived its name from the speed at which it had to be played in order to reach the correct pitch – 78 revolutions per minute. It was ten inches in diameter and made from a brittle black material called shellac.

However, the days of the 78 were numbered and, by the late 1950s, the 7-inch or 45 rpm single as it was known and the 10-inch or 33 1/3 rpm long-playing (LP) record had arrived. Both were made from a flexible black plastic vinyl and this recording format became the norm for the next 20-odd years, until replaced by the arrival of the compact disc in 1982.

SIX-FIVE SPECIAL

In 1957, during my early teens, every Saturday evening at 6.05pm I eagerly switched on my parents wooden-encased black and white television set to watch a music programme called 'Six-Five Special'. This was the BBC's first attempt to cater for the insatiable demand of British teenagers wishing to experience the new American music phenomena called rock 'n' roll, which had recently been infiltrating the British music charts.

The first show was launched in February 1957 and continued through to the end of 1958, although early in that year, the show's producer, Jack Good, resigned following a disagreement with the BBC's management. Good went on to join the opposition channel, Independent Television and for one of their companies, ABC, he produced the 'Oh Boy' show, which went on to eclipse 'Six-Five Special' and forced its demise in December 1958.

The introduction to 'Six-Five Special' was a short black and white film of a steam train travelling along a track. This had been speeded up and was accompanied by a song with the same title – 'Six-Five Special' played by The Bob Cort Skiffle Group. I was immediately transfixed and transformed into another world as the song progressed. 'Over the points, over the points, over the points – the six-five special's steamin' down the line, the six-five special's right on time...........' This was skiffle music at its best.

Skiffle music had originated in America during the 1920s. It was devised by African Americans who, eager to make music but couldn't afford expensive instruments, simply adapted by using everyday items. The household washboard became the rhythm section. It was a simple, flat, wooden frame housing a thin ribbed aluminium plate, and was originally used to rub clothing on the ribbing to help remove stubborn stains from clothing on washdays.

The washboard player would sit with the board between his legs and, with metal thimbles on his fingers, run them very quickly up and down both sides of the ribbed aluminium, thus creating a rapid rhythmic sound.

The second 'cobbled-together' instrument was the bass made from an empty wooden tea chest. String was secured to one top corner of the chest and then on to the end of a vertical broom handle. This was held in position on the opposite top corner edge of the chest. The player stood with one foot on the tea chest and one hand holding up the broom handle. The string was stretched taut by moving the handle and, by plucking the string with the other hand, it created a low bass note. By changing the tension on the string, a different bass note was created and that was the basis of a rudimentary acoustic bass! With a cheap acoustic guitar playing chords, you had a basic three-piece skiffle group. More acoustic guitars or banjos could be added but the simplicity of it all was that any aspiring young teenager, without any real knowledge of music, could form a skiffle group and create music.

'Six-Five Special' showcased British skiffle groups spearheaded by Lonnie Donegan and his Band and the programme was the catalyst for starting the skiffle craze in the UK. Although up-and-coming rock 'n' roll groups appeared on the programme, it was skiffle music that for a few years caught the imagination of youngsters around the country.

The craze was an inspiration for me, and thousands of other young people, to pick up a guitar and play. At around this time in 1957 in Liverpool, a young John Lennon played publicly in a skiffle group called The Quarrymen. He was just one of many guitarists to emerge in the 60s who owed their inspiration to skiffle music.

In September 1957, I switched on the television to watch the 'Six-Five Special' show, quite oblivious to the fact that I was about to watch a singer give a performance that was going to 'blow my mind'. Sorry, a very 70s expression, but so apt in describing what happened to me when I saw this man in action!

During the programme an announcement was made that coming on next was a film clip of a new American rock 'n' roll singer called Jerry Lee Lewis, performing live on a US entertainment show.

There are always memorable events in one's life when you realise you are witnessing a ground-breaking moment, when something reaches out and grabs you, and stays with you for life. Well, this was one of those moments.

I sat mesmerised, watching a trio performing a song called 'Whole Lotta Shakin' Going On'. The sound was so new. It was innovative and totally different from the rock 'n' roll associated with electric guitars. In early rock 'n' roll music, it was quite common for the bass to be played on a floor-standing double bass as used on many of the early Elvis Presley records. But this was the first time I'd ever seen an electric bass guitar. It had an extremely long fretboard and the body shape was so futuristic. It was a very early Fender bass guitar.

Jerry Lee Lewis sat pounding the keys of a white grand piano and sang and moved his body with such intensity that it gave him a slightly wild demeanour. He dressed differently too and, although I was watching black and white television, he appeared to be wearing black trousers with a thin, white belt and a tight-fitting, short-sleeve shirt in broad black and white stripes. White shoes finished the outfit off. Also, he wasn't playing the piano as I'd ever seen it played before. He sat sideways to the piano with a mike stand positioned between his legs and was attacking the keys with great ferocity. When he came to play the high keys, his hands constantly danced around the upright mike stand and his feet were moving and tapping, keeping in time with the rhythm.

When he reached his solo, it was electrifying. He shook his head until long wavy locks of hair hung down over his face. Suddenly the piano stool was kicked out of the way and he was on his feet, standing back from the piano and with outstretched arms he continued to hammer the keys. His whole body shook and his feet stomped to the rhythm. His hands became a blur as they raced up and down the keyboard, and all the time his long wavy blond curls continued to hide his face. Then, with a flick of the head, the hanging curls returned to their original position and it was over. He turned and faced the screaming audience and bowed. The whole experience had only taken two minutes and for a second I felt physically weak but, at the same time, I was exhilarated by what I had just witnessed.

MY FIRST LIVE ROCK 'N' ROLL CONCERT - OCTOBER 1959

I was still attending school in 1959 and one Friday evening I went with my friend Martin to see a rock 'n' roll package tour at our local Odeon Cinema in Romford. Headlining the concert was Cliff Richard and the newly named Shadows. They were originally called The Drifters, but had been asked to change their name as there had been a conflict of interest with a successful US group of the same name. So they became The Shadows.

For me, it was such a ground-breaking experience. Not only was this the first live concert I had attended, I was also witnessing British rock 'n' roll in its absolute infancy. The support acts came and went and were politely applauded as everyone waited patiently for the final act to appear. Suddenly it was time! The final announcement was made and the compere disappeared through the closed curtains. The lights dimmed and, as the curtains opened, the group started playing. There he was, Cliff Richard, resplendent in a pink jacket, black shirt, white tie and black trousers. The girls just screamed their heads off. Behind him, The Shadows moved in unison as they played their guitars, dressed in identical black suits. I was spellbound. It was a magical life-changing moment for me.

When the show had finished, as Martin and I left the cinema, we spotted a small group of female fans that were lingering around in the side road next to the theatre. It was dark by now and, not wishing to head off home just yet, out of curiosity we joined them. Every so often a window on the first floor would open and a head appeared but it was too dark to establish exactly who it was. However, it was enough for the girls to assume it might be Cliff himself and they screamed in expectation. Wow, was I impressed! Fancy being in a group, making music, AND have girls screaming at you! On the way home we both talked about what we had just experienced, how exhilarating it had been and we agreed there and then – let's form a group!

By this time, I had been attending guitar lessons for over a year but was finding it hard going learning to read music and playing old-fashioned songs from another era. My guitar teacher was a professional guitarist and most evenings he played in a trio performing in small club in Soho in central London. I really don't think he'd ever heard of rock 'n' roll or, if he had, he didn't acknowledge it, and I was too shy to mention it. I persevered with my lessons but I was rapidly losing interest. I just wasn't learning to play music that inspired me. I wanted to be a lead guitarist in a group – now that really appealed to me. I suppose being the centre of attraction springs to mind so, as a fledgling guitarist, I elected myself for the job.

At school the following day, I approached a friend in my year, John Wilkinson. He had attended the Royal School of Church Music at Addington Palace near Croydon in South London, a training school for choirboys. It never ceased to amaze me that if handed the sheet music of an unknown song, John could sing the melody line simply by reading the music. John was up for the job of being the singer in the group and then suggested two of his classmates – one played the drums and the other the guitar. When approached, they both jumped at the opportunity and so Malcolm Fowler, a complete extrovert, became the drummer and Pete Weavers became the rhythm guitarist. All that was needed now was a bass guitarist, a rare breed indeed in 1959, and so when Martin asked me 'What instrument shall I play?' I told him 'You're the bass guitarist.' So, by default, Martin became the bass guitarist. Off he went, bought himself a bass guitar and learnt to play the instrument. He went on to become both outstanding and innovative in his playing.

OUR FIRST PUBLIC PERFORMANCE – JUNE 1960

During our last few months at St Edward's in 1960, the school staged a pageant over a two-week period to celebrate the 250-year anniversary of its foundation in 1710. Being part-funded by the local council, the school needed to continually organise events to raise much-needed money. To start off the celebrations, a Summer Fair was hosted in May and was opened by the Lord Mayor of London no less. On 27 May, a thanksgiving service was held at St Paul's Cathedral in London, which the entire school attended. In the evening, over two consecutive nights, a play written by our headmaster entitled 'An Historical Miscellany' was held in the school's assembly hall. The play portrayed historical and social events that had taken place during the school's 250 years existence. Pupils from the school took various acting parts in the play and also made the costumes.

The school had allowed our newly formed group, as yet without a name, to rehearse in a classroom after school hours and we were designated to perform at the very end of the show. We were portraying what present-day pupils listened to and how they looked 1960s style.

Rehearsals for the pageant started many weeks before the opening ceremony and we had been told to perform two songs, which would signal the end of the show. It was decided that, because of the limited space on and off stage, upon the cue 'to the beat of rock 'n' roll', we would enter at the back of the hall and make our way to the stage, passing down the centre aisle with the audience either side of us, carrying our guitars and snare drum up onto the stage. However, the organisers had a problem where to store our amplifier while the rest of the show was being performed and Martin came up with an ingenious solution. The amp was stored beneath the stage and positioned behind a fabric curtain. He then drilled a few holes in the stage close to where we would stand and installed some jack plug sockets. Beneath the stage, the sockets were wired up to the amplifier, so all we had to do was carry our guitars with leads attached, walk onto the stage and simply plug our instruments into the sockets on the floor – problem solved.

All pupils taking part in the show had to have make-up applied beforehand and we were no exception. Photographs taken of us prior to our performance in the school playground show us wearing make-up, which makes us way ahead of our time. Eat your heart out David Bowie! It would take ten years before Bowie came to prominence wearing outlandish feminine-inspired clothes and wearing make-up on stage. He helped to spearhead Glam Rock when many groups took to wearing make-up on stage.

JUST MINUTES PRIOR TO OUR CUE
'TO THE BEAT OF ROCK 'N' ROLL'

The big day arrived. The Lord Mayor of London and the Mayor of Romford conducted the inauguration ceremony with many local dignitaries attending and the event was well covered by the local press. Looking at that photograph taken in the school playground, I can't for the life of me remember why two of our classmates were portraying 'black and white minstrels' in the play, but it certainly wouldn't take place in today's politically correct society!

It was at an early appearance in a youth club in Hornchurch that Malcolm blackmailed us – no drum solo, no drummer. This wasn't part of our act, but not wanting to lose our drummer we relented. To our horror the solo went on for over ten minutes and would have gone on longer if it hadn't been for the club warden's insistence that he stopped playing. Malcolm was so annoyed that he simply picked up his drum kit and left and that was the last time we ever saw him. So now we were on the look out for a drummer. John remembered that his old classmate, John Graham Rixon (JG), had played drums in the local Boys Brigade bugle band, but he had already left school to start his apprenticeship in the printing trade. We contacted him and he became our new drummer. Unfortunately Pete Weavers left to pursue his studies, so this was now the nucleus of the group and would remain so for eight years–

Lead Guitar:	Colin Stoddart
Bass Guitar:	Martin Palmer
Vocalist:	John Wilkinson
Drums:	John Rixon

Two additional members joined a year or so later, Patrick McCarthy on rhythm guitar and Dave Murkin on saxophone. They remained with us for five years, and for a brief period Ray Stevenson replaced Martin on bass after he left, but Martin was soon to regret his decision and returned to the fold.

A FOND AND LASTING MEMORY OF SCHOOL

Before entering St Edward's playground, every pupil had to walk along a drive passing a row of six very tiny, old terraced cottages, a daily reminder of a bygone age. They had stood there for over a hundred years, the brickwork slowly gathering grime and moss. Their size never ceased to amaze me – how could a family live in such small surroundings? But one family did, and that was old Lil and her two young children. They lived in the end cottage on the corner of the school entrance. Built in the traditional two up, two down style, the cottages consisted of two small rooms on the ground floor and two small bedrooms on the first floor. From the appearance of these cottages on the outside, the interior of every room must have been minuscule.

Sometimes, when passing her cottage in the morning, Lil would be standing by her front gate watching us kids walking into the playground. She was a well-proportioned woman, probably in her early 40s, who always wore a scarf tied around her head in a turban style and over her clothes was a tatty, faded pinafore. Remember, this was still the late 1950s. As Martin and I walked past I would always say 'Morning Lil' and she responded with a semi-toothless grin. I always wondered why she couldn't apply the bright red lipstick she wore actually onto her lips, rather then around them, which gave her a clown-like appearance.

Rumour had it at school that Lil was on the game, and this probably explained the odd sighting of different men coming and going from her cottage over the years. We often used to remark amongst ourselves that you'd have to be pretty desperate to end up paying to jump into bed with the likes of old Lil. She never appeared to go to work, or have a husband, so perhaps she had been forced to become a prostitute to make ends meet, so to speak.

In our fifth year, pupils were allowed out of school at lunchtime and quite often, on our return to school, there would be a small gang of us. John was always the vocal one as we slowly passed by Lil's cottage, shout-ing out 'Show us your tits Lil', which usually brought about no response at all from the cottage, but lots of laughter from us. However, I think she recognised us as occasionally the grubby, and rather tatty bedroom curtain would be pulled aside to reveal a grinning Lil, her head looking so large against the tiny bedroom window. Her appearance always brought on a round of applause from us.

Now, only a month away from leaving school and with examinations completed, we were free agents, so there was no rush to return to school after our lunch break and the headmaster fortunately appeared to have turned a blind eye to our comings and goings. On this particular day, there must have been about six or seven of us returning to school after lunch and when we came to Lil's cottage we stopped outside. As usual John called out 'Show us your tits Lil' and suddenly somebody pointed out that the bedroom curtain had moved ever so slightly, prompting John to yell out again, 'Go on Lil, show us your tits.' Suddenly the bedroom curtain was pulled aside and there was a toothless, grinning Lil, still wearing her turban, with fresh, bright red lipstick on, mostly around her lips. We started clapping madly, when suddenly she pulled up her top to reveal her large boobs. One by one we stopped clapping and, for a brief second with mouths wide open, we goggled at the sight. Suddenly she was gone. We were so taken aback by the experience that silence prevailed as we made our way back into school. I've often wondered if she knew we would shortly be leaving school forever and wouldn't be seeing us again, so that bountiful display was a leaving present for us all! Strangely, during the final few weeks before leaving school, John never shouted out again when we passed old Lil's cottage!

Finally my last day at school had arrived. It was a day of mixed emotion. As I walked around the school with friends, saying goodbye to the various teachers, it was hard for me to get my head around the fact that this was indeed my final day as a pupil of St. Edward's. Some teachers I hadn't particularly liked, but saying goodbye to them had brought about big smiles and vigorous handshakes, so perhaps they were quite normal after all. By mid-afternoon, I was clearing my desk out and the reality of it all was starting to sink in. Saying goodbye to people in my class was hard too, even though I had nothing in common with many of them. But I had spent the past five years of my life, five days a week, working with them and now I'd probably never see them again.

With a bunch of close friends, I walked out of school, passing Lil's cottage on the way. We encouraged John to give her one last call for old times' sake, but there was no sign of her from inside. Again he yelled out, but there was no telltale movement of the upstairs bedroom curtain. 'Perhaps she's too upset seeing us leave' I suggested, which brought about a few chuckles, but sadly no last appearance was made, so we moved on and out into the big wide world.

5

WHAT TO WEAR AS A MOD IN THE EARLY 60s

Life in general in the early part of the 60s was still quite formal and I would wear a conventional suit and a tie for every day office work. My work suits were bought locally off-the-peg. However, when the weekend arrived I would head off to the local dancehall dressed in my best tie and shirt and Mod suit which was hand-tailored from mohair fabric and made by a bespoke tailor in Stratford in London's East End.

Certain influences from America were slowly creeping into the British way of life, like refrigerators and washing machines and, of course, rock 'n' roll music. Here in the UK, the wearing of denim jeans was still very much associated with cowboys as portrayed in the popular Western movies. In the early 60s, and pre-Carnaby Street days, Mods were a minority group of youngsters found only in and around the London area, who sought to dress differently. In most towns at this time there were Army and Navy Surplus Stores, which had sprung up around the country after the Second World War. These shops specialised in selling new and old military gear including boots, tin helmets and basically anything to do with the military. They even sold second-hand US leather flying bomber jackets and, most importantly, US parkas – a long, windproof, hooded jacket that eventually became the 'uniform' of the Mod scooter boys.

These shops also stocked a small selection of industrial clothing, which catered for the local work force and one of the initial fashion statements for a Mod in its early manifestation was to wear a pair of baggy industrial jeans, which could be purchased there. It was imperative, when buying an industrial pair of jeans, that firstly they were made from a very dark blue denim fabric and secondly, they had a small pouch running down the right leg, originally intended to house a workman's ruler. No pouch, then no purchase. In the early Mod days, local high street menswear shops didn't stock denim jeans, so when the Mods moved on to wearing US imported Levi denim jeans, it meant going on a buying trip early on a Sunday morning to Petticoat Lane market. Situated in the East End of London, this market was where a few stalls specialised in selling imported American Levi jeans, button-down shirts and T-shirts. The name Levi was vitally important, and the brand could be easily recognised by a leather label bearing the name etc. in red, which was sewn on the waistband at the back of the jeans.

Another piece of important Mod clothing was a sports shirt, nowadays known as a polo shirt. In the 1920s, tennis players wore cumbersome, heavy cotton, long-sleeve shirts, so the famous French tennis player, Rene Lacoste, went about designing a more user-friendly tennis shirt. The outcome was a T-shaped shirt made from a white knitted cotton pique fabric, which had short sleeves, a knitted collar and a two or three-buttoned placket.

At the peak of his tennis career in the US, Lacoste was a formidable tennis player and he was nicknamed 'the crocodile'. Lacoste cashed in on his fame and his nickname and went into partnership with a clothing manufacturer to mass-produce his shirt. To identify his shirt brand, an embroidered crocodile was sewn on the front of each garment.

Now enter Fred Perry, a British tennis player who had achieved enormous success between 1933-1936 by winning the US and Wimbledon Championships three times, and the French and Australian Championships twice. To capitalise on his name, Perry also went into partnership to manufacture a similar tennis shirt to the Lacoste one. His tennis shirts were also only supplied in white and embroidered on the left side of the shirt was a green laurel wreath, the Fred Perry logo.

I'd heard through the Mod grapevine that a Fred Perry tennis shirt was now the shirt to be seen in, but definitely not in white. So I bought one of these shirts and my mum dyed it navy blue. The manufacturer of the white Fred Perry tennis shirt was quick to sense a trend and started to produce the shirt in a variety of colours, all with a contrasting embroidered Fred Perry logo.

Change during the early sixties was understandably slow. Britain was still recovering economically from the effects of the Second World War, which had ended less than 20 years before and food rationing had only finally been lifted in 1954. Most of Britain's youth were employed and so had spare money in their pockets but young people still dressed like their parents. My father never wore a pair of jeans throughout his entire life. When visiting family and friends, he always wore a suit and tie and even in the 1990s he would still wear a suit and tie if invited to our house for Sunday lunch. Dressing casually for my father was to discard the suit jacket and slip a knitted cardigan over his formal shirt and tie.

A MOD PARTY - 1962

A year or so after leaving school, we started to attend a few all-night parties, which meant having to pretend to my parents that that I was sleeping over at John's house. Likewise, John told his mother he was sleeping at my house. This little white lie was essential otherwise we would have been barred from going out at night. We'd heard through the grapevine that it was popular for local Mods to assemble at Romford station on a Saturday evening to learn if and where a party was being held on that night. So, wearing our latest Mod gear, John, Martin, JG and myself all headed off to the station to check out the action.

We arrived to find the station foyer packed with Mods. We didn't know anybody there and the four of us stood around smoking and trying to look pretty cool. Nothing happened for about half an hour, when suddenly a guy came out of a telephone kiosk in the foyer holding up a piece of paper. He had the address of a party, which resulted in a mass exodus as soon as it was read out. Scooters suddenly appeared outside the station making a lot of noise revving up, letting everybody know they were impatient to leave. Any empty pillion seats were immediately occupied. A couple of cars pulled up behind them and most of the girls rushed over and got in the cars. Suddenly they were off, forming a convoy as they made they way up South Street. So there we were, the only four people still left standing outside the station. Decisive action was needed. I hailed a taxi, saying to the driver 'follow those scooters' and we headed off to some unsuspecting victim's house to gatecrash the party. Entering Harold Hill, we continued following the convoy. Ahead of us, the line of scooters turned right and went down a dead-end side road. We instructed the taxi driver to stop by the entrance to the road, paid him, and we piled out of the taxi.

It was dark now and we stood there listening to the taxi disappearing into the night. We could hear music being played, but somewhere in the distance and guessed that was where the party was being held. We headed off down the side road and, as the music got louder, we could see about ten scooters had parked up outside a house. Through the net curtains we could make out people dancing in the front room. After much debate, we walked up to the front door and knocked. Immediately a Mod, with a can of beer in his hand, opened the door and welcomed us in. The place was absolutely packed. We wandered down the hall, into a kitchen and helped ourselves to a bottle of beer each. I stood there wondering who lived here. Fancy having your home invaded by a bunch of unknowns!

I, for one, didn't feel safe there, and I'm sure the others felt the same way. People were wandering in and out of rooms and some had headed upstairs. Suddenly a girl screamed from the front room, followed by glass being broken. We edged our way into the hall and, looking into the front room, we could see a guy retrieving crystal glasses from a broken-fronted display cabinet and handing them out. The girl was crying on the floor and kept screaming out for people to leave. I guessed it was her parents' house and originally she was hosting a small gathering until this hoard of uninvited Mods gatecrashed the party. We looked at one another and JG said 'Lets get out of here.' We all agreed, made for the front door and disappeared into the night. We'd just reached the top of the road when, in the distance, we could hear police cars coming with bells ringing. The next minute three police cars appeared and headed off down the side road. We thanked our lucky stars that we'd left when we did. We'd had a narrow escape from the law and we decided there and then, never again. And we never did gatecrash another party.

But we had an immediate problem on our hands – where do we sleep tonight? We couldn't go home having said we were staying over at each other's house. It was decided to head back to civilisation and the bus conveniently dropped us outside Romford station. 'Anyone fancy a Horlicks?' I called out. Faces lit up, so we crossed the road, walked straight into Sherry's Bar and ordered four mugs of frothy Horlicks. We whiled away the time smoking, talking about the party and our narrow escape, the group, girls and, now feeling a bit peckish, we each ordered the cafe's speciality – a hot dog with fried onions and mustard. After another round of Horlicks, some lights in the cafe were switched off, signalling they were closing. So, at one o'clock in the morning, we headed up Romford South Street, wondering how we were going pass the night away.

We reached the Eastern Avenue dual carriageway and, as we walked along the side of the road, we spotted a private double-decker bus parked in a long layby, opposite some factory gates. The bus would be the works bus and was used to pick up the factory workers every day from designated pick-up points throughout the surrounding areas. We looked up and down the road and, with not a soul in sight, we boarded the bus and cautiously climbed up the stairs – it was empty! Well, at least we had a roof over our heads for the night. I drifted in and out of sleep curled up on a bench seat, but by now the temperature had dropped considerably and I was freezing. After a couple of hours I'd had enough and sat upright on the bench seat, to find John and JG quietly smoking cigarettes. So I lit up as well and within minutes Martin was awake too and rolling a cigarette.

As we sat there in silence, shivering and puffing on our cigarettes, we heard the distinctive sound of a bicycle being wheeled along. It stopped by the bus and we sat there motionless. Heavy footsteps could be heard slowly coming up the stairs. Eight eyeballs widened and looked towards the staircase. The top of a policeman's helmet emerged first, followed by a head, and then a body, and then the light of a powerful torch momentarily blinded us as it was switched on and pointed at us. The policeman called out 'allo, 'allo, 'allo, so what have we here then? We explained the predicament we were in and, although he appeared to be somewhat sympathetic, he certainly wasn't going to allow us to remain on the bus any longer.

GOOD OLD VIC BABY

We got off the bus and walked away – it was certainly a lot colder outside than in! Although dawn was breaking, it was still too early to go home and anyway, what could we say to our parents? John came up with the suggestion 'Why don't we go to the 8 o'clock communion service at St Edward's church?'

Now, why would four young Mods contemplate going to church of all places to kill time? Well, we had all attended St Edward' Secondary Modern School, a self-funded Church of England school which was affiliated to St Edward's Church, both found at opposite ends of Romford Market Place. Vicar Wright from the church had hosted our weekly religious study classes at school, and subsequently he come to know us individually by name. He was a rather tall, rotund and jovial character, and was a sight to behold heading through the market square sitting astride his old Vespa scooter dressed in his flowing black cassock and white dog collar. An early Mod perhaps!

Apart from all that, we were cold and desperate, and John continued 'It'll kill an hour of our time, and at least it'll be warm inside. Then we can head home from there.' I was the first to pipe up 'We can't go into the church looking like this' referring to our Mod gear. 'And besides, not one of us is wearing a tie.' Martin came up with the classic 'I'm sure God won't object to our clothes.' I chirped up again 'What's Vicar Wright going to say when he sees us looking like this?' JG responded, 'I think he'll be surprised but grateful to see us and I bet he won't say a thing.' No one came up with an alternative suggestion, so we made our way into town. Romford Market Place was totally deserted when we arrived and we were early for the service. By now we were freezing and looking more than a bit dishevelled. We needed some warmth, so we decided to go straight in and made ourselves as comfortable as possible on the hard wooden pews at the back of the church.

We were all also extremely tired by this time. As we knelt down on the hassocks, we pretended we were saying a few prayers and were able to briefly close our eyes. At 8 o'clock on the nail the service started, so we were forced to sit up, but we longed for Vicar Wright to say, 'Lets all pray' so we could fall onto our knees and close our eyes again. I had my eyes closed and was drifting into a light sleep, when I caught a whiff of tobacco smoke in the air. Opening my eyes, I looked across and there was Martin, head well down, puffing on one of his roll-up cigarettes. I could see John next to me trying to stop himself from laughing out loud at what Martin was doing. I looked towards the altar to see if Vicar Wright had spotted any smoke drifting up from the pews at the back of the church, but fortunately he was in full prayer with his back to us. Martin, by this time, had extinguished his cigarette, and whispered across to us, 'I just had to have a puff.' The service came to an end within 45 minutes and, when we sat up, the Vicar was already standing outside the church entrance ready to shake hands with his parishioners as they left.

Although I had warmed up somewhat, I felt dirty and sticky, and my clothing was badly creased. I looked at the others and they didn't look any better. We waited until the last parishioner had walked out of the church and began to make our way to the exit. Would we face rebuke from the Vicar for attending church looking like we did? But as we emerged into the daylight Vicar Wright's face lit up. 'How lovely to see you boys' he said and then, as we shook his hand, he thanked us individually for coming. 'Thank you Colin, thank you John, thank you John (JG).' I stood and watched as he shook hands with Martin. 'Thank you Martin', and still he made no reference to our appearance or the smoking episode – good old Vicar Wright! I think that was the last time I attended a service at St Edward's Church, but not the last time I saw Vicar Wright.

BANKING FOR BEGINNERS

U pon leaving school, my brother, who was five years my senior, started an apprenticeship at Ford Motor Company in Dagenham, to qualify as a toolmaker. As a Ford employee, my father had also registered my name well in advance of me leaving school to complete the same apprenticeship. But nearing the end of my time at school, and with very minimal career advice offered, I had to come to a decision fairly soon. A toolmaker! I couldn't even make a simple wooden toast rack correctly in woodwork classes! Toolmaking definitely wasn't for me! I had fancied the idea of becoming a draughtsman but having failed my technical drawing examination, that put paid to that idea. I was running out of options.

Some people had already left school to find work in the printing world, like my good friend JG, our future drummer. But it was a closed shop, a union protected profession, and the recommendation for an apprenticeship had to come from a union member, who could be a member of the family or a close friend.

During our last year at school, the local employment office set up a couple of short meetings to discuss and advise pupils on possible job prospects. Some pupils already knew the career route they were going to pursue, but anyone like myself, still dithering around, was put under pressure to decide on a career for life. Narrowing it all down, the only option open to me was a clerical career in either banking or insurance. I was pretty naive at 16 as to the ways of the world and, looking back, it might have helped matters had the career officer make some reference to creative jobs such as those in the world of advertising for example.

I did suggest to my father that I'd like to go to art school, or even become a window dresser. The latter brought about a look of sheer horror on his face! It was never mentioned again, but he went on to say, 'If you want to go to art school, then you get no financial help from me. You'll be on your own.' So it was back to the drawing board, not literally, as I'd dropped the draughtsman idea. But banking or insurance – what was it going to be? I didn't know anybody who worked in a bank and the only person I knew in the insurance business was our insurance agent, who visited my parents' home every month on his bicycle to collect premiums due on a couple of polices. He was a pleasant enough guy, but pretty boring, so the decision was made. Banking it was, much to my mother and father's delight.

During my early years in the bank I used to complain to my father that I was unhappy at work, not so much with the people I worked with, but with the job itself. His worldly advice was always to 'Give it a bit longer son and remember that you have a job for life, with a good pension at the end of the day.' This statement from my father was understandable as he had experienced being out of work for months on end during the 1930s and 1940s and had to take any job he could get just to pay the bills. Eventually, after numerous jobs, he finally found himself working at Ford Motor Company with an opportunity to make something of himself. He became an industrial engineer or, more commonly known as a time study engineer, and was eventually promoted to a managerial position. He received a gold watch after working there for 30 years, and retired a few years later.

But his advice, well meaning as it was and given in all sincerity, came from his own personal perspective and experiences of life. However, from a young man's perspective in the 60s, to have to work for nearly half a century at a job you disliked and in an alien environment, just to get a good pension 30 or 40 years later, just didn't cut the mustard with me.

MY FIRST DAY AT WORK

The bank and I were strange bedfellows and we were never going to hit it off. We continually clashed during my 11-year career there, even from day one on the 15 August 1960, when I walked into that small banking hall in Victoria Road, a new sub-branch of the main Westminster Bank in Romford.

I really thought I looked the 'bees knees' having dressed that morning in my new Mod suit, but within an hour I was called into the manager's office and reprimanded for wearing such clothing. I was sent home to change into something more appropriate to wear for every day banking!

My Mod ensemble consisted of a plain navy blue three-button jacket, which was nicknamed a 'bum freezer', so-called because it was a lot shorter than a conventional jacket. It had two, three-inch side vents, high narrow lapels and narrow slanted pocket flaps and the three buttons were covered in the identical suit fabric. The matching trousers had a two-button waistband with a double pleated front, medium leg fit, but crucially, no turn-ups.

With the suit I wore a white shirt with a detachable white stiff collar, which was attached to the shirt by collar studs at the back and front, borrowed from my dad's battered old leather stud box. The double cuffs of the shirt had no buttons, so required the use of cufflinks, also borrowed from my dad's stud box.

I was especially proud of my newly purchased white stiff collar, another Mod accessory, which I had found in a local Dunn & Co menswear shop in Romford High Street. Dunn & Co was an old fashioned, well-established chain of menswear shops found in most High Streets throughout the country. I can remember the shop assistant having to fetch a small stepladder and climb to the top of a cupboard to retrieve an old dusty box. As he opened the box he said 'There isn't much call for this shape of collar anymore sir.' Much to his surprise, I said 'Perfect, I'll take two collars please.' Instead of being the traditional pointed collar, the points were replaced with rounded ends, and Mods would complete the ensemble with a very conservative narrow navy blue regimental tie with repeating pairs of thin diagonal stripes of red and gold – dead smart.

Arriving home that morning, my dear mum had been shocked to see me, especially when I told her the bank manager had sent me home as he thought the way I dressed was 'not appropriate apparel for the bank.' He had even criticised my shoes, which he felt were too pointed. It was ironic, as my mum had very kindly paid for my first pair of work shoes, which I'd bought at the local Dolcis shoe shop in Romford. I had initially bought a much more pointed pair of shoes but when I returned home with them, my mother was horrified and insisted they were much too pointed to wear for work. So I was sent back to the shop to exchange them for a less pointed pair, and now the bank manager felt that even this pair of shoes was not suitable!

Fortunately for me, I did have a spare, traditional navy blue suit and a conventional stiff collar with points to wear with my white collarless shirt. I had to make do with my old black school shoes and sod it, the tie I wore this morning was perfectly acceptable, so off I tripped back to work, and nothing more was said.

Towards the end of my first week, a man wearing a dark uniform walked into the branch and was warmly greeted by members of staff. He was obviously expected and four small brown cardboard boxes were handed over to him. He went outside and disappeared into a van. Within a few minutes he returned with the boxes, which he put down on the till. I was intrigued – what was in those boxes?

I was soon to find out when I was called over to the till and asked if I wanted to join the Westminster Bank's stiff collar laundry service. It was explained to me that I could choose in total to have ten collars, and I could also choose from four different collar styles illustrated on the side of the box. They were basically the same style but with varying lengths to the points, a couple slightly more cutaway in appearance. Apparently I didn't have to pay for the collars – they remained the property of the bank, but each week I would have to pay for however many collars I wanted laundered. Needless to say, there were no round white collars available. As all the males in the branch used this service and although I wore detachable stiff collars for a totally different reason, I agreed to join. I selected just six collars, gave him my name, collar size and style, and the details were recorded on the side of the box. He then went back to the van and returned with a box containing my six stiff collars.

Next Thursday, the van arrived as usual and, waiting on the till counter for the laundry man, were five boxes containing a lot of dirty white collars, which were dutifully replaced with identical freshly-laundered collars. This service was eventually phased out as retailers like Marks and Spencer introduced inexpensive cotton shirts with fused, attached collars and buttoned cuffs.

This was 1960. Computers simply didn't exist in the bank and wouldn't be introduced for a further eight years. On a daily basis, after the bank's doors were closed, every cheque and credit paying-in slip received during regular banking hours, were sorted into two categories – external and internal items. The internal items were sorted into alphabetical order and then laboriously written by hand into ledgers later that afternoon, after the bank had closed its doors. The ledgers contained a separate page for every bank account in the branch and every new entry had to be tabbed and initialled, then double-checked and initialled again by a senior clerk. When this task was completed, the cheques and paying-in slips would be handed over to me and, as junior clerk, my job was to ensure that each item was printed mechanically onto each individual customer's bank statement using a semi-automated Burroughs machine.

I would first select the correct bank statement contained in a tray, which corresponded with the name and account number on the cheque. The first step was to enter the customer's balance into the machine, then align the statement in the machine, press a button and the statement was dated automatically. The printing head then moved to the next column. I then entered the cheque number and, pressing the button again, the head moved to the next column and I entered the amount of the cheque. If that was the only entry, I would press the button again, and the head would move to the next column and the new balance was calculated and printed onto the statement.

The following morning, as part of my junior clerk responsibilities, I would deliver the external cheques and credit slips to the main branch in Romford, where a bank messenger collected them from London. They were then sorted and finally distributed to the various banks and branches around the country, from where they had originated.

All banks around the country opened their doors for a few hours on a Saturday morning, except sub-branches and so members of staff at my sub-branch worked at the main branch on that day. The bank's dress code during weekly banking hours for a male employee was a dark suit, navy or charcoal, with a white shirt and tie, and black shoes. However, on a Saturday morning it was a more relaxed code for males who could wear a sports jacket (Harris Tweed or similar) or a traditional navy blue blazer with gold buttons. This could be worn with a relaxed shirt, not stiff-collared, and tie, with cavalry twill beige or plain light grey trousers and brown brogue or even brown suede shoes – how exciting!

I ORDER MY FIRST MOD OUTFIT

I paid a proportion of my weekly salary to my parents and then the rest was mine to spend as I saw fit, but I was encouraged by my parents to save some of the money as well. One Saturday afternoon, after about a month of saving, I went into the Romford branch of Burtons Tailoring, a men's clothing shop, and ordered my first made-to-measure Mod ensemble.

Burtons Tailoring at the time only offered made-to-measure suits, jackets and trousers. Shelves were neatly filled with rolls of different fabrics and pattern books were filled with drawings illustrating various styles of suits. There was a choice of single-breasted jackets with two or three buttons or double-breasted with four or six buttons. Trousers were available with or without turn-ups and a choice of waistbands from zip adjusters to button or simply just having belt loops, and either a zip or a button fly. There was even a page from which to select a variety of buttons, plain black, brown or tortoiseshell, covered buttons for evening suits, and an assortment of metal buttons for blazers.

I wanted everything to be made to the current Mod style, but with a bit of my own artistic licence as to the choice of fabrics. The first major problem I encountered, after I was measured up, was selecting the style of jacket I wanted. I pointed to an illustration of a four-button double-breasted blazer, but said I wanted the length of the jacket shortened to hang just below the waistband and to have two three-inch vents at the back. Eyes were immediately raised. I then pointed to a heavy grey Harris Tweed cloth woven with a faint red criss-cross pattern as the fabric of choice. A look of disbelief was written all over the face of the assistant. At first he said he doubted the factory could make such a jacket as they worked from standard patterns, but I was insistent to the point of cancelling my order.

Before the assistant volunteered to telephone the factory in Leeds to see if making this jacket was feasible, I gave him the details for my trousers. Again I thought his eyes might pop out from their sockets as I described what I wanted. I requested a two-and-a-half-inch waistband with four small fabric-covered buttons in the same fabric at the front, zip adjusters and fly, no turn-ups, and the trousers had to taper to 16 inches in width. On the outside of each trouser leg at the bottom, I wanted a one-inch vent, with a small single cloth covered button sewn on the fabric directly above the vent. I then pointed to the roll of black and grey mottled wool fabric I had selected, from which I would like them to be made.

All the details had been dutifully noted on an order pad. The assistant said nothing. He excused himself and walked over to a colleague, presumably to discuss my order. Heads were shaken, hands were put on hips, and I could tell from the body language that my order had created a bit of wobbly – I had dared to interfere with the rules! A telephone call was made to the factory and, after about 10 minutes, the assistant wandered over to me slightly shaking his head. I expected some bad news but no, the production manager in Leeds had given the OK. Probably my little order would give him an interesting and challenging break from the usual production routine.

A card arrived within about three weeks informing me that my jacket and trousers had arrived. Excitedly I went back to the shop and tried both on in the changing room without showing the assistant, fearing my appearance might produce some sniggering from the staff. They fitted perfectly and I was a happy chappy.

The following Saturday, wearing my new Mod outfit with a casual shirt, leather moccasins and, please note, no tie, I strode into the main branch of the Westminster Bank in Romford. Needless to say there was plenty of whispering, especially from the older members of staff, as I walked around the branch, but in the machine room where all the younger people worked, my outfit was quite well received, but not fully embraced, I hasten to add.

I ended up wearing this outfit every Saturday morning and slowly it must have been accepted as the whispering stopped after a few weeks. I half expected to be reprimanded by the manager at some stage but, looking back, I'm convinced I got away with it because I wasn't a permanent member of staff at this branch.

7

EARLY DAYS AT THE WYKEHAM HALL - ROMFORD - 1961

The Wykeham Hall belonged to St Edward's Church and was located next door to the church in Romford's Market Place. The church had close links with our school, also called St Edward's, which was located at the top end of Romford Market. During our school days, every Monday evening we all attended the St. Edward's Youth Club, which was held in the Wykeham Hall. The club was a useful meeting place to chat up the girls you fancied but Vicar Wright ran the youth club and his presence there rather hindered my feeble attempts. However, we were very fortunate that, during the early days of our band and with our school and church connection, Vicar Wright allowed us to rehearse there.

1961 was the start of our group playing locally on a more serious basis. Although we were without our own transportation, we still managed in that year to perform at 17 different locations, in youth clubs and schools. As soon as we were mobile with our own van one year later in 1962, we suddenly achieved lift-off, performing live 88 times and during 1963 the bookings rose to 133.

Local youth clubs, especially those held in schools, were only open during the week, so weekend work for us was pretty thin on the ground. During those early days of the group, the four of us would spend most Saturday evenings at the Wykeham Hall in Romford watching other local bands play.

The Wykeham Hall was one of the important early venues east of central London for the burgeoning late 1950s and early 1960s music scene. Popular groups at the time, such as Adam Faith, Joe Brown and The Bruvvers, Johnny Kidd and The Pirates, Screaming Lord Sutch and Marty Wilde, were just some of the popular acts that performed there. This venue was also where up-and-coming groups cut their teeth, some going on to greater recognition, like Amen Corner, Chris Farlowe and The Thunderbirds, The Dave Clark Five, The Small Faces and The Love Affair. Neil Christian and The Crusaders also appeared at the Wykeham Hall. Their lead guitarist was a cocky 16-year-old Jimmy Page who, a decade later, would be lead guitarist of Led Zeppelin, one of the world's biggest and most influential groups of the time. Seeing all these various groups was an important learning curve for us at the time, allowing us to watch and gain invaluable insight into individual performances, listening and learning and gaining ideas for our own band.

In America some of the early rock 'n' roll star's careers had already started to dim, but here in the UK they still had a small and loyal following of supporters. One of John's idols was a US singer called Gene Vincent who, with his group The Blue Caps, had a world-wide hit in 1956 with 'Be Bop A Lula', a song which has become an all time rock 'n' roll classic. But eventually the hits started to dry up in the US, so Gene Vincent left America to perform in the UK. When it was advertised that he would be making an appearance at the Wykeham Hall, John was ecstatic. We all loved the song and had seen Gene Vincent and his Blue Caps perform in a small cameo role in a film called 'The Girl Can't Help It' starring the actress Jayne Mansfield. To us, this man was a living legend, and not to be missed.

So there we were, one Saturday evening in 1963, huddled together at the front of the stage, waiting to see this living legend perform. On cue, the curtains opened and there was the man himself dressed all in black leather, even to the point of wearing black leather gloves. The microphone stand had been lowered to allow him to stretch out his damaged leg behind him. Gene Vincent's stance was somewhat unusual due to a motorcycle accident a few years earlier, when his leg was severely damaged and had to be encased in a metal brace for support. He sang clutching the mike stand with both hands for support. His backing band was a six-piece London group called Sounds Incorporated who, with their three sax players, generated a very big and loud authentic rock 'n' roll sound. He rarely acknowledged the audience and sang most of the time looking up at the ceiling with a slightly demonic expression on his face, but we were impressed.

Unfortunately, Gene Vincent died in 1971 at the young age of 36 due to a ruptured stomach ulcer, but his legacy was finally recognised when he was posthumously inducted into the US Rock 'n' Roll Hall of Fame in 1998. He also has a star on the Hollywood Walk of Fame.

Other Saturdays, when no headline acts were booked, there would be two or three local groups performing throughout the evening. For us, these visits to the Wykeham Hall were extremely useful and gave us an opportunity to watch, listen and learn. It was helpful for me to study the lead guitarist and to try and establish what chords were being used in a certain song. Sometimes, if I was lucky, I could even follow the notes that were being played in a guitar solo, which made my job that bit easier at rehearsals. Martin and JG would do the same, watching their respective counterparts, learning what they did. Nothing passed our scrutiny, everything was of interest to us – the guitars, the drums, the amplifiers, the sound systems and the bass speaker cabinets, how the group members moved on stage and the clothes they wore. If not discussed there and then, comments would be made on the way home, or brought up at our weekly rehearsal night. It was all part and parcel of our development as a group. The music industry was changing fast. Guitar-based groups were taking over from traditional jazz bands. Young people wanted their own identity – and their own music.

Martin naturally had his eye on bass guitarists and especially bass speaker cabinets. He soon started to build one of his own and, as we began to play in bigger and bigger venues, so the cabinets increased in size due to Martin's obsession in developing a 'cleaner' and louder bass sound. Bass notes, when produced at high volume, create vibrations and this was causing Martin's bass cabinets to vibrate and move from their original position on stage. To try and cure this problem, Martin put a layer of concrete in the bottom of each cabinet. An innovative idea which had the desired effect, but the major drawback was the weight when transporting them from van to stage and back. Each cabinet was so heavy. It took at least two people to lift, even more if we had to negotiate flights of stairs. Slowly it dawned on us that the one person not helping carry these cabinets was Martin. Cunningly, at the end of a gig, he always managed to find somebody to talk to, or was just about to roll up a cigarette, which meant the rest of us having to lug his speakers back to the van.

We finally got over this problem. Instead of loading the bass cabinets into the van first, as we usually did, we devised an alternative packing format. In went the drums, then the amplifiers and then the PA system, leaving just enough room to pack in the two bass cabinets. Problem solved! We just left the bass cabinets on the stage until the very last and finally Martin got the message!

On one of these Saturday night gatherings, JG watched intrigued as a drummer walked on stage, laid down a square of carpet and then proceeded to set up his drum kit on top of it. When the kit was finally erected, the last job he performed before leaving the stage was to hammer in a number of nails around the two front feet of the bass drum. The carpet and the nails prevented the drums from moving around on the stage – we were impressed! It was fairly common practice for drummers, halfway through a set, to launch into a drum solo. This night was no exception. The drummer was manic, and without the carpet and nails, he and his drums would have moved their position on stage. For a short while after this, JG adopted the same carpet and nail routine, but we were never sure why as he never performed a drum solo, or played his drums that energetically! Now I come think of it, perhaps we never asked him to perform a drum solo, but I do recall the three of us sniggering away behind his back, as he resolutely nailed his kit to the floor. We were still a 'small time' semi-pro group, but we had ambitions – one day we would top of the bill at the Wykeham Hall.

GUITAR CHATTER

Cliff Richard and The Shadows were one of the main inspirational groups during the early British rock 'n' roll movement of the late 50s and early 60s. The music they performed was easier to emulate than their American counterparts. Like the earlier skiffle craze, it needed a more simplistic approach to the music, which encouraged aspiring young men around the country to pick up an instrument and form a group, and the same applied to punk music decades later.

So, for me as the lead guitarist, the American guitarists were way ahead in their technical approach and sound. But that's not surprising because America had already embraced the guitar in its early blues music and flourishing country and western music scene. The acoustic guitar had become intrinsic in American cultural music and acoustic guitars had been manufactured in the States since the turn of the century. Then along came the electric guitar, which was invented in the early 1930s, and it instantly became a key component in the blues and country bands, and in the final development of rock 'n' roll.

Naivety certainly played a major part for me in these early days, as did the lack of money, and I bought my first electric guitar because it was cheap and looked similar in appearance to Hank B. Marvin's guitar. I wasn't aware at the time, or even a few years later, of the importance of buying a guitar that was set up correctly by the manufacturer. Crucial to learning and playing the guitar is to ensure that the strings are set as low as possible over the fretboard. If the string height were too high, as was the case with most cheap guitars bought in the 60s, it would require considerable pressure to press the string down onto a fret to make a note ring. It would be even more difficult attempting to play a chord and to get every note of the chord to ring. This would eventually result in very sore fingers and, in extreme cases, I'm sure it must have put off many aspiring guitarists from playing the instrument all together.

The British government, at this time, had an embargo on importing US-made guitars into the UK. However, on rare occasions a few of these exquisite guitars were brought into the country by British seaman returning from visits to the US, and many of them were eventually sold on to local guitar shops, but it was extremely rare to see a beautiful American-made guitar in a British music shop window. Basically, the only time you ever saw these guitars were on LP covers, being played by visiting American guitarists when on tour in the UK, or making the odd appearance on a TV show. Many of these jaw-dropping American guitars were only seen in cameo shots of artists performing in early rock 'n' roll films.

Seeing for the first time the now-iconic Fender Stratocaster was a memorable experience for me. It was 1958, and I had bought an LP called 'Chirping Crickets' by an American group called Buddy Holly and The Crickets. Two electric guitars were held by two members of the group in the photograph on the front of the LP, but it was the brown sunburst-coloured Fender Stratocaster that stole the show for me. I just couldn't stop studying the guitar on the cover as I sat for hours listening to this album. Its shape was so futuristic and it just fascinated me. The other guitar was a Gibson ES225, equally an interesting but not so futuristic-looking brown sunburst, semi-acoustic model, with a Florentine cutaway. I had never seen guitars like this before and it was sometime before the UK embargo was eventually lifted and they started to appear in music shop windows. These classic guitars – Fender, Gibson, Gretsch and Rickenbacker – are still being manufactured to this day.

The local music shop in Romford didn't help matters either, with the average salesman in his 50s and most probably proficient in playing a brass instrument or a piano. His knowledge of the guitar was non-existent, so no advice on buying a guitar was forthcoming.

The Shadows, as a group, had created their own distinctive sound and it was mainly attributable to Hank B. Marvin's use of the tremolo arm on his Fender Stratocaster guitar combined with an echo chamber.

The tremolo arm was part of a mechanical vibrato system, with the arm being held in the hand of the guitarist. Pressing gently up or down changed the pitch of the strings. So another important factor when choosing my guitar, besides having to look the part, it had to have a tremolo system. Again, the cheaper the instrument, the less sophisticated the tremolo arm mechanism, which would result in the strings going out of tune when used, or even breaking. This sort of problem was only discovered after the guitar had been purchased, and slowly I learnt an early lesson in life – you pay for what you get. Three cheap guitars later I'd had enough. I desperately needed a good reliable guitar, so I splashed out, spending £120 on a second-hand electric, blond, semi-acoustic Gibson 330 guitar, which became my final instrument of choice. A high price to pay for a second-hand guitar, but worth every penny – and I loved it! It had been set up professionally, so was a dream to play, It had an incredible sound and had been fitted with a Bigsby, the best tremolo arm money could buy.

WE DESPERATELY NEED AN ECHO CHAMBER

Any group wishing to sound like Cliff Richard and The Shadows also had to have an echo chamber. With more bookings coming in, we decided that obtaining an echo chamber was imperative and one Saturday John, JG and myself hopped on a train and headed for Charing Cross Road in Central London, where there were a number of large music shops. Our intention was to buy the echo chamber on hire purchase, paying off the debt with regular monthly payments using the money that was now trickling in from our live appearances. Naivety again reared its head. We hadn't realised that, being under 18 years of age, the hire purchase agreement had to be signed by an adult family member, and the signature witnessed by another responsible adult.

This was a world before credit cards and many households throughout the UK relied upon borrowing money from hire purchase companies to buy a variety of items, such as household goods and cars. Raising money this way was commonly known as borrowing money on the 'never, never'. The full amount borrowed, including interest, would then be paid back in monthly instalments, over an agreed period of time.

Apart from JG, who had paid cash for his drum kit as he had been working for a year before us, we had all recently borrowed money from our parents to purchase various other pieces of group equipment. So he was the obvious choice, but understandably he didn't want to ask his father for money to buy an echo chamber when he was the drummer! However, he was confident he could persuade his father to sign an HP agreement. So off we went up to Charing Cross Road and into Selmers music shop to look at echo chambers. Having selected the unit we wanted, the salesman proceeded to complete an HP form and indicated to JG where his father had to sign the form, and where the witness had to sign. JG took the agreement home, confident his father would sign the papers and, as far as we were concerned, the agreement was signed and posted to the HP company. All we had to do now was wait on a call from the music shop confirming that the papers were in order and for us to go and collect the echo chamber.

The following Saturday evening was spent as usual at the Wykeham Hall. On our way home we stopped off at the fish and chip shop and bought ourselves each a bag of freshly cooked chips, sprinkled lightly with vinegar and salt. As we walked along eating our chips and chatting about the groups we'd watched earlier, I just happened to look ahead and said to the others 'Look at this man coming towards us on his bike. I think he's wearing a raincoat over his pyjamas!' It was pretty dark, but as we drew level with a street lamp, the cyclist was passing by and we suddenly recognised him. He braked when he saw us. We couldn't believe it! It was Arty Rixon, JG's dad! Usually quite a placid man but, by the tone of his voice, he was clearly upset as he dismounted his bike. 'Get home immediately young man. We need to have words.' 'What's the problem Dad?' JG asked. 'I'm not discussing this in the street – just get home' was the sharp reply.

JG turned to us, shrugging his shoulders, and very quietly said 'See you tomorrow round Martin's house.' Off he trotted behind his dad, who had crossed over the road and started to cycle home. John and I just stood there, watching them disappearing into the dark. We couldn't for the life of us imagine what this was all about. 'Perhaps somebody had been taken ill at home' John suggested. None the wiser, we then headed off home. We couldn't wait to meet up tomorrow afternoon at Martin's house to find out what had happened.

The following afternoon we assembled at Martin's house, basically for a group practice. I filled Martin in with what had happened and, like John and myself, he was equally mystified. There was no sign of JG. We wondered what on earth had made Arthur Rixon hastily throw a coat on over his pyjamas, leap on his bike and cycle into Romford late at night, looking for his son. It had to be something very serious to take such drastic measures.

Finally JG arrived and it was apparent from his demeanour that he had the weight of the world on his shoulders. 'Are you OK?' I asked. 'Yes I'm alright' he replied. 'But I'm in serious trouble at home.' He went on to explain that when he'd confronted his father about signing the HP agreement, he had refused point blank as he didn't believe in using hire purchase. JG repeated word for word what his Dad had said. 'If you want something, save up your money and buy it. Don't take the easy way out and borrow the money, and then end up paying a lot of interest on top for the privilege.' Sound advice really, but we couldn't hang around trying to save up sufficient money to buy the echo chamber. We needed it now – life was too short!

John fired the question that we all wanted to ask. 'So why did your dad come looking for you in his pyjamas late on a Saturday night?' JG suddenly looked very sheepish, and paused for a moment. He then went on to explain. 'I was so disappointed my dad wouldn't sign the HP agreement, and I didn't want to let you all down, so I forged his signature on the agreement. Also, his signature had to be witnessed, so I simply made up a name and address and signed the form and posted the agreement direct to the HP company as instructed by the salesman at the Selmers. I was convinced the deception would work and I'd get away with it. At the end of the day, I knew we'd make the regular monthly payments on time until we'd paid the debt off, so I thought nobody would be the wiser.'

JG went on to explain. 'When the hire purchase company received the signed agreement, they carried out a check on the names and addresses on the form. It was when they came to check the witness details that they discovered the bogus name and address I'd given them and immediately became suspicious.' Suspecting fraud, they had sent a private detective round to JG's home on that Saturday evening to investigate. Poor old Arty, a very upright citizen and manager of a local hardware store, had got himself ready for bed, and was no doubt watching a bit of TV, when the private detective rang the front door bell. It must have been difficult enough having a private detective knock on your door on a Saturday evening, but even worse when you discover that your eldest son had forged your signature. This had sent Arty into a spin. He waited and waited for JG to arrive home until he became so incensed, he'd jumped on his bike and headed off into Romford in search of him.

I dread to think what the consequences would have been had Arty Rixon left earlier that night and tried to gain entry into the Wykeham Hall where he knew we were. Now that would have been interesting! The bouncers would have prevented him gaining entry into the dance hall thinking he was a bit of a bit of a nutcase with a raincoat over his pyjamas!

Poor old JG – he was really upset by the whole episode and his father wasn't talking to him after they went head to head the previous night. We all sympathized with JG, but at the end of the day, what about the echo chamber? Desperate needs required desperate measures. The four of us dug deep into our not-so-deep pockets and between us we managed to raise the required £35 or so to purchase one. Considering I would be the only one using the echo chamber on stage, what good friends I had!

John and I travelled up to Selmers the following Saturday morning and we paid cash for a Watkins Copycat echo chamber. JG had decided not to show his face there for obvious reasons!

As Martin's parents were away for the weekend, we arranged to meet at his house the following day for an impromptu jam session, basically just to experiment with the different effects we could get out of the echo chamber. I was the first to use it and I plugged in and played a few Shadows' riffs. We couldn't believe the sound! It was just like the record! Unfortunately, JG hadn't been able to get a lift to transport his drum kit so, without drums, the jam session was a non-starter. However, John plugged his microphone in and with full echo, he started to mimic Gene Vincent's singing voice, which had us in fits of laughter. A couple of girls stopped outside the house and started listening, and then a few more joined them. They stood there listening to John singing, giggling away to themselves. To get a better view of the girls, we ran upstairs with the echo chamber and mike, plugged in and, with the net curtains pulled back, John serenaded them. They loved it!

I can't recall who came up with the idea, but to liven things up, we decided to play a practical joke. A dustbin was carried out to the front of the drive and left close to the pavement. Martin put a small speaker inside and carefully hid the wiring from view. We stuffed paper up the sleeve of an old jacket and a leather glove was tied onto the sleeve. We arranged it so that this false arm was left hanging out of the dustbin. The speaker wire was long enough to allow us to take it upstairs to the front bedroom, where Martin wired it up to an amplifier. With the echo chamber and mike plugged in, John started to mimic an injured person's voice moaning in agony. JG and I stood outside by the dustbin and gave the thumbs up sign to John – we couldn't wait to try our little surprise on unsuspecting passers-by.

Martin came rushing out, grinning like mad. He was holding a bottle of tomato ketchup and proceeded to pour some sauce onto the glove, and also onto the ground beneath the glove. We stood back and surveyed the scene. It was certainly pretty realistic now with the fake blood and, for effect, John gave us another rendition of his moaning abilities. The scene was now set. We all rushed upstairs and gathered at the window, hidden behind the net curtains to watch the fun.

'Here comes our first victim' shouted Martin, and we spotted a woman coming along pushing a pram. As she passed the dustbin, John started moaning and crying out 'Help me, help me.' She didn't stop and only glanced at the dustbin, and then carried on as though nothing had happened, which was quite strange. A couple of young lads then passed by, and again John started moaning. They both looked at the dustbin in disbelief and ran off. Our faith was restored,

This little game had lasted about ten minutes and we were slowly getting bored, when we spotted an old man I recognised as living up the road to me. I had often seen him around. He walked with a limp and required the aid of a walking stick. He was out walking his old dog on a lead and, as he drew level with the dustbin, the dog immediately started sniffing around the tomato sauce. John started his moaning sounds and repeating 'Help me, help me' which made the dog bark.

We were huddled behind the net curtains in the bedroom killing ourselves laughing. The old man moved slowly round the dustbin and looked at the arm hanging out. John continued moaning. By now the dog was licking the tomato sauce, so the old man pulled it away. He then stood back from the dustbin and, with his walking stick, prised off the dustbin lid. Simultaneously John let out a blood-curdling scream. Well, we were in stitches by now, and the poor man must have had the shock of his life, because he and the dog took off at high speed. Strangely he wasn't limping anymore! Mission accomplished. I took the echo chamber home and spent the next couple of days experimenting with it, ready for our Tuesday rehearsal.

ENTER PATRICK McCARTHY – RHYTHM GUITAR – OCTOBER 1961

Towards the end of 1961, we were rehearsing and playing more and more Cliff Richard and The Shadows' songs and also Shadows' guitar instrumentals. Using the echo chamber had gone a long way in helping us to obtain the authentic their authentic sound. But to complete an identical line-up, we needed a rhythm guitarist. His presence would also allow me to concentrate more on my lead guitar fill-ins and solos.

A decision was made to advertise for a rhythm guitarist in our local newspapers. Much to our disappointment, we only received one response and we auditioned this young man at my parents' bungalow. Patrick McCarthy arrived wearing a white shirt, a yellow waistcoat and a red wool tie and sported a Teddy boy (Rocker) haircut. His hair was swept back at the sides with a large quiff of hair hanging over his forehead. Patrick was a slightly overweight car mechanic who rolled his own cigarettes. Not that that was particularly unusual – it was just that my mum later found about half a dozen cigarette butts hidden under the rug!

Pat was certainly not the best guitarist in town, but there again, we were a fledgling group and all of us were feeling our way with our instruments of choice. Being pretty desperate to get a Shadows' sound and as Pat was the only person to respond to our advertisement, he was invited to join the group. His appearance could be dealt with at a later stage!

We started to rehearse on a regular basis and slowly Pat integrated into the group. However, he was constantly nagged by us all to make sure his cigarette butts ended up in the ashtray and not on the floor! Fortunately, he decided himself to change his hairstyle, turning up one day with a new Mod haircut, but still he persisted in wearing that yellow waistcoat and red tie.

I was the eldest in the group by a few months so just after my 17th birthday I started taking regular driving lessons. Once I had a license I could buy my own car and drive to work. More importantly, for the development of the group, we needed to be mobile in order to spread our wings. I was close to taking my driving test when, at a rehearsal, Pat mentioned there was an old Bedford van at his works up for sale, and would we be interested in acquiring it at the princely sum of £10? After much deliberation, we agreed it was too good an opportunity to be missed. We were now the owners of an ex-baker's van, albeit 12 years old, which spent the next few months parked on Martin's parents' drive waiting for me to pass my driving test and get behind the wheel.

ROMFORD YOUTH COUNCIL – TALENT COMPETITION

As the fledgling group Beat Ltd, and with our new rhythm guitarist, we entered a talent competition for the first time. It was being held on a Saturday at Quarles Secondary Girls' School on Harold Hill – a new housing estate built close to Romford. Our parents kindly helped us by transporting us and our equipment to the school.

Eight contestants had entered the competition, but we were the only pop group appearing that day. However, we were up against a diverse array of talent, from a solo violinist, twin girls who both sang and played accordions and even a singing tap dancer. Because of all our equipment, we were the last act to appear on stage that afternoon.

The waiting was intolerable and I was so nervous before going on stage that I must have gone to the loo about eight times. The rules stated that each act had to play two songs. With instrumental records riding high in the charts, we started with 'Walk Don't Run' by the US group The Ventures, followed by Cliff Richard's first hit 'Move It'. Much to everyone's disappointment, we came fourth. But this was 1961 and pop groups were still a new phenomenon. By the look of the judges that afternoon, they didn't approve of us anyway.

A few weeks later I received a letter from the warden of the Quarles Youth Centre asking if we would be willing to undertake an audition at the centre on 18 December. We agreed and played for an hour. It was very gratifying for us that we were well received by the young audience. We passed the audition and were booked ahead to appear at the Youth Club on 1 March 1962 and would receive £8 for our troubles. So, although we only achieved fourth place in the talent competition, our appearance that day paid off in the long run.

8

THE BIRTH OF JOHNNY LONESOME AND THE TRAVELLERS - 1962

W hen we first formed the group at school at the end of the 50s, we simply called ourselves Beat Ltd, and we used this name until the middle of 1961. However, as our bookings started to increase, we decided to reinvent ourselves by calling the group The Tremolos. The name was derived from a popular sound effect incorporated in many guitar amplifiers and was commonly used by groups at that time. In the dictionary the word is described as a 'wavering effect'.

However, unbeknown to us, in Barking, a nearby town to Romford, there was a group already performing under the name of The Tremeloes. The name sounded the same but was spelled differently. We had, for a number of months, been 'knocking on the door' trying to get a booking at a popular local dance held in the Masonic Hall in Hornchurch, but without any success. Our endeavours finally paid off when I received a frantic call from the promoter there one evening. Apparently a group booked to appear on Friday had pulled out at the last minute, so this was our opportunity, not only to play at this prestigious club, but also to launch our new name. I told the promoter that we were now called The Tremolos and he made no reference to the fact that the previous week he had booked a group called The Tremeloes from Barking. We were well received by the audience and the promoter, who assured us of further regular work. But still no reference was made to our name being the same as a group he hired from Barking. I suspect the promoter contacted The

Tremeloes from Barking and gave them my address, as this is what happened the very next day.

I had gone into work as usual for a few hours on the Saturday morning and when I arrived home around lunchtime, my dad told me that a couple of young men had knocked on the door asking for me. Finding out I wasn't there, they went on to explain that they were in a group called The Tremeloes and demanded that we change our name. My dad said he would pass the message on and proceeded to close the front door, when a booted foot prevented him from doing so.

Just let me say that if you'd known my father, a stocky fiery Scotsman with a short temper, the one thing you don't do is put your foot out to prevent him closing his own front door! My dad, according to his version of the story, opened the door and politely asked these two young men to leave. Later, my mother recalled what actually happened. With a foot preventing my dad from closing the door, he had apparently opened the door quickly and grabbed the offender, spinning him around and marched him up the garden path to the front gate. He then sent him sprawling out onto the pavement, while his frightened friend looked on. They quickly gathered themselves together and shot off down the street without another word being said.

However, we eventually all agreed that there was a definite conflict of interest in having the same sounding name as another fairly local group, especially as they also played at the Masonic Hall. This was an important new venue for us and we wanted to continue performing there, so it was back to searching for an alternative name. Various names were being tossed around for a few weeks, but we were getting nowhere fast. With more bookings coming in, it was becoming vitally important to come up with a new name, especially as we wanted to have new business cards printed. To try and speed up the process, we all needed to be together in agreeing on the final name, so it was decided to convene in a local pub one evening to thrash the matter out. An hour had passed and still names were being thrown into the pot, when somebody suggested the name The Lonesome Travellers, after a song called 'Lonesome Traveller' recorded in

1958 by the British 'skiffle king' Lonnie Donegan. A US folk group, Pete Seeger and The Weavers had originally recorded the song back in 1950.

At first it was immediately rejected, as we wanted a separate name for the singer and another name for the group. Somebody then suggested Johnny Lonesome and The Travellers and for a moment all went quiet as we contemplated the name. There were no immediate objections, which was promising, but still we continued throwing names around just to be sure. But try as we might, no other names reached the same consensus of opinion as Johnny Lonesome and The Travellers. It just had a certain ring to it. So that was it. Decision made. Glasses were raised and we toasted our new name. We walked out of the pub that evening, job done. Business cards were ordered through JG who was in the printing trade. Finally we were moving forward. Would the birth of our new name bring us luck and eventual stardom!

MOBILE AT LAST – I PASS MY DRIVING TEST – FEBRUARY 1962

Four days before passing my test, my dad and Jim Palmer had taken us and our equipment to Stratford for an audition at Stratford Town Hall. It was an unpaid audition, but it was important to try and get regular work at this prestigious East London town hall venue. We were pretty chuffed to be given the opportunity of performing in this large ballroom. It was the biggest dance hall we had played in so far and we now had our new name, so what could stop us now! On arrival, we discovered that every Sunday evening two groups were booked to appear and that night we found ourselves sandwiched between the two other groups. We had a half-hour slot. Quickly we set up our gear and played our best numbers, but with our fathers waiting outside in their cars, we had to pack up and leave almost immediately after performing. Although we were all quite nervous, it had gone very smoothly. The promoter thanked us and promised to contact us.

Lo and behold, the following day I received a telephone call from Ken Johnson, the promoter, informing me that we had passed the audition and gave us a booking in May to appear at the town hall. When I told the others they were over the moon. All I had to do now was pass my driving test.

So much depended on me passing my test. It would be a major boost, not only for me, but also for the group as a whole, if I passed the first time. We could then travel around independently to pastures green. I was so confident I was going to pass that, in anticipation of the big day, I insured the van in my name. On that auspicious morning in February, I drove around the streets of Chadwell Heath near Romford with the examiner sitting beside me. After half an hour, I was asked to pull over outside the test centre and told that I had passed my test!

After telephoning everyone with the good news, we convened outside Martin's house in the evening ready to drive the old van. The battery was flat, so over to Pat McCarthy to sort things out. Lets face it, he was now the unofficial group car mechanic. With four people pushing the van, I sat inside steering it and when it was up to speed, put it into first gear and let the clutch out. Nothing happened, so up with the bonnet and we all peered in as Pat primed the petrol pump. We started pushing again and this time the engine suddenly sprung into life, but then died within seconds. Pat gave me specific instructions. 'Once the engine fires, increase the revs, and just keep driving.' It was after about three further attempts that the engine finally sprang into life. With a bang followed by a big cloud of exhaust fumes, the van shot forward and I drove the thing up Marshalls Drive all on my own.

I was petrified to say the least in case I stalled the engine but as I turned into Pettits Lane, it was so far so good. I intended to drive round in a circle so I took the next turn left and went hurtling down Parkside Avenue hill. As it levelled out at the bottom, the engine suddenly died on me. I coasted to the side of the road and pulled the starter. Nothing. The battery was flat and it took at least 20 minutes before the others found me. Another push and this time I managed to keep the engine ticking over as they all climbed into the back of the van and we made our way home.

Pat had worn his regular 'uniform' under his coat that night, but that yellow waistcoat was going to suffer a very sad demise, and not of our doing I hasten to add. With all the exertion of pushing the van that evening, and being slightly overweight, Pat's face was very red. He was sweating profusely so he had taken off his outer coat and the famous red tie, and these were thrown into the back of the van. His expertise was called upon again after the engine stalled, fortunately outside Martin's house, so up went the bonnet for the umpteenth time, and he leaned over the wing of the van to manually pump some more petrol into the engine. It was then that tragedy struck. When he stood up, one side of his yellow waistcoat was covered in black oil and a roar of laughter rang out. Suffice to say the waistcoat was never seen again and was replaced by a black leather one, which was very well received. As for the red tie, somebody tied it across the front of the van, where it remained for weeks. It disappeared one night at a booking, taken by a souvenir hunter we think. Well that's the story we told Pat to console him!

A new battery was purchased and apart from the odd occasion when we had to take it in turns to jump out of the van, lift up the bonnet and prime the petrol pump, we were now mobile. But in time our 'mechanic', under extreme pressure, went on to eventually replace the petrol pump.

ME ON THE LEFT AND JG WITH OUR 'NEW' BEDFORD VAN

WE HIT THE ROAD - QUARLES YOUTH CENTRE - HAROLD HILL MARCH 1962

Having passed an earlier audition at this Harold Hill youth centre, we were now being paid for our evening's work and, as it transpired, this was to be our very first booking driving our very own van. We assembled at Martin's house and packed our amps, drums, guitars, suits and three bodies into the back of the small van. Martin was in the passenger seat. I was slightly nervous sitting behind the steering wheel, not with the prospect of driving, more with the reliability of the van. Would we make it there and back to the school in one piece, a round trip of about eight miles? Also, up to a few weeks ago, I'd been learning to drive in a Ford Prefect, which had all-round vision but in its previous life, this van had been a delivery vehicle and had no rear side windows.

My driving instructor had taught me to constantly check in the rear view mirror when driving, but with the equipment loaded up to the ceiling my vision was obscured. All I had to rely on now was a single rear view mirror mounted on the driver's door. But these were minor considerations and nothing I couldn't handle. Besides it was a short journey — what the heck!

There was a palpable air of excitement in the van and a cheer rang out as the engine fired on the first pull of the starter. We slowly pulled away. 'Harold Hill, here we come!' I yelled out.

About 20 minutes later we swept into the school playground and parked the van. We had made it! We unpacked our gear and, with a few girls watching, we proudly carried it into the assembly hall and onto the stage. Some basic sound checks were carried out before tripping off to an allotted classroom to change into our band gear.

Money wasn't plentiful at this time and we couldn't afford custom-made suits for the band. Fortunately, we were all Mods, apart from Mr McCarthy, and we all had a navy blue suit hanging in our wardrobes. We would have to work on Pat at a later date!

However, the lead singer was the front man in any group during the early sixties, so John needed to stand out from the other members of the group when on stage and we had left it with him to find something suitable. At the time he was an apprentice at Honorbilts, a clothing manufacturing company based in Romford. He turned up at rehearsals with a sample jacket he'd found at work – a waiter's jacket made from a bright mustard-coloured fabric. It was tight fitting, with narrow lapels, and the buttons had been covered in the same fabric. It was short and just covered the waistband of his trousers. It was certainly different and he looked really good in it.

Ten minutes later we assembled on the stage, picked up our guitars and checked the tuning. JG did a few drum rolls and made some adjustments. John then walked forward and switched his mike on.

I looked across to make sure everyone was ready before I launched into the opening riff of 'That'll Be The Day' and thought how good the group looked in their navy blue suits. John was standing centre-stage with both hands gripping the mike stand. He reminded me of a Spanish bullfighter standing there in his new short tight-fitting yellow jacket. 'Ready?' I called out. Everyone nodded in unison and I played the opening guitar sequence. The others came in on cue and John started singing – we were off! Although the hall was still only half full, I could see more and more young people drifting in, mostly girls, who quickly moved down to the front of the stage to watch and study us.

We were about half an hour into our set, and already around 30 girls had gathered together at the foot of the stage, mostly staring up at John. Out of the blue something very unexpected happened which caught us totally by surprise. John had just started singing the intro verse to the song 'Dynamite', a Cliff Richard and The Shadows' hit, when a girl screamed, and then three girls next to her started screaming. Suddenly they were all screaming!

I stood there playing away, trying to act nonchalantly, as though this happens all the time, but I had this nervous urge to burst out laughing. I glanced across at John and although he appeared to be handling it well, I wondered what was running through his mind at this precise moment.

He continued singing, staring straight ahead. I watched a bunch of girls in front of me, their eyes firmly focused on John. When he suddenly clutched the mike with both hands, they screamed in unison. It was time for my guitar solo and, as John turned towards me, I could tell from his expression that he was about to grin at me. I knew instinctively that the look on his face was going to start me laughing so, as I started into my solo, I spun round quickly to face the back of the stage. Now I was facing JG who had the most serious expression on his face. Well, that was it. I just couldn't hold back any longer and started laughing. John also had his back to the audience by now and seeing my shoulders shaking, knew I'd lost it. That set him off too and suddenly he was laughing away as well.

We were now both looking at poor old JG who sat there facing the audience, drumming and frowning away, a customary facial expression of his when he was playing. Why was he so serious? This made John and I giggle even more – and still JG remained composed, with not a hint of a faint smile. With my solo quickly coming to an end, I battled to bring about a straight face as I turned to face the audience again and, glancing across at John, saw that he had managed to regain his composure and had moved back to the microphone. He was now singing with a lot more conviction, which brought on even more screaming – he was revelling in the moment. Every now and again I glanced across at Patrick and Martin, who also seemed to been enjoying the attention, but in a more controlled manner than John and I. Wow, what a moment, and what a night to remember!

On the drive home we talked and laughed, and laughed and talked, and none of us could believe what we had happened that evening. Although a totally new experience for us, the screaming had obviously been encouraged in Britain by the enormous popularity of The Beatles. The TV and the national papers talked about this new phenomenon and referred to it as 'Beatlemania'. The screaming was so intense at their concerts that it actually drowned out the music, so much so that The Beatles couldn't hear themselves play. Martin and I had witnessed a few screamers at earlier rock 'n' roll package tours, but nothing like the intensity of the screamers at a Beatles' concert. Never in a thousand years had we expected to be confronted by girls screaming at us and although it had been difficult at first controlling our emotions, the consensus of opinion was – we loved it, bring on some more!

We were booked to perform at the youth club again in May, where we experienced the screaming once again, but this time there were even more girls than before standing at the foot of the stage. However, we were ready for it this time around and just soaked up atmosphere, enjoying the moment and taking it all in our stride. For whatever reason the screaming only took place when we performed at schools and youth centres in Harold Hill, and nowhere else.

STRATFORD TOWN HALL – MAY 1962

This was the 'big one' and would be the first long journey in our own van. Having attended an audition a couple of months ago, I knew where to go, but there was a sense of trepidation as we pulled into the cobbled yard at the back of the town hall that night. I pulled the van over and parked as close as possible to a metal fire escape, which led up to double fire escape doors on the first floor. It was dark by now and, as we climbed out of the van, we could hear music playing. I looked up to where the music was coming from and was fascinated to see small flashes of white light coming through the windows above. I was soon to discover that two revolving mirror glitter balls created the effect and, although I'd seen them hanging in ballrooms, I'd never seen them in action before.

We all picked up some gear from the back of the van and, as we made our way up the fire escape, we could hear 'Do You Wanna Dance' by Cliff Richard and The Shadows being played. John banged on the fire escape doors. A few seconds later the doors swung open and Ken Johnson, the promoter greeted us. As I stood there on the fire escape looking into the ballroom, my heart sank. I just couldn't believe it. It wasn't a record being played – it was an actual group performing the song live! They sounded identical to the record and we looked at one another in disbelief. We were led to a side stage door, which took us up some wooden steps and into the wings on the stage, where we deposited our equipment. I stood there for a moment looking at the group performing on this large stage – and I just wanted to go home! Their name was Joe and The Teens.

With the all the equipment stashed in the wings, Ken Johnson then led us through a door, along a corridor and into an area of individual glass-fronted council offices. We selected an office in which to change. How trusting of the council to let total strangers just wander into their offices! And how times have changed! We were handed a sheet of paper headed up Performing Rights Society and asked to complete the group's name and address plus list the numbers we were going to perform that evening. This was certainly a first for us, and made us feel quite import-ant – we were moving into showbiz life slowly but surely!

The stage was big and high off the ground. We performed our one-hour set looking down on around 200 people, who were just content to dance the night away. All the main ballroom lights were switched off, apart from a few dimmed wall lights. On the floor in front of us was a bank of coloured lights, which provided the only light on the stage. I stood there, playing away, slightly mesmerized by the revolving glass balls, watching the small light reflections swirling around the entire ball-room and bouncing off us and off the dancers. What was slightly unsettling during our performance was looking across and seeing Joe and The Teens assembled in the wings watching us. After each song most of the dancers politely clapped and, looking around, I could tell this was a slightly older audience than the youngsters we were used to performing in front of at the various school youth clubs.

We finished our set to loud applause and the curtains were drawn. As we moved our gear into the wings, Joe and The Teens moved their equipment back into place to play their last set. We were all on a high, confident that we had provided a good set, and the audience appeared to have warmed to us. After watching the group play for half an hour, we returned to our office to change. By the time we came to leave, the other group had finished and were changing in another office. As we were leaving, I couldn't help but spot a beautiful Sunburst Fender Jaguar lying in an open case on a desk in one of the offices, and I stopped to admire it. Its proud owner opened the office door and invited me in. He then encouraged me to pick it up, which I did. I studied it closely, but I wasn't going to attempt to play it on front of him!

Just over a year later, I recognised the same guy while I was watching 'Top of the Pops' on television. He was the lead guitarist, Rick Westwood, and the group was Brian Poole and The Tremeloes. I looked across at my dad to ask him if he was the guy he had ejected onto the street, but he was fast asleep in the armchair.

With all the gear loaded up, and feeling good about our performance that night, instead of heading off home we took a vote and headed in the opposite direction to central London. Why not – we were young and free – and we were all on a bit of a high. This would be my first drive into central London, and a first for all of us in our old jalopy.

All was going well and, up to now, I hadn't experienced any real difficulty relying on a single side mirror whilst driving. However, unbeknown to me at the time, I was heading towards Marble Arch in central London, a notoriously busy and extremely large roundabout, with a number of roads leading on and off it in all directions. John was sitting in the passenger seat up front with me as we headed along Oxford Street in the West End of London, fast approaching Marble Arch which resembled a busy racing track, with cars speeding round the large roundabout. The rest of our group were packed like sardines in the back of our small van, constantly making comments and generally mucking about. As I approached this three-lane roundabout, I leaned forward in my seat, looking left to make sure it's all clear to move out into the flow of traffic ahead. However, because of the angle of my approach and having no side windows at the rear of the van, my vision was somewhat obscured. Panic stations! 'Quickly, anything coming?' I yelled out to John, who was busy chatting to somebody in the back. I had left it to late to brake and I felt like closing my eyes. A couple of cars hooted me up, but there was no sound of metal on metal, and suddenly I joined the traffic in the outside lane of the roundabout. Too late John yelled out 'All clear.' 'Thanks for nothing' I said. Everyone in the back thought it was hilarious.

Already my nerves were rattled, and there we were now travelling in the outside lane of Marble Arch roundabout as I shouted out 'Anybody know which exit I should take?' No response from the back, only laughter, and John, like me, had no idea which road to take. By now I had completed one full circuit of the roundabout. I was starting to panic slightly and beginning to lose my cool. 'Could you possibly concentrate and help me here!' I yelled out to the back of the van. There were numerous roads leading off the roundabout with road signs pointing to places we'd never heard of before and I'm receiving conflicting suggestions as to which road to take. I felt like screaming.

I'd now gone round the roundabout twice, when suddenly a car pulled out in front of me. Instinctively I looked in the rear view mirror as I needed to quickly change lane, but heads and group equipment blocked my vision. My eyes darted to the door mirror. I couldn't see the middle lane and yelled out, 'John, anything coming up in the middle lane?' John spun round and peered out of the window. 'Looks all clear as far as I can see' he called out. I indicated to pull into the centre lane when suddenly a car behind gave a long blast on its horn. I had to take decisive action or else crash into the car in front of me, so I pulled into the middle lane, and within seconds a car passed by on the inside lane. He hooted as he passed – not a happy chappy. John obviously hadn't seen the car approaching from where he sat. I felt like I was driving virtually blind and with hardly any driving experience to my name. I looked in the door mirror. All clear, so I pulled back into the outside lane and slowed down a bit. Complaints immediately came from the back. Apparently, swinging out into the middle lane had caused the equipment to shift position and it had moved forward, squashing them.

I couldn't take anymore of this. I must have driven round the roundabout about four times, if not more. My nerves were really taut so, without any further discussion, I indicated and headed off down a road with signs for Lancaster Gate.

'Anyone heard of Lancaster Gate?' I yelled out. The response was negative. We were now heading into unknown territory, no maps on board, but who needs a map! A good 30 minutes later, we were still none the wiser where we were. Names kept popping up on road signs and some sounded familiar, but we still had no idea if we were heading in the right direction for Stratford. Suddenly we were driving across a bridge over a large river, when I spotted a large floodlit building over on my right and yelled out, 'Look, there's an effing castle!'

We were all dumbfounded. Not one of us could recall ever crossing over a river earlier during our drive. We realised that it had to be the River Thames, but what castle was it? Needless to say, we all had a very limited knowledge of London at that time! It was then that I spotted an illuminated sign declaring the Tower of London and yelled it out to the others. A simultaneous cheer rang out in the van. We were heading in the right direction after all and much closer to Stratford than we thought. About a mile or so later we were driving along the Mile End Road, following signs for Stratford. I was feeling on top of the world now, relaxed and pretty pleased with my driving prowess, but I made a mental note to myself to remember to buy a map and have it in the van at all times!

THE CAPTURE OF HAROLD HILL 1962 – 1964

The heavy bombing of London during the Second World War left many inner London areas facing major housing shortages. In an attempt to alleviate the problem after the war, the government sanctioned the building of new towns around the South East of England, and one of the areas selected for development was a wooded area on the outskirts of Romford, a small market town in Essex.

The designated site was close to a suburb of Romford called Harold Wood. The new town was completed in 1958 and was named Harold Hill. Most of the new residents had been living in temporary pre-fabric-ated accommodation built on many of the derelict bombsites in and around London. These homes were called prefabs and were constructed out of asbestos sheeting. A single prefab could be built in a day making it a very fast and efficient way of housing the thousands of homeless people quickly. Besides the vast number of terraced and semi-detached brick homes that were built, Harold Hill also had its own parade of shops, banks, schools, parks, playing fields and churches.

Harold Hill was immortalised by Ian Dury, a local Essex boy who, with his group The Blockheads, went on to achieve fame in the 70s. He wrote a song called 'This Is What We Find'. A verse describes how Harold Hill from Harold Hill who was a builder, returns home to find another man with his wife and so proceeds to carry out some serious surgery on the man with his electric drill!

HUNTING ON THE HILL

Our van was looking very tired, so we decided to give it a bit of a face-lift by painting over a lot of the bad rust marks. We hand-painted the wings, roof and bonnet in black, leaving the bodywork in its original royal blue colour. I remember one evening getting all spruced up in our latest Mod gear, overdoing the Old Spice, which was something we were all guilty of. This was a cheap American male fragrance recently introduced commercially into Britain, and one of the first fragrances used by men in the early 60s. We set off from Martin's house and, as we entered Straight Road on the outskirts of Harold Hill, a policeman stepped out from nowhere and signalled for me to pull over. This was becoming a regular occurrence because the van was old and decrepit and looked un-road-worthy.

Having pulled over, the constable walked up to the driver's window just as I wound it down. 'Good evening officer' I said, handing him the insurance and MOT (roadworthy) certificate, together with my driving licence. Calling him officer had the desired effect to his ego as I could see him grow a couple of inches in stature. Without saying a word he poked his head through the window and immediately reeled back when he smelled our Old Spice saying 'Where are you lot off to this evening smelling like a bunch of flowers?' We couldn't help but laugh at the comment, and I made some crack about hoping to meet some girls tonight, which brought a wry smile to his face. So far so good. It looked like we'd been pulled over by a friendly copper. He then proceeded to walk around the van inspecting the bodywork. He even stood on the front bumper making the van bounce up and down, no doubt hoping to dispute its roadworthiness, even though we had a genuine certified MOT test certificate. Fortunately nothing fell off the van, and he sauntered up to my window and handed back the papers. He made a final comment before departing 'Good luck with your search tonight boys' and smiled – now that's what I call a friendly cop. And we drove off into the wilds of Harold Hill on our search.

We had really loved the screaming from the girls on both sessions at Quarles Youth Club and we wanted to show our appreciation in so many ways! Evenings were spent riding around Harold Hill in our empty van, trying to chat-up any girls walking the streets. Sometimes luck was on our side, other times we were totally blanked. I'm convinced the appearance of our van was putting them off. Even when we told them we played in a group it simply didn't work. Obviously most of these girls hadn't yet heard of Johnny Lonesome and The Travellers. But this was early days yet and within a year things would drastically change on the Hill.

Out of the blue, I received a call from the warden at the Harrowfields Youth Centre on Harold Hill. He told me that many of their members had been pestering him for months to book Johnny Lonesome and The Travellers and also, in a conversation with the warden at Quarles Youth Centre, he had been told how well we had been received there a few months ago. We were now booked to appear at Harrowfields Youth Centre in November. Arriving on a Thursday evening outside this rather large school, I jumped out of the van and went inside where I was told to drive round to a specific side door, which would be opened for us. This side door led us directly to steps leading onto the stage and, with my guitar case in my hand, I walked across the stage and joined Martin and John. We stood there surveying the scene, marvelling at how large the stage was and also at the size of the assembly hall with its high ceiling. A good crowd attended that night and we went down well. Before we left, the warden booked us again to appear in February.

Slowly but surely our appearances on the Hill were increasing and, wearing our navy blue suits on stage with John in his new jacket, we were more confident in ourselves. We looked 'the business' and were certainly on an upward roll. A further appearance at Quarles in March had the girls screaming again, and we lapped it up.

WE BUY A BEDFORD DORMOBILE – MAY 1962

It was decided that the old van wasn't particularly reliable and also it simply wasn't big enough for our needs. It was pretty uncomfortable in the back for three growing lads and our expanding equipment and, most importantly, no room for additional female passengers! So our trusty mechanic Patrick was dispatched to locate a replacement van and one was found in Dagenham. It was a cream and blue eight year-old Bedford van, similar in style to a Bedford Dormobile camper van. It had the distinctive large sliding side doors, which gave access not only into the front of the van, but also into the back. However, it didn't have any side windows as the van had been used commercially in its previous life. We were now moving up in the world! The garage gave us an allowance of £5 on our old van and in total the new, albeit second-hand, van cost us a cool £36.

This was a major step-up for us. It had a much larger interior, which covered all our needs and, importantly for the group's image, this van was still in production, so it still looked a modern vehicle. Having been checked over by the group's mechanic Patrick, we were assured that for its age, the van was in fairly good nick all round – rust-wise and engine-wise. In fact, it lasted us exactly one year to the month before it expired.

It had been worked literally into the ground, so we did in fact get our money's worth out of it.

ENTER DAVE MURKIN – SAXOPHONE – AUGUST 1962

It is interesting to note that in obtaining regular work in ballrooms and dance venues around this period of time, promoters expected a group's repertoire not only to be varied but, most importantly, to contain a number of popular songs that had recently, or were currently, in the top 20 hit parade. Coincidentally, we were also being made aware by promoters, when looking for work, that there were plenty of two guitars, bass, and drum line-ups like us in the area, all searching for work, and all sounding very similar. So we were acutely aware that in order to compete with the other local groups, and to give us an edge over them, we needed to sup-plement our current standard line-up with either an organist or a saxophonist.

In and around the East End of London, having 'live' music in your bar attracted more people, and more people meant more money, so good groups were in big demand.

Pat McCarthy had mentioned on many occasions that he had a friend and neighbour in Dagenham who played the saxophone and was looking to join a group. At a regular Tuesday evening practice session, a decision was made and Pat was dispatched off that evening to find out if his pal was interested in joining our group and if so, to invite him along for an audition.

Dave Murkin turned up the following Tuesday, a jovial character with plenty of jokes to tell, but he wasn't a Mod and overall, with his black horn-rimmed glasses, he looked pretty straight. However, could his playing make up for his lack of dress sense? We started rehearsals with an instrumental song Dave already knew. He told us the chords to the song and before we knew it, we were playing it almost fluently. We then continued through our repertoire of songs, and when Dave recognised a particular song he knew, we gave him the key, and immediately he was playing along with us. For me personally, Dave would be extremely useful in the group, not only because of the added sax sound, but also because of his knowledge of written music. Plus he would be able to help us establish what chords were required when learning new songs at rehearsal time, especially if the sheet music wasn't available.

After Dave left that evening, we had a discussion amongst ourselves and came to a unanimous decision almost immediately. Introducing a saxophone into our line-up would give us the edge – and the bigger sound we needed. Pat left in high spirits with full instructions to tell his friend and neighbour the job was his if he wanted it. Pat called me the next evening with the good news that Dave wanted in. Our line-up was now complete – AND he owned a navy blue suit as well!

With a saxophone in the group, we now had that fuller sound which the promoters liked, and this gave us an edge over our local rival groups who only had a standard line-up.

OUR NEW LINE-UP PERFORMING AT HARROWFIELDS YOUTH CENTRE

9

THE FRENCH CONNECTION

My passion for all things French started when I was about 15 years old. I was obsessed with Brigitte Bardot, a popular French actress and sex symbol of the time. With her long blond hair, pouting shiny lips and husky sexy voice, she could have me any time! I would read every article at my disposal about this actress and avidly studied every photograph published of her. I wanted to know what was going on in her life, the men she dated, what they looked like, where they went, where she lived, and when her next film was coming out.

This love of all things French took another turn while on a skiing holiday in Champery in Switzerland, during the Easter of 1959. For the first time in its history, my school had organised a week's skiing holiday for pupils in the fourth year and, much to my delight, my parents agreed to pay for me to go, as did Martin's parents.

In the Swiss hotel's dining room one evening, I was eating at a table with Martin and two other friends, when I overheard a family talking in French. Looking up, there at the far end of the dining room, sat a family of four. They must have arrived earlier that day as I hadn't seen them before. I continued with my meal, but every so often kept glancing across at this family. They fascinated me, especially the young attractive girl who was sitting next to a man who was presumably her papa. I left the dining room and went to the hotel's reception desk and very cheekily asked the name of the French family who had recently arrived. The receptionist very kindly opened the hotel register. There were four entries made that day under the surname of Frey. Firstly there was Mr and Mrs Frey, followed by Sacha Frey, and then Jacqueline Frey, a family from St Étienne in France.

Brigitte Bardot was still haunting my mind at the time, so I was ripe for meeting a French girl. Although Jacqueline unfortunately didn't resemble Brigitte, she was an extremely good substitute. She had very long straight brown hair that cascaded over her shoulders, olive-coloured skin, and an unusual but attractive face. Most importantly, she was French! Over the next few evening meals, she caught me staring at her and would blink and look away. I was getting hooked. I just couldn't take my eyes off her. Then one evening – surprise, surprise. As we sat eating our evening meal, I glanced across to the Frey table. At the same time she looked up and for a brief lingering moment our eyes met. I could feel my heart racing but she just went back to slowly eating her meal. Not wanting to look too keen, I didn't let temptation get the better of me, so I fought not to look across to her table for a while. Then, after about five minutes casually talking with friends around our table, I glanced across and it happened again. Our eyes met briefly. Now my heart was really pumping fast – she was showing some interest in me! Eventually the Frey family rose, left their table and headed out of the dining room with the father leading, followed by the mother, the son, and last was Jacqueline. I was watching her intently – was she going to look back at me or not? Just as she was just about to exit the dining room, she looked across, dropped her head slightly and, with a demure roll of her eyes, she gave me a wonderful smile. That was enough for me – I was well and truly besotted!

At the time I was a shy 15 year-old youth with the odd pimple growing on my chin. How on earth was I going to get around to talking to this lovely French girl who had given me that lovely smile? Normally after our evening meal, Martin and I and a few friends would walk up the village high street to join our other school pals and sit in a typical Alpine bar, sipping our Cokes and listening to music being delivered by a large colourful jukebox that stood in the corner. But that evening I made a very quick decision – the Cokes and the jukebox would just have to wait – I had more important business to attend to! I apologised to my friends for leaving, leapt up, ran out of the dining room and followed the French family up the stairs. They sauntered into the large lounge and the entire family gathered round a piano. As Mrs Frey started to play and sing, I sat down a few yards away, pretending I was reading a German magazine that I had picked up from a small coffee table.

After about 20 minutes, the Frey family decided to retire to their bedrooms and, as they left the lounge, Jacqueline turned to me and again she gave me that wonderful smile. Now my mind was racing. I couldn't just sit there. I had to do something. It was now or never! I quickly followed them up the stairs. Her parents had already disappeared into their bedroom and Jacqueline's brother had turned the key in the door of the adjoining room. As Jacqueline started to follow him into their bedroom, I called out her name and she stopped and turned to face me. Fortunately she spoke quite good English, so my schoolboy French wasn't needed.

I soon established that the family was heading back to France early the following morning. I was crestfallen. So was that it – I wouldn't ever see her again. I'd left it too late. Suddenly her father's head appeared from the next room and said something to her. She made her apologies to me and turned to enter her bedroom, when I blurted out that I'd love to write to her and could I have her address. She smiled that wonderful smile once again, went into the bedroom, and a minute later emerged with a piece of paper with her address in St Étienne. We said our good-byes and that was it. But I now had her address! I must admit to feeling pretty proud of myself, so much so, I couldn't wait to tell all my pals. Off I ran, back down the stairs two steps at a time, and headed up the high street to tell everybody.

The next day the Frey family left. For the rest of that holiday, I joined my friends each evening at our favourite bar. It was always very dark and well below freezing as we made our way up the village street, trying to avoid the large mounds of snow on each side of the road. It was a welcome relief, lifting the catch and opening the door, to be hit with a rush of hot smoky air plus music and laughter. Once seated with our drinks, I loved going over to the jukebox, watching it operate, and studying all the names of the various artists.

The jukebox, which was just below my height, had a revolving internal coloured lighting system and the chromed speaker grill at the front resembled the radiator grill of a 50s American car. I was mesmerised by this machine and a good portion of my allotted spending money on that trip disappeared into its slot. Not only so I could listen to my favourite songs, but also I just loved watching the machine go about its work.

Once a coin was dropped into the slot and the song number selected, the machine would spring into life. More lights would come on illuminating the inside, and an arm would spring into action, travelling along a track as it searched through a library of about 50 records that stood vertically side by side in their individual cradles. Sometimes the arm would pass the correct number and I felt like shouting out 'Hey, you missed it,' but upon reaching the end, it would start to make its way back along the track. The arm would abruptly stop when it located the correct number and it appeared to think for a moment before reaching over and magically grabbing the record from its cradle. Then it was off on its travels again. As it reached the turntable in the centre of the machine, the arm stopped, twisted around and gently placed the record onto the turntable, swung back and stopped again. A few seconds later another arm, bearing the stylus, swung into action and slowly dropped down depositing the stylus at the very beginning of the record. This process was reversed when the record finally came to an end.

Twenty years later, while living and working in South Africa, I came across a warehouse full of old jukeboxes. My fascination for these old music machines had never left me, so I bought three quite cheaply, and these were shipped back to England with our household effects when we returned to the UK. But settling back in the UK in the late 70s, after being abroad for five years, was difficult as the rate of inflation had risen to 22% and the mortgage interest rate was 16%, forcing me to sell the jukeboxes at Sotheby's auction house.

This was where I met Hilary Kay, who organised the sale and who, years later, has become one of the regular faces on The Antiques Road-show, the long-running BBC television series. This was the first sale of its kind for Sotheby's and was attracting a lot of attention in the press and on TV. In March 1979 my jukeboxes were sold at an auction in Bel-gravia and, although not making the amount of money made at a private sale of jukeboxes in London in 1975, when famous rock stars like Jimmy Page of Led Zeppelin and Brian Ferry of Roxy Music, splashed out thou-sands of pounds, I did however make just over one thousand per cent profit.

After returning home from Switzerland, I wrote to Jacqueline a few weeks later, and enclosed a small silver identity bracelet with 'Colin & Jacqueline' engraved on the name bar. Please remember I was only 15! I anxiously waited for a reply and one morning a letter arrived from St Étienne. I rushed into my bedroom to read it. I opened the envelope and the silver bracelet fell out. I quickly read her letter. Apparently Jacqueline was Jewish and therefore could not accept a gift from a Christian boy! I couldn't understand it! I was young and naive and hadn't realised that religion played such a strong role in some peoples' lives. I was sad for a number of days after the disappointment and, with French egg on my face, I never disclosed to anyone until years later what had happened.

A TRYST OF FATE

During the summer school holidays of that same year, I was invited to stay with Martin and his family in a caravan on a site in Clacton, Essex. On a day's outing with the whole family, Martin and I were sitting up front in the car when Jim, Martin's dad, said 'Shame we haven't got any more room in the car – we could have given these girls ahead a lift.' I looked up from my comic just as we passed two girls who were hitch hik-ing. I couldn't believe it! One of girls was Jacqueline! I shouted out for Jim to stop the car and was half out the door before it stopped. I ran up to Jacqueline. 'I don't believe it! What a coincidence seeing you here!

What are you doing in England?' A slight sign of recognition appeared on her face. She smiled, but basically showed no surprise or excitement at seeing me. How odd was that!

We only spoke for a few minutes, but I was able to establish that she and her friend were staying at a summer school for a month in Wood-bridge, Suffolk. 'Can I come and visit you?' I asked. 'If you want to' came the accented reply. We said our goodbyes with not a kiss in sight, not even a French peck on the cheek, and off we went on our journey.

Now, what are the odds of meeting someone who came from France, whom you had met in Switzerland a few months previously, on a quiet country road in Essex!

Ten days later, along the same stretch of road, there I was sitting in the back of a Ford Zephyr Zodiac heading for Woodbridge. Martin couldn't make the trip, so another school friend, Trevor Jacobs, and I decided to hitchhike to Woodbridge to see my little French dream girl. After various rides in lorries and private cars, we were kindly dropped off right outside the gates of Woodbridge School. We later discovered that the school was an independent day and boarder school and, during the normal summer holiday closure, the school was opened up for a month as a summer school for Jewish children of all nationalities.

It was just after five o'clock in the afternoon and we had been 'thumbing' rides since nine o'clock that morning. We were both feeling tired but now, as I walked up the long drive towards a large imposing building, which presumably was the school, my tiredness melted away with thought of seeing Jacqueline again. As we approached the entrance there were a few youngsters laughing and chatting outside, a couple of them smoking cigarettes. I strolled over to them, explained who we were and why we were here. Yes, they knew of Jacqueline, but she had left not half an hour ago and gone into town with a friend for a fish and chip supper. We were given directions where to find the restaurant and off we went into town. We found the place quite easily. My heart was beating fast with excitement as I peered through the glass door and there, sitting at a table towards the back, was Jacqueline and a friend.

By now, my friend Trevor had lost interest in this entire escapade and was worried that, at this time of the day, we definitely wouldn't make it home, so where were we going to sleep that night? I told him we'd discuss it inside – he wasn't going to spoil this moment for me. I pushed open the door and in we went. As we walked towards the table, Jacqueline looked up. As before, when we met up at the side of the country road in Essex, she smiled slightly and said hello, but again, didn't show any real emotion at seeing me. I was beginning to think she was a very cold French fish indeed! We joined them for supper and then made our way back to the school. We were taken in and introduced to a crowd of their friends in one of the day rooms and, as we talked together, somebody asked us how we were going to get home.

Having now accomplished my mission of a somewhat disappointing reconciliation, the moment of truth reared its head. Where were we going to sleep that night! There was certainly no way of making it home that evening. Somebody suggested we should stay the night at the school and volunteered to ask one of the teachers if it was OK. A teacher arrived and asked us what we were doing here. I explained that I was visiting my French friend but, unfortunately, it had taken longer than expected to get to Woodbridge. He nodded his head. Yes, we could stay just the one night, but insisted that we call our parents and tell them where we were, which we did.

Job done. We were taken upstairs to a dormitory, given bed linen, and shown our bunks. We shared that night with six other lads.

In the morning, after we were kindly given breakfast, we gathered on the steps and said our farewells to our new friends. I went up to Jacqueline and we shook hands. Neither of us made any attempt to give the customary French peck on each cheek. I had most definitely been blown out, and that was the last I ever saw or heard of Jacqueline Frey from St Étienne.

I don't like going through life with any regrets and I've always consoled myself in rejection with the old saying 'there's always plenty more fish in the sea.' However, in my experience, fishing in the warmer Mediterranean waters has always been more difficult than fishing in the colder British waters!

'MOVE IT' ENTERS MY LIFE

My little trip to the school at Woodbridge was not entirely wasted! The night we shared a dormitory at the school, I was shown how to play the lead guitar intro to 'Move It'. This was Cliff Richard and The Drifters' first 1958 UK hit, The Drifters later evolving into The Shadows. Being shown that intro was inspirational and became a pivotal moment for me. Six months later our group was formed and the first song we learned to play was – 'Move It'.

I have read a book written by Andy Summers, lead guitarist with the mega 80s group The Police, entitled 'One Train Later' in which he tells the story of befriending a slightly older boy at school simply because this boy could play the all-important lead guitar riff in 'Move it'. He gets his new friend to show him how to play it, and it becomes a life-changing moment for him. I wonder how many aspiring guitarists around the UK were influenced by that simple guitar lick?

During our last year or so at school, John, JG and I would spend most Saturdays travelling up to central London. Our first port of call was always Charing Cross Road, where we would spend hours trawling the musical instrument shops. I especially wanted to study the array of guitars on display as I was determined that once I started working for a living, I was going to treat myself and buy an electric guitar. But the selection was so vast that I'd change my mind after each visit! One week I fancied the black Framus, then the following week the bright red Kay or the blond Hofner Veri-thin looked good because it had so many controls on it. But there again, Bert Weedon played a Hofner guitar, and how square would I look playing the same guitar as Bert Weedon!

Bert was the first British guitarist to enter the hit parade in 1959 with a guitar instrumental called 'Guitar Boogie Shuffle'. His guitar tutorial 'Play in a Day', first published in 1957, became the bible for many pimply youngsters who wanted to play the guitar. What an enticement for such a gullible schoolboy like me! If I bought the book, by the end of the day I could play the guitar – wow!

Using money I had earned from delivering newspapers before heading off to school, I went out and bought the book. However, much to my disappointment, I found I couldn't play the guitar in a day! What a load of bull to publish a tutorial making such a bold statement. But I suppose if you learned to play one or two notes in a day you were, very loosely, playing the guitar, and that was a start.

The problem for poor old Bert was that he was in his late 30s at the time of his success and therefore much too old to become a guitar hero. I was horrified when a decade or so later, successful guitarists like Eric Clapton, John Lennon, Hank Marvin, Mark Knopfler and Pete Townsend, to name just a few, admitted that the book was a great influence on their learning to play the guitar. Had I become a successful guitarist, I would have probably slagged the book off!

FRENCH FILMS

At this time in our lives all things French were very fascinating to us, and having had our fill of the music shops, we liked to have lunch in a French bistro in Soho called the Kardom. Afterwards, we would stroll down Charing Cross Road to our favourite cinema, the Cameo Royal. Although this cinema specialised in showing foreign films, the majority were French and occasionally starred my favourite actress, Brigitte Bardot. Some of the films might be advertised as sexy but, don't forget, this was the early 60s and sexy meant perhaps catching a fleeting glimpse of a bare breast, or bare breasts if you were extremely lucky!

One French film really caught my imagination and that was 'Plein Soleil', later re-named 'Purple Noon' when it was released on the US cinema circuit, and 'Blazing Sun' in the UK. It starred the French actor Alain Delon who had it all – the looks, the accent, great hair, and he dressed so very French. This film was later remade and released in 1999 under the title 'The Talented Mr Ripley', featuring the actor Jude Law, with Matt Damon playing the Alain Delon role.

In a memorable scene from the film, having killed the person he is going to impersonate, Alain Delon buys a slide projector and rents a hotel room. He projects the murdered man's signature onto sheets of paper pinned to the wall and then, by writing over the projected signature, he slowly learns how to duplicate it, all in preparation to draw money from the dead man's bank account. Taking a moment's rest, he extracts a cigarette from a packet of Disque Bleu, lights up, and lets it dangle from his mouth. Every so often, with the smoke drifting into his eyes and up his nostrils, he used the tip of his tongue to roll the cigarette over his lips to the other side of his mouth. Now how cool was that to an impressionable young lad!

I was new to smoking and this action really impressed me, so much so that after the film had finished, I dragged my pals back into Soho to a tobacconist that sold a variety of foreign cigarettes and bought a pack of the same French cigarettes, Disque Bleu. As we walked through Soho, I quickly opened the pack, took out a cigarette and put it in my mouth. I attempted to emulate Alain Delon's action of rolling the cigarette from one corner of my mouth to the other but just couldn't get it to roll. John suggested that perhaps moistening my lips slightly might do the trick. That sounded like a good idea so, having moistened my lips, I tried again and immediately the cigarette stuck firmly to the skin of my upper lip. I finally managed to separate skin from paper, but in doing so ripped a portion of skin from my lip, which was very painful and made it bleed. So much for trying to look cool – my mates were doubled up laughing!

Disque Bleu, and a number of other French brands at the time, produced their cigarettes from a very dark brown tobacco leaf exported from Syria and Turkey. This tobacco was strong in flavour and had a very distinctive aroma compared with the lighter Virginian tobacco used in British cigarettes, which were mild in comparison. Smoking cigarettes made from black tobacco was an acquired taste – and required iron lungs. Rumour had it that the dark tobacco was less harmful for you than Virginia tobacco, so that in itself was an encouragement to persevere with smoking French cigarettes!

I can remember conveying this healthy message to a friend a year or so later, but the myth was soon to be exposed. He disagreed with me and suggested we try a little test. He told me to fill my mouth with smoke from my Disque Bleu cigarette, then place an open handkerchief over my mouth and blow the smoke through the fabric. This revealed a large black stain. He then did the same but using his Virginian tobacco cigarette, and this only produced a light brown stain. The biggest shock came when performing the same experiment but this time inhaling the smoke and then blowing it through the cloth. Both tobaccos produced just very light stains. My God, where did all that black sticky tar go!

This experiment always lurked around in the back of my mind and, years later, I finally convinced myself that smoking was endangering my health. I had become a nicotine junkie and was well and truly hooked. It took a lot longer than I had anticipated to eventually shake the habit.

Looking back at this period in my life, I realised that watching those early French films influenced me very much and played an important factor in shaping my formative years, leading to holidays in France and a lifelong fascination with all things French. I just loved the way French films gave you an insight into their way of life, the clothes that were being worn and the futuristic design of many French cars. But most importantly, the three of us would watch and study how, in these films, couples kissed with their mouths open. Now that was a revelation in itself. Also, little things like a kiss behind the ear and on the neck, the hand stroking the hair at the same time. It was like watching a lesson in seduction! How great would it be to be able to apply this newly found knowledge!

10

THE BRIDGE HOUSE PUBLIC HOUSE – CANNING TOWN
SEPTEMBER 1962 – FEBRUARY 1963

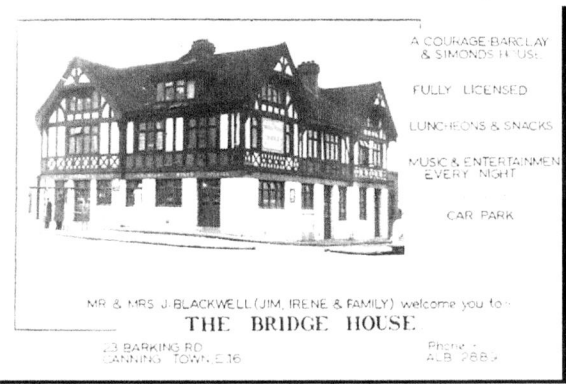

In the space of five months, we performed at this pub a total of 36 times, if you count performing there twice on a Sunday – once at lunchtime and once in the evening. Near the end of our tenure there, it began to feel like a second home and our family was the publican and his wife, Jim and Irene Blackwell, plus the two barmen, Bill and Harry. Drinks were on the house and when food was prepared, we'd always be offered some. When we acquired our new band suits in January, we were even allotted our own changing room upstairs, which meant we had access to the private quarters of the pub where the landlord, his wife, and the two barmen lived. It was a monster of a place, built in a Tudor style, and stood on the edge of the busy Barking Road, just over on the Canning Town side of the concrete bridge that crossed the River Lea at Bow Creek. Prior to a five-span iron bridge being constructed in the early nineteenth century, the area where Canning Town now stands was largely marshland. But when the Royal Victoria Dock was built in the middle of the nineteenth century, houses were erected for the dock-workers and the area expanded and flourished. However, by the time we came to play at the Bridge House, Canning Town had become a badly deprived area, very tough and gritty.

Just 20 miles away in Tilbury, the docks were being expanded and this had a knock-on effect in Canning Town. As fewer boats used the London docks and off-loaded their cargoes at Tilbury, many of London docks were slowly closing down. This resulted in increased unemployment in Canning Town and the surrounding areas. In 1970, the Port of Tilbury had been re-developed and with the global change to container-isation, it became the largest container port in the UK. Work started on building a further container port at Felixstowe to handle the overflow. But it was the development of the Tilbury Docks that sounded the final death knell for the London Docks. At its peak, it had become the largest port in the world, but the decline was quick and most docks remained dormant for many years until re-development started during the 1980s. The area has now become a major commercial and residential site called London Docklands, and is an extension to the City of London's financial district.

Inside the Bridge House, the dividing wall between the saloon bar and the public bar had been removed, which gave access to a large central bar. The saloon bar area was filled with tables and chairs but the public bar area housed a large stage where people could drink and watch the various groups perform. Playing away on stage, I often wondered why it had been built to the same height level as the bar. When I asked the pub-lican why it was built so high, he informed me it was to help prevent the groups from being attacked should a fight break out! I think if I'd known that was the reason, I might not have accepted so many bookings there!

There was one seriously bloody Saturday evening at the pub. Thank-fully we weren't playing there that particular evening, but we heard all about it when we arrived the following day to play our Sunday lunchtime and evening sets. We had become quite friendly with a group of regular Bridge House female drinkers, all in their 20s, and they told us what had happened. A dozen or so Dutch seamen, all off a boat moored locally, had wandered into the pub just after six o'clock. By nine o'clock, the pub was heaving with bodies and the Dutch sailors were very drunk. They had started to try and chat up various females sitting on stools at the bar, but the girls weren't interested in them. However, the sailors were persistent and just wouldn't take no for an answer. This alerted some of the local drinkers who took offence at what was going on and told them to leave the girls alone. Stronger words were then said, a fight broke out and the Bridge House became a battleground.

We had only witnessed a few minor confrontations during our tenure there, although we had heard reports of many more incidents that took place on other evenings.

It was a week later, when I met up with my banking pal, John Jenkins, for a drink, that I discovered it was his group that were performing at the Bridge House that Saturday evening! He told me the full story. His group was on stage playing when the fighting started and they heard the publican yell out for them to keep playing. A few minutes later, when in the middle of playing a guitar solo, he was aware of something wet on his trousers and just assumed it was beer. Finishing his solo, he looked down at his trousers – it was blood! Apparently seconds previously, a guy in front of the stage had walked up to another man and pushed a broken pint glass into his face, hence all the blood. The injured man was clutching his face, blood pouring through his fingers. The whole pub then erupted, with bottles, glasses and chairs being hurled around. A couple of chairs went through the front window and, to John's disbelief, he recalled seeing somebody holding a chair up high and throwing it at the bar, bringing bottles and glasses crashing to the ground. In his words, it was 'pandemonium'. The landlord had by now called the local police, while all the time John and his merry men were feverishly playing away. It wasn't until the police arrived, that the group was told to stop playing.

People from all sides were marched out to waiting police cars, and some to waiting ambulances, which took them to hospital.

We arrived the following Sunday morning to play our lunchtime session and as we alighted from the van, we immediately spotted the boarded-up windows. Carrying our gear into the pub, it was then we realised that something serious had happened. The place was totally deserted apart from five men wearing trench coats with the collars turned up, sitting at a table in the saloon bar close to the entrance door. The two barmen were standing behind the bar chatting quietly amongst themselves, and nodded to us when we came in. No music was being played and we later discovered that the jukebox had also taken a severe beating the night before and wasn't capable of playing any records.

As we set up our equipment, everywhere was eerily quiet. I left the stage, went to the bar and asked Harry for half a pint of lager. While he was pouring my drink I asked him why it was so quiet and he explained in detail what had taken place the night before. He pointed to the broken windows and then to the bloodstains on the ceiling and the walls. How the hell did blood get on the ceiling! He went on to tell me that after the pub was closed last night, they worked for hours removing the damaged chairs, sweeping up the broken glass, mopping up the blood and replacing the glasses and bottles of spirits at the bar, ready for opening time this morning. I was intrigued by the men in their trench coats and asked Harry who they were. Harry lowered his voice. 'They're plain clothes policemen, here in case the trouble-makers return.' I couldn't resist a bit of sarcasm, 'Well, they look exactly like plain clothes policemen, not regular punters, and stand out a mile.' Harry smiled. 'People aren't daft around these parts. They know the police are here and that they will want to talk to the regulars to try and identify some of the trouble-makers. But nobody wants to get involved, hence why it's so quiet.'

That lunchtime, only a handful of regulars came into the bar, and when we came back to perform in the evening, a different bunch of policemen sat at the same table near the door. No more than about 20 people came into the bar that evening, which was very unusual – normally the bar would be packed.

It would take a few more weeks before the pub returned to some sort of normality. Slowly punters started returning to their pub and although the fight wouldn't be forgotten, they had put the incident behind them. Standing on the high stage while playing, I was able to spot a number of regular faces at the bar. We later discovered, talking with our female friends, that they had had the foresight to leave the pub as soon as the fighting started and that this was, in fact, their first evening back.

When we were booked to perform consecutively on a Saturday evening, Sunday morning and Sunday evening, although tiring, at least we didn't have to pack up our gear each night, so we could head back home straight away. One Saturday evening, having played our last number, we said our goodbyes and left. As we climbed into the van, I could see the girls from the pub waiting at a bus stop and called out, 'Can we give you a lift?' 'Yes please' came the response. 'Any chance you could drop us off in Silvertown?' 'Sure' I said, 'jump in.' Silvertown was only a few miles away.

Once in Silvertown, one of the girls, Gina, pointed to a bus stop ahead and said, 'Just drop us anywhere near that bus stop.' Silvertown was no better than Canning Town and, at close to midnight, not a place for young women to wander around by themselves. I insisted we drop them outside the apartment block where Gina lived. The others apparently lived in the same block or very close. A bit further on, Gina pointed to a building ahead saying 'That's where I live' and I pulled up outside this dismal grime-covered block of flats. 'Would you like to come in for a drink?' she said. I looked at the others and they all said they'd love to. We parked the van and made our way up the external staircase to the first floor. We followed Gina and her friends along a dimly lit outside walkway until she reached her flat.

I didn't know quite what to expect, having seen what the block of flats looked like from the outside, so when we walked into her lounge, I was pleasantly surprised. It was nicely decorated with quite stylish furniture. We sat down and made ourselves comfortable, while Gina went off to get the drinks. I was dying for a cigarette, so I got up to get an ashtray off the top of the sideboard just as Gina came back into the room carrying a tray of drinks. Next to the ashtray was a framed photograph of a man I guessed to be in his mid-30s. I called out to Gina 'Who's the guy in the picture? A member of your family?' 'Yes' she responded. 'That's my husband.' 'Your husband!' I blurted out. 'You never told us you were married.' 'You never asked' she said. 'So where is he now?' 'Serving time' she responded.

The shocked expression on my face made her smile. 'Go on. Ask me. What's he inside for?' she mocked. 'OK, what's he inside for?' I said, and her response shocked us all. 'GBH' she said. My God, grievous bodily harm! All I could say was 'Bloody hell!' I looked across at the other group members and they all had the same anxious expression on their faces. What have we got ourselves into here! Her husband might find out that she's been entertaining a group from the Bridge House called Johnny Lonesome and The Travellers and assume the worse case scenario. I glanced at the photograph again but now, knowing this man was serving time for GBH, I was looking at it differently. He suddenly looked menacing with his rather large head, deep set eyes, broad shoulders – and, was that a broken nose! You'd think he could have made an effort and smiled at the camera, instead of scowling at it. Trying to sound as nonchalant as possible, I asked 'So, how long is he in for?' '18 months to go' was the reply. Well, that was good news. If we backed off now, hopefully he wouldn't hear through the grapevine that we'd been in his flat with his wife and her friends late one Saturday evening. If Gina was my wife and I was inside for GBH, I certainly wouldn't have believed some cock 'n' bull story that nothing untoward had happened when she and her friends had entertained a group from the Bridge House!

That was it! I made up my mind and after only one beer, I suggested to the others that perhaps we should make a move as it was getting late. We said our goodbyes and set off for home. In the van we all said how surprised we were to discover that Gina was married – to a convict who was in prison for GBH! What about the other girls – were they also married? And where were their husbands – also serving time? We unanimously decided there and then that it wasn't worth taking any more chances. We'd acknowledge them when we next saw them, but that was as far as it would go. We didn't really fancy them. They were just nice friendly girls. We certainly didn't want to risk being pursued by some nutter of a husband or husbands, who thought we might be giving his missus one!

After five continuous months at the Bridge House, we eventually got bored of playing there. There were a few more minor incidents at the pub when the police had to be called, and the brewery then installed a new landlord who talked about cutting down on the live music nights. We felt it was time to move on to greener pastures and, with more and more bookings coming in, we never looked back.

During the 70s and early 80s, the Bridge House pub reinvented itself and became the seminal live music venue for aspiring musicians around the country, many going on to greater heights. It hosted acts from all music genres – Iron Maiden, Rory Gallagher, U2, Depeche Mode, Stray Cats and Dire Straits, to name just a few. It finally closed its doors as a pub in 1982 and became a private club and then a hotel, until it was finally demolished in 2002 to make way for a new flyover.

However, the legacy of the Bridge House still continues to this day. Just a few yards away from the original site, a new music venue provides live music in Bidder Street. Its name is the New Bridge House. This club has its own website and a Bridge House shop selling CDs, DVDs and digital downloads of old and new recordings but none, unfortunately, going as far back as the early 60s when Johnny Lonesome and The Travellers performed there.

Up until recently, Canning Town was still one of the most deprived areas in the UK, but slowly the town is beginning to breathe once more due to government-assisted regeneration programmes, with most of the old houses demolished and replaced with modern housing.

11

NICE - FRANCE - 1962

Our diary was beginning to fill up with bookings on a regular weekly basis. Slowly we were spreading our wings and although we still mainly performed at schools and youth clubs, we were also getting booked to appear at local sports and social clubs and at weekends at the odd local dance hall. We were on a roll! Regular practicing combined with plenty of bookings, meant we were becoming a tighter band and improving all the time. The money we earned was being ploughed back into funding the groups' continuous needs. Performing more often and increasingly at bigger venues meant that we needed a better and more reliable sound system for John and improved amplification for the guitars. But with more equipment, two additional band members and extra 'baggage' after gigs, our Bedford van simply wasn't big enough. We needed to buy a larger and more reliable van.

At this stage, the drums and guitars were exchanged for better models at the individual's own expense, but within a few years the group would finance the purchase of the very best equipment money could buy, even buying JG one of the best drum kits around at the time. The guitarists however were always responsible for buying their own instruments, stemming probably from the fact that the guitar was a more personal item and also a lot cheaper than replacing a whole drum kit.

By early summer, I was beginning to feel pretty jaded and I'm sure the other group members felt the same way too. Holding down a day job, regular late nights playing in the group and then, on top of that, the extra-curricular activities in the back of the van after the bookings, was taking its toll. I was constantly tired and needed a well-deserved holiday. It was now a year since our disastrous caravan holiday at St Osyth and our brush with the police, so we all wanted to stay well away from any Mods and Rockers. A holiday abroad was the obvious choice. Martin had met the love of his life, so he couldn't bear to be apart for a whole two weeks. As for the two new members of the group, they wanted to do their own thing, so it was up to John, JG and myself to make up our minds where to go.

I had read that Brigitte Bardot had bought a villa along the coast from Cannes, just outside a small town called St Tropez, once a small sleepy fishing village on the French Riviera. It had been discovered by the international jet set and had now become the holiday destination for the rich and famous. The international press coverage given to Brigitte Bardot's move there had put 'St Trop', as it was nicknamed, firmly on the map. Apparently the local mayor, in appreciation of the publicity the town was receiving and the influx of more tourists, had made her an honorary mayor of the town for a year.

The three of us were Francophiles, so it was an easy choice – it had to be somewhere on the French Riviera. Decision made. The following weekend, the three of us went to visit our local travel agent and found that the only package holiday to the south of France that fitted our budget, was a two-week holiday in Nice, travelling there by train. The holiday brochure boasted that, as part of the holiday's attraction, a single carriage on the train had been converted into an all-night disco with flashing lights, a bar, and music supplied by a DJ. This was ground breaking stuff indeed for 1962! I hadn't seen or heard of such a thing before! What a way to start a holiday! Once again a unanimous decision was made. We paid our deposits and booked a two-week holiday to Nice, courtesy of Lunn's, the travel people.

We had the option of booking couchettes for the entire journey, but to keep prices down, we opted to share a carriage with three other people and simply sleep where we sat. We decided that with a disco on board, most of our time would be spent there, and we could always catch up on any missed sleep stretched out on a beach when we arrived. We did, however, reach a compromise for our return journey – with no disco on board we booked couchettes, guaranteeing us a good night's sleep.

On arrival at the Paris, Gare du Nord railway station, we transferred onto our overnight train to Nice. Eventually we found our carriage and met our travelling partners who were already in their allotted seats nearest the window. They were rather large northern gentlemen, whom we later found out to be beer-swilling Geordies. Soon we were under way and finding we didn't have a lot in common with these guys, we kept much to ourselves, just occasionally exchanging the odd word with them.

Later that evening our Geordie friends announced they were heading off to investigate the disco and invited us to join them. We had really wanted to investigate the disco by ourselves, but it was rather difficult to say no. However, we did have to share the carriage with them over the next 12 hours, so we didn't want to offend them.

The six of us snaked our way along the corridors through a number of carriages, eventually arriving at the entrance to the disco. My expectations were running high but as we entered, instead of being hit by loud music, stale smoky air and the noise of lots of people enjoying themselves, we were confronted with a dark, near empty carriage. What a let down! The walls, ceilings and windows had been painted black, and there was a bar on our left. The small disco unit at the rear of the carriage just had three constantly flashing coloured lights. Apart from six fixed stools at the bar, the only other seating provided were pull-down seats, similar to cinema seats, which lined each side of the carriage. Looking back it was all very basic but on the other hand, the idea of trying to attract young people on a holiday by operating an all-night disco on a train was pretty advanced thinking for 1962. However, the SNCF (French Railways) were obviously not prepared to spend a lot of money on the disco itself. Although it was near midnight, only a few dozen youths had bothered to turn up and they sat facing one another down the carriage.

Nobody was dancing, but who could blame them – French rock 'n' roll music at the time was pretty dire.

We decided to have a beer and sat at the bar with our three Geordie friends. After a few rounds with them, it became abundantly clear that our new friends were determined to drink the bar dry, and so we made our excuses and left.

Back in the carriage we made ourselves as comfortable as possible before switching off the main light, which automatically switched on a small blue light in the centre of the carriage ceiling above us, casting an eerie glow in the dark. One by one we slowly drifted off to sleep. It was hard to get comfortable in a sitting position and so sleep was pretty fitful. A few hours must have passed when suddenly the door slid across with a mighty crash and in rolled three very loud and very drunk Geordies. They made their way noisily to their seats, one falling on top of me and another stamping on my foot. Plenty of apologies were made, but that didn't make up for the fact they had woken us up. The three of them fell into their seats, tossing and turning, trying to get comfortable. Numerous belches later, all was blissfully quiet.

I was drifting into a deep sleep, when the roller blind of the main carriage window suddenly shot up and one of the Geordies jerkily got to his feet, slid the two small top windows apart, thrust his head out and after a moment of retching, proceeded to empty the contents of his stomach. He noisily shut the window and somehow managed to hang on to the blind cord. As he fell back into his seat, he also pulled the blind down. Instantly he was comatose. John, JG and the other two Geordies appeared to have slept through all the noise and the carriage was silent once more. I sat there for a while, listening to the distant steam engine and the sound of the wheels racing over the tracks. Eventually I fell asleep again, rocked by the gentle swaying movement of the carriage.

Narrow rays of light flickered across my face. I slowly opened my eyes and watched as the blind swayed in time with the moving train, allowing a small chink of daylight to penetrate the carriage with each movement. I looked around at the five bodies slumped in a variety of positions, all asleep. As I drifted in and out of sleep for a while, I was aware of move-ment and distant noises as everyone began to wake up, stretching arms and legs, and groaning. I lay there for a moment but had to stand up just to ease the stiffness in my back. The light coming into the carriage had now intensified as daylight was mixed with the first rays of a Mediter-ranean sunrise. Someone suggested pulling the blind up, so a Geordie nearest the window obliged and up shot the blind. The intense light momentarily blinded us, but as our eyes adjusted, our first sunny view of the south of France was marred by large deposits of what looked like Heinz vegetable soup splattered across the window. Everyone groaned in unison!

At Nice station we said our goodbyes to three well hung-over and very subdued Geordie gentlemen. Our courier bundled us into a taxi and gave instructions to the driver to take us to our hotel.

It was a hot sunny morning as we shot out of the station and slipped effortlessly into the stream of busy morning rush hour traffic. Our taxi driver was fearless and drove as though his life depended on getting us to our hotel as quickly as possible. As we approached an extremely large roundabout, amazingly he didn't even consider slowing down and we left the roundabout with tyres screeching, heading down a typical French boulevard lined on both sides with trees. Ahead we could see the spark-ling blue Mediterranean Sea and the beachfront. A sharp right turn and we joined the traffic along the Promenade des Anglais, passing very large imposing hotels. Another right turn with a squeal of tyres and we pro-ceeded up a hill into a quiet residential area. Upon reaching the top of the hill, the taxi ground to a halt and the driver pointed to a small tradi-tional French hotel shaded by fir and palm trees at the end of a short driveway.

It wasn't a very big hotel and looked pretty old. The walls of the hotel had been painted dark pink and all the doors, window frames and louvre shutters were in turquoise green. The name, Hotel Sollar Son Charmant Parc, was picked out in blue and ran along the side of the hotel wall.

Having collected our suitcases from the boot of the taxi, we thanked the driver and started to make our way down the short drive. It was incredibly quiet apart from a soft wind rustling the palm fronds and some cicadas nearby trying to keep cool. The only sign of life was a lady's old-fashioned bicycle propped up against the trunk of a palm tree.

We climbed a few steps that led into a darkened foyer and rang a small brass bell on the reception desk. Within seconds, a young French girl appeared wearing an old-fashioned maid's cap. After the usual pleas-antries, she asked us for our passports, and then handed us each a registration card to complete. As she was putting our passports into a small wooden rack and taking a bedroom key off a hook, we quickly agreed in whispered tones that we were professional musicians, so the three of us entered 'musician' in the occupation box. The young recep-tionist glanced at the cards, and then looked us over and smiled. She was obviously suitably impressed and I saw her glance at the guitar case slung over my shoulder, which I felt added to my 'street cred'. I wondered how impressed she would have been if I'd simply entered bank clerk as my occupation!

It didn't take us long to settle into a daily beach routine, but a day of lying in the sun and then having to make that trek back up the hill to our hotel in the hot, late afternoon, was very tiring for us musicians. On the second day, making our way back to the hotel, we came across a small bar in a side road running adjacent to the Promenade des Anglais. We stood outside deliberating whether to go in or not, when a man came out and approached us. 'Are you English?' he asked. 'Yes' we replied in unison. 'Well, come on inside. It's cooler than standing out here.' The decision had been made for us – and he spoke English!

We followed him inside, ordered three Cokes, and made ourselves comfortable on stools facing the small bar. 'Welcome to my bar. My name is Philippe and I'm the owner.' We were very impressed, shook hands and introduced ourselves. It wasn't a very big bar, more like a small club, with another room leading off from the main area, where small tables and chairs had been placed around the perimeter of the room. 'So, what do you boys do for a living?' he said in almost flawless English. 'We're musicians' came John's reply. Philippe appeared to be impressed and asked if we'd like to play in the bar one evening. 'Sorry, no amplifiers, mikes or drums' came our automatic response. 'We only have an acoustic guitar with us.' But Philippe wasn't that easily deterred. 'Don't worry, just bring your acoustic guitar along and we'll have a bit of a sing-along, nothing serious, just for half an hour or so.' What a hole we had dug ourselves into! 'Perhaps we'll try and pop in later' I said. When we'd finished our drinks, we said our goodbyes and headed back to the hotel.

Over dinner we decided it wasn't a bad little bar and, as it was going to be a casual performance, we'd give it a shot. So later, with guitar over my shoulder, we headed out. There were a few extra customers inside since we'd left earlier and there, behind the bar, was our mate Philippe, cleaning some glasses. 'Glad you could make it boys' he said, and insisted on buying us each a beer. He went on to say, 'Why don't you take your drinks into the other room and I'll put some music on.'

Inside this small room, the windows had been blackened. It was pretty gloomy and the only light came from small candles in the centre of each table. We made ourselves comfortable and sat with our backs to the window, listening to the music and slowly sipping our beers. After about five minutes three rather attractive young women walked into the room and sat at a table opposite us. 'Now that's a stroke of luck' said JG. We couldn't believe it – three attractive girls – one for each of us! I particularly liked the one with the long dark hair and kept glancing across at her. She caught me looking and smiled back. Then John got a lovely smile from the blond girl. 'I'm going to ask my one for a dance' I said, and strolled over to her, stretching out my arms. She immediately stood up, and the next minute we were dancing very close together. Over her shoulder, I watched as both John and JG walked across the room, and the next minute they were dancing with the other two girls.

We continued dancing through a couple of songs and then I asked her if she'd like a drink. 'A whisky please' she said. We went through to the bar and Philippe poured the drink. As he handed it over to her, he turned to me and said '12 francs please.' 12 bloody francs! Making a quick calculation I realised that that equated to just about £1. A £1 for one drink! I was shocked – we'd only brought £25 each as spending money to last the whole two weeks! Then I watched as John and JG came up to the bar. 'Two whiskies please' said JG. I remember thinking 'strange they all drink whisky.' Two drinks were poured. '24 francs' said Philippe, and I saw JG's jaw drop. What was going on here! But then the penny dropped. We were so naïve and gullible. We'd been set up – these girls were hostesses!

The girls remained at the bar chatting, while the three of us went back into the other room and sat down. 'We've obviously been well and truly shafted' said John and we nodded in agreement. I suggested we ought to make a hasty exit before these girls wanted their glasses re-filled. Without saying a word, JG stood up and pulled on a handle to see if the window opened. Sure enough it did, straight out onto the street. 'Shall we?' John asked. 'Quickly then' I said. So JG opened the window and climbed out. I handed him my guitar, and then made my exit with John following me. We closed the window and sprinted up the street, laughing our heads off. Needless to say we didn't see Philippe again.

Top of the agenda on this holiday was exploring the local area and definitely a trip to St Tropez. But what was the best and cheapest way to get around? On one of our walks down to the beach, we'd spotted a shop where mopeds could be hired for a day or more. Problem solved, and we hired a moped each for a week. A moped was not much more than a motorised bike and, at the time in the UK, not the most popular or fashionable mode of transport. Also, mopeds were usually associated with being driven by older men. But in the south of France, it was a common sight to see young people riding their mopeds. It never ceased to amaze us how many young and attractive girls with long flowing hair and wearing hot-pants, would zoom past us – in France at this time it was not necessary by law to wear a crash helmet.

Watching all those French films in London, we had a pretty good idea what the trendy young French men were wearing. With our newly tanned bodies, we would ride into town during the day or at night, dressed in our dark denim Levi jeans, tight-fitting black T-shirts and black leather moccasins. We looked the business, very French, and had great fun racing around the endless narrow streets of Nice.

It was during one of our evening escapades into the centre of Nice that we inadvertently discovered the local red light district. We'd found a small yard just off a quiet side street where we could safely park our mopeds. As we headed back to pick up our mopeds later that evening, we spotted a rather lovely looking woman standing in a doorway in the dimly lit street. She was casually smoking a cigarette and as we walked passed, she smiled at us. Before we could say anything, we had passed another doorway with an equally lovely woman standing there, and she also smiled at us. As we continued walking up the street, across the road we could see another couple of young ladies who were deep in conversation. All were dressed quite provocatively. We then spotted more women standing in doorways and another under a streetlight. She was stunning. It was then that the penny dropped and we realised where we were. We stopped at the top of the street and decided amongst ourselves that we'd head back down again, but this time on the other side of the street just to study the lovely ladies once again.

The only prostitute I had every seen in England up to that time was old Lil, who lived in a tiny end-terrace house close to the entrance of our school – and she was pretty grim. Now these French ladies were something else! Very attractive, well dressed and, most importantly, they knew how to apply their lipstick, unlike Lil who always ended up with it all over her face. To us they looked like film stars. We finally ended up at the alleyway leading to the yard where our mopeds were parked. 'Do you want to go home?' John said. 'Not particularly' was the not unexpected response! 'Well let's continue down the street. I must have another look at these amazing women.' I could tell John was enjoying himself. We passed more women standing under a lamppost and one gave John a lovely big smile. John had a great big grin all over his face too!

We walked back up the street, unsure as quite what to do next, and stopped again in the alleyway. Of course, one of us had to ask the inevitable question, and it was John who piped up, 'I wonder how much they charge?' 'Why, are you interested?' I said. 'You bet, if they're not too expensive' he replied. We agreed that if it wasn't too much, collectively we'd pay for John to have a session – and to test the water so to speak! He was now raring to go and raced up the street. JG and I peered around the wall to watch the proceedings. He went up to one of the women under the lamppost, then came striding back. He was quite excited. 'You won't believe it, only four francs.' 'Are you sure?' I said, 'that does sound cheap. Did you ask her in English?' 'No' said John. 'I simply said 'combien' and she replied in French. Because I didn't quite understand her, she went one, two, three, four, counting out the numbers on her fingers.'

We just couldn't believe how cheap it was! I'll see how John gets on and perhaps have a go myself I thought. 'Good luck, we'll wait for you, but don't rush' said JG, which made us smile. With four francs in his hand, John shot off down the road. Once again we watched excitedly as he approached the same woman again. She put her hand out and we could see John hand over the money, but instantly there appeared to be a problem. She kept shaking her head and John hurried back looking quite dejected. 'I don't believe it – she wants 40 francs, not four!' Well, that put paid to any notions we might have had about sex with a French prostitute. Even collectively, we couldn't afford that sort of price.

ST TROPEZ, HERE WE COME

The weather in Nice was beautiful and breakfast, lunch and evening meals were always served in the exotic gardens at the rear of the hotel. The dining tables stood under a cluster of pine trees and were covered in freshly starched pink tablecloths. It was over an evening meal there that we planned our pilgrimage to St Tropez. We'd spent the last five days stretched out on a beach and now we were mobile. It was time to head off along the coast. After dinner we ordered three packed lunches for the following morning. We had breakfast the next day, and then we folded up our hotel bed sheets, collected the packed lunches and packed it all in the individual panniers attached to the back of our mopeds. As we headed off, it simply never occurred to us to inform anyone at the hotel of our intended journey, or that we needed to carry our passports in case we were stopped by the police for any reason.

We estimated a journey of about 70 miles and our route would take us along a coastal road with breath-taking views over the Mediterranean, travelling through the lovely towns of Cannes and Juan-les-Pins. We calculated that if we maintained a speed of around 30 mph, we should arrive in St Tropez around mid-afternoon. Our first and only stop on the way there was for a quick snack in St Augulf, preferring to eat our packed lunches from the hotel later in the day.

We left St Augulf with only 20 miles to go and arrived in St Tropez an hour later. We'd seen photographs of the harbour in magazines and this was where we headed, as it was the central focal point of the town. Driving along the narrow streets of this once small fishing village, we entered the harbour area and were confronted with the most wonderful sight. The harbour was not filled up with fishing boats, but with beautiful yachts moored side by side in all their expensive splendour. People were ambling along the harbour front in the afternoon sun, admiring the plethora of amazing boats. Many of the yacht owners and guests sat at tables in the stern of the boat, eating and drinking. It seemed very strange and slightly rude of people who walked along the harbour front, to suddenly stop and gape at the people eating their meals, with only yards separating them.

The old buildings along the harbour front were painted in an assortment of pastel colours and the louvre shutters, closed to keep out the heat of the summer sun, were painted in contrasting pastel shades. Most of the ground floor properties were either bars or restaurants packed with people sitting under extended canopies, eating, drinking and talking, or some simply watching the world go by. We quickly parked our mopeds in a small side street and walked down to the harbour, ambling along the waterfront and taking in all the wonderful sights.

When the sun finally sank behind the buildings, it was decision time. We intended sleeping on a beach somewhere, so our first priority was to find a suitable beach before it got dark. That wasn't so easy. We had discovered that St Tropez didn't have beaches immediately close by and that the coastline was incredibly rocky, so off we went on our mopeds to try and locate somewhere suitable. After a couple of miles, outside of the town along a quiet narrow coastal road, we spotted a hand-painted wooden sign with the single word 'Bar' pointing down a rocky footpath. We parked up, taking with us our panniers, and made our way down the steps. We were well rewarded and had cracked it in one. There before us, at the bottom of the steps, was a small sandy cove, and towards the back of the beach stood a small ramshackle wooden bar, where a handful of people were sitting eating and drinking – a perfect romantic location.

We ordered our usual Fanta orange drinks and sat on the sand talking about our day's experiences, while slowly the sky grew ever darker and darker until the bar was the only source of light on the beach. By now we were getting peckish, so it was time to open our packed lunches. To our horror, the cold chicken legs, tomatoes, hard-boiled eggs and rolls were covered in dozens of large ants. It was our own silly fault. We'd just dropped the panniers on the sand when we first arrived, and it had never occurred to us there might be ants around, especially on a beach, so our evening meals hit the bin.

We were ravenous, but when I enquired at the bar, they informed us that they had finished cooking some while ago. It wasn't long before the few remaining people sitting at the bar left and headed up the steps. The young couple that ran the bar cleared up the empty glasses, pausing now and again to kiss each other. How romantic! I watched enviously, and daydreamed that I would eventually find a similar location and build myself a bar like this. That was probably the easiest part. I first had to find a beautiful French girl who looked like her with soft tanned olive skin, a beautiful body and long sun-bleached hair!

I came out of my dream with a jolt as the couple called out 'bonne nuit' and then turned off the lights, locked up the bar and, holding hands, made their way up the steps. We sat there for a while in the sudden darkness, listening to the sound of the waves washing up on the sand a few yards away and to the constant high-pitched buzzing of the cicadas. My tummy rumbled. I was starving but I thought the best thing was to try and sleep so I didn't have to think about food. The others thought that was a good idea too, so out came the sheets and we bedded down for the night.

I lay there, but I wasn't tired. Suddenly JG jumped up shouting 'bloody ants' and started patting himself all over. Then I started to feel things crawling over my body and just as I leapt up, John also shot into the air. The ants weren't just content to eat our packed lunches – they now wanted to eat us as well! We'd all had enough. This wasn't fun, so we decided to head back to town and after packing our panniers, we made a hasty retreat up the steps and set off in the direction of St Tropez.

By the time we rode into town, it was about four o'clock in the morning and as we made our way down the narrow streets to the harbour front, we were surprised to see it was still pretty busy. The restaurants had closed, but some bars were still open, with quite a few people still sitting outside drinking. We parked our mopeds in a dark alleyway and then wandered along the front until we found a bar that was still serving snacks. We ordered a plate of toasted sandwiches, which we washed down with our favourite Fanta.

Sitting there eating our food, I noticed that at the back of the café was a tall jukebox with what looked like a large TV screen perched on the top. It was pretty plain in appearance, unlike the usual flashy and colourful jukeboxes I was used to seeing. I was intrigued. I'd never seen anything quite like this machine before and I watched intently as someone walked up to the machine, dropped a coin into the slot and selected a song from a small list of song titles. A button was pressed and suddenly the machine sprung into life. My God, this was unbelievable! The music was loud and there, on the screen in full colour, was Vince

Taylor and The Playboys performing 'Twenty Flight Rock', a song that we all knew and which was part of our own repertoire.

We couldn't believe our eyes! The last time we'd seen this group in action was on stage at the Wykeham Hall the previous summer. We'd seen them again a few times, but then suddenly they didn't seem to be around anymore. We just assumed they had disbanded. John had always enjoyed watching Vince Taylor perform. John was a fan of Gene Vincent, and Vince Taylor had blatantly copied Gene Vincent's appearance on stage by dressing in black leather. He even wore black leather gloves and his jet-black hairstyle was pure Presley. He was such a great mover on stage and here we were, watching and listening to him in a bar in St Trop. How did that happen!

The singer Vince Taylor was born in Britain, but spend his childhood growing up in the United States where he was heavily influenced by the emerging rock 'n' roll stars of the time, namely Elvis Presley and Gene Vincent. He arrived back in the UK to pursue a singing career and formed The Playboys, playing around the country in small dance halls. Their careers suddenly took off after a chance appearance at the Paris Olympia in 1961 and they became big stars in France for a few years.

TV programmes back home in the UK were still being broadcast in black and white in 1961. It would be another ten years before colour television became available and nearly another 20 years before the video boom exploded. The three of sat there mesmerised, watching this group in action in full colour! It was pure magic and, without realising it, we were witnessing the advent of the music video. However, a few years would have to pass before it became the norm for groups and artists to make a music video to accompany their latest record release. The emergence of MTV, the US music TV channel, would prove its popularity.

The French had invented a method of simultaneously combining music with visuals in the late 50s, with the images delivered via 16mm film tape and a magnetic soundtrack delivering the music. It would be another two years before I saw another such machine standing in a Soho cafe in London. This machine, the Scopitone, was a sensitive picce of equipment, requiring regular servicing and it would only survive another few years before being phased out.

Having watched the 'Twenty Flight Rock' video at least five or six times, we decided to head off before we used all our spending money. Dawn was just breaking as we emerged out of the café and headed to the edge of the harbour to study the boats once again. Most were shrouded in darkness, but one or two still had people sitting on their decks, drinks in their hands. We stopped at some steps to watch as a large and powerful speedboat made its way slowly towards us, its engine making a deep throbbing sound. It was beautifully appointed and the first rays of the early sun reflected off the curved varnished mahogany decking and all the assorted chrome fittings. Sitting in the front and steering the boat, was a guy dressed all in white, wearing a white peaked cap. Behind him, in another seating area stood a second man, holding what looked like a glass of gin and tonic. He was slim and good-looking, probably in his mid-thirties, tall, well tanned and with longish blond hair. He was wearing navy blue canvas deck shoes, white trousers, white shirt and a lightweight grey linen double-breasted jacket with a turquoise sash over one shoulder. He just stood there, legs apart, one hand in his jacket pocket, the other holding his drink.

The revs dropped and the boat silently glided to the side of the steps. As it gently touched the side of the quay, the man elegantly stepped off the boat and made his way up the steps. He strode past us, still holding his drink in his hand, and disappeared across the harbour front into a bar. I'm surprised he didn't turn to us and tell us to close our mouths as he passed by! The boat was pushed away by one of the crew and the revs increased again. The boat reversed, turned, and slowly made its way out of the harbour. We were amazed – who the hell was that? Now that's what I call an impressive entrance into St Tropez harbour – slightly more impressive than us arriving by moped! But perhaps the most intriguing thing was why was the man wearing a sash? What was that all about?

Before leaving St Tropez and heading back to Nice, I wanted to take a distance photograph of the harbour front, so we rode along the coast and just outside town we spotted a picnic area where we could park. No sooner had I taken the photograph, than a white police car, a Renault Dauphine, pulled up behind us. Two gendarmes, both sporting pistols, got out and approached us. I suppose three young lads on mopeds whizzing around the roads of St Tropez at 6.30am in the morning did look a bit suspicious.

They addressed us in French and even though I was the only one with a smattering of schoolboy French, I hadn't the foggiest idea what they were saying. Suddenly I recognised the word 'passeport'. Of course, they wanted to see identification! I responded by asking them if they spoke English, which wasn't very well received. In a deep guttural voice one of them replied with a curt 'Non.' I tried to explain. 'Passeports dans hotel dans Nice.' They just stared at me in disbelief and remained silent. It was obvious they weren't out to promote 'entente cordiale!'

We then tried emptying our pockets in the hope of showing them some English money and so prove we were British and didn't really understand what was going on. But all we had were French notes and coinage. Looking back, what was I thinking! Did I really think that showing the police a couple of English pennies would have satisfied them! John then suggested we look for labels on our clothes – perhaps we could find a few 'Made in Great Britain' labels to convince them. What must we have looked like! Three young guys pulling T-shirts away from the back of our necks, straining to make out the country of origin on the attached label, while the police looked on in bewilderment. Unfortunately, being the Francophiles that we were, all our t-shirts had 'Made in France' labels on them!

In one sense we had achieved what we set out to do and that was to look French. Now it was getting us potentially into deep shit. I lifted up my foot to look on the sole of my shoe. Perhaps there was some form of mark or wording showing they were from the UK. I could just make out some raised letters on the rubber sole, so I twisted my foot slightly to get a better look. One of the gendarmes had joined me and as we looked together, oh shit, there it was again, 'Made in France'.

The two policemen were now getting impatient and quite agitated and the language barrier wasn't helping matters. I couldn't face another entanglement with the police on holiday, especially in another country. Please, not another session in jail. In my mind's eye I could still see the interior of that jail in Clacton and I'm sure the others were thinking along the same lines.

The older of the two gendarmes walked a few steps away from us and beckoned over his partner. They stood there talking in low whispers. Surely by now they realised that even if they shouted we still wouldn't understand what they were talking about. But luck was with us. The older one looked across at us, motioned us to leave with the flick of his hand and they both made their way back to the police car. 'I don't believe it' I said, 'I think they've given up on us.' 'I hope you're right' said John. 'I'd hate them to think we were trying to escape and start shooting at us.' We carefully rode out of the picnic area at a nice respectable speed and left St Trop behind us.

Back in Nice, we parked our mopeds at the side of the hotel and with the bed sheets under our arms, we boldly walked into the foyer. Immediately the hotel manager confronted us. In broken English he pointed out that it was forbidden to take the hotel's linen off the premises and that we should have informed him, or at least a member of staff, where we were going. We made our apologies, collected our key and went to our room. Within minutes we were all fast asleep. We had lunch in the garden and then went back to our room where we spent the afternoon attempting to write some songs. Our little adventure was over!

12

THE 'MUSICIANS' HIT CANNES WITH A BANG – AUGUST 1962

With only four days of our holiday left and having returned the mopeds, our movements around Nice were now somewhat restricted. We decided to spend the last few days on the beach, topping up our tans, before we headed back to the UK.

We sat outside in the hotel garden at our usual table and wondered who was going to serve us dinner tonight – the lovely Swedish waitress or the usual skinny, and rather plain, French one. Much to our delight it was Brit, the Swedish girl, who greeted us with a beautiful smile and as she was serving the soup, she asked us if it was true that we were professional musicians. She said she'd noticed that we had each entered musician in the hotel register and that she'd also heard a guitar being played and singing coming from our bedroom. I was the first to respond 'Yes, we are musicians. In fact, we are part of a popular six-piece pop group from London.' She smiled and nodded her head. Then quite uncharacteristically John piped up 'And I'm the singer!' She looked at him and gave him a great big smile.

While we sat waiting for the next course to be served, we all said how much we fancied her, but as usual in these situations, John the singer always managed to pull rank over us. It couldn't be because he was taller and slightly better looking than the rest of us, could it! It had to be because he was the singer in a group. How true this would turn out to be! It was pre-Beatle time and the singer in a group still ruled. However, our day would soon come when girls either preferred the lead guitarist or the drummer or the bass guitarist, and not always the bloody singer.

While Brit was serving our main course, she suddenly put us on the spot. 'My boyfriend Jacques is a teacher at a school in Cannes and they are having an end-of-term party tomorrow. I wondered if you would like to perform for the children.' All this was spoken in beautiful English of course, with only a hint of a Swedish accent. I blurted out 'Er, we'd love to, but we haven't got our full gear with us. I only have an acoustic guitar with me.' JG was quick to point out that as a drummer he needed his full drum kit and he wasn't expecting the response he got back from Brit. 'Don't worry about drums. My boyfriend is a drummer and I'm sure he won't mind you borrowing them.'

We were all beginning to squirm a bit. We had lied about being 'professional musicians' and Brit didn't appear too concerned that I only had an acoustic guitar with me. It was time to put the tall dark-haired one to the test. 'How do you feel about performing John?' I asked. I knew this would put him on the spot and, as expected, John tried to wriggle out of the situation. 'I would love to be able to sing at the school, but nobody would hear me without a microphone and amplifier.' But Brit wasn't going to be deterred. 'I've heard you singing and you have a very strong voice' she said. JG and I tried not to burst out laughing – John was now seriously struggling. He looked across at us, hoping for some sort of support, but none was being offered. He turned to Brit. 'We'd love to do it, but the problem is, we simply don't have any transport.' The hole was about to become too deep. 'Don't worry about that' Brit responded, 'I'll get my boyfriend Jacques to take us in his car.' So that was it – fait accompli!

Two days later we were standing outside the hotel in the warm evening air, waiting for Brit and her boyfriend to arrive, everyone wondering how we had got into this situation and thinking how easily we had succumbed. Why hadn't we put our foot down and just told her no, instead of trying to make our feeble excuses. We could hear a car coming up the hill. It was a Renault Dauphine and it screeched to a halt in front of us.

Brit and her boyfriend got out. 'Hello boys, this is Jacques.' There stood this African gentleman with a big smile on his face and Brit explained that Jacques was from Senegal. He immediately extended his hand and we all shook it. The Renault Dauphine wasn't a particularly big car and couldn't possibly hold the five of us, and a drum kit as well. JG suddenly realised this and thought there might be a get-out clause from this evening's event after all. 'You know we can't perform without a drum kit' he piped up. 'Don't worry' replied Jacques, who walked to the front of the car, lifted the bonnet, which was the boot in a Renault Dauphine, and held up a tall slender African wooden tom-tom. We realised then that we were sunk. 'You can use this' he said. This was going from bad to worse! To think that shortly we'll be playing live, using an acoustic guitar and an African drum. John and I looked at JG, fighting to keep straight faces, as he sheepishly pointed out that he'd never played a drum like that before, but nobody took a blind bit of notice of him.

The three of us sat quietly in the back of the Renault as we made our way along the coast road to Cannes, the same road we used recently to get to St Tropez. The moment of truth was about to hit us – this was going to be one of the most embarrassing situations we'd ever encountered and how could we ever face Brit again back at the hotel after she'd heard us play – she'd know we weren't professional musicians!

We learned during our journey that the school was in fact an orphanage, with just over 100 boys and girls boarding there, the average age being around 12. This evening was their end of term party, and we were their party surprise. I sat there thinking to myself, what a surprise they're going to get! They'll think we are a comedy act not a pop group. I personally blamed Brit for getting us into this mess – she just wouldn't take no for an answer. If only she really knew what it was like to play in a pop group that relied heavily on using electric guitars, microphones, amplifiers and a full drum kit to boost their sound. We had never played as a group without the help of electricity before!

We could see the lights of Cannes ahead, but before entering the town centre we turned off onto a quiet road that led us inland and eventually into a quiet residential area. Most of the large houses were obscured from the road by high walls and shrubbery. We drove up a narrow, winding tree-lined road and as we emerged through the trees at the top, there facing us was this large, old and imposing building partly covered in ivy and softly lit by outside lights.

We climbed out of the car and a female teacher appeared in the doorway, coming down the steps to greet us. Jacques introduced us and we shook hands. Then she went on to say in near perfect English 'We really do appreciate you taking the time off from your holiday to come and perform for the children. They will be thrilled. Please follow me.'

As we made our way round to the side of the school, ahead I could see JG carrying the tom-tom, and in my mind's eye I could see him trying to play the thing. The very thought made me smile and, as I looked across at John he was grinning at me, and nodded towards JG, obviously thinking the same thing. We passed a large glass conservatory and beyond, in the garden, were rows of trestle tables covered in gingham table clothes, strewn with abandoned paper plates and cups. The children hadn't long eaten as a few teachers were still clearing the tables of any remaining food and ferrying the debris into the kitchen.

We eventually reached the rear of the school where a small fire was burning in the distance. As we followed the teacher down a flight of concrete steps, we could now see about 40 children assembled in a large semi-circle on a slope facing the fire. A teacher stood the other side of the fire and was leading them through a song, which they were singing with great enthusiasm.

We were told we would be playing in about ten minutes' time. JG requested a stool to sit on while playing the drum and we had to laugh when he was handed a child's stool. While we sat down on the grass, awaiting our fate, I took my guitar out of its case and tuned it up. Then I sat back on this warm, balmy evening and tried to enjoy listening to a bunch of kids happily singing their hearts out. I was quite nervous, but slightly relieved, that we had at least rehearsed earlier in the day and short-listed four songs, although we had been in fits of laughter at the sound of John singing along to a single acoustic guitar. But the best was yet to come – these songs hadn't been subjected to the additional rhythm of an African tom-tom!

We were told to get ready, so we assembled a couple of yards behind the teacher. JG had positioned his stool and sat down with the tom-tom upright between his legs. John and I moved and stood together just in front of him. The singing finally came to an end and the teacher turned around to make sure we were ready. I turned to JG quickly and although he was fidgeting somewhat, he nodded and I nodded back to the teacher.

By now the children were getting quite excited at the prospect of listening to us, and started to chatter and giggle amongst themselves. The teacher raised both hands slightly and immediately the children were quiet. She then came over to us and asked for the name of the group and where we were from in England. For simplicity's sake we said London, and she made a short introduction in French. I could only recognise a few words near the end, '…de Londres, Angleterre, Johnny Lonesome and The Travellers.' The children all clapped and cheered – you could see they were genuinely excited to have us at their party.

We hadn't noticed however, that while the introduction was taking place, JG was struggling to find a comfortable position in which to play the tom-tom. He had never held or played a drum like this in his life before. It was over three-foot tall and shaped like a long thin torpedo. With the stool being so very low on the ground and with the drum in an upright position between his legs, his chin was just a few inches above the drum skin!

The teacher moved aside and we nodded our thanks. I quietly counted us in – one, two, three, four – and I began playing the intro for 'I Like It', a recent European hit for the Liverpudlian group, Gerry and The Pacemakers. I cringed. My guitar intro was so quiet – I could even hear the bonfire crackling in front of me as I played! John began to sing and I started to play full barre chords which gave a bigger sound, but the overall effect was, to say the least, strange! Not forgetting, of course, the funny tapping noise coming from JG behind us!

Whatever it sounded like to us, we apparently couldn't do anything wrong. The children simply loved us. The clapping and cheering intensified as each song ended. It was during our third number, 'Shakin' All Over', that things nearly fell apart for us. We had just started playing this old British rock 'n' roll standard by Johnny Kidd and The Pirates, when I realised something was wrong. JG seemed to be having difficulty maintaining a constant rhythm and I turned round to find him in the weirdest of drumming positions.

JG later told us that, playing the drum in the original upright position during the first couple of numbers, had been extremely uncomfortable because the drum head was so high that it had been difficult to hit the drum skin with any conviction. So, in sheer desperation and between songs, he had quickly re-positioned the drum by angling it down and resting it on top of his left thigh, pressing the inside of his right thigh against the drum to keep it in place. On reflection, we should have given him more time to get comfortable before launching into the next song.

We were into the first few bars of the song, when a combination of events started to happen. Because the body of the drum was very smooth, and with the vibration of the constant beating, it had slowly started to slip down between his legs. Subsequently the bottom of the drum started to slide across the ground. While still playing, JG had somehow managed to bring his right leg over the drum in an attempt to try and stop it sliding any further. When I turned round, there he was, half-standing, straddling the drum, and desperately trying to prevent the tom-tom from sliding further away. No wonder he was struggling to maintain a constant rhythm! But the more he beat the top of the drum, the more it was slowly sliding away between his legs. His face was contorted in concentration, but he was slowly loosing the battle.

I had to turn back and face the children, otherwise I'd have burst out laughing. I fought to contain myself and somehow still managed to continue playing my guitar. John sensed something was up. He turned round to look and caught sight of JG in the most uncomplimentary position. Turning back, he looked across at me, eyes bulging. I daren't look at him otherwise it would start us both off laughing. Fortunately for all concerned, it was coming up to my guitar solo and I used the opportunity at the end of the solo to finish the song. I don't think John could have carried on singing. As for JG, I'm sure he would have ended up lying prostrate on the ground, while still attempting to play his tom-tom! John and I turned to face JG and doubled up laughing. The children were a wonderful audience – they were so innocent and thoroughly enjoyed the spectacle and I'm sure they thought the antics of our drummer were part of the act. The last song was thankfully completed without a hitch. JG continued as before, but this time around he placed his right foot behind the base of the drum thus preventing it from sliding away. So easy when you know how! As I played the final chord signalling we'd finished, John thanked the children in his well-rehearsed French, 'Merci et bonne nuit.' The children all stood up, clapping and cheering and before the teacher led them off to bed, they all waved us goodbye and we waved back.

We just stood there smiling at one another thankful it was all over. Jacques and Brit wandered over and congratulated us on our performance. But I couldn't stop making excuses for our sound. 'We would have sounded so much better if we'd had our normal gear with us.' But Jacques appeared to be genuinely impressed with our performance and asked is if we would like to join them in the school's conservatory for supper.

We made our way back up the steps and along to the conservatory. As we entered, various teachers approached us and shook our hands, thanking us profusely. We sat down at an enormous table covered with a giant starched white tablecloth. It was all very informal as plates, wine glasses and utensils were handed around the table. Over the centre of the table hung a large twinkling crystal chandelier, but before long that was extinguished and candles were lit. Corks popped and wine was poured. More teachers arrived carrying large gleaming white porcelain tureens filled with piping hot food. In all there must have been about 15 or so people sitting around the table eating, drinking and talking. The teachers who could speak English chatted to us, wanting to know what life was like being professional musicians, where we lived, what age were we and did we still live at home with our parents? For the non English-speaking teachers, our stories were translated for them.

A teacher sitting next to me asked if I had ever heard of the brutal murder of a British family called Drummond on a campsite in Northern Provence in 1952, ten years ago. In fact I had. Although I was only nine at the time, the murder of this British family was well reported in both countries, and embittered relations between France and Britain existed for a while. Sir Jack Drummond was a nutritionist, but was also working secretly for the British government. Eventually an old French farmer confessed to the crime and was convicted of the murders of Sir Jack Drummond, his wife and ten-year-old daughter. One of the farmer's two sons was also imprisoned for complicity in the murders. That son had two children who were being looked after at the orphanage and were amongst the children here tonight. For many years after, there was speculation that the Russian KGB had murdered the Drummond family, but it was never proven.

What a wonderful end to a rather eventful evening. We had been made to feel so welcome, and the food and wine was delicious. But, although we didn't realise it at the time, there was further torment to come. As the table was being cleared, Jacques came up to us and said that because this was an end-of-term party for the teachers as well, they had already booked a table at a nightclub in Cannes and would we like to join them. How could we resist such an offer?

The night club was situated right on the Cannes' beach front and once inside, we were directed to a table towards the rear of the club, which had been reserved for our party. There must have been around 30 or 40 tables, all occupied by people eating and drinking. At the front of the club performing on a small stage, was a four-piece French group playing some rather average electric rock 'n' roll music.

While we waited for our drinks to arrive, I spoke to Jacques as I was determined to convince him that if we had been able to play at the school using our electric guitars, mikes, amplifiers and with a full drum kit, how much better we would have sounded. A statement I was soon to regret making. I must have been distracted, because I certainly hadn't noticed Jacques get up and make his way to the front of the stage, where he talked to members of the group. I was talking to John when there was a tap on my shoulder. It was Jacques. 'I've just had a word with the group and they're prepared to let you borrow their instruments and also their bass guitarist. So now you can get up and show us how you normally sound.' I couldn't believe what I was hearing! I thought we'd finished performing for the night and could relax and enjoy the rest of the evening. This really was the last thing I wanted to happen and John and JG looked at me in disbelief when I explained the situation to them. I was fresh out of any more excuses, so there was nothing left for us to do but get up on the stage and show them how good we were.

'Come on boys, follow me' said Jacques. As we reluctantly left the table, our new French friends were very encouraging and started cheering us as we made our way to the stage. Jacques spoke to the group, and we shook hands with our respective counterparts. The lead guitarist handed over his guitar, which I slung over my shoulder. I played a couple of notes – it was nice and loud. JG sat behind the drum kit and made a few adjustments and the singer showed John the microphone and where the on-off switch was located. In case some extra sound was wanted, he also showed him the volume switch on the amplifier. The group left the stage except for the bass guitarist who, fortunately, besides speaking a little English, also knew the songs we were going to perform, starting with 'Lucille'.

The club owner came up on the stage, switched on the mike and announced that we were a famous group from London, and had agreed to play a few songs tonight. I made some minor volume adjustments on the guitar and also to the amp. Now this was feeling more like it! John did his usual sound balancing 'one, two, three testing' through the house mike. I turned round and said 'All set?' Nods confirmed they were ready and I started with the lead guitar riff. When it came to the repeat of the riff, the bass guitar followed in and then the drums. We were off, playing our interpretation of the classic Little Richard number. John, meanwhile, had stood back from the mike and as we approached the start of the first verse, he moved up, gripped the mike with both hands and started singing his heart out. His voice thundered around the club. By the time we finished, a small group of girls had gathered at the foot of the stage. We kept the tempo up by going straight into 'That'll Be The Day', a Buddy Holly and The Crickets' song.

Just as we were coming to the end of our third and last song, the Chuck Berry classic 'Johnny B. Goode', there was a blinding flash on the stage followed immediately by a loud bang. We were momentarily stunned, but our French bass guitarist quickly assured us that a firework had been thrown onto the stage by way of appreciation – or we think that's what it was! The people in the club didn't seem at all fazed by the bang and were now on their feet clapping and cheering as we came to the end of the song. John thanked the audience, and before we left the stage, we turned and shook hands with the bass guitarist, thanking him for his support. John led us off the stage and immediately a Brigitte Bardot double rushed up to him and gave him a long lingering kiss. JG and I stood behind him waiting, but nobody rushed up to kiss us!

The audience continued clapping as we made our way back to our table. We'd only just sat down when the club owner came up to the table and offered free drinks on the house for everybody. He spoke to Jacques who translated for us. Apparently he was so impressed with our playing that he asked if we were free next summer to do a residency at the club during July and August! He handed me his business card and, with Jacques translating, I told him we would check with our manager when we returned to the UK and get back to him in due course. As far as I was concerned, our reputation had been restored. We'd played well, the locals liked us, and when the drinks arrived, we all raised our glasses and toasted one another.

Now we had proved ourselves, hopefully Jacques would leave us alone. All I wanted to do was relax, enjoy my drink and soak up the atmosphere. Suddenly, without any warning, the entrance doors to the club swung open and in charged about ten gendarmes brandishing semi-automatic weapons. The last two stopped and stood either side of the door to prevent anyone from leaving. The others were circulating around the club giving instructions in French and one went and stood in front of fire exit door to prevent anyone leaving that way.

Whether it was the firework exploding on the stage which had spooked someone in the club to report it to the police, or whether it was just a regular police raid, I'll never know. Perhaps the police were understandably a bit jumpy as it was only fairly recently that a French extreme right terrorist group calling itself the OAS had called a ceasefire. They had orchestrated a series of bombings and assassinations throughout France in an attempt to prevent Algeria, then a French colony, from gaining its independence.

We all stood nervously around our table watching and waiting to see what this was all about and what was going to happen next. The main doors swung open once again and in walked another gendarme. He stood by the door and in a loud voice made a short announcement. One of the teachers translated what he had said. Apparently there had been a security alert and the club was now closed. People were free to leave, but everyone had to show their identity card or passport to the two policemen waiting at the main entrance on their way out.

Oh no, not again! We looked at each other. Again we didn't have our passports with us and these gendarmes looked slightly more menacing than the ones that had confronted us the other morning in St. Tropez.

'Excuse me.' I turned to find one of the teachers talking to me. I recognised his face but none of us had spoken to him before. 'Is there a problem?' he asked. 'Yes, we've forgotten to bring our passports with us this evening' I replied. He glanced at all three of us. 'So, where are your passports then?' 'Back at our hotel in Nice' I replied. 'Right, come with me – quickly' and we left the table and followed him, walking briskly towards the entrance door. It was all so quick, we didn't even have time to say our goodbyes to anyone, but as he spoke good English, with a bit of luck he could explain our predicament and get us out of here.

He strode right up to one of the gendarmes standing guard at the door who, upon seeing him, immediately stood to attention and saluted. In hushed tones the teacher spoke to him and the gendarme turned and opened the door. We walked out of the club closely following our new friend. Outside another gendarme approached us but again, when he saw who we were with, he also stood to attention and saluted. I was impressed – this teacher was obviously well known in town and luckily had lots of friends in the police force. The teacher turned and acknowledged him but didn't say anything, and continued to make his way to a car parked in the corner of the car park.

I was really thrilled when I saw that his car was a 'Shark' as we called them. This was my dream car! The styling of the Citroen DS19 was renowned for its aerodynamic futuristic body design. This was the first car to introduce hydro-pneumatic self-levelling suspension. The appearance and technical innovations of this model put it years ahead of its time. In its all-black livery and chrome, this was going to the first time I'd ever ridden in a Citroen DS19. The teacher opened the driver's door, climbed in and started the engine. He switched on the lights and slowly this magical beast rose up from its hunched position to allow us to climb in – fantastic! We quickly got in and the car automatically found its correct driving height. We sat there silently as he drove towards the exit. Again a gendarme was on guard and as we pulled up, a torch was shone in the face of the driver. Instant recognition brought the gendarme to immediate attention and he saluted. The car accelerated out of the car park and along the promenade road, heading for Nice. I just hoped Brit and Jacques saw us leave otherwise I was sure they would be wondering what had happened to us.

From the back seat, the three of us thanked our saviour, but there wasn't much response from him, apart from a cursory nod, and so we sat for most of the luxurious journey in total silence. As we approached the outskirts of Nice, our teacher friend asked the name of our hotel and where it was situated. We travelled along the Promenade des Anglais and just before our turning, he pulled up outside the entrance to a hotel. 'Let me buy you a drink – you deserve it' he said. Who were we to argue! As we approached the revolving doors of the hotel, the doorman standing outside saluted. Why would a doorman salute a teacher? I was now beginning to doubt this man was simply a teacher – he appeared to be known by a lot of people and under normal circumstances, the doorman would have insisted that the car was moved and parked in the hotel car park.

We followed him into a small bar, drinks were bought, and we sat down in the corner. I had noticed he smoked a lot on our drive back so I pulled out a pack of Gauloises and offered him a cigarette. 'Thank you. So you smoke French cigarettes? That's unusual – most British people find the black tobacco far too strong' he said. I told him that in fact all three of us smoked only French cigarettes and that we loved them. As he sipped his drink, the teacher appeared more relaxed and now a bit more talkative so, out of sheer curiosity, I just had to ask him if, in fact, he was a teacher at the orphanage in Cannes.

'Certainly not, I'm the Chief Commissioner of Police in Nice and I was invited to attend the end-of-term celebrations as I am on the Board of Directors at the school.' We were most impressed – the Chief Commissioner of Nice Police no less! Wow, Johnny Lonesome and The Travellers were certainly moving in higher circles these days!

We all had another drink, this time on us, and he accepted another Gauloises cigarette. Then after chatting for a while, he stood up to leave. We all got up and thanked him profusely for helping to get us out of the club and for the lift back to Nice. We shook hands and his final words to us as he left was 'Now, don't forget to carry your passports with you at all times.' He smiled and was gone.

What an evening! My head was spinning with everything that had happened that night and I found it hard to get to sleep.

We missed breakfast but sitting in the garden for lunch, we were served by Brit. She thanked us and hoped we'd enjoyed ourselves. Apparently the teachers all carried their identity cards, so they were able to leave the club without any problem. It was Brit's afternoon off, so John invited her to join us on the beach. JG and I sat on the sand, enviously watching as John and Brit held hands and ran into the blue Mediterranean sea. The good-looking one had struck it lucky again!

RETURNING HOME

Walking along the platform at Nice station, we located our carriage and climbed on board, shuffling awkwardly along the narrow corridor with our cases. When we found our compartment, we discovered three young English girls making themselves at home. I looked at my ticket and checked the compartment number. It was correct. 'Excuse me' I said confidently, 'I think you're in the wrong compartment.' They hastily rummaged through their handbags and retrieving a ticket, one of them looked at it and replied, 'I don't think so' and thrust the ticket at me. As I quickly looked at the ticket, I could see she was right. They obviously had different seat numbers to us but the date, carriage and compartment numbers all tallied. 'My apologies' I said. 'I think Lunn's must have made a mistake.' This being 1962 and all of us being quite naive, I couldn't believe that three females and three males would be put into the same sleeper compartment!

I volunteered to go and sort the problem out with the French courier. I got off the train and went down the platform to where he was standing, organising people who were boarding the train. I showed him my ticket and explained that there must be some mistake as three girls had been allotted seats in our sleeper compartment. At first he looked at me with a quizzical stare and then a broad grin appeared on his face. 'So what's the problem? You're in France – it's quite normal here for males and females to share a sleeper carriage.' That being the case, I was sorely tempted to say that at least he could have made sure we had three beauties in our compartment! He shrugged his shoulders and moved off down the platform and as I made my way back I thought to myself, bloody Frenchmen, they think they're God's gift to women.

Returning to the compartment, I sheepishly explained to everyone that there wasn't a mistake and we had in fact been allocated the correct compartment. There was a brief moment of stunned silence from both parties. I decided not to repeat to the girls what the courier had said as they looked very straight-laced and demure.

It was a very uneventful journey. The girls kept very much to themselves and when it came to bedtime, we volunteered to use the higher bunks. Each side of the compartment converted into three bunks, one above the other, and I made sure I was on a top bunk. I didn't want some strange girl on the bunk opposite watching me while I was asleep.

John was on the opposite top bunk to me. We both ended up having a fit of the giggles in the morning. He had rolled onto his side and looked down below. He suddenly shot up and silently indicated for me to take a look. I leaned over and on one of the bottom bunks, a leg was sticking out and a pair of hands was delicately rolling on a nylon stocking. Seeing a sight like that that might sound very tame now but believe me, in those days it was very sexy and provocative. Just a pity the leg didn't belong to a better-looking female!

During this holiday, we had managed to write two completely new songs – 'Miss, I'm Missing You' and 'Keep a Looking'. Due to the lack of writing paper in our room, both song lyrics were written on sheets of white toilet paper, but that was not necessarily an indication that the songs were a load of shite! However, due to our heavy schedule of bookings ahead, it would take a further 14 months before I eventually booked a recording studio so we could commit both songs to acetate.

13

SUPPORTING B. BUMBLE AND THE STINGERS – OCTOBER 1962

Ron King was the promoter who ran the Wykeham Hall in Romford on a Saturday evening. We wanted to talk to him about playing there but it took six months for us to be confident enough to do so. We were watching the bands as usual one Saturday evening and decided amongst ourselves that it was time to approach the promoter. I was chosen to do the talking and so, after the last song of the evening had been played and the lights switched on, the four of us headed for the exit doors. Ron King was sitting at a table chatting to a couple of his bouncers. These were rather large gentlemen who were employed to quickly quell any confrontations and eject the troublemakers. As I walked up to him, he stopped talking and looked up at me and said, 'What can I do for you young man?' I explained that we were a local group and would love to be given the opportunity to play at the Wykeham Hall. I handed him a business card and after looking at it, he asked 'So tell me, who's Colin Stoddart?' 'That's me' I said. 'How long has the group playing and what's your line-up?' was his next question. 'We've been performing together for two years and have two guitars, bass, drums and a sax.' I just knew that the sax would create a bit of interest and, sure enough, I was right. He thought for a moment, then went on to say 'A sax, well that's a bit different.' I then started to list the local clubs where we had played and added a few more where we hoped to play just to make it sound a bit more impressive.

He suddenly put his hands up, obviously to stop me rabbiting on any more. 'Well boys' he said, 'I run a small club in High Barnet, North London every Monday evening and if you want to play at the Wykeham Hall, you'll first have to come along for an audition at High Barnet. If you think you're good enough, then just turn up any Monday between 8.00pm and 9.00pm and play for about 15 minutes or so.' Having thanked him and obtained the address of the club in High Barnet, we walked out, trying not to run and show our excitement, but as soon as we were out of sight, we started leaping around congratulating ourselves. However, as we made our way home the excitement started to give way to trepidation – would we be good enough to pass the audition? If we only had 15 minutes in which to impress Ron King, what numbers should we do? 'I reckon we should start with 'Lucille' – the sax solo should impress him' said John. 'Maybe, but what about 'Down the Line' I suggested, a safe number for me as the guitar solo was quite easy to play. 'But there's no sax solo in that' Martin pointed out.' Of course, Martin was right – we had to select our most impressive numbers and exploit the fact we had a saxophone in the group.

Not to lose the momentum, we decided to head off to High Barnet in two days' time for our audition. We set off in pouring rain and by the time we arrived in High Barnet it was dark and still raining. We found the club, which was an old army drill hall, and made our way inside where there were about 40 youths milling around and dancing to music being played on an old record player. I spotted Ron King sitting in a corner and approached him. 'I spoke to you last Saturday' I said, and he put up his hand and stopped me. 'Yes, I remember' and then proceeded to give us instructions as to where to stack our equipment, pointing to an area half-way down the hall on the right. It was then we noticed other piles of amplifiers and guitar cases and realised that we weren't the only group auditioning that night.

We were told that because of the lack of space in the hall, and to speed up the auditions, all drummers would be using the first group's drum kit, so no more drum kits needed to be brought in. In total four groups auditioned that night, which provided free live music to an audience that had earlier paid money to gain entry. We were informed that each group had only ten minutes in which to perform and after each performance they had to quickly remove their gear to make way for the following group. Our ten-minute slot went well, although JG made a lot of excuses about his playing. I suppose having to play on a strange drum kit couldn't have been easy.

As we packed everything back into the van, we discussed our set and came to the unanimous decision that we had played pretty well. Feeling quite confident, we set off back into the hall to discover our fate. But luck wasn't with us that night. Ron King had apparently left by the rear exit immediately after hearing the last band play. We were devastated and also we felt ripped off. 'How rude is that! Leaving without saying a word, when we've gone out of our way to attend the audition at our own expense!' John said, sounding really indignant. It wasn't often John got wound up, but we all agreed with him.

A few weeks passed and Ron King still hadn't bothered to call to let us know if we had passed the audition or not. We were all eager to know his decision. We planned to call on Ron King after we'd played at a local youth club in Romford one Saturday and to confront the man himself. But to my amazement, he eventually called me and said we'd passed the audition in High Barnet. He went on to apologise for giving such short notice, but could we audition again, this time at the Wykeham Hall on Saturday and play for an hour. Although I knew we were already booked to play in Harold Hill, I didn't hesitate. I said yes we were free, knowing full well we were being ripped off again. I called the other group members and they all agreed to do it just this once, but no more auditions after that. The Wykeham Hall was one of the most prestigious venues for miles around. Considering the opportunities that could open up for us, it was well worth playing for free just one more time. I didn't like doing it, but I called the local youth club in Harold Hill and made my apologies and excuses. Surprisingly, we managed to get re-booked for a few weeks later.

We arrived as instructed at seven o'clock and parked our van facing St Edward's Church in Romford Market Place. John and I hopped out of the van and made our way into the hall. Sitting at a table with a money-box, a couple of rubber stamps and an inkpad was Ron King, no doubt waiting for the first people to arrive. Looking up he smiled 'Hello boys, bring your equipment through and set up on the stage right away. I want you to play from 8 o'clock for an hour, before the main group appears. By the way, it's the American group B. Bumble and The Stingers you'll be supporting.' 'OK' I responded nonchalantly. As John and I turned and walked out of the hall, we both drew breath. We were supporting B. Bumble and The Stingers! They had had a number one hit in the British charts the previous year with 'Nut Rocker', a fast raucous piano-led instrumental, based on Tchaikovsky's 'March of the Wooden Soldiers' from the 'Nutcracker Suite' ballet. We excitedly ran back to the van to tell the others.

Our equipment was taken in and assembled, we tuned up and completed a sound check and then drew the stage curtains across. Earlier, we had all spotted a piano parked in the wings, together with an assortment of drums and amplifiers, so we assumed the group had most probably arrived already and were relaxing in the small ante-room that adjoined the stage. But when we entered, it was empty – perhaps they'd gone across the marketplace for a drink in an English pub to sample the local beer. We changed, and close to eight o'clock we climbed up the few wooden steps and strolled onto the stage. 'Sod it' I said to myself. I now needed another pee even though I'd only been just five minutes ago. Always a sign for me that I was nervous, so off I went to the loo in double quick time.

We checked our tuning for the fourth time, which wasn't really necessary, rather a sign of our nerves. Suddenly the curtains opened slightly – it was Ron King. 'OK boys, whenever you're ready' he yelled out, and with that he disappeared. I looked across and said 'Everybody ready?' Heads nodded, and I then nodded to the caretaker to open the curtains. As they opened, we went into our first song of the evening.

We'd written out our song list beforehand, making sure our best sax-orientated songs were included. We were very conscious that Ron King had probably given us this audition just because of the fact that our line-up featured a saxophone. All went well despite our nervousness and in no time at all, we were playing our last number. We didn't get a big response from the audience but as the curtains closed, we could hear some clapping, which was encouraging – or were they pleased we'd finished! Ron King's head suddenly appeared again. 'Good set boys. Can you move your gear into the wings as soon as possible' and he was gone. As we quickly moved everything into the wings, two guys appeared on stage and started to pull out the piano. Within minutes the equipment was set up and ready to go. We were impressed.

We came down the steps into the small ante-room near the stage. The group was there, waiting for their signal to go on stage. They acknowledged us, but you could tell they wanted to keep very much to themselves and did not enter into any small talk, which was fine by us. As I slowly put my guitar back in its case, I surreptitiously looked across the room to study them. I was slightly in awe of this group. Fancy having such a massive worldwide hit and only last year to boot. They all looked at least a couple of years older than us. One guitarist was intent on putting a new string on his guitar, while two other guys just sat there smoking. As we quietly changed, I looked across at a very large gentleman who was standing with his back to us. He appeared to be getting something out of a little leather case. I thought to myself that that was probably B. Bumble himself and, sure enough, later when watching them perform, he indeed was the pianist. I was rather fascinated what this big guy was up to. The next minute he took off his jacket and started to roll up his shirtsleeves. As I moved to lean my guitar case up against the wall, I glanced across at him and was stunned to see that he had started to inject himself with a syringe!

This was the early 1960s and I'd vaguely heard about drug use but didn't really know anything about it, apart from pills called Purple Hearts, which the Mods took to keep themselves awake at all-night parties. It wasn't until the late 60s, during the psychedelic music era, that drug taking became more prevalent amongst the youth of the day. It was discussed openly on TV and in the newspapers and drug use was portrayed in films. But still, even to this day, the sight of a drug user injecting with a dangerous drug is quite alien to me.

Researching B. Bumble and The Stingers on the Internet recently, I discovered a black and white photograph of the group. I instantly recognised B. Bumble, most probably because of his size, but not the other members of the group. I went on to discover that his real name was R.C. Gamble and that he had retired from the music scene a few years later in 1965. He went on to become an economics professor at a college in Kansas and died in 2008. This man didn't sound like a drug addict to me, which I had naively assumed he probably was at the time. Perhaps because of his size and weight he was a diabetic and required regular injections of insulin.

We all thought we'd performed reasonably well on that night, but there was always room for improvement. As we left, Ron King told us that he'd be in touch shortly. I really wanted to establish that hopefully we'd passed the audition, but I bit my tongue. I just hoped he'd call me as promised and let me know when our next engagement at the Wykeham Hall would be. Weeks went by and as much as I tried calling him, he never answered his phone. It wouldn't surprise me if the number on his business card were a fictitious one. He was a likeable character, but in business terms a very cunning individual. Did he perhaps have one business card for the likes of us and dozens of other groups who pestered him constantly, and another for the serious contenders?

Auditions were a necessary evil – no auditions, basically no work, unless you were an established artist, of course. The audition potentially gave the promoter free music for an hour or so, even though he'd charged an entry fee. However, for the group involved, it was the one opportunity of selling itself and possibly obtaining regular work. The Beatles, in their pre-hit record period, must have also experienced the same audition process. They performed their last-ever live concert in 1969 on the rooftop of their offices at 3 Savile Row in Central London and John Lennon, in his usual sharp-witted way, said at the end of the concert 'I would like to say thank you on behalf of the group and ourselves and I hope we've passed the audition.' It was a short concert and was filmed for inclusion in a Beatles' film called 'Let It Be'.

TRAVELLING FROM A TO B

Throughout the eight-year existence of our group, we all lived at home with our parents and so, before we could head off to any gig, each member of the group had to be individually picked up – a bit of a pain really as this always took around half an hour. The routine was always the same. With four of us living in Romford, it would start with me, the lead guitarist, walking up the road with my guitar to our van, which was parked on a drive of a rented garage next to Martin's house.

Martin was the bass guitarist and his parents' house adjoined a block of six garages. This was ideal and we had managed to rent the garage immediately next to their house. When we started hiring the garage, the intention was to store our equipment in the locked garage and then to park our van right up against the garage door, giving it greater security. After a booking, Martin and I always arrived home late, having dropped the others off first, and unloading the equipment became our responsibility. We would then have to load it all up again, just us two, within a few days for the next booking, so we gave up doing this. We took our chances and it became routine to leave the gear in the locked van, except for our guitars. Nobody ever queried it and anyway, why should Martin and I have to do all the work, knowing the others were probably either already tucked up fast asleep in bed or sat at home relaxing, watching television waiting to be picked-up! It would have helped matters if we could simply have driven our van straight into the garage, but it was too tall. So, apart from our guitars and Dave's sax, the bulk of our equipment always remained in the van.

After knocking for Martin and putting our guitars in the back of the van, we then drove a couple of miles to the drummer's house, JG. We sounded the horn to let him know we were outside and with JG on board we would then drive another couple of miles to pick up John, the singer. Hearing the van's horn, he would often appear at the front door wearing a silk dressing gown and smoking a cigarette in a cigarette holder, like some precious Hollywood actor! This was all for effect of course and always provoked a few choice words and rude sounds from us. He would give a cheeky grin and close the door, then join us a few minutes later in the van.

It was then another few miles drive to our last pick-up point in Dagenham where we collected Patrick, the rhythm guitarist, and Dave, the saxophonist, who lived opposite each other. Finally, we then set off to the gig. The journey en-route was always light-hearted as we joked and talked about our day at work or our recent conquests – or rejections. With five young lads bundled together in a van there was always going to be lots of ribbing and laughter.

John loved having the star role as singer and was a great mickey-taker as well. On our way to and from longer haul gigs, we'd occasionally stop off at roadside cafes for food and drinks. Invariably, if a young waitress served us, John would go into one of his many routines. Looking straight into the girl's eyes, he would say 'My God, you're beautiful. Why are you wasting your time in a dump like this? Have you ever thought of break-ing into the movies?' The poor girl would blush like mad and rush off to get our orders.

We wanted to advertise the fact that our van belonged to a group, so in the back two windows there were photographs of the group plus, in bold print, our name, Johnny Lonesome and The Travellers. When some of our female admirers discovered where our van was parked at a gig, the odd message like 'I love Colin' followed by a name and a telephone num-ber would be written in lipstick on the side of the van. Over time the van was literally covered with lipstick messages made to various members of the band, but it was always Johnny Lonesome who had the most! Having a name and telephone number to call could be viewed as all very convenient for five hot-bloodied young men, but as far as I can recall, none of us ever took the gamble of calling a telephone number for a date, probably in case it was left by Lonesome himself, just to get a laugh!

On the road our van was pretty conspicuous and often during a journey that took us through local high streets, girls would wave and call out to us.

Sometimes after finishing a gig, there would be a group of girls waiting around the van, wanting to talk with us as we loaded up our gear. When we came to leave we felt bad leaving these girls to make their own way home in the dark at such a late hour, so being very chivalrous, we would offer to drop them home! The return journey could be delayed as we dropped off these girls close to their homes, sometimes having had a bit of fun together on the way. As far as I can remember, none of the girls ever complained that we had taken advantage of them. In fact, I think they took advantage of us!

Our return journeys from gigs were generally full of light-hearted banter as we discussed how well we had or hadn't played and how well we had gone down. And was anyone going to see the girls again that we had just dropped off? If the journey was a long one, the talking would slowly dry up as we started to fall asleep except, of course, the poor old driver! Finally, very late at night, one by one group members would be dropped off outside their home and the next booking and pick-up time would be confirmed.

LEYTON BATHS - LEYTON, EAST LONDON

On one of our rare free Saturdays towards to end of 1962, Patrick and I went to check out Leyton Baths, a prestigious music venue in the East End of London, which both of us had heard about, but neither of us had visited before. It was a very large Victorian indoor swimming pool, which during the winter months, would be covered with wooden planking and was hired out by the local council for dances. The promoters, besides hiring local groups to perform on a Saturday evening, also hosted well-known groups as well and in 1963 both The Beatles and The Rolling Stones played there on separate occasions. Our task that Saturday evening was to check out the place and to chat to the promoter with a view to getting an opportunity of hopefully performing there. No doubt we would be expected to give the customary audition before any serious work was offered.

When we arrived, I found the promoter and gave him the full background of the group, the line-up, the venues where we had played, and handed him a business card. He invited us in to have a look around. We entered the hall and were both astonished at its size. It was enormous, and packed with people. The group on stage was no other than Johnny Kidd's backing group The Pirates, who had recently released a solo album and were no doubt on tour to promote it. There were only three of them in the group but collectively they produced a really big sound, helped by the wizardry of their guitarist Mick Green. They wore identical pirates' outfits consisting of black baggy trousers, black and white striped T-shirts, black leather waistcoats and eye patches. Mick Green went on to join Billy J. Kramer and The Dakotas for a number of years, his career culminating in playing alongside Dave Gilmour of Pink Floyd in a band handpicked by Paul McCartney for his historic re-appearance at The Cavern Club. This would be the first time McCartney had played in this now-famous club in Liverpool since his early days with The Beatles, before they achieved international stardom.

As we left, we thanked the promoter and he said he'd be in touch. Yeah, yeah, I've heard that many times before! So I was quite surprised when I received a call from him in early January asking if we were available to appear at the Baths in two weeks' time, which we were. And no audition! That was a first!

SO VERY COLD - LEYTON BATHS - JANUARY 1963

During the winter of 1962/63 Britain was gripped by one of the coldest winters on record which continued for months, a period now referred to as The Big Freeze of 1963. Snow had lain on the roads for weeks on end with temperatures daily dropping well below zero.

On the evening of our booking at Leyton Baths, the cold weather hadn't abated and the temperature was dropping rapidly as I set off up the road carrying my guitar. There was a heavy frost in the air, which sparkled in the moonlight. Mounds of dirty snow lay in the street where people had cleared their paths after the last fall over a week ago. Most front gardens were still covered in frozen snow but the road itself wasn't too icy. However, many quieter side roads were still quite dangerous for vehicles.

When I arrived at Martin's house, the Bedford Dormobile van was white with frost, so I thought I'd quickly open the door and start the engine to get the interior warmed up a bit and the windscreen defrosted before we set off. But as hard as I tried, the door simply wouldn't budge – the doors and the locks were frozen solid. Minutes later Martin came to the rescue with a kettle of hot water, pouring it over the lock and around the doors and, hey presto, the door slid back. I climbed in and to our surprise, the engine fired on the second try. With a freshly filled kettle of boiling water, Martin set about de-frosting the passenger's door, but wasn't as successful this time. The two of us put our combined weight behind the door. Suddenly it broke free and slid back along the track at speed. Before we could stop it, it crashed into the rubber stops at the end of the tracks, shearing them off and the door fell to the ground. We struggled in the dark and the freezing air to realign the door back on to its rails, but our hands by now were so cold that we just couldn't do it. As hard as we tried, we just couldn't engage the small wheels on the top and bottom of the door with the rails.

Time was now against us – if we didn't make a move soon, we'd be late arriving at Leyton Baths – and we still had to pick up the rest of the group! There was no choice. We opened the back doors and together we lifted the door, placing it on top of our gear. Climbing into the van I turned and said to Martin 'With a bit of luck, perhaps Dave and Patrick will be able to put the door on.' Martin agreed and off we went – with no passenger door! It was less than a ten-minute drive to collect JG. I was driving and although I was cold, I wasn't being buffeted by the freezing cold air streaming in from where the passenger door used to be. I could feel a bit of warmth coming from the heater and through the engine cover, which was next to me, but still my feet and body were very cold. Poor old Martin just sat there huddled up in the passenger seat and didn't say a word during the entire journey. By the time we stopped outside JG's house, Martin was frozen solid, so it was decided from then on that we would rotate positions and take it in turns to drive.

Every new pick-up sat in the passenger's seat and the coldest person took the warmer seat in the rear of the van. We rotated drivers, and this was how we made our way to Dagenham. By the time we arrived to collect Dave and Patrick, we were all shivering quite badly. We pleaded with them to try and get the door on, but after five minutes of trying, they gave up. For whatever reason, the wheels on the door simply didn't want to engage with the rails on the van and so with time seriously against us, the door went back into the back of the van. Using the rotation system, we eventually made our way into East London, pulled up outside the Baths and five frozen bodies struggled to get out of the van. Now ahead of us was the most tortuous job – hauling the gear out of the van and getting it on to the stage. Luckily, it was extremely warm inside and for once the gear was unloaded in record time.

We had half an hour in which to set up our gear and change into our band suits before we played our first one-hour set. Thankfully, by this time we had all thawed out. Just before starting, the promoter came up and spoke to me and it was then I discovered we were the support band to The Viscounts. They had had a couple of slightly humorous novelty hits a couple of years ago and I had seen them a few times on TV. Originally they were part of a large theatrical harmonica group but now performed as a trio. They were a few years older than us, and a leftover from the late 50s/early 60s music scene.

We hung about in the wings of the stage to watch their set. With only three members in the group, they were dwarfed as they performed in the centre of this gigantic stage. Personally I found their music pretty tame and we were pleased when we received more applause than they did from the audience with our modern music.

In just under two years' time our paths would cross again with a member of The Viscounts when we supported Tom Jones at the Club Noreik.

14

SUPPORTING JOHNNY AND THE HURRICANES - JANUARY 1963

HERE WE ARE IN OUR NEW BAND SUITS

had used Montague Burton Ltd to make my very first Mod outfit. They were situated in Romford's South Street and supplied made-to-measure suits to the public. When it came to having our own bespoke band suits, we commissioned Burtons to make them for us, and we excitedly took delivery in early January 1963. Amazingly, the company is still around today but trading under the name of Burton and selling ready-to-wear clothing for younger men.

Our first public appearance in our new suits was made at the Pettit's

Lane Youth Club on 17 January. Not a particularly impressive venue to launch our new look but for us, the transformation was immediate. By wearing the suits on stage, we became a professional-looking band, elevating us above other local groups.

In 1963 the singer in a group was the main front man and had a separate name to that of the group who stood slightly behind him when performing on stage. Popular groups around at the time reflected this trend – Cliff Richard and The Shadows, Shane Fenton and The Fentones, Johnny Kidd and The Pirates, Marty Wilde and The Wildcats and much further down the scale – Johnny Lonesome and The Travellers.

Our suits were made from a lightweight fabric in moss green with contrasting rounded lapels in maroon. In keeping with trends of the time, the jackets were short, no vents and with slanting pockets. The trousers were high waisted with narrow bottoms and no turn-ups. To give our singer a different appearance to the rest of the group, John's suit was in black mohair, the same style as our suits, with the identical rounded lapels in maroon. Our new band suits were worn with a white shirt and a narrow maroon tie which co-ordinated with the lapels.

We had been really pleased with our performance supporting B. Bumble and The Stingers a couple of months ago and I couldn't understand why Ron King hadn't called me with more work. Martin and I decided that before picking up the other group members and heading off to play at a club in Ilford, we would first pay Ron King a quick visit at the Wykeham Hall.

Fortunately we managed to find parking in Romford Market, even though the local council workers were still dismantling the market stalls and clearing up the rubbish. As we made our way up the cobbled path towards the hall, I could see the entrance door was open. We strolled in and there, sitting at the usual table, was the man himself. When he saw us, he broke into a big smile and in his usual loud voice said, 'Hello boys, meant to call you. Sorry it's such short notice, but could you make next Saturday? I need a support group for Johnny and The Hurricanes.'

I was completely taken aback and certainly hadn't been prepared for this. Presumably he did like us after all. This was a great opportunity not to be missed, supporting another top American instrumental band. However, I knew we were tentatively booked to play in Dagenham next Saturday, but still hadn't received final confirmation. Without consulting Martin, I just blurted out 'Yes, we are free as it happens. What time do you want us here?' 'Good' he said 'We open the doors at seven – be here around then. That'll give you time to set-up. You'll start at eight and finish at nine and the fee will be £8. Is that OK?' Oh yes, it was OK – and we were actually going to be paid at last!

We said our thanks and goodbyes and casually walked out in stunned silence. We were so excited when we climbed back into the van and couldn't wait to tell the others. But what a strange way to operate. Suppose we hadn't turned up unannounced when we did – would he have called me with the booking? When we picked up Dave and told him the news, the first thing he said was 'Well, that puts "Crossfire" off the playlist.' All went quiet while the penny dropped. Of course, 'Crossfire' had been one of a string of saxophone-based instrumental hits for Johnny and The Hurricanes and had been one of the first sax-based songs that Dave had encouraged us to learn when he joined the group.

I did feel a little guilty when I telephoned the entertainment manager at the Ford Social Club in Dagenham to explain that the gearbox had broken in our van and so we wouldn't be able to make Saturday's booking. He was very sympathetic and hoped it wasn't a Ford van! I told him it wasn't. Fortunately, he then proceeded to give me another date two weeks later.

I was extremely nervous and I'm sure the others were too – this was only the second time we'd supported a well-known group, let alone another top American band. Johnny and The Hurricanes were even more well known than B. Bumble and The Stingers, with a string of instrumental hits in both the US and British charts behind them.

We arrived early and set up our gear, using the small anti-room next to the stage to store our band suits. We were making last-minute adjustments and checking our tuning, when the curtains parted and Ron King's head appeared at the foot of the stage. 'Whenever you want to make a start boys.' 'OK' I called back and turned to the others. 'Are we ready then?' Everyone nodded, so I gave the caretaker the signal to pull the rope and as the curtains opened we started our set.

We'd been playing for about 20 minutes or so, when a shaft of light suddenly lit up the corner of the hall as the anti-room door swung open and I could just make out some silhouetted figures rushing into the room with guitar cases in their hands. Obviously Johnny and The Hurricanes had arrived. We were just about to play the last number of our allotted one-hour set, when Ron King appeared at the foot of the stage and shouted out 'OK boys, you can wind it up now.' We finished our last number, the curtains were drawn and we hurriedly moved our gear into the wings. I opened the door leading into the changing room, walked down the steps followed by the others and there they were – Johnny and The Hurricanes in the flesh! A couple of them turned and gave us a cursory nod.

The only person I recognised from my LP cover was the main man himself, Johnny Paris, a tall good-looking guy with slicked-back hair and big quiff, Elvis Presley style. As with B. Bumble and his mates, these guys were a few years older than us, having had hits in the late 50s and early 60s.

As we changed out of our band suits, so they changed into their outfits. They all wore black trousers, white shirts, black bow ties and shiny silver grey jackets. Within about ten minutes the door leading onto the stage opened and a face appeared telling them their gear was all set up and ready to go. With that announcement, guitars and a saxophone appeared out of cases, a quick tune-up session followed, then they were off up the staircase and onto the stage to a warm reception. This was our cue to take up positions at the front of the stage and watch in awe as this famous group performed, and hear the hit songs we'd all danced to at parties.

Ron King was on stage in front of the curtains with a mike in his hand. He turned and peered through the curtains for a brief moment. The group was ready, so he made a brief announcement. 'Good evening everyone. Let me introduce to you, all the way from America, Johnny and The Hurricanes!' As the curtains parted, stage lights came on and they launched into their first big hit, a number we also performed, called 'Red River Rock'. They then proceeded to play the A and B-sides of their various instrumental hits. Johnny Paris was centre stage, playing his sax raised up in front of his face. They were a very tight band consisting of a keyboard player, bass and lead guitars, drums and, of course, a sax.

They were well into their set and we were watching their every move, when suddenly the lead guitarist looked panic-stricken – a string had broken on his turquoise Fender Stratocaster. He quickly left the stage via the side door and I just assumed he was in the changing room fitting another string. As the group continued into their next song, there was a tap on my shoulder – it was the lead guitarist. 'Have you got a spare high E string man?' he asked. 'Sure' I said and he quickly followed me into the room. I opened my guitar case, rummaged through a bunch of spare strings and handed over a high E string in its little paper wallet. 'Thanks man' he said in his American drawl and within seconds he had removed the broken string and replaced it with my string. He quickly tuned up, gave me a wave of thanks and ran up the steps onto the stage. I went back to the front of the stage and was in seventh heaven during the rest of their performance knowing that the lead guitar solos were being played with the help of my E string!

Carrying out some recent research work on Johnny and The Hurricanes, I discovered that prior to us supporting them in January 1963 at the Wykeham Hall, a month before they had played at the Star Club in Hamburg, Germany and their support band had been a relatively unknown group from Liverpool called The Beatles!

15

SUPPORTING THE DAVE CLARK FIVE - MARCH 1963

Ron King had started to take us under his wing and would occasionally insist on taking us across the market square in Romford and into the White Hart pub to buy us drinks and now and again he would give us a little pep talk. He had specifically chosen us to support a north London group from Tottenham called The Dave Clark Five, who just happened to have a sax player. He emphasised that we should watch them, see how they interacted with the audience and suggested we should do the same.

Having completed our set on the night of this gig, we changed out of our band suits, while they changed into what would become their customary outfits – white trousers, navy blue blazers and white polo-neck shirts. We watched their set from the front of the stage ready to take notes, but were quite disillusioned at the way they fooled around and I'm sure the quality of their playing suffered. They invited girls up from the audience to try and play the sax or the organ and even Dave Clark's drums. A couple of the band members went as far as donning ladies' wigs and generally larking around while they played a number. This certainly brought on plenty of laughter from the crowd, but that type of show wasn't for us. However, when they did concentrate on the music, they were really good. Their singer, Mike Smith, had a great voice. Besides being the singer, he also played a keyboard and had a very distinctive stance while he played. The lead guitarist, Lenny Davidson, must have joined the band fairly recently as I recognised him from when he was lead guitarist for another band that used to play at the Wykeham Hall. As for Dave Clark, the drummer, he was a good-looking guy and the girls obviously adored him.

A few months later, I saw them performing at the Basildon Locarno just as 'Glad All Over' had entered the lower rungs of the charts. Presumably they still had a few old bookings to honour under their Mecca contract. I was there with my new girlfriend Pat, who eventually became my wife, and we were unaware that The Dave Clark Five were the live band that night. It was mid-week and wasn't very busy. W were standing at the bar sipping our drinks when who should come up to the bar to order a coke – Mike Smith. I whispered in Pat's ear, 'He's the singer in the group.' She looked him up and down and watched him as he had his drink. When he was gone she said 'Oh, I rather fancy him' which immediately provoked an argument on my part. We hadn't been together very long and I was extremely jealous if she just looked at another man! Just a few weeks later, the Dave Clark Five had lift-off.

It had been nine months since we'd supported them in Romford and now The Dave Clark Five had toppled The Beatles from their number one position in the British singles chart with their self-penned song 'Glad All Over'. The music press loved anything to do with The Beatles and having replaced The Beatles at the number one slot in the charts, the story was really hyped up. They labelled The Dave Clark Five as having the 'Tottenham Sound' and said they were a threat to the 'Liverpool Sound' of The Beatles and the other numerous groups from Liverpool. Of course this was a load of old rubbish. There weren't dozens of groups emanating from Tottenham suddenly entering the charts. Considering our line-up was similar to The Dave Clark Five, we could have said we had the 'Romford Sound'.

It is quite amazing that, even when 'Glad All Over' was fast climbing the charts, the group were still self-managed. However, managers and agencies around the country were clamouring to sign the group and they held out for the best and most lucrative deal. They went on to have 12

Top 40 hits in the UK and 17 hits in the Top 40 in the US, going to number one in the US with their song 'Over and Over'. They became one of the most popular British bands to tour the US in the 1960s.

Ron King made no reference again to us adding a touch of comedy into our act until over drinks a year or so later in the White Hart. This time he seemed determined to press home the point and we could all sense that this time round, it wasn't simply a case of think about it – more about getting on and doing something about it. So we promised to go away and work on it and assured him we would have something in place when we next appeared at the Wykeham Hall.

At our rehearsal on Tuesday, we discussed how we were going to introduce some humour into our act. Dave, always the comic, opened his sax case and took out a blond wig with pigtails tied with ribbons and plonked it on his head. Without any further discussion, we all agreed that Dave looked good in it and he could wear it on stage. That at least let the rest of us off the hook. Now we had to decide when he would wear it. Certainly none of our current songs were suitable for our sax player to suddenly put a woman's wig on. We put our heads together and it was suggested that perhaps we should rehearse a comedy song that had been in the charts recently. It was called 'Shame and Scandal in the Family' and was sung with a Caribbean accent to a calypso rhythm by a comedian/actor/TV performer called Lance Percival. We agreed I'd buy the record, and sheet music if available, and we'd make a start on it at our next rehearsal.

I recalled watching Joe Brown and The Bruvvers performing a guitar instrumental called 'Hava Nagila' (Let's Rejoice) a few years ago. It is a very old traditional Jewish folk song and when it came to the chorus line, Joe and his group danced around on stage. We had also performed this instrumental on stage, but without the dancing of course, and the song had been dropped from our playlist well over a year before. I suggested resurrecting the song and working out some sort of dance routine, which would add some additional visual interest to our stage act. Not that I really wanted to show myself up in public by dancing around on stage, but it wouldn't take us long to relearn the song and we were collectively short of any decent ideas. The whole humour thing just wasn't us. However, Ron King was important to us and was the one real possibility we had of getting a recording contract, so it had to be done.

That evening we rehearsed 'Hava Nagila' and after a few attempts, we perfected it. Now for the tricky part – could I play this song, which started slowly and built up to a crescendo towards the end, and dance at the same time? This, of course, also applied to Martin, Patrick and Dave but John and JG, the lucky beggars, didn't have to worry at all about the dancing bit. We practiced standing close together in a line and then kicking out our right legs like chorus girls, at the same time moving across the floor from left to right and back again. After many failed attempts and in between a lot of laughing fits, we slowly began to get the hang of it.

The following week, with the sheet music and the record at hand, we'd learned 'Shame and Scandal in the Family' within one hour, and then we concentrated again on 'Hava Nagila' and our dance routine. It was decided unanimously at the end of that night that two silly numbers were enough and we certainly weren't going to make fools of ourselves at any other venue. This was strictly for the Wykeham Hall.

Within a few weeks we were back on stage at Wykeham Hall. No longer the support group, we were headlining, with another group supporting us! On arrival, I mentioned to Ron King to keep an eye on our performance tonight as we had a couple of surprises for him. Dave was the only one that didn't mind making a fool of himself on stage, but I still had reservations about playing 'Hava Nagila' and dancing around like a chorus girl. However, having spent time at rehearsals learning these two numbers, hopefully Ron King would be impressed.

During the early part of our set, John announced that we were going to play a new comedy song that we'd never performed in public before. As Dave donned the pigtails, I realised it bore no relevance at all to the story of the song but I suppose it did have the required effect on the audience. We couldn't stop laughing at Dave for being such an idiot, but I think he enjoyed the attention he was getting. With us laughing and joking on stage, it was obviously infectious, because the lines of girls at the front of the stage started laughing along with us and looked like they were having a great time.

We waited another half an hour or so, and then John announced we were going to play an instrumental song called 'Hava Nagila'. He then left the stage sniggering away to himself and loud enough for us to hear. The four of us formed a tight line in the centre of the stage and started to play the song. Slowly, as the song increased in speed, it was our cue to start our chorus girl routine. We moved across stage to our left, kicking out with our right legs and, as the song got faster, I had to concentrate more and more to avoid making any mistakes. Getting close to the wings, I thought it was time to start making our way back across the stage and I stopped too early, resulting in Martin and the others tumbling into me which brought about a howl of laughter from the front of the stage. We managed to recover and started to make our way back across the stage, kicking out in time, but only just. So far, so good. We made another return journey successfully, but I was distracted for a moment by John standing in the wings taking the mickey out of us. I missed my timing as I told him to piss off and then had to move quickly to catch up with the other three. By the time we reached the other side of the stage again, we looked more like a professional line of chorus girls, lifting our legs to the same height, and our timing was spot on. We started to make our final shuffle back to the centre of the stage and, with one final kick in the air the song came to an end.

A big cheer rang out from the audience and some clapped and whistled. Looking at the grinning faces at the foot of the stage, it was obvious they had enjoyed it, certainly more than we had, so mission accomplished. Were there any lessons to be learned from this stressful episode? Yes, never do it again – and we didn't! As we ferried our gear out to the van later that evening, I was dying to get some feedback from Ron King. He was busy counting the takings for the evening, but stopped and looked up at me. 'So Ron, what do you think? Did you like our new stage act? I asked. 'Oh, sorry about that' he replied. 'I had some trouble outside the hall tonight which needed sorting out and I had to wait outside to make sure the culprits didn't return.' So it was all a waste of time! Then, without any prior warning from Ron King, the Wykeham Hall closed its doors to Saturday dances a month or so later.

Not long afterwards, I received a call from an unknown London agency called Galaxy Entertainments offering us work. They insisted we had to undertake an audition, which was fair enough, at a club where people were charged an entry fee. Of course, Ron King sprang to mind but we did the audition and passed. We then went on to work with Galaxy on a regular basis for a few years. Occasionally I'd jump on a tube train in my lunch hour to go and collect a bunch of contracts for advanced work from their offices in Carnaby Street. Unbeknown to me until many years later, Ron King had gone on to work for Don Arden at Galaxy after he stopped running the Wykeham Hall dances. Don Arden was a notorious promoter with a reputation for getting what he wanted by intimidation. Although Ron King eventually ended up running Galaxy Entertainments, I never bumped into him at the agency on my visits and never ever saw him again. He obviously still had my contact details and must have recommended us to the agency when he joined, which was why they got in touch with me. As we'd worked with him for quite a few years, an audition wasn't really necessary, but old habits die-hard. We performed for free while people paid to dance to us!

THE CO-OP HALL - GRAYS - MAY 1963

I have fond memories of playing in this stark Victorian hall on a Saturday night. Not because it was such a great venue to perform in but it was where John, after a lot of persuasion from the rest of the group, decided to put a bit more effort into his performances. He had a great voice and delivery, but he was extremely shy and self-conscious on stage. None of us were extroverts on or off the stage, but he was the singer, the frontman of the group, and besides, he was Johnny Lonesome.!

A few of us, including John, had been fortunate enough to see the great American singer Gene Vincent perform live a few times, and he always ended his show with a grand finale, played out with great emotion. While singing a fast raucous rock 'n' roll number, he would drop down onto both knees, with eyes tightly shut. He would finally end up prostrate on the floor, singing his heart out, while all the time clutching the mike stand close to his body, just as the curtains closed.

During one of our rehearsals, we had persuaded John that he should put a bit more effort into his stage act. He agreed to talk more to the audience, not only announcing some of the songs he was about to sing but also, if we finished with his favourite song 'Whole Lotta Shakin' Going On', he said he would do this with, in his words, 'a Gene Vincent ending.' One further very important factor remained, which John insisted upon. The venue had to have curtains that were fully operational in order to perform his finale. We knew the Co-Op Hall had curtains, so that was it. When we played there in a couple of weeks' time, John would perform his new and very own grand finale. We couldn't wait!

We arrived at the hall, set up our gear and had our usual sound check. I went off to look for the caretaker as we needed somebody to close the curtains at the end of our set as per the stipulation set down by John. I tipped him, with instructions to be in the stage wings a minute or so before 10.30pm. We agreed that when I nodded across at him, he would then slowly draw the curtains across. I went off and joined the others to change into my stage suit and informed John that the caretaker was cooperating with us. While changing, John suddenly produced a large cloth serviette, rolled it up and stuffed it down his trouser leg, getting a lot of ribbing from us as he did it. Apparently he'd recently seen a documentary on Elvis Presley and it said that, in his early days, Presley had stuffed a hosepipe down his trouser leg to impress the girls at the front of the stage. We teased John that he was taking the re-launch of his career a bit too seriously using the serviette, but he was determined to impress the girls tonight with his act – and the size of his serviette!

Our performance, and especially John's, got off to a good start when, for the first time, he announced the opening song. Behind him eyebrows were raised – things were looking up. We had just performed our fifth song of the evening, when John announced our next number would be 'Woolly Bully'. This song would get the audience livened up a bit. By this time there were about 20 girls milling around at the front of the stage – perhaps word had got around about John's serviette!

Well into the song, we reached Dave's sax solo, and I glanced across at John who was standing bolt upright with an intense expression on his face. He was gripping the mike stand with both hands, the only movement coming from his left leg that shook in time to the music. Suddenly something white fell to the floor. I looked, and then looked again. Oh no, how embarrassing! There on the floor next to his left foot, was the white serviette, still rolled up. A few of the girls had spotted it at the same time and were nudging one another, pointing to it and giggling. All the time John was totally oblivious that the serviette had become dislodged, travelled down his trouser leg and now lay on the stage floor. By now he was singing the last verse of the song and I couldn't wait to see the expression on his face when I pointed to the serviette. The final chords were played and John stood back from the mike. I nodded discreetly to the serviette, expecting a look of blind panic to appear on his face. But, like a real trooper, he simply bent down, picked up the serviette, wiped the sweat off his brow and casually put the serviette into his pocket.

We were reaching the end of our penultimate song and I glanced across into the wings to make sure the caretaker was there. He was sitting in a chair rolling a cigarette and acknowledged me with a nod of the head. John announced the final song and we were off. Well into the song, with the guitar solo out of the way, Dave launched into his sax solo. John, now with beads of perspiration running down the side of his face, slowly started to lower himself onto his knees, at the same time sliding the mike stand away from his side. Next minute, with eyes closed, he slid down onto the floor and lay there, clutching the mike, singing the last verse of the song.

We all watched in utter amazement. The girls at the front of the stage were getting quite restless. We'd never seen our singer so active before. I daren't look at John for too long, otherwise I might burst out laughing.

The timing had to be just right, the curtains needed to be slowly drawn any minute now, so I quickly glanced over to the wings – an empty seat! Bloody hell, where was the caretaker? I looked to the side of the curtains – he must there be holding the rope ready to close the curtains, but no, he wasn't there. I started to panic. John was still flat out on the stage floor singing the remainder of the last verse of the song and had now opened his eyes. He was looking up, directly at me, in utter panic. He had expected to see the curtains closing in front of him by now. Then the reality of it all suddenly set in. He turned his head. The audience were still watching him. This would be John's worst nightmare. He looked back at us, eyes pleading for help. But what could we do – we were still playing away. I looked down at him squirming on the floor when suddenly he started laughing. Not a genuine laugh but an embarrassed and very nervous one.

Instead of getting up and rushing into the wings, he just lay there laughing which in turn got us laughing and the people watching started laughing as well. Poor John, I thought to myself. I'd have hated it to be me. Slowly he started to drag himself across the stage, still laughing nervously, but I knew he wasn't going to make it to the wings before the song finished. Then it was all over – the last chord and crash of the cymbals signalled the end of the song. And there he was, still slowly crawling along the stage floor, but now in total silence – he wasn't laughing any more. We didn't help the situation – we just stood there watching those final agonising seconds as he finally made it into the wings. By this time we were all doubled up with laughter and when he got to his feet, understandably he didn't look very happy. We put our instruments down and made our way over to John, who was pretty angry. 'Why didn't one of you close the curtain rather than all stand there laughing at me?' 'How could we' I said. 'We were still playing. You should have got up and made a run for it.' Needless to say, John never ever attempted the 'Gene Vincent ending' again – what a shame. But he did however go on to announce more songs. We found the promoter to find out where the caretaker was in order to have a go at him but his response was 'problem at home, had to leave early and left me to shut up shop.' Oh the trials and tribulations of being in show business!

HARROWFIELDS YOUTH CENTRE - HAROLD HILL - JUNE 1963

The engine in our Bedford Dormobile had started to smoke a lot over the past few months and was steadily getting worse. Although there was a cover clamped over the engine, in the middle of the two front seats the rubber seal had corroded badly and so poisonous exhaust gases were escaping into the inside of the van. Its final journey was to take us to Harrowfields Youth Centre. I drove and Martin accompanied me, while the rest of the group travelled in their own cars. We drove off from Martin's house with the doors slid back to allow the exhaust gases to escape and with great difficulty the poor old van limped its way there and back. The only photograph of the van shows it parked in Martin's drive, with me sitting in the driver's seat, a few days after our performance on Harold Hill. It was never driven again after that and had literally expired on the drive and was towed away to a breaker's yard. Now whether Patrick, the group's mechanic, should have been towed away with it, is debatable.

ME SITTING IN THE BEDFORD DORMOBILE VAN
BEFORE IT WAS TOWED AWAY.

This was to be our fourth appearance at Harrowfields and our third this year alone. There was a noticeably larger crowd there than on the other occasions.

As soon as we started playing, the lights were lowered, and quite a few girls made a beeline for the front of the stage. By the time we started playing our fourth number, there must have been at least 50 to 60 girls crammed at the front of the stage, their faces illuminated by the stage lighting, and I could see most were watching John's every move, although I did get a few smiles myself which was always gratifying. As I looked at the crowd, I recognised quite a few of the girls from our last appearance at Quarles Youth Centre. I could sense our reputation was growing – and so was the audience.

As we launched into 'Whole Lotta Shakin' Going On', a bunch of girls burst out screaming. More and more girls joined in until it was quite deafening. This had happened before at Quarles Youth Centre and was certainly a great and flattering experience. Hearing Dave launch into his amplified sax solo made me glance across the stage in his direction. I couldn't believe my eyes – there he was, kneeling on top of Martin's large bass speaker cabinet, playing his heart out, with his head tilted back and the sax raised high. This action alone appeared to get the girls quite excited and they seemed to scream even louder. When John started singing again, he was in top form, in his usual stance of holding the mike stand with both hands.

Most of the girls at the front stood there screaming with their arms outstretched across the floor of the stage. I watched in fascination as a girl, pressed up against the front of the stage was suddenly hoisted up by her friends. With her body now flat on the stage, and with outstretched arms, she grasped the base of the mike stand. Her friends then started to pull her back while she grimly held onto the mike's base. Slowly the mike edged towards the front of the stage. John was trying to concentrate on his singing, fully aware his mike was moving forward, but unaware that outstretched hands were about to grab his ankles and when they did, he lost his balance, tipped forward and fell head-long into the crowd, while still gripping the mike stand.

We continued playing with difficulty during fits of laughter. There was no sign of John at all but we could still hear him singing through the vocal speakers, even with girls sprawled on top of him! An old showbiz adage springs to mind 'the show must go on.' I gave the signal to carry on playing and went into a second guitar solo. Suddenly John's head appeared above the girls' heads and he slowly stood up, looking rather embarrassed. Smiling slightly, he moved to the front of the stage with the mike stand in his hand and lifted it back onto the stage. Dave went forward and helped pull him up. I brought my guitar up, indicating to finish the song, which we did.

The girls were laughing, we were laughing, and John was smiling, albeit his nervous smile. Although he loved the attention, he was really suffering with the embarrassment of it all. However, they were such a great crowd, you just couldn't be annoyed at what had happened. We finished playing that evening with no more screaming. It was while we were packing up our gear that two young girls approached us and asked if we had a fan club. When they found out we didn't, they offered to start and manage one for us. I was handed a slip of paper with a telephone number and name written on it. Her name was Mary Bennett. I said we'd discuss this later and we'd get back to her – we were well chuffed to have been asked. Imagine – our very own fan club!

A BIGGER AND BETTER VAN – JUNE 1963

Without transport now, we urgently needed a replacement van. We were earning more money these days and it was decided we should splash out on something a bit newer and grander. We all agreed on one thing – it must have windows all round. During my lunch hour I walked to Maryland Point, a ten-minute walk from the bank in Stratford, where there were four second-hand car dealers.

Luck was on my side. There, standing at the back of the forecourt in the very first dealership, stood the ideal van. It was large with windows all round and a side opening door – just what we wanted. What a find! I made my way to the van to have a closer look and to find out the price. It was just perfect and, making my way round to the front, there stuck on the windscreen was a large sticker stating 1959 AUSTIN J2 – £199. Although the price was more than we really wanted to pay, it was just four years old and fitted the bill. However, the others needed to see it as well, especially our in-house mechanic Patrick, who needed to give it a quick inspection. Instead of attending our usual band rehearsal on Tuesday, we drove over to Stratford. Everyone instantly loved it. Patrick started checking the tyres, then lifted up the interior engine cover for inspection, switched on the ignition and started it up. He listened for a moment before nodding his approval. Finally, looking at the speedometer, he confirmed it had quite a low mileage for the year. It was thumbs up all round. I handed over the required £22 deposit to the salesman and arranged that we'd collect the van at the end of the week after it had undergone a full service.

LIPSTICK MESSAGES FROM FANS ADORN THE SIDE OF OUR NEW VAN

THE CARTOON – 1963

George Murdock, a colleague of Martin's, drew this cartoon of Johnny Lonesome and The Travellers during a lunchtime break. Both were attending the Ford Motor Company's Trade School at the time. George must have seen us performing live quite a few times and he was able to really capture personal characteristics of the group.

Dave (far left) sometimes looked as though he might burst a blood vessel when he played a raucous sax solo. Next to him is Patrick, a little overweight, who often stood with his feet splayed. On drums is JG with his determined look when performing a fast drum roll. George even remembered the make of his drum kit, Ajax, which was also the name of a popular washing powder at the time and he's included the punch line from an Ajax advertisement 'Ajax Washes Whitest'.

There's John, known for his shyness on stage trying to hide behind the collar of his jacket. Next is Martin playing bass and holding the guitar in the same way as Bill Wyman of The Rolling Stones. He has captured Martin's side profile perfectly. Next is me with the grim face. I can only assume I was upset about something, probably with Martin who constantly, after a sound check, would turn up the volume of his bass guitar, much to my annoyance. We'd quite often have a little verbal spat in front of the audience going something like, 'Why have a bloody sound check, when all you do is turn up your bass?' which usually resulted in Martin telling me to 'piss off.' As to my expression, I thought I had only got aggressive as I got older, but looking at the cartoon I must have had the ache with some poor soul at the front of the stage even then. Finally, in the bottom left-hand corner, 'a music lover' who didn't appreciate our music, tossing a bomb onto the stage!

When sound checks were carried out, it was to make sure we had an overall balanced sound. We didn't want the guitar and drums drowning out the vocals. In smaller venues it was essential not to be too loud and in the larger halls more volume was required. Sometimes the larger empty halls also suffered from echo, which played havoc with the amplified sound, so the sound balance was very important. It's quite deceptive when a bass guitar is played on stage – the notes may not sound very loud standing in front of an amplifier, but at the back of a hall, the bass notes could be bouncing off the wall and distorting our sound.

We relied on John on most occasions to stand at the back of the venue, while we played an instrumental song and to signal what instrument needed more or less volume. So it was a bit annoying when the bass was suddenly booming away on stage, as it meant it was blowing out eardrums at the back of a hall. It wasn't just me who complained about this to Martin but other members of the group too. But he never seemed to take any notice!

16

THE JOHNNY LONESOME AND THE TRAVELLERS FAN CLUB

**Johnny Lonesome
and the Travellers**

Official Fan Club

NAME..No...............

Signature of President.................................

At a rehearsal towards the end of 1963, having been approached with the idea by some girls during a gig at Harrowfields Youth Centre, we discussed the idea of having our own fan club. Were we getting ahead of ourselves? Was it a bit presumptuous of us to even to consider it? But there again, it wasn't our idea. Could we make it work? What were the practicalities? And could we afford it? The one big plus on our side was that JG was completing an apprenticeship in the printing industry. After checking first with his employers, he said he would be able to provide the required stationery at a much-reduced cost. We were all in agreement and I called Mary Bennett to arrange a meeting to go through things with her. Quite understandably, as Mary was only 15, and this being 1963, she said her father insisted on meeting us as well.

Mary greeted us when she opened the door and ushered us into the front room. I guessed from the décor in the room that this family still followed the old British tradition of reserving the front room for formal occasions and entertaining visitors. Normally the living room was at the back of the house and was where a family ate and relaxed. I had witnessed this tradition first hand in my grandmother's house when visiting her during many summer holidays to Ayr in Scotland. But my parents had broken with tradition, as many families started to do in the 60s, by removing the dividing wall between the lounge and the living room.

We huddled together on a large settee in this small front room, with Mary in attendance, waiting for her father to appear. Facing us was a classic 50s Formica and glass, mirror-backed display cabinet filled with gaudy cocktail glasses and small coloured glass animals. At last Mr Bennett entered the room, which was a relief, as making small talk with Mary was proving to be rather difficult. We all stood up and shook hands. He was quite an impressive figure and was wearing a white tight-fitting singlet, which showed off his firm muscles and tanned skin, and his trousers were tightly belted with an old army belt. We later learned that he worked on a building site, hence his tanned appearance. He was a real London cockney, and spoke like one. The 'salt of the earth' kind of guy, proud to be working class. No doubt he had lived in temporary accommodation following the bombing of London and had recently been relocated to Harold Hill.

While we settled back in the settee and before I could start proceedings, he immediately apologised for having a plaster stuck across his nose. 'Did it on the job, like' he explained. Perhaps we were being a bit childish, but we frantically tried to cover up our giggles with bursts of coughing and nose blowing as we visualised him head-butting his wife while 'on the job', that being a euphemism for making love in those days. We apologised profusely for the interruption and he said it must be the amount of pollen in the air, which brought about another burst of coughing and nose blowing.

Once we'd settled down, we went on to explain that Mary's role would initially be to sign up new members. Then JG took over and produced some prototypes of the application form to join the club, and a club membership card. He also mentioned that we proposed sending out a printed monthly newsletter and that all new members would receive a free photograph of the group. I think Mr Bennett was suitably impressed. He could tell we were serious in our endeavours, especially when we explained that the small annual membership fee of 2/6p (12.5p decimal money) would hopefully cover the cost of the stationery and postage. The group would finance any additional money required. Mary asked if she could have her close friend Kathleen Merrit to act as the club secretary, and of course we agreed. We appointed Mary as the president of the fan club. You could see her father was so proud of his only daughter. He thanked us, shook our hands vigorously and said his goodbyes.

Application forms and membership cards were printed and handed over to Mary and she and Kathleen set about enrolling members while I, in the meantime, drafted our first newsletter. This first issue gave us an opportunity to introduce the group members, giving our names, height, colour of eyes and hair and our birthdays. John, who had recently been taken into hospital with a serious throat problem, thanked his fans for all the get-well cards he'd received while in hospital. Most importantly, in every monthly newsletter we would list our bookings for the following month and if we were playing locally, we asked for their support on the night. In the second issue, we homed in on individual group members, listing their likes and dislikes and their favourite singers. The first to get this treatment was the man himself, Johnny Lonesome.

The first newsletter went into print, photos were collected from the photographers and these were given to Mary to distribute to new fan club members. Mary and Kathleen couldn't wait to tell us that within a couple of weeks they had already enrolled over 70 new members and, with great confidence, assured us that there were many more people still out there who wanted to join. To coincide with the launch of the club, I put an advertisement in the classified section of the New Musical Express on Friday 20 September. Our name and Mary's full address was listed under the banner heading of Fan Clubs. The listings were laid out in alphabetical order and our fan club was sandwiched between the Johnny Cash Fan Club and the Judy Garland Fan Club.

JOHNNY LONESOME AND THE TRAVELLERS WITH FAN CLUB PRESIDENT
MARY BENNETT (RIGHT) AND KATHLEEN MERRIT FAN CLUB SECRETARY (LEFT).
THIS PHOTOGRAPH APPEARED IN THE ROMFORD RECORDER
15 NOVEMBER 1963

In the newsletter we also encouraged existing members to introduce new members to our fan club, the reward for doing so being an exclusive signed photograph of the group. In addition, every now and then, a member's number was selected at random and a prize of a record token was sent to the lucky winner.

We ran a competition with Mr Lonesome making the draw. The prize was a token for an EP (an extended 45 rpm record) and together with a friend, the winner would accompany us to the booking of their choice. The first winner was Maureen Long who had recently joined the fan club. She was a paraplegic and confined to a wheelchair. I asked Mary to talk with Maureen's parents to make sure it would be OK for her and a friend to join us one evening at a booking. Her parents were delighted to hear the good news and Maureen chose to join us at a forthcoming appearance at the Lorain Club in Chingford.

On 11 October, we drove to Maureen's home where we met Maureen and her friend, also a new fan club member. We gave Mr & Mrs Long our assurances that they would be well looked after and, with some assistance, she was seated in the back of the van. Her wheelchair was folded up and put on top of the equipment.

On the drive over to the club we chatted to them both and it was easy to tell that they were both quite shy and in awe of us, and slightly intimidated to be in the group's van. On arrival outside the club, the wheelchair was unfolded and Maureen was escorted into the club. I had pre-warned Eddie Caswell, who ran the club, and he seated them at a table close to one side of the stage. John even dedicated a song to them both, which really pleased them and we could see them grinning at each other. On the way home they were more relaxed and chatted away to us, asking questions about the group and telling us how much they had enjoyed themselves. They thanked us over and over again for such a lovely evening. I saw the curtains open slightly as we pulled up outside Maureen's house and two anxious parents came to the door as we wheeled Maureen up the path. When everyone had thanked us, we said our goodbyes and made our way home. With the van parked, I walked down a dark Seymer Road with my guitar case in hand, thinking about the evening. It sounds rather pompous now but at the time I felt pretty proud of what we had done for someone less fortunate than ourselves and had a warm glow inside. After all, I was still only a teenager and up until then hadn't thought of anyone but myself.

SHANDON DANCE HALL - ROMFORD - OCTOBER 1963

Although we had encouraged our fans to support us at this new club in our first newsletter, we hadn't anticipated such a large turn out or for the reception we received. The screaming started fairly early on into our set and continued in waves throughout most of the evening's performance. With the stage only about a foot high, it gave easy access for a few over-enthusiastic fans to rush the stage and gather mementos while we were still playing. We all had our ties removed from around our necks, buttons were ripped off our jackets and JG lost a pair of spare drumsticks. There's one particular photograph taken during the evening that I'm rather proud of and, for once, Johnny Lonesome didn't get all the attention. It shows me happily playing my guitar, minus my tie, with three young girls sitting on the stage, two of them clutching my legs. Eat your heart out Johnny!

STOP PRESS – I have to interrupt this story and turn the clock forward to early 2016, nearly 53 years later. My son Daniel had set up a website a few years prior to 2016 to advertise the fact that he was producing music for short films and advertisements. He needed to give the site a name and so he used Johnny Lonesome, a name apparently he thought sounded pretty 'cool'.

In February 2016, Daniel forwarded an email to me from somebody who had contacted his website. It basically said 'Is this the Johnny Lonesome and The Travellers that played at our youth club at Harrowfields Secondary School in the early 60s?' It went on to say 'My girlfriend Kathy and I were the "screamers" and accompanied the band in this role to a few gigs…. definitely not groupies but swept up in the magic of music.'

So here I was emailing someone called Jean from my past life and discussing the events of that time. Amazingly it turned out that it was her and her friend Kathy who were photographed clutching my legs during a gig at the Shandon Dance Hall! Jean then put me in touch with Kathy, who turned out to be our fan club secretary, known then as Kathleen. Kathy sent me a photograph of items she'd kept in her 'memory box' as she called it. There was an original fan club membership card, a broken guitar string I'd discarded, a broken drumstick and various newspaper cuttings – a real 'lifelong' fan of the group! In one of her emails Kathy went on to say 'I remember that Jean and I used to rally up support from everyone at school to attend the gigs when you were playing at Harrow-fields and to lead the screaming horde.'

KATHLEEN (WITH THE DARK HAIR) IS CLUTCHING MY LEFT LEG
WHILE JEAN IS CLUTCHING MY OTHER LEG ON THE STAGE
AT THE SHANDON DANCE HALL

Interestingly Kathy went on to become assistant secretary of the UK's Roy Orbison Fan Club. In one of Jean's emails she made a very touching comment 'You gave us, and many others so much pleasure, a part of our growing up.'

Back to 1963 and the Shandon Dance Hall. When we went to load up our gear, we found the van had been covered in lipstick messages and telephone numbers. It was now becoming abundantly clear how import-ant it was to have a fan club and how, by asking our fans to support us, it paid dividends on the night. The audience response was fantastic and we were so impressed by the turn out of fans. Even more impressed was the promoter!

The next morning over breakfast, my brother Dave commented that he was walking up South Street in Romford at around 10pm the previous night, when he heard a commotion going on in the old snooker club. He said it sounded like a lot of screaming and music being played, but couldn't figure out was going on. I quickly and proudly pointed out that his younger brother and his group had caused the commotion. 'But why were girls screaming?' he asked. You had to make allowances for him as he was five years older than me!

The Romford Recorder, a local weekly newspaper, had recently introduced a full-page feature reporting on local 'pop' news, and was always interested in a good story. I called them and explained that the group had formed their own fan club and was being run by two local Harold Hill girls. They liked the story and a meeting was arranged. A photograph was taken of us together with Mary and Kathleen and it appeared in the paper a few weeks later.

With the festive season fast approaching and our December newsletter at the printers, we desperately wanted to give our fans a small Christmas gift as a way of saying thank you for their support. At rehearsal one evening, we put our heads together and between us came up with what we thought would be an appropriate and much-appreciated gift – an autograph book. Being in the print business, JG made some enquiries and discovered there was a large stationery wholesaler in Petticoat Lane in East London. One Sunday morning in November, John, JG and myself took ourselves off to Petticoat Lane, knowing also that the market would be in full swing, which gave us a chance to look around and perhaps buy some Mod clothing.

We purchased sufficient autograph books for every fan and JG suggested having a sticky label printed with a message. We decided it should read 'Thank You for Your Wonderful Support During 1963 – Johnny Lonesome and The Travellers' and was stuck on the inside cover of the book. On the opposite page we all signed our signatures – I won't call them autographs because the Oxford Dictionary states that an autograph is 'a celebrity's signature written for an admirer.' We didn't qualify as celebrities yet but we certainly had admirers!

17

ALL HELL BREAKS LOOSE - THE WINDMILL HALL
- UPMINSTER - NOVEMBER 1963

Playing in a group was not all 'wine, women, and song' and at times it did have its dangers. The following incident took place, not in the rough and tumble of London's East End pubs and clubs, but in a small hall in the leafy suburb of Upminster in Essex.

Known by many a late night reveller returning home from London, as the station at the end of the line, Upminster was the last stop on the eastern section of the District line on London's underground system. It was a case of catching the last train home after a heavy drinking session in London and then slowly being lulled into a deep sleep by the soporific atmosphere of a hot stuffy carriage. Then, the indignity of being woken up in an empty carriage by the gruff voice of a railway guard, 'Upminster, end of the line mate.' The last insult was having to dig deep into your wallet to pay for a taxi ride home as you had missed your stop.

By November 1963, we were performing on average at least three times a week and practiced every Tuesday in a council-owned large wooden hut in Dagenham. Johnny Lonesome and The Travellers had become, by sheer hard work, one of the top groups in the area and able to pull in the crowds. Being the opening night of this new venue called The Windmill Hall, the promoter had advertised the event in the local newspaper and had put up posters all over town many weeks before.

With our excellent local reputation and heavy advertising, a good attendance was expected. On a good night the hall could accommodate around 150/200 people.

The small narrow hall, built by the local council as a community hall, was a prefabricated concrete structure with a corrugated roof and had a very utilitarian appearance. It stood in the corner of the sprawling Upminster Park and its name derived from a windmill that stood just down the hill from the park. It is necessary to describe the interior layout of the hall in order to understand what happened on that night. The hall was entered via double doors that led into a long narrow hallway with a small cloakroom on the right and a small kitchen on the left. At the

end of this narrow hallway, a stage had been built leaving a natural passageway either side, which, to the right, led to the male toilets and the left, to the female toilets. On the back wall of the stage, and separating each side of the stage from the passageway, hung long dark curtains.

This was 1963 and it was quite normal for any dance promoter simply to hire a hall, stick up some posters around town or place an advertisement in the local paper announcing the event. Then hire a couple of bouncers, turn up on the night with a cash box and a roll of tickets, sit back and hopefully make a profit. Some promoters would offer soft drinks for sale, if the facilities allowed and on this particular night, no alcohol could be blamed for the trouble. No attempt had been made to provide any additional interior lighting or decoration inside the hall. But, it didn't matter. In those days we were all 'rock pioneers' in a way. People turned up just to listen and dance to the latest pop hits provided by a live group. Controlled coloured lighting rigs with smoke machines and lasers would eventually become the norm but that was a decade away.

The reputation of weekly dance clubs and their longevity relied heavily on the quality of the groups. Occasionally, when playing the old ballrooms or town halls, they still had a mirror ball on the ceiling, a leftover from the ballroom dancing days of our parents. With spotlights trained on the slow moving mirror ball, it created hundreds of moving small squares of lights, which circled the dance floor and walls. This did at least create some form of atmosphere, as the main lights would have to be dimmed to be effective.

By the time we had set up our gear and carried out a quick sound check, people were buying their tickets and the hall was slowly filling up. We went off into the gents' toilets to change into our band suits and by the time we emerged and climbed up the steps onto the stage, the hall was already packed and still more people were being let in. It was a council-owned building, so presumably there had to be fire and safety regulations in place. But tonight, without council supervision, the promoter just let more and more people into the hall – money ruled.

Although it was November, with so many people packed into the hall the temperature and humidity level had risen quite dramatically and was giving us problems. We had to keep fine-tuning our guitars before we could start and with so many people now packed into the hall, John had to increase the volume of his mike. JG performed a couple of rolls across his drums and adjusted his snare drum skin and his drum stool. Fortunately, Dave's saxophone liked the increased humidity level. By now the crowd was heaving and, from our elevated position on the stage, we could clearly see that nobody was going to be dancing tonight. The crowd had now become shoulder to shoulder and was swaying through sheer numbers. One minute moving forward, the next moving back, and then from side to side. It was like watching a field of wheat in the wind.

God, it was hot! Combined with a low ceiling and with us standing on a fairly high stage, the air was hot and sticky. Beads of sweat were trickling down my back. I turned to John and said 'ready' and he looked around to get the nod from the others. As agreed, our first number was to be 'Lucille', an old Little Richard song that had been covered by a multitude of artists. This was always a good first opening number guaranteed to get the crowd jumping. Martin and I would in unison start the opening riff. I looked across at him and shouted in the count above the noise of the crowd. 'One, two, three, four', and we were off. The lights were dimmed in the hall and the crowd appeared to freeze for a moment, just listening. As we completed the full riff, the rest of the group came crashing in and the audience became alive – jumping, laughing, cheering, clapping and swaying around the entire hall. In front of me, I could see people having to fight not to get crushed against the stage. When we had completed a full second riff, John came screaming in 'Lucille, you won't do your sister's will. Lucille…!' It was mayhem, but we lapped it up, and so did the crowd. We simply couldn't do anything wrong and when the last chords of 'Lucille' rang out, there was a massive cheer.

The crowd were really enjoying themselves now and as the cheering continued, I went straight into the lead guitar intro to 'Please Don't Touch', a number by Johnny Kidd and The Pirates. As the last note of my riff was played, the band came thundering in. Sweat was running down John's face as he sang his heart out and the crowd loved it. This song was a crowd pleaser. I really enjoyed the section when the group simultaneously stopped playing and I carried on with the lead guitar intro again. Then, apart from JG, we all moved forward into a line across the stage and with our right feet banged hard four times on the floor as John simultaneously yelled out 'one, two, three, four' and in unison we kicked our right legs high into the air. The crowd roared out their appreciation.

The temperature in the hall was still rising. It was so damned hot we had to loosen our ties. John then deliberately introduced a slow song – we all needed to catch our breath and cool down a bit and that included the audience. Following a second slow song, we instantly brought the crowd back to life with 'Woolly Bully', a fast rocking number that had been a recent international hit for Sam the Sham and The Pharaohs. As we approached the sax solo, Dave climbed up and knelt on top of Martin's big bass speaker and, with the horn of the sax pointed at the ceiling, he performed his raucous solo to the delight of the crowd.

We were close to finishing the song, when I looked across at John and could see that blood was pouring down his chin. Although I didn't see it happen, John told me later that he had been watching a guy at the front of the stage who was apparently pushing and shoving people around. This had caused someone else at the front of the stage to put up their arm to protect themselves and in doing so, had inadvertently hit the mike stand that had, in turn, hit John in the face, splitting his lip.

Without any warning, John stopped singing and literally dived off the stage into the crowd and directly on top the guy responsible. They disappeared from sight amongst all the swaying bodies. John, although six foot plus, was normally a very placid guy and this aggressive action was totally out of character. I'd never seen him do anything like this before and we all looked across at one another in amazement. We knew from experience that if a fight breaks out in the audience, just to keep playing in the hope of keeping the trouble localised. So, although we didn't have a singer, we carried on playing and fortunately Dave had the foresight to break into an extended sax solo. But where the hell was John? I was getting concerned when I spotted him amongst the crowd. He moved forward and started to climb back onto the stage, when suddenly a girl came up behind him and banged her fist into his back.

We found out later that this was the girlfriend of the guy John had just punched. But John, thinking it was the guy attacking him, instinctively swung has arm round, knocking the girl for six. Well that was it! All hell let loose! Suddenly, about 12 guys started climbing up onto the stage, with more following. John pushed a couple of them back into the audience but three rushed towards me, pushing me back and I fell through the curtains, landing on my back in the narrow passageway, still clutching my guitar. Momentarily stunned, I stood up and lifted the curtain to reveal total chaos on the stage. John was exchanging blows with two guys and JG had left his drum kit to protect my new amplifier as it was about to topple over. As he grappled with the amplifier, three guys were punching the hell out of him. Across the stage Martin was pushing two guys away, but there was no sign of Dave or Patrick.

Just as I started to climb back on the stage, two burly bouncers had finally made their way there and were literally throwing young men back into the audience. The promoter followed them and went up to the mike pleading with the audience for calm, informing everyone that unless the fighting stopped, he would be forced to call the police, and the local council would most likely shut him down. He turned to John and told him to speak to the audience and apologise for hitting the young girl. John spoke into the mike, 'Please, I didn't mean to hit the girl. I thought it was the guy who was responsible for the microphone hitting my face. Let's get back to enjoying ourselves. I'm really sorry.' That did the trick. One or two people clapped and the audience calmed down. The promoter turned to us saying 'Come on boys, let's get the music started otherwise it might all start up again.' I turned to see Dave and Patrick climbing the small wooden staircase at the far side of the stage. Later we discovered that when the trouble first started they had high-tailed it down the narrow passageway and locked themselves in the ladies' toilets. So much for loyalty!

Quickly we started playing, the lights were dimmed and all was calm again in the hall. We were all pretty shaken up by the experience and I felt a bit of a sham having contributed nothing in helping my mates in their time of need. However, deep down I was thankful I had been pushed through the curtains into the passageway. Apart from John's split lip, the rest of us were only nursing a few bruises, but Dave and Patrick were obviously untouched. By now, things were back to normal and everyone appeared to be enjoying themselves once again. I did notice about six menacing looking guys standing together close at the front of the stage, just eye-balling John. But they soon disappeared when records were put on and we had a half-hour break. However, not to chance our luck, we decided to keep together at the back of the stage and not to venture out into the audience. We drank our soft drinks and discussed what had taken place, with John filling us in on what had actually sparked the whole affair.

We started our final hour's set with no further disturbances. It was like nothing had ever happened – people were back to laughing and chatting as they swayed back and forth and a few even managed to dance in the odd small space. The two bouncers had left the front of the stage and from my elevated position on the stage, I was able to see them now both standing at the back of the hall, presumably getting ready to keep control when the music finished and people filed out. We had about five songs to go before finishing for the night, when I spotted the same six guys who had been at the front of the stage before our break. They were there again, just staring at John who appeared unaware of their presence. Out of the blue, these guys made a dash and climbed onto the stage. It was déjà vu all over again. Immediately two of them came rushing over to me and, as I was punched, I stumbled backwards and again fell through the curtains clutching my guitar and into the passageway leading to the gents' toilets. Getting onto my feet, I climbed back onto the stage, not easy to do with a guitar strapped around your neck and curtains hindering my progress, but this time the scene was different. Only the five of us remained on the stage. Even Dave and Patrick hadn't had time to make a run for the ladies' toilets this time. But John had disappeared and so had the thugs. The gang had obviously singled John out – nobody else in the audience had attempted to get on the stage.

Martin told me he'd been rushed by a couple of guys and they had pushed him over his amplifier, but in the skirmish nobody had seen what had happened to John. The promoter suddenly appeared on the stage again, panic-stricken. We learned later that the stupid man had already paid the two bouncers off and they had now left the hall. The crowd watched and listened intently as the promoter once again pleaded for calm. Turning to us, he said 'Quickly boys, start playing for Christ's sake.' Still no sign of John, but we knew we had to start playing and, after a quick consultation, we launched into 'Tequila', a saxophone instrumental, originally a hit for the American group The Champs. By now I was extremely concerned about John.

We were halfway through the next instrumental number when John suddenly appeared at the front of the stage. My God, what a mess! He'd been severely beaten up. There was blood trickling down from his nose, his lip was bleeding and his right eye was badly swollen. While the group continued playing, I stepped forward and helped him up onto the stage. He was badly shaken up, but determined to carry on, so while we finished the number he moved to the back of the stage and tried to clean up his face the best he could with his handkerchief.

We finished the instrumental and turned to look at John to see what we should do next. He walked up to the microphone and, in an attempt to divert a third wave of attack, John spoke to the audience, appealing for calm. In a faltering voice he repeated that he was really sorry and had had no idea, when climbing back on to the stage earlier, that it was a girl who had punched him in the back.

We went on to play for a further quarter of an hour, but really we just wanted to finish and get out of the place. After the last number of the evening, John said 'Thank you and goodnight' but there was no reaction from the audience. The lights in the hall were switched on and people quietly started to make their way out of the hall.

We were all eager to find out what had exactly happened to John and, as we started packing up our gear, he explained what had taken place. During the second attack, while we were all looking after ourselves, he had been dragged away and bundled out through a fire escape door at the side of the stage. Then, in an outside toilet, three of the older lads just laid into him, while the others watched and cheered. 'I wonder where they are now?' Martin asked. 'I don't know' replied John. 'Perhaps they're outside waiting for us' I suggested, which didn't go down at all well judging by the looks on their faces.

We quickly changed out of our band suits and agreed that, before loading up the van, we'd each carry a microphone stand or a base for protection and go outside together to see if anyone was still hanging around.

As we passed the promoter by the front door counting his takings, he assured us that the gang had gone and told us that the troublemakers were in fact gypsies from a local gypsy caravan site. But we weren't convinced they had gone and wanted to make sure for ourselves. Who knows, perhaps they had left, but before doing so had damaged our van in retaliation and maybe even slashed the tyres.

We cautiously stepped outside into the darkness, holding the mike stands and bases at the ready, and walked around the car park. We then checked around the sides and the back of the hall, just in case they were ready to ambush us. No one was around. Thankfully it looked like they had all gone. We breathed a sigh of relief and walked over to the van, happy to find it was still intact. We certainly wouldn't be hanging around tonight but a slight panic was triggered when someone suggested that perhaps they had gone for reinforcements, which was quite conceivable. Taking no chances, it was then agreed that two of us should remain outside with the mike stands for protection and guard the open van, while the others quickly loaded up the equipment. We broke any previous records and within minutes the van was hastily loaded up, the back doors locked and we all climbed into the van, accelerating out of the small car park at record speed.

It was a very subdued drive home. John was nursing his wounds and was especially quiet. I think we were all shaken up by the whole episode. After we had dropped Pat and Dave off in Dagenham, Martin told us that they had jumped down from the stage as soon as the first lot of trouble started and had hidden in the gents' toilets. We noticed that they had been very quiet on the journey home – presumably they were slightly ashamed of their actions. We were never asked by the promoter to appear there again and even if we had, we most certainly would have turned him down. Fortunately for us, that was the one and only time during our eight years of performing, that the group had been attacked in such a way.

18

AMERICAN RHYTHM AND BLUES MUSIC ENTERS THE UK CHARTS

The young record-buying public in the UK had already been listening for some time to rhythm and blues songs on recent record releases by The Beatles and other Merseyside groups but were probably unaware that some of the songs had originally been written and recorded by American blues artists. The Beatles had become immensely influential, not only with the record companies, but also with many other groups around the country, who then started to record original R&B songs, many entering the hit parade. In addition, with the help of the various weekly music papers and TV, young people were being made aware of American R&B artists such as Chuck Berry and Bo Diddley.

In June 1963, The Rolling Stones' first hit single was a Chuck Berry song called 'Come On'. An LP entitled 'The Rolling Stones' was released in 1964, which mainly consisted of American rhythm and blues songs, apart from three self-penned numbers. Another Chuck Berry song appeared on the LP but even more importantly, various groups were recording relatively obscure songs by American blues artists such as Rufus Thomas, Muddy Walters and Jimmy Reed and this was having a strong influence on the record-buying public.

In their earlier days, The Rolling Stones were blues purists and had a residency in one of the few blues clubs that had emerged around the Greater London area. It was called the Crawdaddy Club and operated out of the Station Hotel in Richmond. They also performed in another blues club located a couple of miles away in Twickenham. It was located on Eel Pie Island, an actual island in the River Thames. After The Rolling Stones found fame, they ceased playing at the Crawdaddy Club and were replaced with another aspiring blues band, The Yardbirds, whose lead guitarist at the time was Eric Clapton. He eventually left the group citing differences over their choice of recording material, which was moving away from the blues. He was replaced by Jeff Beck and in due course before Beck finally left, Jimmy Page, who had tired of session work, joined the group. When the Yardbirds finally split, Page went on to form Led Zeppelin.

Some astute promoters in the UK soon sensed the interest and the demand for R&B music and lured many of the original blues artists – some old, some not so old – over to the UK to undertake small blues' tours around the country. A number of these artists had been out of the public eye in the States for decades and some had even come out of retirement to play!

Chuck Berry was a black R&B artist who had emerged during the late 50s rock 'n' roll era, singing infectious fast blues songs, and his guitar technique was admired and copied by aspiring guitarists everywhere. Rock 'n' roll was the white American answer to the black American rhythm and blues music. But rock 'n' roll had evolved from many music genres, not only from rhythm and blues but also from gospel, jazz, bluegrass and country music. Out of this mix came many black and white rock 'n' roll artists. Elvis Presley came from a poor white family living close to the segregated black areas in and around Memphis in the southern state of Tennessee. The black music he listened to influenced the young Presley. Many of his early songs recorded at the Sun Studios in Memphis had originally been recorded by black artists.

Segregation was all encompassing in the Southern States of America in the late 50s and early 60s and local radio stations mainly played either only black music or only white music. Elvis Presley's first official single release was 'That's Alright Mamma', originally written and recorded by an African/American eight years earlier. This song was issued as the Aside and the B-side was an old bluegrass number called 'Blue Moon of Kentucky', also recorded eight years before by The Blue Grass Boys and written by a group member, Bill Monroe. Bluegrass music was a sub-genre of country music and was predominantly performed and listened to by white Americans. In 1954, when this record was made, there was a dilemma – which local radio station would air it? What a situation it must have been for Sun Records at the time! Give the record to a station catering for the African/American community and upset the listeners by playing a song originally written by a black artist and now sung by a white singer. Or, alternatively, give the record to a local radio station that catered for the white community and upset their listeners with a singer that sounded like a black performer!

A few local radio stations dared to play a mixture of both black and white music. These local radio stations relied heavily on advertising to fund the station and therefore, for obvious reasons, it was very important not to upset the advertisers. In fact, it was one of these controversial local radio stations in Memphis that agreed to air the A-side one evening and after it was played, calls came in requesting to hear it again and it was played a number of times during the evening show. Many of the callers wanted to know the background of the singer and the DJ, Dewey Phillips, promised to try and carry out an interview with the actual singer that evening.

A call was made to Sun Records who in turn called Elvis and he was asked to go along to the radio station. To avoid a direct question during the interview as to whether he was white or black, he was discreetly asked what school he had attended in Memphis and when Elvis responded, listeners knew then that he had attended a whites-only school. The record was played regularly on air and the record-buying public made it a local hit. Sun Records also took the record along to a white radio station that specialised in playing country music and they agreed to play the B-side as they had no problem revealing on air that the singer was a local white lad. The response from the listeners was encouraging and the record was played regularly. Again the public responded by buying it and so the B-side also became a local hit. Fortunately times have changed. It now sounds quite shocking to live in a society where people were segregated because of the colour of their skin. The owner of Sun Records, Sam Phillips, who is no relation to Dewey Phillips, the local DJ who first aired the song, certainly knew how to play the game of record promoting. He was a pretty controversial figure at the time. Although he was white, he mainly recorded local black artists and I wonder if it was all a cunning move on his part, in light of the segregation problems, to make a record that catered for both communities, thus getting two bites of the apple!

In the UK during the 60s this urban music, performed by black Americans, was referred to as either rhythm and blues or simply the blues, and clubs that were opening up around the country using either term to denote the type of music that would be played there. From my personal perspective, I suppose if you wanted to differentiate between the two terms, then a slow 12 bar blues song would simply be referred to as the blues, while a faster 12 bar blues song would be called rhythm and blues. However, every artist who played this form of music would play both fast and slow songs. A decade or so later, in the USA, the term rhythm and blues had a total shift in meaning and was applied to soul and funk music, and this still applies today.

On reflection, it is strange why it took a bunch of young English lads to adopt a music genre generally associated with music that evolved from the African slaves who had been taken to America centuries before. When the Rolling Stones started to tour the Southern States of America in 1964, it was amazing to learn that many white Americans were shocked to discover that The Stones were actually playing blues songs that had originated from the USA and had first been performed and recorded by African Americans.

Segregation still existed in the Southern States when The Stones first went to America and when touring the South, they encountered a lot of resentment and hatred, as had The Beatles before them. There were still many white 'Middle America' prejudices to overcome. Some accused The Stones of being homosexuals, simply because they had long hair. It was during 1964 that President Johnson finally passed the Civil Rights Act banning segregation, but after decades of discrimination against the black African American population, it would take a long while for many white people to change the habits of a lifetime.

JIMMY POWELL AND THE FIVE DIMENSIONS – FEBRUARY 1964

In 1964, when R&B had come of age, there were a few instances when the term was used flippantly and some groups were put in potentially embarrassing situations when supporting the true R&B groups or artists. Although we had introduced a number of R&B songs into our repertoire, we were still primarily a pop rock 'n' roll band.

Towards the end of January of that year, I received a contract from the Cana Variety Agency in Central London for us to appear on 8 February at the Coronation Ballroom in Kingston-Upon-Thames. On the outskirts of town, we started spotting posters advertising the event. We hadn't heard of the group before, Jimmy Powell and The Five Dimensions, and above their name in bold print it stated 'Rhythm And Blues – Non Stop – No Interval'. Their name was a bit of a mouthful and received banner heading, so poor old Johnny Lonesome and The Travellers was just about squeezed in below. With more groups around with one word for their name, we had already been thinking of perhaps changing ours to something more compact, and in circumstances like this it would make sense.

Jimmy Powell and his group did play R&B music and were pretty good at it. They even had their own harmonica player, which authentic-

ated their sound, but we had also been billed as being an R&B group –
and we weren't! Fortunately, by limiting our repertoire and omitting any
pop songs, we were able to get away with it. But quite frankly, I don't
think the large audience that night gave a monkeys as long as they could
dance to the music.

It was a large stage and we stood in the wings when Jimmy Powell
and his group started their set, curious to see how good they were. It was
fascinating watching the harmonica player. He wore a wide leather belt
across his chest, which reminded me of an ammunition belt, with the
bullets replaced with at least ten harmonicas. When the opening number
finished, he would grab a different harmonica from the belt and replace it
with the one he'd just used, ready to play along to the next number. He
was a jovial character, with thick, slightly sticking up blond hair, cut in a
Mod style. He would acknowledge us in the wings every so often and on
one instance, seeing me drinking a bottle of Coke, he came rushing over
to me and snatched the bottle out of my hands, took a big swig, smiled
and said 'I owe you one' and rushed back on stage.

After playing about five numbers, Jimmy announced the next blues
song and immediately their harmonica player ran off the stage towards
us. He complained jokingly as he opened a battered old leather suitcase
close to where we were standing, and started rummaging around. Inside
were lots more harmonicas, each with stickers attached displaying the key
of the instrument. 'Unbelievable' he said. 'We'd worked out our playlist
for the evening and I'd selected all the harmonicas I needed' pointing to
his belt, 'then the silly bugger wants to do a song that isn't on the playlist.' The group had started without him but suddenly a great yell rang
out as he found the correct instrument and he rushed back onto the
stage, up to a mike and started playing.

With the harmonica currently being used by a lot of R&B groups,
John had a hankering to get one. In the dressing room, just before we
went on to play our final set, and with a bit of persuasion from me, John
went up to the harmonica player and asked him a couple of questions on
how to suck and blow the instrument. He was only too pleased to show

John and taking a harmonica from his pocket, he proceeded to give John a five-minute lesson. John did eventually go and buy one, but he just couldn't get that wailing blues sound, and so it never saw the light of day on the stage.

Apart from chatting up the promoter and getting a copy of the poster, that was the only permanent reminder I had of that evening. In the early 1980s, married by then and decorating a bedroom in our house, I was listening to a programme on BBC radio about the life and times of Rod Stewart. After about half an hour of interviewing Rod, and in between playing records, he was asked the question, 'Was it true you were a harmonica player in your early days?' and Rod replied 'Yes, that's quite right. I was asked to join a blues group called Jimmy Powell and The Five Dimensions.' I made the ladder shake with my excitement. I couldn't believe my ears – all those years ago, that harmonica player wearing the denim jeans and striped shirt, with the thick spiky blond Mod haircut was the man himself, Rod Stewart, who by now had become an international star!

So now my stories of the group, regaled at so many dinner parties and most times boring the pants off people, now included Rod Stewart. Also, when boasting that we had supported some top groups in our time – The Who, Tom Jones, Jerry Lee Lewis, The Merseybeats, Dave Clark Five, Johnny and The Hurricanes, Bee Bumble and The Stingers – I could now add Rod Stewart. Only if questioned further would I reveal that at the time he was the harmonica player for Jimmy Powell and The Five Dimensions!

While researching on the Internet to double-check my facts, I had a massive disappointment. Indeed, Rod Stewart had been the harmonica player in that group, but following a disagreement with Jimmy Powell who apparently wouldn't let Rod sing any numbers, Rod had walked out of the group whilst playing at the Ricky Tick Club in Windsor in November 1963. We had played with the group a couple of months later! I have subsequently seen photographs of the group with their replacement harmonica player, the one we met and, in my defence, he did have a mop of blond hair, cut in a Mod style, and looked very similar in appearance to Mr Stewart.

OPENING AT THE KAVERN CLUB - FOREST GATE - FEB 1964

Now that R&B music was slowly taking hold, blues groups were emerging out of the woodwork from all over the country and some even had records entering the national charts. Eddie Caswell, our manager, was still running the successful Lorain Club that he operated every Friday evening from the Royal Forest Hotel in Chingford but he was now itching to expand and open another club. He finally found suitable premises in Forest Gate, East London, located above Courts, a local furniture store. It was known locally as the Lotus Ballroom. Eddie renamed it the Kavern after the now-famous club in Liverpool where The Beatles and other popular Merseyside groups performed before becoming famous. But the name was spelt with a 'K' not a 'C'. The reason why will be revealed a bit later on.

Eddie had traditionally always booked local semi-professional groups to appear at the Lorain Club, with himself as the resident DJ, and he continued with the same format at his new club. His workload was increasing. He was now running two clubs, managing us, and working as an agent for some other local groups. In addition, with his experience as a DJ at the Lorain Club and now at the Kavern Club, he was hiring himself out as a mobile DJ, under the professional name the Ed Williams Sound System. This was also proving to be a great success.

I joined Eddie one evening in Kent, when the Ed Williams Sound System was supporting The Kinks, an extremely successful London band.

I sat behind the stage while Eddie played his records, just before The Kinks went on stage. While I was sitting there, minding my own business, who should come up to me but Ray Davies, the singer/composer and frontman of The Kinks. He smiled and asked me if I was working with the DJ and I explained that the DJ was a pal and also the manager of our group. He wanted to know about the group, what our line-up was, and when I told him that we had a sax, he became very interested and said he had just written a song especially with a sax in mind. He asked for the group's business card, said he'd be in touch, and left. Minutes later, I stood in the wings and watched the group perform their famous hits. Needless to say, I never ever heard from Ray Davies!

Eddie also had a full-time job at Ford Motor Company and decided to give this up in order to concentrate on building up his growing entertainment empire. We paid Eddie a commission and I was pushing him to promote us and get more bookings and ultimately a recording contract. We had become personal friends and over drinks one evening, he mentioned that trying to work from home was proving too restrictive because of space and so he was looking to rent an office. We both knew that if he was going to be taken seriously in the music business, he needed to operate from a bona fide commercial office address, and so the search began to find suitable premises.

At the time I was working in Stratford at the Westminster Bank, situated on Stratford Broadway, which coincidentally was just a mile or so down the road from Forest Gate and the Kavern Club. It was only a few days after my drink with Eddie that I spotted an 'Office To Let' sign outside a small Victorian building just along from the bank on the Broadway. I called Eddie and after inspecting the property, he decided it was perfect, and within a week he had set up office there. It consisted of two small rooms at the top of a small narrow Victorian tower-like building. He was especially chuffed when he showed me his new business plaque by the entry door which stated '4th Floor – Kaz Enterprises – Variety Agency', Kaz being the abbreviated version of his surname

Caswell, but using a K just to be different. Now I knew why he spelt Kavern with a K!

In Forest Gate it wasn't proving particularly successful for Eddie to book semi-professional groups to appear at the Kavern Club, although I have to say we were the exception, having built up quite a reputation in and around the area over the last year or so. He changed tactics, and having witnessed the recent rise of R&B groups, he started booking some professional London-based blues bands. These bands were more blues purists than the hit parade commercial blues groups and, most important, they didn't command such high fees. Although our repertoire was eclectic, the number of R&B songs we performed was on the rise. Eddie really wanted to promote us and so he started to book us on alternative Thursdays at the Kavern. We never had to support these blues purist groups as this would have been a disaster all round. However, with Eddie playing his selection of blues records for part of the evening every week, and us playing our blues and rock 'n' roll songs, leaving out the pop numbers, we were well received which was good for us and good for Eddie.

If for some reason we weren't actually playing at the Kavern on a Thursday night, John, JG, Martin and I would visit the club just to listen to these new blues groups. My favourite was The Downliners Sect, a great band live who played fast blues music, whereas the likes of The Graham Bond Organisation were pretty hard going and slightly verging on the jazzy side. Two of the band members, Jack Bruce and Ginger Baker, would later go on to international success with the forming of the super group Cream, together with Eric Clapton.

19

SUPPORTING THE BLUES LEGEND JIMMY REED - 1964

A call from an unknown promoter brought us on a Tuesday evening to a large first-floor ballroom, situated above a pub called the Red Lion in Leytonstone, East London.

I knew nothing about this ballroom. It was new venue for us and the promoter asked me if the group played any blues numbers. This was becoming quite a fairly common question and, not wishing to lose a booking and the money it gave us, I always answered yes. However, I always covered myself by also saying that we weren't a full blues band and that we also played quite a few rock 'n' roll numbers. I purposely didn't mention the pop songs we also played.

We were able to conveniently park our van in a small dead-end side road, right outside the side entrance to the ballroom. Carrying our gear up the stairs and through some double swing doors, this led us into a typically large oblong ballroom with a wooden parquet floor and a stage at one end. No effort had been made by the promoter to titivate the interior, apart from having a single bare light bulb dangling above the stage. No doubt, in its heyday, this had been an elegant ballroom with expensive drape curtains at the windows. Now the windows were simply painted black.

As we assembled our gear on the stage, the promoter came and introduced himself. It was then that he dropped a small bombshell by telling us 'We have the American blues artist Jimmy Reed performing here tonight, so if you start at eight o'clock and finish at nine, he'll play for an hour with his band and then you go back on again at ten and finish at 11pm prompt. OK?' We just nodded in agreement. After he'd left the stage, I looked at the others and said 'I don't believe it, Jimmy Reed! We'd better get 'Shame, Shame, Shame' out of the way early. He might not like our version!' John looked at me and said 'I didn't know this was a blues club – how are we going to play R&B for two hours?' 'We'll get by' I said. 'We can do a few repeat requests and Dave and I can double up on our solos. I'm sure we'll manage OK.' I think I sounded more confident that I felt!

For the first hour we played our repertoire of assorted R&B songs in this depressing venue under the eerie light of the single bare bulb. I doubled up on guitar solos, John repeated a few extra verses and Dave added a sax solo here and there. By nine o'clock, we'd managed to play only blues songs to a half-full hall. I turned to the others and said 'I wonder if this guy's spent any money on advertising the fact that Jimmy Reed is appearing here tonight?' 'I didn't see any posters outside the entrance' said Martin. Nobody had seen him arrive and he was due on stage now. The promoter came up to us looking concerned and asked us if we could keep playing as Jimmy hadn't turned up yet. As we had already exhausted our repertoire, to fill up the time we pretended we had had a few requests for earlier numbers we had played. We also improvised by making up our own slow 12-bar blues songs and again, by extending our guitar and sax solos, we managed to make just one song last nearly ten minutes. We congratulated ourselves – we were beginning to sound like an authentic blues band, but the audience appeared indifferent to anything we played. It was getting close to nine-thirty and still Jimmy Reed hadn't arrived. Suddenly there was a commotion over by the entrance door and in the darkness of this dimly lit hall we could make out people coming in carrying guitar cases. 'Thank goodness they've finally arrived' said Martin. 'I'm dying for a pint.'

The promoter came scurrying across the hall and spoke excitedly to us from the foot of the stage 'They're here boys. To save time, all right if they use your equipment?' We didn't have a lot of choice really, and we certainly didn't want to play any more extended slow blues songs, so I looked at the others and they all nodded in agreement. Five minutes later we were shaking hands with Jimmy Reed's backing group for this UK tour – two guitarists, a bass guitarist and a drummer from London. I showed the lead guitarist the controls on the amp, and the others were doing the same with their counterparts. JG adjusted his drum stool for the drummer, who then proceeded to rearrange the height of the various cymbals. Guitars were tuned and then a group member walked up to the mike and brought the height down a bit, presumably for Jimmy Reed himself.

'So, where's Jimmy Reed then?' I asked. 'He's in the van, no doubt having a last drink. He only flew into the country yesterday. We met him for the first time this morning and we've only managed one short rehearsal with him earlier on. That's why we were late arriving.' Apparently Jimmy Reed had been drinking all day and they were dreading playing with him.

We left the stage and they broke into a blues instrumental, followed by another. Was the famous bluesman ever going to make an appearance? Suddenly the entrance door swung open and hit the wall with a bang. Standing there was this big guy, silhouetted against the light outside in the hallway, surveying the scene. He then staggered across the floor heading for the stage. It wasn't until he got closer to the stage and the light fell across his face, that I thought I recognised him from an old LP cover I had. Once he'd stumbled up the stairs and onto the stage, I realised it was him all right, but he'd put on a lot of weight. A group member quickly pulled up a chair behind the mike and Jimmy sat down with a jolt. He was handed a guitar and then the mike had to be re-adjusted and brought down to his sitting position. A harmonica was then locked onto a wire frame that was put around his neck. This man was clearly well under the influence of alcohol and obviously he had to sit down. No other choice, otherwise I'm convinced he would have probably fallen over!

I was waiting for the promoter to jump up on stage and introduce the man. If he had planned to, then he had left it too late – suddenly Jimmy started a 12-bar blues intro on the guitar and then the harmonica came in. He hadn't even timed in his backing group who looked at one another in bewilderment, but quickly caught up. His words were slurred as he sang his way through his repertoire, but his guitar playing and harmonica playing were spot on – he was obviously used to performing in this condition.

The backing group was pretty average, but I felt sorry for them. They'd been booked to back Jimmy Reed at the last minute and thrown together without any quality rehearsal time. On top of that, they had to try and follow a singer who was nearly out of his mind on booze. No songs were announced and I doubt they even had a playlist. Fortunately many of Jimmy Reed's songs followed the same 12-bar blues format and a lot of them sounded very similar. Song after song followed and slowly the music started to gel as the group managed to establish a working format of coping with a drunken singer.

He went on to play the song I desperately wanted to hear 'Shame, Shame, Shame.' It was OK, but it just didn't have the magic of the recorded version. Then followed 'Bright Lights Big City', which unfortunately was a bit shambolic. He ended his set by playing one of his big hits 'Ain't That Lovin' You Baby.' Again, he didn't quite reach the high spot with this song. The audience was odd, again quite indifferent to his entire performance, as they were to us. Most had just danced all evening. Reed rose to his feet, handed over his guitar and harmonica, stumbled down the steps, and somehow made his way across the floor and out into the night.

This had been a poorly organised event and the lack of advertising hadn't brought in the type of person who appreciated the blues and wanted specifically to see Jimmy Reed, a blues legend. But there again, like me, they would have been very disappointed with his performance. Whoever the agent was who brought him over to England in the first place, probably ripped him off. I've subsequently read that he suffered from rampant alcoholism, which affected his career badly, and it had been two years since his last hit record. His recording contract hadn't been renewed and, due to his drinking problem, he wasn't in the best of health when he came to England at the age of 38 and by the age of 50 he was dead.

Jimmy Reed had been a successful recording artist and a few of his record releases crept onto the bottom rung of the US top 100, plus he did have 14 entries in the US R&B charts. 'Ain't That Lovin' You Baby' and 'Bright Lights Big City' both peaked at number three, but he never had a hit record in the UK.

We only had to play for a further 20 minutes and then it was all over. The promoter handed over our money and we started to load up the van. Presumably the backing group had gone into the pub downstairs for a drink, as their van was still parked outside. All packed up and ready to go, I pulled out and did a three point turn at the end of the road. It was only then, as I started to move forward, that I suddenly spotted him. I brought the van to a standstill and we peered out at the pathetic sight of Jimmy Reed. He sat, propped up against a lamppost, fully illuminated in this darkened street, drinking from a bottle of whisky. I started to move forward slowly and as we drew level with him, he raised the bottle to his lips to take another swig. That was my last enduring image of the American blues legend – how very sad!

BROMEL CLUB – BROMLEY COURT HOTEL – NOVEMBER 1964

Our old friends, Galaxy Entertainments, had recommended us to another London agency and it was late one Friday afternoon while still at the bank that I received a panic call from them. They apologised for giving me such short notice, but they had been let down at the last minute and were we available to play at a club in Bromley the next Monday? Generally most venues never opened on a Monday so I knew we were free. I told him we were available that night. You never knew, helping them out might just lead to more work. We agreed a fee, and they gave me the promoter's name and the full address and telephone number of the club.

I was at the wheel as we entered the outskirts of Bromley and had just pulled up at some traffic lights, when suddenly there was a loud shout from the back of the van. 'Look at that bloody poster!' Turning around, I saw John pointing to a poster stuck on the wall of an empty building. It read 'Bromel Club – Monday 16 November – Rare London Appearance of Blues Legend, Memphis Slim'. For a moment there was stunned silence, then slowly it sank in – we were supporting Memphis Slim! As we pulled away from the lights, I assured the others that the agency hadn't mentioned we were supporting anyone tonight, least of all Memphis Slim. Basically we were just a pop group and here we were, once again, booked to support another well-known blues legend. Worse news was still to come.

We would soon be approaching the centre of Bromley and I asked everyone to keep their eyes peeled as according to the directions, the hotel was somewhere in this area. Martin spotted it first and pointed to a row of terraced buildings up ahead on the other side of the road. A large illuminated sign told us we had found the Bromley Court Hotel. I drove into a small service road and pulled up outside the hotel entrance. On the right was a small awning emblazoned with the words Bromel Club with steps leading down to a basement door.

I told the others that Martin and I would check out what's going on. We jumped out of the van and made our way down the steps. Pinned on the entrance door was a message – 'Unfortunately, due to unforeseen circumstances, Memphis Slim will not be appearing here tonight'. I sensed trouble ahead! As we made our way into the club, we noticed it was quite impressive inside, tastefully decorated and with fitted carpets. There were a number of tables and chairs close to a large bar at the back. All in all, it had a rather cosy feel about it, which made a change from some of the rather bleak ballrooms we often played in.

I spotted a man sitting on a stool at the far end of the bar, reading a paper. He looked up as we approached, smiled and asked if we were the group. I replied that we were and he introduced himself as the promoter. As we shook hands he said 'Boy, am I pleased to see you! Thanks for making it tonight at such short notice. You've no doubt read the message on the door. Unfortunately Memphis Slim was refused entry into Britain last week, as apparently his entry permit was not in order. The problem is, I had posters put up around town a couple of weeks ago, but being let down at the last minute like this, I haven't been able to let people know in advance, so they'll only know of the non-appearance of Memphis Slim when they turn up tonight. That's why I was desperate to at least put on some live music here tonight.'

We had been well and truly been stitched up by the agency. Had I been told initially that we were a replacement for Memphis Slim, I would most certainly have turned the engagement down. Now we weren't even sure what the agency had said about us to the promoter. For all we knew, he'd probably been told we were an authentic blues band. Martin and I looked at one another. I felt I had to bring the matter up before we went any further. 'Did the agency by any chance explain that we're not an official R&B group. We do play a few blues numbers, but our repertoire is mainly chart songs.' The promoter just stared at us for a brief moment in stunned silence and then said 'Well, I appreciate your honesty, but I was told you were an R&B group and the agency damn well knew I run a blues club here. Now I'm really stuffed.'

I wanted to put things straight and to be honest with this guy, so I explained that we had never worked with this agency before. They had been put in touch with me via another agency that we worked with who knew full well that we were not an R&B group. I went on to tell him about our experience last week with Jimmy Reed and how, due to a late appearance by him, we had played our blues repertoire. Also by doubling up, extending the guitar solos, making up a few extra verses and repeating a few of the songs as requests by the audience, we had managed to play blues music for well over an hour. This seemed to calm him down a bit, so I was hopeful that we could reach a compromise. It had taken us an hour to get here and it would be an evening wasted if we didn't perform.

I also wanted to make sure that if we played, we would get paid at the end of the evening. I told him how much the agency was paying us, but he didn't flinch. I suspect it was a lot less than he would have paid Memphis Slim! His dilemma was that it was supposed to be a blues evening at the club and people would be arriving soon to listen a night of blues music. We were a poor compensation for Memphis Slim not being there and we weren't even an authentic blues group! No doubt the promoter wanted to earn something from the evening but he also had to maintain his and the club's reputation.

The promoter pondered for a while. 'OK then, you play this evening and play R&B music for as long as you can. Perhaps between us we could make an announcement later on in the evening, explaining the mix-up by the agency.' I looked at Martin and he nodded his approval. However, I felt I had to make it clear to him that we wanted to get paid before we left that night and didn't want to leave it to get paid, or possibly not get paid, by the agency. He agreed and said he would sort some form of discount from the agency when one of their acts next played there.

Thank goodness, a deal had been reached. As we turned to leave to go and get the gear in, I noticed more seating for about 20 people, this time arranged in front of the small stage. That meant only one thing – they took their music really seriously here! Perhaps we should have refused to play there and then, but it was too late now to change our minds. However, we really didn't fancy playing in front of serious die-hard blues' fans. I then decided to let the promoter battle it out with the agency. We were simply pigs in the middle of an embarrassing situation, which was not of our doing – or the promoters come to that.

We explained to the others what had happened and what we had agreed with the promoter, but John especially was a bit disgruntled. He was the singer and the front man and he knew that all eyes would be on him tonight. It certainly wasn't an ideal situation and none of us particularly wanted to play under these circumstances, so it was with some reluctance that we unloaded the gear. As we set up our equipment, people were slowly trickling in and some had even started to sit in the seats facing the stage. We were informed later that many people, discovering that Memphis Slim wasn't performing tonight, simply turned away and left.

We were ready to start our set. John switched on the microphone and spoke to the half-filled club wishing them good evening and telling them that we would be starting with a Rufus Thomas number called 'Walkin' the Dog'. We couldn't believe it when we finished the song and a few people clapped politely. What a morale booster that was! Our confidence grew immediately which was reflected in our playing. We completed our first hour playing most of our blues' repertoire and received a reasonable reaction from the audience. But we weren't out of the woods just yet. Although we still had a couple of blues songs in reserve and we could also include a couple of dummy requests, there was only so long that we could keep playing.

We started our second set with 'You Can't Judge a Book by its Cover' with John frantically shaking his newly acquired maracas in his right hand, Mick Jagger style. So far so good, but within about 15 minutes we had reached the end of our blues' repertoire. We daren't try and get away with any more dummy requests and we still we had a further 45 minutes to go. It was then that John suddenly decided to speak to the audience. He apologised, explaining our predicament of not being an out-and-out blues band and that we had accepted the booking through an agency at the last minute to help out the promoter. He went on to say that unfortunately we had no more blues numbers left and would spend our final 45 minutes playing some old rock 'n' roll numbers. John turned to the rest of us and said 'Lets give them 'Lucille' then' and so we gave them some real down to earth music with links to the blues. We finished our set to loud applause from an appreciative audience.

The promoter later came over and congratulated us and to our relief, handed over our money. I had half expected him to renege on the deal. I doubted we'd ever be invited back to this club or that we'd ever hear from the agency again. We didn't, although I did point out to Galaxy

Entertainments the problems we had experienced. I really had to make sure that in the future we weren't being booked into a blues club as a blues band. Fortunately, we never went through the same experience again.

20

THE DAWNING OF 1964

The power and influence of popular music had risen extremely quickly over the past couple of years, spearheaded of course by The Beatles. It had reached such a pitch that even the national newspapers reported regularly about The Beatles and The Rolling Stones and other well-known groups. Nearly every day, The Daily Mail had a small column just devoted to what The Beatles were up to. It was easily spotted on the page because, at the top of the article, were four 'mop-tops' as they were sometimes called, a simple flourish of an artist's pen denoting four Beatles, haircuts only, nothing else.

During that year, even one of our local papers, The Romford Recorder, devoted a whole page to pop music information, headed up 'The Beat Page'. It gave information about major artists and groups and which venues they were appearing at in the area. Besides listing the top ten records currently in the charts and any snippets of pop music news, it also included news about local groups like ours.

QUEEN'S THEATRE HORNCHURCH - FEBRUARY 1964

Apart from featuring in the local press now and again, we were also starting to realise the advantage of having our own fan club. It was an extremely useful tool in which to encourage fans to support us when necessary and when Hornchurch council approached us to headline a concert featuring five local groups at the Queen's Theatre, we of course accepted. We knew we could rely on our fans for their support.

Following renovation work on a disused cinema in Hornchurch, its doors opened as a repertory theatre in 1953. It was the year of Queen Elizabeth's coronation and so it was named Queen's Theatre. It eventually became well known throughout the area for staging plays, musicals and pantomimes. As the theatre's reputation grew in stature, new premises were needed and a new Queen's Theatre was purpose-built nearby. In 1975, the old theatre closed its doors and the new theatre took over the mantle.

With the country gripped in a frenzy of pop music, the Queen's Theatre did its bit by hosting an evening to showcase local groups from around Essex. I was approached by the trust and following a meeting, I received a letter from the producer offering us a 15-minute top of the bill position, for a fee of 15 guineas (£15.15/- = £15.71p).

This forthcoming event had received a lot of local newspaper coverage and the evening itself would be well reported so it was time to call in the troops. Once again we asked our fans to support us on the evening. Eddie Caswell, our manager, took this booking very seriously. He spoke with the trust and insisted that we had a separate dressing room, as we were top of the bill. Perhaps he took it a little bit too seriously. We arrived to find a large gold star on our dressing room door and the other four groups had to share a dressing room opposite!

The show was advertised well in advance and tickets for the event were sold out. The theatre's stagehands were well versed in moving scenery around, but they now found themselves shifting amplifiers and drums. Organisation behind the scenes was extremely professional and, according to the order of appearance, each group was allotted an area at the side of the stage to store their gear. All the vocalists would use the in-house sound system and with five groups playing that evening, there were five drum kits and dozens of guitars and amplifiers laid out in the wings. Most importantly, to avoid any hold-ups and to facilitate a smooth transition between each group's appearances, the stage crew would be on hand to help move the equipment. While we busied ourselves on stage, I couldn't help but notice a very large white sign, which stretched across the entire width of the stage. It was suspended high up by ropes at the back of the stage and would not be visible to the audience until lowered into position. Printed on it in large black letters was Johnny Lonesome and The Travellers – we were certainly being given the star treatment tonight!

Eddie Caswell had been talking with the organisers and discovered that after the appearance of the fourth group a reconstruction of a popular TV programme of the day called 'Juke Box Jury' was to take place onstage. Like the programme, there would be a host who would play a newly released record to a team of panellists, who would then judge the record as either a 'hit' or a 'miss'. Eddie, being our dutiful manager, had insisted one of the panellists had to be the star of the evening, Johnny Lonesome. You have to appreciate that although John had a great voice and could sing in public, talking in public was another thing altogether. It was only after a lot of persuasion from within the group in the earlier years, that John had finally started to announce the songs as we performed them.

So you could say this came as rather a shock to John when Eddie told him he was the star panellist on the programme and although he protested profusely, it was to no avail – Eddie had already made a commitment. Of course, the rest of the group found it hilarious and we teased him mercilessly.

The Queen's Theatre was packed to its 500-seat capacity when the curtains opened and we could hear, in the distance, the first group kick off the evening. We were spending our time relaxing in the 'star' dressing room. As the fourth group started their set, there was a knock on the door and John, now wearing his distinctive black mohair stage suit with a curved maroon velvet collar, was summoned to the stage. We all cheered as he left and stood in the wings to watch the fun. When the group had finished playing, the curtains were drawn and instantly the crew was at work clearing the stage. Various props and pieces of furniture were being brought out and slowly the stage started to resemble the layout of the TV programme.

John was asked to take a seat with the other panellists, made up of a young councillor, a member of the theatre staff and a person selected at random from the audience. The host, a local actor, also took his seat. As I peered through the curtains, John saw me and I blew him a kiss, which brought on a stilted smile, but I could see poor John was suffering badly from nerves. Suddenly the theatre was filled with the 'Juke Box Jury' signature music and the front curtains opened to rapturous applause. The music faded and the host, sitting at his desk, introduced himself and the panellists one by one. When it came to introducing Johnny Lonesome, there were screams from girls in the audience. Seeing John squirming in his seat had us in fits of laughter behind the backdrop curtain, but we also felt sorry for him.

Three records were played and each panellist gave a brief review of the song, John keeping his comments to a minimum. Following the various reviews, the panellists voted by holding up a 'hit' or 'miss' card. After the third song, the signature music was played again and the curtains were drawn. I think John must have been glad it was all over!

Within a few minutes the stage was again cleared and our equipment was brought on and put into place. Guitars were quietly checked for tuning and as we assumed our usual positions on stage, I saw the large black and white sign with our name on it being lowered into position behind us. I nodded to the others to have a look – what a proud moment that was for all of us!

When we were ready, spotlights were switched on above us and the lights were dimmed in the theatre. Somebody walked onto the stage in front of the curtain and announced 'Ladies and gentlemen, may I present to you, Johnny Lonesome and The Travellers.' This was our cue and as the curtains drew back, JG launched into the opening drum sequence of our first number. The curtains were now fully open and with perfect timing, John sang the opening line, 'You say that you love me' and Martin and I sang the next line in harmony 'Say you love me.' This song had been a recent number one hit for The Dave Clark Five and with a sax in their line-up too, we sounded very similar to the record, which in those days was extremely important.

There were loud screams from the audience and I was in seventh heaven being up on the stage that evening. I gazed out into the darkened auditorium, seeing only the first few rows of faces lit up by the stage lights, but knew there were at least 500 faces staring back at us. Not only did we look good in our new suits, we also sounded good and, to top in all, we were going down a bomb. Yes, we had encouraged our fans to come along and support us and they were doing just that, but the whole audience wasn't only made up of fans and we were clearly liked by every-one.

We saved the best till last. Our penultimate song was 'Summer Time', a slow classic number, which showcased John's strong vocals. We had arranged beforehand with the lighting engineer to dim the lights at the start, which added to the atmosphere of this haunting song. At the end of the song, there was a tremendous response from the audience and, as pre-arranged, the lights were brought up on stage and in the auditor-ium. We then stood to attention on stage, while JG did a long drum roll, and slowly but surely everybody in the audience started to stand up, thinking that the National Anthem was about to be played. The drum roll continued until the final person rose to their feet and then JG sud-denly stopped and John yelled out the opening words to our last song 'Mashed Potato Yeah'. As we broke into this fast raucous rock 'n' roll number, the spotlights came on but the auditorium was dimmed. We had fooled the audience. Most started to sit down but some remained standing and just danced along to the music, From my viewpoint on stage, I could see plenty of smiles in the first few rows, so thankfully it hadn't been taken too seriously. As the last chord was played, the curtains closed to a rapturous response – we were well chuffed with our perform-ance. The reception we'd received was unbelievable – what a night to remember!

Back in the changing room, with the star still on the door of course, we chatted excitedly about the whole evening. After we had changed out of our band suits, we went back to the stage area and started to pack up our gear and take it along to the back entrance of the theatre where our van was parked. The last few pieces of equipment were being loaded into the van, when a very excited Eddie came rushing up to us shouting 'There's a crowd of girls gathered outside the front of the theatre waving autograph books!' We made our way through to the front of the theatre where there were about 30 highly excited girls gathered on the steps. Within seconds we were surrounded. Some just wanted to talk to us, others wanted our autographs, and so we happily obliged. It had all happened very spontaneously and was such a thrill for us to be appreciated in this way.

However, an article appeared in the Hornchurch and Upminster News that week, obviously written by an older reporter. The first give-away was the banner heading 'Square's Eye View', square being a late 1950's word which described a person who was old-fashioned and boring and who obviously wouldn't like or appreciate rock 'n' roll music. We were heavily criticised in the article for being 'too cleverly professional to win a lasting affection' which referred to our mock National Anthem drum roll. It went on to say it 'was a trick too questionable for a group of any standing'. In addition, criticism was made of our fans, 'a well-rehearsed bunch of screamers out front'. A photograph of us taken on the night with Mary Bennett, our fan club president, was displayed below the article.

A follow-up letter to the article was published in the paper the following week from a very upset and loyal fan. Under the heading 'Don't Jump to Ridiculous Conclusions' it stated 'I must comment on that sarcastic report written about Johnny Lonesome and The Travellers.' She went on to say 'I am one of the supposedly 'well-rehearsed' screaming teenagers. Our admiration for the group is perfectly genuine, therefore no rehearsals are necessary.' It concluded 'the fans scream, shout and applaud because they know how hard the group work to please them.' It was signed Kathleen Merrett – Harold Hill. Kathleen was our fan club secretary and, I can assure you, wrote the letter without any prompting from us – hand on heart.

The idea of the National Anthem ploy came from a talent competition we'd entered in May 1962, which had been held at the YMCA Hall in Romford. One of the judges was Joe Brown, a highly influential singer/guitarist of the early British rock 'n' roll scene who fronted the group Joe Brown and The Bruvvers. We came second and were pretty pleased with ourselves, especially when Joe Brown announced the results, saying he thought we had a lot of talent. After the competition ended, Joe Brown and The Bruvvers played for half an hour and when they'd finished their penultimate song, they all stood to attention while the drummer carried out a long drum roll, bringing the audience to its feet, expecting the National Anthem to be played. Suddenly they broke into their final song and everyone laughed. Some sat down again while others remained standing or started dancing. No one complained then!

When I was a young boy, the British National Anthem was always played in cinemas across the country at the end of an evening's screening. Many people would make a hasty exit for the door as the credits rolled up at the end of a film to avoid standing quietly while the Anthem was being played. Some even left as the National Anthem was being played, which at my young and innocent age, I thought very disrespectful, but perhaps they had a last bus to catch. For me then, it was quite normal to stand to attention while the National Anthem was played and watch on screen as the Queen, in full military uniform, sat side saddle on a horse and saluted. It concluded with just the Royal Standard flag fluttering in the wind. However, as a rebellious teenager, I also started making a hasty exit while the credits were being shown – and I didn't have a bus to catch!

In those days there was only one channel of television being broadcast throughout Britain – the BBC. I would often fall asleep on the settee at home while watching a late night programme, only to be woken up with the National Anthem playing and the Royal Standard flag flapping around in the wind on the screen. This always signalled the end of transmission for the evening. The British Empire was slowly disappearing and the BBC, in line with the cinemas, would eventually drop this tradition.

At this point in time in 1964, it had come to a point when having to write the monthly newsletter was putting me under a lot of pressure. Our workload was increasing as we accepted more and more bookings and then JG's firm put their foot down and no longer allowed him to print our newsletter there. We would now have to employ a local printer, which would cost us a lot of money.

Reluctantly, we eventually announced that the July 1964 issue would be our last newsletter. Perhaps it was a blessing in disguise when Mary Bennett also announced that unfortunately her parents were moving out of the area and she wouldn't be able to continue as club president. Although Kathleen offered to pick up the reins and continue to run the fan club, we all agreed that enough was enough. The annual membership fee was now due and the number of new fans joining had slowed down dramatically.

The membership had consisted mainly of young schoolgirls who lived on Harold Hill. However, we were now performing further afield and making fewer appearances there so it was obviously time to call it a day. It had been an interesting experience for all concerned and had given us an insight into how supportive fans can be. It was a natural progression really. As we had grown up, so had our fans.

SUPPORTING THE BACHELORS – FEBRUARY 1964

The Bachelors, as far I was concerned, was an old-fashioned group. They sang close harmony country-type music and accompanied themselves using two acoustic guitars and an upright double bass. They were an Irish trio from Dublin and although I had seen them many times appearing on various television shows, their music left me cold. In 1961 their song 'I Believe' went to number one in the American charts and number two in the UK. This was followed by more chart entries. In February 1964, when we supported them along with two other groups, they were riding high in the charts at number four with a song called 'Diane'.

The East India Dock Hall was part of the Poplar Baths situated in East London, a massive structure built in 1852 to provide washing facilities for the East End's poor. It also housed a large swimming pool. It was only when the pool was covered with a temporary floor that it became the East India Dock Hall and was hired out by the local council for dances and private functions.

East India Dock Hall was large and cavernous and The Bachelors were really best suited to performing in a theatre, where the audience just

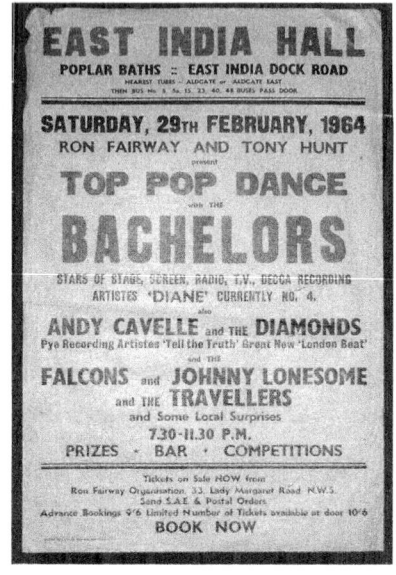

sat and watched and listened. They weren't part of the new British music scene and although they had a large record-buying public, it was an older generation who listened to their music. The event was poorly attended which didn't really surprise me. The hall needed at least a thousand people in the audience to make it look crowded and there were a lot of empty seats. The evening was already off to a bad start.

We were the second group to go on the stage and we played a very uneventful set. We weren't happy with our sound and this affected our performance. With the lack of people in the hall to help absorb the sound and the hall itself being so large with a high ceiling, we were troubled with echo, which muddied our overall sound.

When The Bachelors finally took to the stage, we had already packed most of our gear into the van but, out of curiosity, we decided to watch them perform from the wings of the stage. Their sound also suffered from the poor acoustics of the hall but for me that didn't make any difference – I just didn't like their music.

All in all it was a very disappointing evening for us and a disaster for the promoter. We returned to our dressing room to get our band suits and instruments and then headed out. By now The Bachelors had departed and as I passed their dressing room I took a look inside. There was no litter of any description lying around the room, no ashtrays full of cigarette stubs, no odd newspapers left behind, in fact the room was spotless. So it would appear that they hadn't eaten anything during their stay there and also that none of them smoked or read. In fact, the only sign that any human beings had occupied the room were three empty half bottles of beer sitting on top of a table. I couldn't believe it! They must have spent a couple of hours cooped up in that room and in all that time they'd only consumed half a pint of beer each! Irishmen are normally renowned for enjoying a drink or two, so it just about summed it all up for me – The Bachelors just weren't very rock 'n' roll!

'HERE COMES VICAR WRIGHT – IGNORE HIM'

We went on to play many dates at the Wykeham Hall over the years and as our local reputation and pulling power grew, we became the headlining act, with groups supporting us for a change. It was all very gratifying. During one of those headlining bookings an incident occurred that, even today, I feel quite ashamed about.

With the curtains closed and the support group's equipment replaced with our own, we carried out a final tune-up and were just about ready to start. As a headlining act, and without the support of a DJ playing music at this venue, time was of the essence for a quick and smooth turnaround between acts, otherwise the audience grew restless. As a support band in the past, we always had time to carry out a sound check before people started arriving but now time just didn't allow us this luxury. However, with our top-end sound system, large powerful amplifiers, expensive drum kit and guitars and, most importantly, from experience we knew the settings required to give us a good sound balance.

I nodded to the caretaker to drop the lights in the hall. This always triggered a rush to the front of the stage by young girls wanting to study the group. Behind the curtain the sound of these impatient girls could be heard as we stood in a line across the stage ready to start. John always brought a smile to my face with his usual remark 'OK girls, settle down.' I then looked across and called out 'all set?' Everyone nodded and we started with our usual big sound number '(Do the) Mashed Potatoes'. I had pre-warned the caretaker not to open the curtains until I gave the word. We were loud, but still the curtains remained closed, muffling our sound in the hall. The effect, especially for the girls at the front of the stage, was one of excitement and expectation. I nodded to the caretaker. The stage lights were already blazing away but the hall itself was dark. As the curtains slowly drew back, the effect was dramatic. The sound and light suddenly escaped and hit the audience full on. John walked forward holding the mike stand and started singing 'the mashed potato yeah, ah yeah, ah yeah, hot dig it…'

We had just started into our third number and things were going extremely well. We still held the attention of the girls at the front of the stage, which was always reassuring as sometimes, if they didn't like the group, they simply drifted away. I was standing there in my element, looking over the sea of bobbing heads as people in the distance danced, when I was distracted for a moment by a shaft of light at the back of the hall as a door was opened. I could just make out Ron King. He was talking to somebody, and suddenly that somebody came through the open door and into the hall. Oh no, I thought. It was Vicar Wright himself! What on earth was he doing here on a Saturday evening?

How embarrassing for Ron King to have the Vicar coming into the packed hall, dressed in his flowing black cassock and white dog collar. One of the drawbacks, I suppose, of hiring a hall that belonged to St Edward's Church, which was situated immediately next door. Vicar Wright had very kindly allowed us to rehearse in the Wykeham Hall during our school days, so he knew we played in a group, and if he recognised us this evening he might attempt to talk to us. John stood back from the mike and I suddenly realised it was time for my guitar solo. As soon as I'd finished the solo I looked to the back of the hall again. They were still there, talking away, but now both men were looking directly at the stage.

I couldn't wait to tell the others and so when the song finished, I quickly shouted across 'Don't all look at once but Vicar Wright's standing at the back of the hall with Ron King.' Immediately of course, Martin, John and JG all looked towards the back of the hall and my worst nightmare happened – Vicar Wright waved to us! 'Now look what you've done' I said. Nobody waved back. We certainly didn't want to encourage him! We were deciding what number to do next when Martin yelled out 'Shit, he's started to make his way through the crowd towards us!' I don't mean this nastily, but our group image and street cred could be badly tarnished if Vic Baby, as we affectionately called him, came up to the stage and wanted to chat to us. My head was in a spin. 'Quickly, lets do 'Lucille'. All ready?' Everybody nodded and I immediately started the solo guitar intro. Martin came in on bass following my riff, and then the drums, guitar and sax all came in and we were in full swing. John started singing 'Lucille, you won't you do your sister's will. Oh, Lucille…' I looked over the heads of the audience. Vic Baby was now halfway down the hall, weaving in and out around the dancers, and stopping occasionally to talk to people.

In no time at all he was standing close to the front of the stage. Fortunately, the girls lined up there were three deep and thus prevented him from getting any closer. I just pretended he wasn't there and the others did the same. I don't think Patrick or Dave had an inkling of what was going on as they hadn't attended St Edward's School and so didn't know the Vicar. I surreptitiously glanced in his direction. He was just standing there smiling away at us, hands on his hips. Oh please go away, I said to myself. It wouldn't be long before the song came to an end and then we'd be in serious trouble.

Fortunately John took the initiative and saved the day. He indicated to me to play another guitar solo and I obliged. When the solo was nearly over, and with the Vicar still standing there, John then encouraged Dave to repeat his sax solo. However, we couldn't keep this up – we had to finish the song soon. I glanced again out of the corner of my eye to where the Vicar was standing but he'd gone. Where was he? I searched the crowd, looking from left to right, when I spotted him making his way to the back of the hall and hopefully heading home to the vicarage. That was the last any of us ever saw of Vicar Wright and I read in the local paper that not long after he had retired from the church.

So, sorry Vicar, it wasn't our intention to be so rude to you. Hope we didn't prompt your early retirement, but what else could we do under the circumstances! He most certainly would have hated the loud music, but still he braved the wall of sound just to say hello to his boys.

SO SORRY VICAR....

21

BIRTH OF THE CANDLES - AUGUST 1964

By the summer of 1964, our popularity was at a peak. Not just a well-known group locally, we were now playing in other major towns around Essex. We were also performing regularly in the East End of London and in south London.

More Liverpool groups were conquering the music charts – The Fourmost, The Searchers and The Merseybeats just to name a few. Other groups from around the country were also entering the charts as well including The Hollies, The Kinks and The Yardbirds. Over a relatively short period of time, groups with short names were dominating the music scene. The name Johnny Lonesome and The Travellers suddenly sounded dated. It had served us well but sounded like we came from another era. It was time to move on. We were also acutely aware that squeezing our long name onto posters was proving pretty restrictive, so once again we put our heads together to come up with a new name.

To gain some publicity for ourselves while we searched for our new name, I telephoned the local rag, The Romford Recorder, and explained that we were changing our current name, Johnny Lonesome and The Travellers, to a shorter name. The July 3 issue of the newspaper then ran a short story on their Music Scene page, with the banner heading GROUP HAS A BILL POSER. When I was originally talking to the journalist about our name change, he mentioned that he had received quite a few letters asking the paper if Johnny Lonesome was married. I was able to clarify the situation with a straight 'no' and under the main article, it simply stated that Johnny Lonesome was not married, which must have pleased his hordes of fans!

After much deliberation, and many pints of beer, we democratically agreed our new name should be The Candles. This name was chosen because essentially it was short, but we were also looking to have our own logo as well. For the logo itself, we finally settled upon pure simplicity – a candle with a large flame that sat in an old-fashioned style candle holder with the handle shaped as an 'S'.

To launch our new name, our manager, Eddie Caswell, placed a series of weekly advertisements in the Record Mirror, which at the time was one of the UK's major weekly music papers. The first ad appeared on August 8 and consisted of a black square, 4cms x 4cms, with the wording 'Have you heard THE' in white. At the side of this wording our candle logo appeared, but no name. Directly beneath, it gave a list of where we were performing for the next week or so, but still no name, only 'Direction: Maryland 2026/2052' which were the telephone numbers of Eddie's office in Stratford.

Have you heard THE

If not—see them at—
10th: Back from hols.
11th: Shopping for gear.
12th: Recording.
13th: Kavern, Forest Gate.
14th: Loraine, Chingford.
15th: Grays, Co-op Hall.
16th: Cooks Ferry Inn, Edmonton.
17th: Flamingo.

Direction:
Maryland 2026/2052

The following week the same ad was run again, but the wording was replaced with 'Get A Thrill With THE' plus our logo, but still no name.

GET A THRILL WITH THE

Direction:
Maryland 2026/2052

On the third and fourth week, there was still no wording, simply our candle logo in white, centred in the black box.

It had the desired effect and attracted the 'curious'. This national weekly music paper hit the news stands every Thursday and as soon as the first entry of the ad appeared on 8 August 1964, Eddie started getting numerous enquiries from promoters wishing to know about the group. Most importantly, these enquiries resulted in more work for us.

Direction:
Maryland 2026/2052

To create some additional interest, and to promote our new name, JG had some large sticky labels printed at work, which just displayed our newly designed logo. Wherever we went, we stuck these labels all over the place – on windows, doors, walls and pavements. To cater for the smaller promoter who didn't go to the expense of advertising his club with posters, Eddie designed a full-sized poster with plain white panels at the top and bottom so that the promoter could enter the name of his club and the date of our appearance there. I particularly liked the wording 'Raving Excitement', which featured on the poster. At the base it had Eddie's agency name and telephone number.

All the colours on the poster were printed using fluorescent ink which when exposed to ultraviolet light would glow in the dark. Our name and logo from one of these new posters was cut out and stuck on the front of JG's bass drum and would glow in the dark whenever an ultraviolet light was in use. Ultraviolet lighting was one of the first lighting effects to be used in clubs, and on a dark dance floor any white on the clothing of the dancers glowed in the dark plus there was the added bonus of highlighting certain items of female underwear! Also particularly fascinating was the way that the ultraviolet light made peoples' teeth glow extremely white in the dark. On a crowded dance floor, it looked like lots of teeth moving around by themselves in the dark!

A few years later, when psychedelic music became popular, a lot of psychedelic art would be painted on walls in clubs using fluorescent paint and, combined with the ultraviolet lighting, this created some great effects.

SHOPPING FOR GEAR - AUGUST 1964

The first advertisement that Eddie placed in the Record Mirror after changing our name to The Candles listed our future bookings and also mentioned the fact that we were 'Back from hols' and 'Shopping for gear'. Gear was a trendy word used at the time to describe young fashion and often the expression 'Fab Gear' was used.

To coincide with our change of name, we decided that we needed to refresh our appearance on stage as well and so, after eighteen months of wear, our band suits were finally hung up for good. The music scene was constantly on the move and although the old band suits were dead and buried, many groups still dressed with some sort of uniformity. In their early days, The Rolling Stones wore identical black leather waistcoats, but would soon push the boundaries even further and, being non-conformists, they started to dress individually when performing. One Saturday, together with Eddie, we all travelled up to the West End of London to buy new gear at Harry Fenton's in Shaftesbury Avenue, a well known London outfitters,

We had seen Georgie Fame and The Blue Flames and The Moody Blues on TV wearing the fashionable, and distinctive, Madras cotton jackets. Even John Lennon was photographed wearing one. These jackets were becoming all the rage for young men. They were single-breasted with three buttons and, as they were unlined, extremely lightweight and easy to wear. The fabric was manufactured in Madras in India and although many patterns were available, only striped fabrics were selected for the jackets. The colours used in the manufacture of the fabric were traditionally quite muted in appearance and when the fabric was cut, the stripes ran vertically on the jacket.

The jackets we finally chose had vertical narrow block stripes in royal blue and grey, with thin royal blue stripes running through the centre of the grey ones. We selected white shirts plus light grey trousers to compliment the jacket, but still we chose to wear a tie. Old habits die hard and although we'd up-dated our appearance, a tie was still a must – but not for much longer.

So, it was farewell to Johnny Lonesome and The Travellers and hello The Candles. Our first engagement as The Candles was at the Kavern Club on 13 August and it was very exciting to see large posters around town with our new name advertising the next two forthcoming appearances at the Club. We shared the poster with John Mayall's Blues Breakers who were appearing there the week before us. Eddie always designed his own posters and so he had the name John Mayall printed in large blue large letters and below, in much smaller letters, Blues Breakers. Our name, The Candles, was depicted in bright orange letters and, being a smaller name, it meant the overall size was slightly bigger than even John Mayall's name and, most importantly, the poster could be read from a fair distance away. It was mission accomplished – sorry about that John Mayall's Blues Breakers!

Unfortunately, we were playing elsewhere on the night John Mayall's Blues Breakers were playing at the Kavern, which was a shame as I had heard a lot of good things about this group. The bass guitarist that evening was John McVie, who later joined the British blues band Fleetwood Mac and went on to worldwide fame. John Mayall's band became famous as a breeding ground for great British guitarists. In 1965 Eric Clapton joined the group after leaving The Yardbirds, but later left to form Cream. He was replaced by Peter Green who also eventually left and joined Fleetwood Mac. Peter Green became a casualty of drug taking and ended up a recluse for many years. His replacement was Mick Taylor who later joined The Rolling Stones, replacing Brian Jones who had just died.

Over the years people have asked why choose a name like The Candles and commented that they didn't particularly like the name. My response has always been, why not? Is The Beatles such a good name? Without seeing it written, why name a group after an insect? However, it was spelt differently and used the word 'beat' to emphasise the musical connection. Clever and slightly corny really, but that name didn't hold them back!

THE EAST HAM GRANADA - AUGUST 1964

Although primarily a cinema, the East Ham Granada was on the theatre circuit for touring rock 'n' roll and pop package tours, which proliferated during the early sixties. Two of the biggest names in music history appeared there – The Beatles twice in 1963 and The Rolling Stones once in 1964. Many cinemas throughout London had started introducing groups to play for half an hour during matinee performances on a Sunday.

BACKSTAGE AT THE EAST HAM GRANADA
WEARING OUR MADRAS JACKETS

Within two weeks of changing our name to The Candles, we were booked to appear at the East Ham Granada one Sunday afternoon.

We brought our equipment into the theatre and stored it in the wings ready to move it out onto the stage when the time came. It was amazing, standing in the wings and looking across at the giant screen while a film was being shown. What I hadn't realised was that a cinema's screen was perforated with tiny holes and I discovered that by looking through the little holes you could actually see about the first six rows of people staring at the screen. But they couldn't see me! We were shown into a large dressing room with a large mirror surrounded by bright light bulbs across one wall. We'd seen this sort of mirror in movies, with the star sitting at the mirror applying make-up before being called to go on stage, so this made us feel like we were really breaking into show business!

Now wearing our new Madras cotton jacket outfits, we stood in the wings as the film finished and the curtains were drawn across the stage. Cinema staff immediately lifted a wooden rostrum into position, which was our cue to start shifting our amps and other equipment onto the stage. John was handed the house microphone. This was on a long lead and allowed him to move back and forwards across the stage. After a last minute tune-up, we were ready to start and took up our positions.

WEARING OUR MADRAS JACKETS AT THE
WALTHAMSTOW ASSEMBLY HALL – SEPTEMBER 1964

The cinema manager came on stage and took the microphone off John, parted the curtains and addressed the audience. 'Ladies and gentlemen, we have for your entertainment this afternoon, The Candles.' He handed the mike back to John and we started to play as the curtains opened. Immediately there was a problem. I could hardly hear John singing and the others were struggling to hear him as well. Even John was having a bit of a problem hearing his own voice – we were simply drowning out the vocals. The problem was that the in-house vocal sound system speakers were set into the sidewalls of the theatre area. Nowadays this problem is resolved by using stage monitor speakers, which are relatively small wedge-shaped speakers that are positioned at the front of the stage and which direct the mixed sound of the singer and group to the performers. Alternatively, the singers can have in-ear units fitted, which are wireless driven and again, the mixed sound of the band is relayed back to the singer.

John got around his problem by using the long microphone lead, which allowed him to walk nonchalantly to the front of the stage where he could hear himself in the theatre. The rest of us had to improvise, at times lip-reading if possible while John sang. At least when it came to a guitar or sax solo, John turned to the respective person and nodded, whereas JG could hardly hear John at all, but took the cue from me to end the song when I raised my guitar up and brought it down on the final beat.

I'm not sure how the 60s package tour groups coped with this sound issue, but we had never been faced with this problem before, so it was all a new experience for us.

But it wasn't long before the Madras jackets were also discarded and we went on stage wearing our own individual casual clothing. And that's how it remained until we called it a day in the summer of 1967.

BANKING – STILL HANGING IN THERE!

I was transferred to the Westminster Bank's East Ham branch during the summer of 1964. This was not in any way a promotion, simply replacing a cashier who had retired. By now I was just going through the motions of everyday banking and, with my busy evening activities, I just didn't have time to consider looking for another job. The group for me was all encompassing and had really taken over my life. I loved it, but going to work in the same office day in and day out was something I really hated. Because I had my own car, an opportunity arose to become a relief cashier, which I grabbed with both hands.

Although I was based at the East Ham branch, I could be summoned to go to any branch in and around east London. This suited me down to the ground as it got me out of the normal banking routine, which I rebelled against, and allowed me to meet new people, which I enjoyed. It also took me into new areas of London where I hadn't been before and the bank even covered my out-of-pocket expenses.

DRESSED TO KILL IN OUR MOD GEAR

BURNING THE CANDLE AT BOTH ENDS

This old saying is very apt for us considering what would be our new name and also the fact that we were literally burning ourselves out, working full-time jobs during the day and then performing as a group in the evenings four to five times a week. 1961 was the start of the group playing locally and in that year we performed live at youth clubs and schools 17 times. By contrast, in 1962, when we became mobile with our own van, we suddenly reached lift-off, performing live 88 times. In 1963, it rose to 133 performances.

When I was still working at the Stratford branch of the Westminster Bank, the sustained late nights began to take their toll on the group. I was the first to suffer the consequences and was diagnosed with a suspected stomach ulcer brought on by erratic eating habits. Martin and Patrick were both treated for bronchitis, Dave ended up having pleurisy, and JG suffered from lumbago. We were all treated for our ailments and recovered completely, but John was the last to drop – literally. He collapsed with quinsy, a severe throat disorder, and had to go into hospital to have his tonsils removed.

Our manager, Eddie, seized this opportunity to get some extra publicity for the group and the Romford Times was dispatched to John's hospital bedside. A photograph was taken showing him in bed pouring a glass of champagne for one of the nurses. The photograph and an article appeared a few days later in the paper under the heading 'Johnny's Not Lonesome'. The article also mentioned that the group would shortly be changing their name to The Candles. So, while John was recuperating from his operation, the rest of the group took advantage of the break and went on holiday. We returned to find John in good health with his strong singing voice still intact, even though his tonsils had been removed. With all our batteries recharged and all recovered from our various ailments, we were now ready to return to battle.

22

FOR BETTER FOR WORSE

We had performed at quite a few wedding receptions in the East End of London and all had passed without incident until one Saturday evening in 1964. A regular customer from the Bridge House pub in Canning Town had asked us to play at his wedding reception.

The reception was being held in a small community hall in Canning Town and when we arrived, the guests had already made their way from the church and drinks were flowing. Chairs had been positioned along each side of the hall and the bride's family sat along one side with the bridegroom's family facing them on the other side. There was no stage as such and we had to set up our gear on the floor at the far end of the hall.

As the evening progressed, I found it fascinating to watch the guests while we played. I could see certain members from both families slowly and surely getting pissed. As the drink flowed, the talking and the laughter got louder, forcing us to increase the volume – and still the two families sat facing one another, keeping very much to themselves. For me, the whole atmosphere was not dissimilar to playing in an East End pub.

We had just started into our second slow song and I was watching the bridegroom drinking and chatting in the corner with a bunch of mates. The thought crossed my mind that if he didn't slow down on the drinking, he certainly wouldn't be in any fit state to perform his conjugal rights later that night! Then it all happened very quickly. He put down his drink and staggered over to a woman who was sitting down talking to some friends. Next minute, they were on the floor, dancing and smooching together and I could see trouble ahead. I spotted the bride, resplendent in her white wedding dress, deep in conversation with some guests. Suddenly she spotted them. In a flash, she ran across the floor and started screaming obscenities at the woman. She then grabbed her by her hair and they fell to the floor, exchanging blows. Immediately people rushed over to try and separate them. Some men in the bride's family were now up on their feet and started hurling abuse across the hall about the morality of the bridegroom. That, of course, angered the bridegroom's relatives and a number of men responded with rude comments about the bride.

I remember seeing a beer glass arching across the hall and exploding against the wall. Suddenly the hall erupted – it was every man for himself. We just kept playing, as we knew from past experience performing in East End pubs, that if we stopped we could become the next target. Punches were being thrown everywhere, male against male and female against female. Two men quite near to us were grappling away and getting dangerously close to where we were performing, when suddenly they both fell across the drum kit. JG was knocked off his stool, drums and cymbals rolled across the floor and we were forced to stop playing. As the men continued fighting and rolling on the floor, we took evasive action, quickly moving amplifiers and mike stands back to avoid any damage.

By now the bride was standing in the middle of the hall, crying her eyes out, being consoled by her new husband, who had sobered up very quickly and was apologising profusely. Suddenly, the doors to the hall swung open and two policemen came rushing in blowing whistles. The hostilities quickly stopped and within minutes of talking to both groups, peace reigned in the hall once more. After assurances from both sides that the trouble was over, the police left and the best man came over and asked us to continue playing. Some people started to leave, but for the rest of the evening there were no more incidents, although the atmosphere was pretty tense – what a start to married life!

ROAD RAGE – 1964 STYLE

A few months later we found ourselves heading back into the wilds of the East End of London to play at another wedding, this time being held in a church hall in Stepney Green. Fortunately for all concerned, this wedding reception was a very happy affair, as weddings should be, and although the alcohol flowed all evening everyone remained in good spirits, with plenty of dancing and laughter. The best man paid us at the end of the evening and we packed up our equipment and headed off home for a reasonably early night, oblivious to what lay ahead.

Up front in the van, Dave was driving and Martin sat in the passenger seat. The rest of us were lounging in the back of the van on the bench seat. Although it was quite late, it was a Saturday night and the roads were still busy as we crossed the wide bridge that dropped down into Canning Town. We were chatting away in the back of the van, when we suddenly swerved, and the driver of a car behind us kept his hand on the horn for a few seconds. Apparently Dave must have accidentally cut somebody up as the road narrowed from three to two lanes on the approach to a set of traffic lights.

As we sat waiting for the lights to turn to green, Dave looked in his mirror and saw that the driver of the car behind had got out and was walking towards us. Dave locked his door and just as this rather large gentleman got near the van, the lights turned green and we accelerated away leaving him standing in the road in a cloud of exhaust fumes. As we pulled up at the next set of traffic lights, the car had caught us up and was now level with us on the inside lane. He wound down his window and was mouthing off, when Martin pulled down his window and told the guy in no uncertain terms to get lost.

The lights changed and we were off again, but this was the A124, a long road leading out of London, and the road was full of traffic lights. By now we were travelling through Plaistow and we were all getting quite anxious as the car, identified by Martin as an Aston Martin DB9, was sitting on our tail. This time we pulled up at traffic lights on the inside lane and the Aston Martin screeched to a halt alongside us in the outside lane. Immediately, this big guy got out of his car and and instead of coming to the driver's door which we had all expected, this time he walked around the front of the van, obviously wanting to have words with Martin.

He was extremely tall, so tall in fact that, as he marched past in front of the van, we could only see his body and his head was above the top of our windscreen. Our van was quite high off the ground and you had to climb into the cab to drive the vehicle, so this guy was BIG. Martin quickly locked the door just as he gripped the door handle of the van and tried to open it. Martin yelled out 'There's six of us in here!' Unfortunately that didn't have the desired effect. He yelled back 'I'll take you all on!' Luckily the lights turned to green and, as we accelerated away, we could hear him swearing at us. Looking out of the back window, I could see he was standing in the middle of the road, nursing his right hand, and shaking his fist at us. I reckoned from his reaction, that his hand must have still been holding the door handle when Dave accelerated away. Somebody in the van said 'Oh shit, now were in trouble.'

However, there were six of us and only one of him, so what was the problem? Surely between us we could tackle him. Martin must have been getting extremely worried by now and regretting shouting at him as this big guy was obviously after him. We managed to cross three sets of green lights, but still the Aston Martin sat on our tail. What were we going to do – we had to have a plan of action. We all agreed that this guy must be as hard as nails as he would have seen all of our faces at the windows and calculated that inside the van were about five or six young men. But that certainly didn't appear to deter him at all!

A thought crossed my mind and I decided to share it with everyone. 'Perhaps he's a gangster and works for the Krays (the Kray Twins were notorious East End gangsters at the time). Actually, when you come to think of it, we've just played at a wedding in Stepney Green and that's not far from Bethnal Green where they operate from.' From the expressions on most faces, I could sense that my comments weren't going down particularly well! 'Aren't you getting carried away a bit' said John. 'OK' I said, 'Let's face it, not many people in the East End of London own an expensive Aston Martin. The guy's huge and seems quite prepared to take us all on.' And then it suddenly occurred to me, 'Perhaps he's totally fearless because he packs a gun and is prepared to use it.' I was beginning to scare myself now. John tried to put on a brave face but the nervous laughter that followed confirmed that my comments had worried him and everyone else.

John suggested that we just keep driving around, hoping the guy would eventually lose interest and leave us alone. We turned a corner, coming into Barking, and there ahead were traffic lights, just turning to red, and still we didn't have a plan of action. We sat there silently at the lights with our hearts in our mouths. The car was directly behind us, but the guy wasn't getting out this time around. We moved off again with the Aston Martin inches from our back bumper. With John's suggestion in mind, we started to extend our journey to Dagenham, driving down roads we knew with roundabouts rather than traffic lights. Dave pointed out that we only had less than a quarter of a tank of petrol remaining, but we definitely didn't fancy stopping at a garage to fill up with fuel!

We started to realise that we may have to come face to face with this guy after all but a mass exit by four of us through the back doors of the van would be hindered as the group equipment was piled so high. We could only get out of the van slowly, one at a time, via the small side door, which was just back from where Martin was sitting in the passenger seat. Conceivably, this guy could wait by the side door, knock us out one by one, or shoot us one by one, as we exited, and still get Martin when he tried to get out of the van! Dave, being the driver, possibly had the best chance of escape – if he was lucky. How could we defend ourselves? JG suggested 'We could use the mike stands and the heavy iron bases.' These were close at hand, but still the most important question had to be answered, who would exit the side door first? Then John made a suggestion. 'Suppose we brake suddenly and catch him by surprise. That might give a chance for all four of us to get out.' I then suggested that we should toss a coin to determine the order of exit, as I didn't fancy being the first one out.

Someone then came up with the thought that if we stopped suddenly, without any warning, the guy was likely to crash into the back of the van. We could only imagine his reaction if he damaged his lovely car. All this time, Martin had been sitting quietly in the front, no doubt contemplating his predicament, Suddenly he spoke out. 'I think we should just stop the van and all make a quick getaway.' It was then pointed out that this guy would then be free to damage or take our equipment, or even to torch the van. Not a good idea Martin!

The seriousness of our situation was beginning to sink in. In desperation I blurted out 'I think we are just going to have to take our chances when the occasion arises. If we pull over and exit the van as quickly as possible, that should give us some advantage, and if the six of us confront him with mike stands in our hands, he's bound to back off.' 'But what if he pulls a gun on us?' said John. The silence said it all. We continued along the Barking Road, with no real solution at hand. I looked over my shoulder and still the car was sitting on our tail. This guy was certainly playing mind games with us and just biding his time. He must know we were spooked.

It was almost an hour since we had cut this guy up in Canning Town. He was obviously extremely determined and was not going to give up. We continued driving along familiar roads on the outskirts of Dagenham, with our petrol gauge showing close to empty. We had been in this situation before but not with a maniac on our tail! 'How much petrol is left in the tank when the gauge is on empty?' I asked Patrick. 'Probably enough for about ten miles' he responded. Then Dave came up with the near perfect solution. 'Why don't we drive to Dagenham police station and park right outside! Surely this guy isn't going to want to cause a scene there and risk getting arrested.' 'That's it, well done Dave, you're a genius!' I said excitedly. Finally, we had a plausible solution and hopefully with a non-violent ending. We all agreed it was the best option and so we headed for the local police station.

The petrol gauge needle was now resting on empty. 'How far is the police station from here Dave? asked Martin. 'About a couple of miles I reckon' was the reply. This was nail-biting stuff and for the next few miles nobody spoke. I checked again and, yes, he was still following us. As we turned into Rainham Road South, Dave broke the silence. 'It's further down this road somewhere on the right-hand side.' We all peered anxiously ahead trying to identify a police station as we passed the various shops and houses. Suddenly there it was, the familiar blue light and, as we got closer, we could read the single word in white 'Police'. We'd made it! Dave indicated and swung the van over to the other side of the road, pulling up sharply outside the steps leading up the main entrance. We all looked back anxiously. We had made our move, now it was up to him.

The Aston Martin had stopped on the other side of the road with its engine ticking over and headlights ablaze. No doubt the driver was contemplating his next move. The car remained motionless for a while and we all sat there silently wondering what he was going to do. Then, very slowly, the car performed a U-turn and accelerated off. The relief inside the van was palpable. We unanimously agreed to stay parked outside the police station for a while, just in case he came back. Or perhaps he had cunningly circled around and was waiting for us further down the road. Paranoia had well and truly set in.

We desperately needed to get some petrol but to find a petrol station open at 1.30am in the morning wasn't going to be easy – this was the 60s. The only petrol stations open 24 hours a day were to be found on the few new motorways and dual carriageways. Remaining where we were at the moment at least gave us some sort of police protection, but once we drove off, we became highly vulnerable again. Besides not knowing if this nutter in the Aston Martin was waiting for us somewhere close by, we simply didn't know how far our meagre petrol supply would take us. Then I had the bright idea of asking in the police station where the nearest garage was and, much to my relief, was told there was a garage open about 2 miles away.

The officer on duty gave me directions to the garage and then took great delight in lecturing mc about always making sure, when travelling late at night, that you have sufficient petrol in your tank. He said how lucky I was because this particular garage was the only one open at that time of night for miles around. Apparently it remained open at all times to cater for the comings and goings of the shift workers employed at the gigantic Ford Motor Company production plant nearby. I did contemplate telling him what we had just gone through, but thought better of it.

I raced down the steps and climbed into the van. 'Our luck's in boys – there's a garage open a couple of miles away.' Everyone cheered, basically relieved that we must be close to getting out of this mess, and would also hopefully be climbing into bed very soon. Dave started the engine and we drove off slowly as I gave Dave the directions, fully aware that we had to conserve as much petrol as possible. We realised that we weren't completely out of the shit yet and it remained pretty low key in the van as we drove along. Suddenly Dave yelled out, 'There it is' and ahead of us we could make out the familiar illuminated Esso sign, shining brightly in the sky. Everyone cheered. As Dave got out and began putting some petrol in the van, we sat there quietly looking around in all directions, wondering if the Aston Martin would suddenly appear.

Dave climbed back in the van and we drove off. But still we were edgy – this guy had really unnerved us. We looked up every side street we passed and kept glancing out of the rear window. Slowly but surely we all came to the conclusion that the guy must have given up on us and we started to relax. It wasn't long before we'd dropped everybody off and Martin and I were able to park the van. We quietly said our goodbyes.

It was now 2.30am and as I walked down an unlit road to my parent's bungalow, I contemplated our lucky escape and how close we had come to a possible bloody confrontation. Although the street was dark, as I approached the bungalow I could just make out my cat Spud, sitting on the low wall, waiting for me as usual. As I turned the key of the door, I could feel him rubbing his body against my legs. Was he really just pleased to see me or was it because he knew I'd feed him before going to bed!

REHEARSAL TIME

When the group first started to perform at Pettits Lane School Youth Club on a Thursday evening, we had approached the school secretary, as we needed somewhere to rehearse. We were kindly allotted an empty classroom, which we could use every Tuesday evening. It wasn't an ideal situation as people attending night school classes could hear us playing and, out of curiosity, would come and check us out. With people constantly peering into the classroom, it was a distraction for us, especially if they were young females!

We didn't really have an alternative choice in those early days, but as soon as we had our own van and became mobile, Patrick found the ideal place for us, not far from his home. A collection of huts in varying sizes had been erected at the rear of an old fire station and could be hired out from Dagenham Borough Council for regular use. So we entered into a contract and hired hut number five on an annual basis. It had its own power, water supply and heating during the winter months. It was perfect for our needs and we could rehearse in total seclusion and not worry about disturbing other people. There was a local cub meeting every Tuesday in a much larger hut, but it was a fair distance away and we never received any complaints during our five-year tenure.

We had found from experience that simply turning up at a rehearsal evening without any basic ideas of what we wanted to learn was generally a waste of time. We often discussed what song or songs we wanted to learn at the next rehearsal, or while we travelled to and from gigs. It then became my task to buy the record and, where possible, the sheet music of the song we wanted to learn. This was always transcribed for a piano, but it provided the words, the correct key and also the piano bass lines, which helped Martin to work out his bass guitar requirements.

As the lead guitarist, I needed the record as I had to work out in advance any lead guitar parts and solos of the particular song we wanted to learn. On occasions it was quite easy to copy a guitar piece but, with a complicated solo, it had to be painstakingly learnt by playing the record over and over again and slowly picking out the notes until the solo was perfect.

It would take a few years before the music publishers started to offer sheet music specifically transcribed for the guitar. Besides the musical notation, it listed the individual letter of each chord and eventually progressed to actually printing a small illustration of the fretboard with dots indicating the finger formation of each chord. This was designed to assist the aspiring guitarist who didn't read music. In the meantime, I had to make do with listening to the record!

We always took along a portable record player to rehearsals, which enabled us to sit down and play the record a few times to familiarise ourselves, not only with the melody and the construction of the song, but also with our own individual parts. If I hadn't been able to find the sheet music, then John would continue to play the record over and over again, writing down the words. Patrick and I would get together to try and work out the final chords we had to play, sometimes with the help of Dave via his sax. I would try out any lead guitar parts I had worked out and Martin would work out his bass riff, sometimes by playing a 45 rpm record at the faster speed of 78 rpm which, for some reason, highlighted the bass riffs, albeit at a faster speed. When we were all satisfied that we had a good idea of our individual parts, we would have a trial run of the song. Bit by bit, the song slowly took shape and, where necessary, we'd go back over each section until it was correct. We'd continue until we were all happy and if sufficiently confident with our arrangement, only then would it be premiered at our next live performance, which in most cases could be within a couple of days. A particular evening springs to mind for me, when we decided to premier a song we'd rehearsed the previous Tuesday.

THE DUKE'S HEAD - EAST HAM - SUNDAY OCTOBER 1964

I can distinctly remember a moment of near disaster when we came to play this particular song live for the first time. We'd rehearsed the latest hit record hit by The Kinks called 'Till The End of the Day' and, although overall we were pretty pleased with our interpretation of this song, I wasn't entirely happy with my guitar solo. I promised myself I'd perfect it at home and had persevered with the solo until I was happy I could play it live. It was pretty rare not to have an opportunity of premiering any new song within a couple of days as Thursdays was usually when we performed at various school youth clubs. But on this particular occasion, we had to wait five days before our next booking and the opportunity of performing the song for the first time.

We were booked to play for the first time in a very popular venue in East Ham, which was held in a ballroom above the Duke's Head public house. We arrived on the night to find we had to perform on an extremely small stage and shared the cramped conditions with an upright piano. Huddled together, we had hardly any room to move as most of the free space was taken up with JG's drum kit and our various amplifiers and mike stands. Before we went on stage to play, the main lights in the ballroom had been switched off and a revolving mirror ball hanging from the ceiling provided the only lighting. For the group, the only light we had on stage came from a small table lamp housing a low wattage light bulb.

All evening I struggled to see what I was playing on the guitar because although the lamp was behind me and only a few feet away on top of the piano, my body was blocking out its direct light. As the penultimate song ended, we decided to finish on the latest song we had learned last Tuesday. John turned to the mike and announced 'Well folks, that's it for tonight. We'd like to finish by playing 'Till The End of the Day', the latest hit from The Kinks.' Looking around and making sure everybody was ready, I counted us in 'one, two, three, four' and, in unison, we started with the four-chord introduction. Then John started singing and we were off and running.

We were into the first few bars of the song when suddenly I thought, I can't remember the guitar solo I'd practised that morning! I started to panic. John was singing the last line that led into the solo, when suddenly it went dark on the stage. I heard someone curse 'The bloody bulb's blown.' I attempted to carry on, but looking down at the fretboard, all I could make out was a dark thin oblong shape and not a fret in sight. I launched into an improvised solo, but instantly I could hear I was playing in totally the wrong key! In a panic, I took a chance and moved my fingers up the fretboard. It now sounded even worse! I kept moving the guitar around hoping that a chink of light from the mirror ball might just illuminate my fretboard, but no such luck.

Martin was having similar problems in the dark and so was JG, who was just about keeping the rhythm together. But even he started to falter when he heard my disastrous solo. John just wasn't able to carry on singing and I gave up. One by one, the others followed suit until we ground to a halt. If only the promoter had just left us in darkness, we could have scurried off back to the dressing room. But no. Suddenly all the lights came on in the ballroom!

I felt such an idiot. John turned to me and with his usual wit said 'I dread to think what that solo would have sounded like if you hadn't practiced it this morning.' All I could say in response was 'Get stuffed' and his final quip was 'I hope so.' The rest of the band were looking at me with big grins on their faces, which then turned into great howls of laughter. Fortunately we'd played a good set and members of the audience also saw the funny side and were laughing with us. That helped me unwind a bit and I started to smile as well. 'Bloody light bulb' I managed to blurt out. But I never did confess to anyone that I'd actually completely forgotten the guitar solo that night!

THE LORAIN CLUB – OCTOBER 1964

Over the past 12 months we'd been performing regularly at the Lorain Club, located in the Royal Forest Hotel, Chingford and situated just on the edge of Epping Forest. We all enjoyed playing there because the club had a great a atmosphere and over the past year we had built up a good steady following of supporters. Our growing popularity meant regular appearances at the club, which was good for us, and good for the management.

The night before we played at the Club Noreik supporting the then unknown Tom Jones, we'd arrived at the Lorain Club an hour before opening time, and already a long queue of people had formed, waiting to gain entry. Apparently many club-goers were turned away each week as the club reached its capacity. But knowing Eddie Caswell, who ran the club, he would take a chance and squeeze in quite a few more bodies before shutting the doors. Eddie the promoter was a really nice guy who would eventually become our group manager, and a close lifelong friend.

23

SUPPORTING TOM JONES AND THE PLAYBOYS - OCTOBER 1964

In 1964 I was working as a cashier at the Westminster Bank in East Ham. During quiet moments in the bank, I would daydream that one day stardom would beckon and whisk me away to a better life. Basically, I knew that I didn't want to spend the rest of my life working every day in a high street bank, but the problem was that I didn't know what I really wanted to do. Deep down, I suppose I hoped the group would be my meal ticket out of this dilemma, but realistically the odds of making it were a million to one.

At times like this, I would complain about the job to my dad and he would say 'Stick at it lad, you'll eventually get used to it. Don't forget, it's a secure job for life, with a good pension at the end.' I used to think to myself, my God, retiring at 60 meant I had another 40 years ahead of me before I was free from the bank and could get my hands on that pension! I looked up to my father. He had experienced a jobless existence for months on end during the depression years of the 1930s, so he was happy with the thought that his son was in a very secure job for life. I used to console myself by telling friends that I was simply biding my time, learning how to count and control large sums of money, ready for the day when it would be my money I was counting! To this day, I am convinced that my dalliance with the Mods and Rockers and my subsequent court appearance back in 1961, had put paid to any long-term banking career.

This was fine by me. Besides the police, the bank had also marked my card, so at some stage it would be farewell.

The telephone rang and somebody called out 'A call for Colin.' I turned my till sign around to Till Closed and made my way to a small telephone booth at the back of the branch. Picking up the telephone, I recognised the voice. It was Gary at Galaxy Entertainments and he wanted to know if we were available on Saturday 10 October. I always carried a small diary in my pocket for such an event and was able to tell him there and then that we were free on that night. He told me it was at the Club Noreik, Tottenham, with a start time of 11.30 pm and two one-hour sets. I put the telephone down and quickly jotted the booking into my diary.

Receiving calls like this was now becoming quite routine – the more we worked with various London entertainment agencies, the more they needed to be able to contact me during normal working office hours, to confirm bookings.

It was now Friday morning, 9 October, and nothing ever changes. Once again I was running late for work. As I rushed into Romford station, an announcement came over the Tannoy system 'The train now standing at platform three is the all-stations to Liverpool Street.' Oh shit, I thought, if I can just catch this train, I might make it into work on time. I broke into a run and quickly flashing my weekly season ticket at the ticket inspector, I dashed through the barrier and made my way up the stairs, two steps at a time. As I ran onto the empty platform, the guard blew his whistle and I heard that familiar hiss as the doors started to close. Without slowing down, I leapt onto the train just as the doors closed automatically behind me. One or two newspapers were lowered briefly to see what the noise was all about and then with a jolt, the train started on its journey.

I was breathing heavily as I glanced around the carriage. Well, well, wonders will never cease – there was one empty seat, which I quickly occupied. I sat there quietly for a moment, catching my breath – now I could relax. Being a Friday morning, in my hands was a fresh copy of the

NME, the New Musical Express, which was a national weekly music paper. First things first, I had to know who we were supporting tomorrow night at the Club Noreik. I opened the paper at the classified section and scoured the columns. Nothing, no ad, which meant most probably that it was just us and the in-house DJ supplying the music. If we were supporting a named act, then the Club Noreik would have advertised the fact. Shame, so no star acts to support this time around.

I had my little routines and next I turned to the inside page as I liked to scan the charts. Herman's Hermits were still riding high at the top of the singles chart with 'I'm Into Something Good' and The Beatles' LP, 'A Hard Day's Night', was still topping the album chart. Towards the end of July, both The Beatles' single of the same name, and the album, were top of the respective British charts. That was an achievement in itself. However, as if that wasn't enough, during the first two weeks in August, The Beatles were still top of the singles and LP charts in the UK and were also top of both charts in the USA! It remained that way for two consecutive weeks. This was simply unbelievable! Never before had a British group had such success in the US – the Americans were certainly taking a bashing – and I simply revelled in it.

Although soon to lose the number one position in both singles charts in both countries, the album remained at the top of the album charts right up to near the end of October, when it lost its top spot in the States. However, it continued to remain at the top of the British album charts right into early December. 'A Hard Day's Night' had topped the UK album charts for 21 weeks, which was record-breaking stuff. It was finally knocked off the top in early December 1964 when their follow-up album 'Beatles For Sale' was released. This went straight to the number one album spot, all quite routine for the Beatles no doubt, but very exciting for me – these were heady times indeed.

WE MEET TOM JONES

Saturday evening I left home early, guitar in hand, contemplating another gruelling night of rock 'n' roll ahead as we had been booked for two consecutive sessions that night.

The first was at the Double D Club in Hackney, North London from 7.30pm to 11.00pm, doing the usual two one-hour spots. The only trouble with this club was that it was above a row of shops in Hackney High Street, which meant having to haul our gear up a few flights of stairs – always a pain. However, the good news was that it was only four miles away from the Club Noreik, so we shouldn't have any trouble getting there for around 11.30pm.

We drove away from the Double D Club after an uneventful evening and, as we turned into the Seven Sisters Road and approached the Club Noreik's entrance, I could see a poster on the wall announcing 'Saturday 10 October Tom Jones and The Playboys plus The Candles'. Pulling up outside the double fire exit doors at the side of the club, someone in the back of the van yelled out 'Who the hell are Tom Jones and The Playboys?' 'Never heard of them' came the response.

The fire doors were opened and we started to unload the van, taking in our equipment, up the wooden stairs and straight on to the stage. Once the gear was set up, we carried out a quick sound test and then retired to the dressing room to don our stage gear. In the meantime, the DJ pumped out a selection of soul numbers at the usual high volume. We kicked off our set at 1.00pm. Within minutes, the fire doors opened and the mystery band arrived and started to pile their gear up at the side of the stage.

We were about 20 minutes into our set when I couldn't help but notice a slightly older guy behaving rather oddly. One minute he was standing at the front of the stage listening to us, and the next he was darting up to one of our vocal speakers and appeared to be listening to John's vocals. I then spotted him standing at the back of the hall and again he appeared to be listening to us, then the next minute he was standing once more at the front of the stage. The stage lights caught his face and I could make out his features. I knew that face, but I couldn't place him. Suddenly it came to me – he was a member of the group, The Viscounts, that we had supported at the Leyton Baths a year or so back. Now what was he doing here and what was he up to?

As I stood there playing my guitar, I couldn't help but think that maybe he was here to watch us. Perhaps he was a scout for a record company or a music agency! When the song finished, I excitedly moved across to the other members of the group to tell them who I'd had spotted in the audience and suggested we put a bit more life into our rather lethargic stage act, just in case he'd come to see us. Throughout the remainder of our set, we really pulled out all the stops, but only once did I spot the guy again.

Our hour was up and the DJ started to play his customary soul music, which was a signal for us to start removing our equipment from the stage to allow the other group to start setting up their gear. When we'd finished, we made our way to the bar at the back of the club, ready to listen to Tom Jones and The Playboys. JG told us he'd spoken with their drummer who said that they had travelled up from Wales for the gig. That was all we knew about this group. There was still no further sign of the guy from The Viscounts – what was that all about?

The Playboys walked onto the stage wearing yellow frill-fronted shirts with black string bow ties and black trousers. The singer, Tom Jones, wore the same outfit, but the shirt was white and his appearance vaguely reminded me of P.J. Proby, an American singer, who had hit the charts earlier in the year. They all looked slightly old-fashioned, with swept back hairstyles, so when they opened with 'Whole Lotta Shakin' Going On', an old rock number, I wasn't surprised.

John was the first to pass comment when the first song finished. 'My God, can that guy sing – what a voice! You watch when he sings, his voice is so powerful, he holds the microphone well back from his mouth.' John had a trained voice, so if he was impressed, so were we.

As they continued, we all agreed that The Playboys were an average band, but that singer – wow, he was good! He had a deep, slightly operatic-sounding voice, very strong and resonant. The group played loud, but the singer's voice just bounced off the four walls of the Club Noreik. This guy was from Wales and the Welsh miners' choirs were noted for their powerful voices. It was more than just a loud rock 'n' roll voice, it was very controlled, and it was certainly very different.

It was while we were back on stage setting up our gear again, that Martin and I briefly got into conversation with Tom Jones. He told us that they had travelled up from Wales during the day and that they were shortly going to drive back as they couldn't afford accommodation in London. 'We've done so many auditions recently, and not getting paid for them. It's all a bit of a rip off. All they gave us tonight was ten shillings (50p) to cover our petrol costs. If nothing comes of this audition, I'm certainly not doing any more – we'll just play locally in Wales. I bet you're getting paid for tonight's performance.' Neither of us responded. We didn't want him to know that we were being paid £20 for tonight's work. But to try and make him feel a bit better, I did go on to explain that we had done our fair share of auditions, providing the promoters with free music for the evening. I added that sometimes it pays off – an understatement considering what lay ahead for him!

Just before playing our second set, Martin and I wandered into the small dressing room we shared with Tom Jones and The Playboys. There, huddled together in the far corner and talking in hushed tones, was Tom Jones and the guy from The Viscounts. They looked at us momentarily, nodded, and then continued with their conversation. It seemed strange there was no sign of the rest of the group. They continued their conversation while Martin and I sat there having a last cigarette before going back on stage again. As we got up to leave, I glanced across and Tom Jones was putting his signature on a printed document, which was balanced on his knee.

We were about ten minutes into our last set, when I heard somebody shouting to us from the side of the stage. Looking around, there was Tom Jones standing at the bottom of the steps wearing a black leather jacket with a scarf wrapped around his neck. He smiled and raised his arm to give us a cheery wave. We waved back and then he was gone. As we started our next song, I thought to myself 'Oh well, obviously the guy from The Viscounts wasn't interested in us after all' and never gave it another thought.

It was just after six-thirty in the morning when we wearily loaded our gear into the van. Before driving off, I did my usual, and went up and removed the promotional poster from the wall and put it on top of the amps in the van. I had it framed years later and it hangs on a wall in my home today.

FOOTNOTE:

A bit of rock history had taken place during the early hours of that morning as I sat there with Martin in the confines of the small dressing room at the Club Noreik. Tom Jones and the guy from The Viscounts had been deep in conversation and then Tom Jones was handed a sheet of paper, which he signed. I often wonder, was he was signing a contract, or just signing a receipt confirming that he had been paid ten shillings for petrol expenses!

It couldn't just be a coincidence that four weeks later, on 11 November 1964, Tom Jones went into the Decca Recording Studio in West Hampstead to record a couple of songs. The A-side of this forthcoming single release was 'It's Not Unusual' and it was released in the UK during January 1965. By early March it was at number one in the British charts.

Released in the US in March, by early April it had peaked at number ten in the American charts and had also entered other charts around the world. Tom Jones' career had gone into orbit!

That guy from The Viscounts was Gordon Mills. He had co-written 'It's Not Unusual' and became Tom Jones' manager. His career also went onto even bigger things when he ended up managing two other highly successful singers, namely Engelbert Humperdinck and Gilbert O'Sulli-van. However, his relationship with Gilbert O'Sullivan didn't last as, following a contractual dispute between the two men, the court awarded in O'Sullivan's favour the reputed sum of seven million pounds.

Tom Jones went on to have an enormously successful worldwide career and he is still performing around the world today (2015). With numerous number ones, and selling over 100 million records worldwide, in 1999 he was awarded an OBE, and in 2006 he was knighted by the Queen in recognition for his services to the music industry. Arise Sir Tom Jones! Who would have thought that, back in October 1964 when we received £20 for our performance, Tom Jones only received the equivalent of 50p!

A few years ago I approached the online UK branch of the Tom Jones Fan Club website with a view to selling the poster. They suggested I contacted the USA branch of the Fan Club, who in turn put me in touch with Tom's US agent in San Diego. I was asked to forward a copy of the poster, which aroused interest, but we couldn't agree on a price.

24

SUPPORTING THE MERSEYBEATS – NOVEMBER 1964

Eddie's original aim, when he started the Kavern Club in February 1964, was to slowly introduce some of the emerging professional rhythm and blues groups and so take advantage of the rising popularity of this 'new' music genre. Unfortunately, although many of these groups were booked to appear there, they just didn't have the pulling power that Eddie expected, and needed, to cover his costs.

So it came as a bit of a surprise when, on one of my frequent visits to Eddie's office during my lunchtime break, he announced that he'd just that morning booked The Merseybeats to appear at the Kavern Club and he wanted us to support them to give us greater exposure. This was a bold move by Eddie, and a bit of a gamble booking a 'chart' band that would command a high guaranteed fee, but extremely good kudos for the club and hopefully it would bring in more people. If it was successful, then he would book more bands of this calibre and we'd be supporting them.

For us, it would be the first time we had played with a 'famous' Liverpool band and I was pretty excited at the prospect. They'd had two single releases in 1963 and both had gone into the charts. The second release called 'I Think of You' went on to sell over a million records, earning them a Gold Disc. During 1964 they had a further two top 20 hits and an EP was released in March called 'On Stage'. This was followed

by an LP release in June, simply titled 'The Mersey-beats' and again, both went into the respective charts. When we came to support them in November of that year, they were still a 'big' band.

As we drove into the East End of London that Thursday evening we were all curious about what lay ahead – what would this group be like? We'd all listened to their records many times, but how good would they sound live? And would they be friendly towards us, or play the 'star' role.

We were on stage first and were carrying out a sound check, when the group arrived accompanied by screams from fans outside the club. They were quickly ushered into a stockroom close to the entrance. Two roadies appeared carrying some of their gear and proceeded to stack the equipment next to the stage. In the meantime, we went off to change and Eddie suggested we use the stockroom together with The Merseybeats. Normally we would quickly dash into the gents to change, but tonight was different. Already there was a large audience waiting outside and shortly the loo would be busier than usual.

Knocking on the door, we gingerly entered the long room, which was filled with folding chairs. Towards the back of the room was a large table and around it sat the group, each with a girl on their lap. Nobody bothered to look up but I suppose, when you're engrossed in such important matters, why would you!

We kept close to the door and moved some chairs around as quietly as we could so not to disturb the goings-on at the back of the room. However, I don't think they were even aware of our presence. It was a bit embarrassing, having to change our trousers with four females present in the room, but nobody was taking any notice. Suddenly the group dismissed the four girls and they hurriedly made their way past us, giggling away as they went out of the room. I looked down the room, hoping to catch the group's attention, really just to acknowledge them, but they were huddled up together, talking and laughing and lighting up cigarettes. Suddenly the door opened and a voice called out 'I've got another four girls out here. Are you ready?' and a voice from the back answered 'Yes, send them in.' In walked another four young girls, who glanced at us as they made their way to the back of the room and, after a few mutterings and giggles, the group started again with their fun.

It was difficult not to sneak a glance towards the back of the room, but they were all huddled together and we couldn't see very much so, apart from the odd giggle and bursts of laughter, it was rather left to the imagination what was going on. We weren't particularly surprised – it was more the fact that they just carried on in our presence as though we were totally invisible. We finished changing, quietly left the room and headed for the stage. We had to push our way through to the front as already a large crowd had gathered, eager to get the best viewing position before The Merseybeats came on stage. We'd played at the club many times and fortunately we had our own local following, so after each number we received a good response. Every so often, I couldn't help thinking about the scene in the stockroom and wondered how many more girls had been led into that room after we'd left!

We finished our last song to thunderous applause and immediately started to move our gear to the back of the stage and allow the roadies to start setting up The Merseybeats' equipment. Ten minutes or so later, and after a few 'one, two, three testing, testing' into the microphones, the gear was finally set up and the two roadies left the stage. I wanted to watch and listen to this band, so I remained close to the front of the stage, which by now was mobbed with people, mainly young girls. The lights dimmed in the ballroom and suddenly the excitement was palpable. Everyone was here to see the group whose music they'd listened to on the radio and whose faces they had seen regularly on 'Top of the Pops' and in numerous weekly girly magazines.

The group was waiting in the dark at the side of the stage holding their guitars. Eddie came on stage, walked up to a mike and tapped it to make sure it was live. He then announced in a loud voice 'Will you please give a big warm London welcome to The Merseybeats.' The crowd instantly erupted as the group rushed onto the stage amid screams from some of their more avid admirers. A couple of spotlights above their heads came on and there they were, four young Liverpudlians, all in their early 20s, three with guitars slung over their shoulders, and all wearing the identical clothing that they wore on the front of their new LP – tight black trousers, white shirts, narrow black ties and black leather waistcoats. All were sporting the now popular 'moptop' hairstyle, made famous by The Beatles. My eyes dropped to the floor and yes, they all wore the obligatory black Beatle boots, ankle-high pointed leather boots with elasticated sides and high Cuban heels. The drummer quickly made himself comfortable behind his drums and picked up his drumsticks, while the others plugged in their guitars.

Tony Crane, one of the guitarists and a vocalist, walked up to a mike and in a broad Liverpudlian accent announced 'Good evening one and all. Nice to be here in London. We'd like to start with a number called 'Fortune Teller', originally on the B-side of one of our hit records.' I couldn't wait to hear what they really sounded like playing live. Liverpool groups, for the past two years, had dominated the charts and they all had such a distinctive sound.

The atmosphere in this dark, low-ceilinged ballroom was now electric. The hushed crowd waited in anticipation. The drummer suddenly raised his sticks in the air and hit them against each other as he counted out 'One, two, three, four.' Simultaneously, the two guitars, bass and drums crashed in with the opening chord sequence. They were loud and I watched intently as the two guitarists strutted up to their separate microphones in their high heel boots and, in close harmony, started singing the opening line 'Went to a fortune teller, had my fortune read, didn't know what to tell her….' Around me more and more girls started screaming. This was a great opening number and the crowd, packed liked sardines around the foot of the stage, swayed in all directions. The final chords were played to thunderous applause, but before the cheering and screaming had died down, they launched into their second song.

After playing a couple of fairly fast numbers, they slowed the tempo down and, without making an announcement, they launched straight into playing their last hit 'Wishin' and Hopin', which immediately brought about more screams from their female fans. This was followed with their first hit 'It's Love That Really Counts' and, of course, that instantly brought about even more screaming from the girls. A quick announcement was made that the next two songs were from their latest EP and they launched into 'Shame', a fast blues song. This was followed by 'Long Tall Sally', a number The Beatles had popularised on an EP released in 1964. The Merseybeats did a frantic version of this old song originally performed by the rock 'n' roll legend, singer Little Richard.

They were such a tight band and I was enthralled by their performance. The drummer, John Banks, who every so often would start moving his forehead up and down extremely quickly, injected humour into their set. This made his 'moptop' fringe move up and down and the audience loved it. But for me personally it was Aaron Williams, the rhythm guitarist, who stood out. On stage he was such a live wire, constantly smiling and grinning the whole time. His exuberance was infectious and I envied him. He was doing what he loved to do and was obviously enjoying every moment. Who knows, perhaps one day I would be in a similar position. One thing that sticks in my mind from that evening, is that every so often throughout their set, Tony Crane, their vocalist and guitarist, would suddenly stare at me for a few seconds. I just assumed he must have recognised me as a member of the support group but, even now, I wonder why he did this.

They were now getting close to the end of their set and were playing the opening chord sequence to 'Milkman', a song I particularly liked, which was written by Johnny Gustafson, their bass player. For me, this number exemplified the 'Liverpool' sound, a melodic song with the lead riff played on a twelve-string guitar and sung in a two-part harmony.

Finally, as this song came to an end, they announced they were going to finish with their million-selling hit song 'I Think of You'. The crowd erupted and, amid all the cheering and the screaming, they launched into their final number.

This was by far the crowd's favourite song and many people were singing along to it. For me though, finishing on a slow number was a bit of an anti-climax. Most groups would usually end on a rousing number. However, the crowd still cheered and shouted, showing their appreciation, but strangely no encore was forthcoming. That was it – it was all over. They thanked the audience and ran off the stage to further cheering, clapping and screaming. Within a few minutes the road crew were on the stage packing up their gear, making way for us to set up once again. By the time we had finished our last set, the group and their entourage had left the building – a year later the group disbanded.

'It's Love That Really Counts', the Merseybeats' first minor chart hit in 1963 was a slow number. Their record company, seeing the encouraging sales, decided that the follow-up single release should also be a slow number and their second single, 'I Think of You', became the biggest selling record of their career. The die was now firmly cast and the record company executives continued to milk this success. More singles followed, but they were all slow songs. However, they managed to break the pattern briefly when an EP was released in March 1964 featuring four fairly fast rocky numbers. It was called 'On Stage' and it sold very well.

Their next single release reverted back to form with a slow song called 'Wishin' and Hopin', which charted in the top 20. The public then started to tire of the same old format and the chart positions reflected this. Their last single release only made number 38 in the charts and in 1965 it was all over.

I enjoyed their EP record 'On Stage' so much so that we introduced two of the songs on that record into our own play list. 'Shame, Shame, Shame' had originally been performed by the legendary blues singer and guitarist Jimmy Reed and was a chug-along 12 bar blues. The Merseybeats' recording was a lot faster and this was the version we performed on numerous occasions. It turned out to be a great favourite with our audiences. The other song was also a fairly fast blues number recorded by another legendary blues artist, Bo Diddley. Called 'You Can't Judge a Book By It's Cover', again we followed the Merseybeats' rendition which was a more rocking and frantic version of the original's mid-tempo, slightly Latin rhythm.

Although the event had been well publicised with large posters displayed throughout Forest Gate and surrounding areas, The Merseybeats had only managed to draw in about 300 people. This was extremely disappointing for Eddie, who had expected more people to attend. When he finally counted the takings for that evening, he was out of pocket. So, no more chart groups at the Kavern Club.

25

SUPPORTING - JERRY LEE LEWIS - NOVEMBER 1964

Travelling to Tottenham in the van, the air was full of excitement and expectancy and the main topic of conversation was Jerry Lee Lewis. We just couldn't believe that soon we would be sharing the same stage with the man himself, a rock 'n' roll legend who had influenced our musical ambitions just a few years before. Our group repertoire had always included some Jerry Lee Lewis' songs, but on this special occasion we collectively decided that, for diehard fans in the audience, playing any of his songs might be a little provocative.

We had all heard and read stories about this man. In 1958, Lewis undertook his first tour of the UK. During a routine press interview on arrival at London Airport, it came to light that although Jerry Lee Lewis was only 22 years old, he had already been married three times. It was then discovered that his third wife, Myra Lewis, who accompanied him, was only 13 years old and was, in fact, his cousin. The story became front-page news in the national newspapers and caused such a

CLUB NOREIK
HIGH RD., TOTTENHAM, N.15
SAT. 21st NOV.
JERRY LEE LEWIS
PLUS
THE CANDLES
ADMISSION 12/6 IN ADVANCE 15/- ON THE NIGHT
11.30 P.M. TILL DAWN

furore that, after only performing three concerts, the tour was cancelled and Lewis returned to America. The story followed him back to America and hit the national newspapers there, resulting in his records being blacklisted on the radio, which nearly wrecked his career.

He continued performing, but could only find work in small town clubs. However, after a change in musical direction, he slowly resurrected his career and with a few hits under his belt, Jerry Lee Lewis became a country and western star.

I particularly like the story behind Jerry Lee Lewis' appearance in the now famous 'Million Dollar Quartet' photograph taken at Sun Records studio in Memphis on 4 December 1956. That day, Carl Perkins had been given studio time at Sun to put down some tracks as a follow-up single to his first rockabilly hit 'Blue Suede Shoes'. Elvis later recorded the song when he left Sun and signed to record for the giant RCA Victor label and it became a massive worldwide hit a year later. Jerry Lee Lewis had only recently been signed to Sun and had, on this particular day, been asked by Sam Phillips, the studio owner, to attend the recording purely as a session pianist, a session incidentally, which spawned Perkins' second hit 'Matchbox'.

However, earlier that day Johnny Cash had come into the Sun offices to sort out some paperwork. While he was there, Elvis Presley, now a big star, had arrived early in the afternoon quite unexpectedly with his girl-friend, to say hello to Sam Phillips.

When the Perkins' session had finished, Presley wandered into the small studio to have a chat, and not long afterwards in strode Johnny Cash to do the same. A jam session ensued and, unbeknown to the four Sun artists, it was recorded and eventually released as an album.

The ever-resourceful Sam Phillips, never wanting to miss a public relations opportunity, got in touch with the local newspaper 'The Memphis Press-Scimitar' and a reporter and photographer were duly dispatched. The resulting photo shows Presley at the piano, talking with his three friends who were standing directly behind him – Carl Perkins, with a guitar slung around his neck, and either side Jerry Lee Lewis and

Johnny Cash. An article and the photograph appeared a few days later in the Memphis newspaper with the banner headline 'Million Dollar Quartet'.

Over 50 years later, a stage musical was written about this chance meeting at Sun Records in Memphis and the show was named after the article headline, 'Million Dollar Quartet'. It was premiered on New York's Broadway in 2010 and then in London's West End in 2011.

With his infamous 1958 tour now behind him, Jerry Lee Lewis was still heralded in the UK as one of the icons of rock 'n' roll and so, in 1964, he undertook another tour of Europe. He was using The Nashville Teens, a British band, as his backing group and in April of that year he appeared at the Star Club in Hamburg, where The Beatles cut their teeth before fame came along. One of his shows was recorded live and an album released entitled 'Live at the Star Club in Hamburg'. This is now widely considered as one of the greatest live rock 'and' roll performances ever recorded.

With Jerry Lee Lewis now in the UK as part of this European tour, we were privileged to be his support group that night. Pulling up outside Club Noreik's double fire escape doors was now routine to us, having played there many times before. However, as we banged on the door to be let in on that particular night, we were unusually apprehensive and nervous. The doors swung open and we said our hellos to the bouncers. We then proceeded to unload the van and carry our equipment straight onto the stage. The Noreik's stage wasn't very large at the best of times and the only access was via a small wooden staircase at the side, so climbing up the stairs and coming face to face with a full-size grand piano, although expected, came as a bit of a shock, as space was at a premium. I then felt butterflies in my stomach as I realised that the great man himself would soon be sitting there, playing away.

As we assembled our gear on the stage, I kept wondering if Jerry Lee had arrived and was holed up in the small dressing room next to the stage. Normally we had access to that dressing room, but on this particular night we were informed that Jerry Lee had exclusive use of the room.

The show was a sell-out. I recognised quite a few regular faces in the front row leaning against the stage so with a bit of luck, having performed at the club on a fairly regular basis in the past, people knew us and hopefully we wouldn't get heckled to leave the stage early in order to hasten Jerry Lee Lewis' appearance.

We played the first of our two one-hourly sets to quite an appreciative crowd and when we finished the last song, to our pleasant surprise we were clapped and cheered and hadn't been heckled at all. Being a realist, I did wonder if the audience was clapping because we'd finished and next on was Jerry Lee, or did they genuinely enjoy our playing! I'll go for the latter following a comment made later by the man himself.

The excitement in the audience was palpable. After all, it wasn't every day you got to see a rock 'n' roll legend appearing in the flesh and playing his hits. As we started to pack up our gear and carry it off the stage, the roadies for The Nashville Teens quickly started to bring their equipment onto the stage. The drums had been assembled beforehand and were now positioned on the rostrum.

By the time we had removed most of our equipment, The Nashville Teens' gear had been assembled and the group were now on the stage making final adjustments to the drums, tuning guitars and adjusting microphones. I was impressed at the speed in which all this was done. We had just performed for an hour and it was now 2.00am in the morning, but we didn't have roadies to help us with our gear!

Picking up the remaining mike stand base and a couple of electrical leads, I was the last to leave the stage. Although I kept glancing around, I still could see no sign of the man himself.

As I approached the narrow wooden staircase, the dressing room door suddenly opened and a figure rushed out and immediately made for the staircase. I stopped at the top of the stairs to let this person come up and instantly recognised him – it was Jerry Lee Lewis himself! The next second he was standing next to me and turned and said 'You in the warm up band?' 'Yes' I responded. 'Well, you did a real good job warming up my audience. Go and get the rest of your band – I want you gathered round the piano while I perform.'

The lights came up over the stage as he walked over to the piano and sat down to a great cheer from the audience. From the top of the steps, I hurriedly beckoned to the others to come up. 'He wants us to stand around the piano – quickly!' There was disbelief on their faces. We all went over to the piano and leaned on the top, directly facing Jerry Lee. He looked at us and nodded, then turned to face the audience and, without any introduction, he started playing the intro to 'Whole Lotta Shakin' Going On'. After a couple of bars, the group came thundering in. Without any warning, he suddenly stopped playing and turned and motioned to The Nashville Teens to stop as well. He twisted round in his seat and then shouted across to the drummer 'You come in like this' and proceeded to beat a rhythm on top of the piano. Nothing else was said. He swung back round and started playing the intro once more, but as soon as the group came in, he still wasn't happy and stopped playing again. He left the piano, walked across the stage, mounted the rostrum, and motioned for the drummer to get off his drum stool. He then sat on the stool, picked up some drumsticks and literally demonstrated to the drummer exactly the rhythm he wanted. The poor drummer just stood there and watched, looking highly embarrassed, but he nodded that he understood what was required.

I felt for the drummer – how embarrassing to be given a lesson in playing the drums in front of the entire audience. You could have heard a pin drop as Jerry Lee made his way back to the piano and sat down. He started to play the intro again and I held my breath, willing the drummer to get it right, as I'm sure many others did. The band came in on cue and this time there was no stopping as he started singing 'Come along a baby, whole lotta shakin' going on..........' Thank goodness, the drummer had cracked it. I dread to think what would have happened if he hadn't got it right on the third attempt.

When it came to the end of the song, the audience erupted, and I suspect Jerry Lee had by now relaxed off a bit. It was straight into 'Down the Line', another one of my favourites. I glanced across at John and we grinned at each other. Who would ever have thought that we could be in such close proximity to one of our rock 'n' roll idols!

As song after song finished, people in the audience yelled out their favourite numbers. Sometimes they were lucky and he sang them, but for me he still hadn't sung his most famous song. It was now getting close to the end of his set, when he announced that he'd like to finish with 'What'd I Say'. A big cheer went up and he was off, playing that wonderful piano solo introduction. I was so close to him, I could see beads of sweat dripping off his chin. Suddenly he lifted his right foot, complete with leather cowboy boot, and started hitting the high keys on the piano with it. The crowd lapped it up.

The song finished and Jerry Lee stood up, faced the audience and bowed, then moved quickly towards the wooden staircase. The crowd were going crazy. As though changing his mind, he stopped, turned quickly and ran back to the piano, sat down and nodded to the band. The drummer counted in on his drumsticks and immediately they were playing those wonderful opening chords to 'Great Balls of Fire'! My prayers had been answered! We were all well and truly caught up in the moment as we clapped and sang along to this great number. As he reached his solo Jerry Lee was up, the piano stool was kicked away behind him and he just stood there, legs apart, his arms outstretched, his fingers a complete blur as they pounded the keys. He appeared to be in a trance – his body shook and his long damp blond curls hung over his face. As the last chord was played signalling the end of the song, he was off down the wooden steps and straight into the dressing room.

Nothing was said for a moment – we were in shock. We just looked at one another, aware that we had been privileged to witness 'The Killer' in action and at such close quarters – a rare moment, never to be forgotten!

Sluggishly, at around 4.00am, long after Jerry Lee Lewis had departed the premises, we started to re-assemble our gear, ready for the final hour set. We were very tired by then and played on automatic pilot, but thankfully that final hour seemed to pass quickly. The audience had thinned out as most of the die-hard Jerry Lee Lewis fans had already drifted home.

Just after 6.00am on a frosty November morning, the van was loaded up and we were ready to head home at last, but before driving off I carried out my usual routine and peeled off another poster from the wall to add to my collection.

On reflection, regarding the unfortunate start to Jerry Lee Lewis' set that night, you had to give the man his due. He was a true professional. He wasn't prepared to compromise. He wanted the song played right and certainly wasn't prepared to ruin his reputation, especially as that number was one of his biggest hits. I suspect the cause was a lack of quality rehearsal time between Jerry Lee Lewis and The Nashville Teens prior to this particularly short tour. However, they had toured and recorded a live album with him in Hamburg earlier in the year, so you would have expected them to be a fairly tight band by now. But this wasn't The Nashville Teens' full line-up – there was no lead singer or pianist so, who knows, perhaps that wasn't their original drummer who played that night. Also, I've subsequently read that Jerry Lee Lewis wasn't an easy person to work with, and I can quite well believe that.

FOOTNOTE:

In 1983, Jerry Lee Lewis' wife Myra Lewis, who had accompanied him on that fateful tour of the UK in 1958, wrote a biography entitled 'Great Balls of Fire' in conjunction with M.M. Silver Jnr., a noted music journalist.

Six years later, a film script was written based upon her book and a film was released in 1989, also called 'Great Balls of Fire'. The plot of the film was described as 'The Story of Jerry Lee Lewis, arguably the greatest and certainly one of the wildest musicians of the 1950s'.

The film starred the actor Dennis Quaid who gave a very life-like portrayal of Jerry Lee Lewis, not only in appearance, but also his character and mannerisms. The actress Winona Ryder played Myra Lewis, his wife, and Alec Baldwin played the firebrand evangelist Jimmy Swaggart, a real-life cousin of Jerry Lee. The soundtrack to the film had Jerry Lee playing many of his early Sun Recordings, especially re-recorded for the film.

Jerry Lee's lead guitarist was portrayed in the film by the blues guitarist Jimmie Vaughan, the brother of Stevie Ray Vaughan, the famous and renowned blues guitarist who died in a helicopter crash in 1990.

The Nashville Teens had their own top 10 UK hit record in August of that year called 'Tobacco Road', which also entered the top 20 charts in America in November.

THE KING ALFRED PUBLIC HOUSE - BELLINGHAM, KENT 1964 - 1967

On many occasions, if we had just completed a Saturday 'all nighter' in Tottenham, I had the unfortunate responsibility to remind everyone, when dropping them off, that in 12 hours' time we'd be back to pick them up as we had a Sunday booking at the King Alfred. This announcement was always greeted with dismay and lots of moaning. It was tiring enough when we played a normal Saturday booking from 8pm–11pm even though we had all Sunday in which to recover before making the journey to Bellingham in Kent that evening. But when it followed an 'all nighter', it was particularly gruelling. However, once there, the King Alfred was always a good venue and we were extremely well received. The building was a purpose-built, large, detached 1930s pub that had a live jazz band playing in the saloon bar on a Sunday evening and we played upstairs in a large, sprawling ballroom, run independently to the pub.

In the mid-60s, promoters generally didn't go out of their way to 'tart' up the premises they were renting and the old ballroom at The King Alfred was no exception. The promoters who ran this weekly Sunday dance were a couple of smart 'thirty something' guys. Sometimes, if we arrived early and were in the van waiting for the doors to open, we would see them arrive in their respective sports car. One drove a new off-white

E-Type Jaguar and the other, my favourite car of all time, a new red Triumph TR4A. I often thought to myself, watching enviously as these two sports cars came roaring into the car park, 'Who's got it right, us or them?' All they had to do was open the doors, set up a table close to the door and sit there collecting the money as around 250 punters arrived, each paying an entrance fee of five shillings (25p). Each evening they must have earned over £60, plus a share of the profits on the drinks consumed on the night. We played for two hours and received a fee of £12 in total!

The ballroom was oblong in shape with a dark wooden parquet floor and leaded windows overlooking the car park. Single chairs lined the perimeter walls and lighting came from two large hanging ceiling lights. On the walls were numerous small wall lights covered with old-fashioned lampshades. The toilets and a bar were close to the ballroom entrance door at one end and the small stage was at the opposite end. As soon as the records started playing, the two main ceiling lights were switched off and the wall lights provided the only lighting for the entire evening. On the stage, two wall lights on the back wall gave us our only light.

The promoters paid us in cash and, as far as clearing up after the dance, I'm sure that would have been included in the rent. The publican who ran the large pub downstairs, always provided the bar staff and the booze, so he was a 'happy chappy', sharing the profits made on the drinks with the two promoters. Usually, as we carried the last few pieces of equipment out of the hall, the lights would be switched off behind us and the promoters would climb into their gleaming sports cars, giving us a final wave as they left the car park, pockets bulging with money!

We played regularly at the King Alfred over a three-year period and it was during our early performances there that we purchased our top-of-the-range gear. The £12 we received in 1965 would be the equivalent of around £150 in today's money. We'd just spent over £1,200 on new equipment, which in today's spending power is equivalent to £18,250. Our monthly outgoings were high and so there was never a lot of spare money. However, for me, earning the money wasn't the driving force and

I'm sure the others all felt the same. We loved playing the music and had the added bonus of being great friends together, just enjoying ourselves. But personal circumstances over the next year or so would change within the group and then money became the all-important factor.

It might have been a pain to have to trek across London to get to Bellingham, but once there and on the stage, it was a real pleasure to play in front of an appreciative audience of around 250 people. During the 20 times we must have played at the King Alfred, I can't recall ever seeing any trouble break out, even though alcohol was served. It probably helped that the average age of the people who attended on Sunday evenings was slightly older than some of our other audiences, about 20 to 25 years old. Our association with the two promoters who ran the King Alfred was a productive one and eventually led to other bookings, one of them being a memorable evening at the Savoy Hotel in Central London.

PANCAKES AND CREAM PLEASE!

There was never any delay in packing up our gear after playing at the King Alfred as, on our way home, it became a tradition to stop off at a Wimpey bar just on the outskirts of Lewisham, to enjoy some delicious pancakes served with warm maple syrup and a large dollop of cream. We looked on this as our reward for our night's work at the King Alfred and the group's kitty always paid.

Very rarely were we ever delayed because nothing was more important than eating that dish of hot, sweet sticky pancakes! By the time we arrived at the Wimpey bar, it was always near closing time and as we drove along the road, all eyes would be focused ahead – was it still open? If the lights were on, then we would quickly park the van and make a mad dash into the restaurant.

Once seated, we could hardly wait to be served. On rare occasions, having written down our order, the waitress would return, saying 'Sorry, we're out of maple syrup' or 'We've run out of cream' and there would be groans all round as that meant no pancakes that night! For the first

minute or so after placing our order, we quietly waited, praying the waitress wouldn't immediately return from the kitchen with the bad news. If
she didn't appear after a few minutes, we knew everything was alright.

Finally, after about ten minutes, stainless steel pans would be placed
in front us and there would be four small pancakes swimming around in
a sizzling sea of maple syrup and on the top, a mountain of aerated
cream, which came from a pressurised aluminium flask. Nowadays, this
type of cream comes in an aerosol can and can be purchased in most
supermarkets, but not then! This was a real treat! The test then was,
could you devour all the pancakes before the mountain of cream simply
melted into a small white pool at the bottom of the pan and the answer
was yes, every time! Pure heaven!

26

SUPPORTING THE WHO – 1965

Dawn had already broken on that grey cold morning in March 1965 in north London as we packed away our gear after our second gig that night. I realised it would be another one of those weekends when I would miss my Mum's delicious Sunday roast dinner as I needed to sleep before another gig tonight. What a shame, as I could do with some solid fuel after playing two gigs within 12 hours, 50 miles apart. The Seven Sisters Road was deserted and the last 'die-hard' club members had already scurried away to catch up on some lost sleep. There was precious little time to do any chatting up of fans and even if I wanted to, they probably would have fallen asleep as I tried, exhausted by a long night of drinking and dancing.

We had been booked to perform at the King Alfred pub that night so we had to get home and get to bed, post haste. I knew that in about 12 hours we would be back in the van travelling across to Bellingham in Kent. Another late night and then back to work on Monday morning.

I put the last mike stand and base into the back of the van and closed the double doors. By now, the rest of the group had already scrambled in, waiting for me to drive them home. Lazy buggers, but I didn't mind really – it was a pleasure to drive home so early in the morning, when the roads were so uncharacteristically quiet. As I started to pull away from the curb, I suddenly spotted a poster advertising our gig stuck on the side of the wall next to the club's entrance. Being an addictive collector of anything relating to the group – our official archivist if you like – I stopped the van, left the engine running, jumped out and started to try to carefully remove the poster. I knew the silence from the van wouldn't last. 'Come on, we want to get to bed. Anyway, what do you want that stupid poster for?' someone moaned.

Our poster had been stuck on top of about half a dozen other posters from previous gigs and separating ours from the rest was proving rather difficult. Again more abuse spewed from the van and I was in half a mind to abandon the operation. Just one last try. I pulled on a curling thick top edge and, assisted by an early morning dew, a fat wodge of posters came away freely from the wall. Feeling pretty chuffed with myself, I opened the back doors of the van and laid the damp posters over the amplifiers and off we went. A successful gig, and now a successful mission in archiving.

Galaxy Entertainments had booked us for two one-hour spots at the Wilton Hall in Bletchley, Buckinghamshire for the first of that Saturday night's two gigs. This venue was a popular local Saturday night dance club and was within walking distance of the town centre. I had also accepted a late booking from Ajax Entertainments to perform our usual supporting role at the north London 'All Nite Rave' at Club Noreik in Tottenham. The club opened its doors at 11.30pm every Saturday evening and closed at around 6.00am Sunday morning.

We played two uneventful hour-long sets at Bletchley, finishing at 11 o'clock. Under normal circumstances there was no rush. We would take our time and there was always somebody hanging around who wanted to chat while we were packing up. Just as bands have, and always will, attract young women, they also attract opinionated young men, often drunk on both booze and their perceived sense of superior musical knowledge.

But on this particular night, we had to drive 50 miles south to Tottenham to play at the Club Noreik, and get there as soon as possible as the club opened its doors at 11.30pm. So there was no hanging around that night, however stunning any of the female music lovers might be, or how much any of the big-mouthed males wanted to give us a slap. We were packed up and on our way within half-an-hour of playing our last number and under normal driving conditions we would arrive in Tottenham around midnight. Fortunately, we had reserved parking outside the fire exit, which was situated at the side of the club in Seven Sisters Road. It was adjacent to the stage, which helped matters considerably.

It was the usual ritual – we would pull up outside, bang on the fire exit doors, which would be opened by Big Paul, the bouncer and a member of the staff there, who usually offered us a handful of purple hearts. He knew we'd performed earlier that evening and were tired and assumed we needed something to keep us awake. But no way! I had heard about these 'uppers' and considering I could last on a couple of alcoholic drinks all night, why would I want to experiment with something I knew nothing about. The others were of equal mind – our refusal must have stemmed from our secure family upbringing. My high was to play a good set and receive a good response from the crowd and should any female attention be forthcoming, then that was the cherry on top of the cake. But on this particular night, Martin, our bassist, suddenly decided otherwise. He helped himself to all the purple hearts on offer and with one quick movement, they were all down his throat. We were shocked, but I wasn't surprised. Martin was always the first person to try anything new. It certainly had the desired effect – he remained hyperactive all night and I can't remember ever seeing his fingers move so fast!

Whereas we all hit the sack as soon as we arrived home on Sunday morning, not Martin! He was still full of energy and still hadn't gone to bed when I knocked on his door later that Sunday evening, ready to drive over to Bellingham in Kent to play at the King Alfred. I never thought any more about it until I called in to see him three days later and when he opened the door, he looked like death warmed up. His skin had a sickly pallor about it and his eyes were dark sockets sunk into his face. Since downing the tablets early on Sunday morning, he hadn't slept a wink! He had managed to attend his apprenticeship course at the Ford plant on the Monday, but the next two days were spent at home trying to sleep. He appeared punch-drunk and was swaying slightly from side to side. He finally got to sleep that evening and didn't go in to work for the rest of the week.

As we entered the club and began hauling our equipment onto the stage, the local DJ would be playing some popular Tamla Motown or soul music to the audience that consisted mainly of Mods.

GREEN ONIONS BY BOOKER T AND THE MG'S

Inevitably at some stage, my favourite record would be played. It had become a Mod anthem and was played in all the Mod clubs. The name of the song was 'Green Onions' by Booker T and The MGs, who were a four-piece US band consisting of organ, electric bass, drums and electric guitar. This bluesy instrumental number with a lot of attitude was played on the Hammond organ, which gave the song its distinctive sound. It is a wonderful moody song and when this track was played, I would wait with anticipation for one minute and 13 seconds for that loud, searing, single note played on the electric guitar to leap out from nowhere and grab you. The guitarist responsible for this was a young 16-year-old American called Steve Cropper. That single note was basically the only time the electric guitar came to the forefront throughout the entire song, although the guitar played a big part in the overall sound of the group.

I subsequently learned that the technique was achieved by pressing either the first, second or third string down on the fret, striking the note and stretching the string by pushing it either up or down with your finger. It helped immensely using lighter gauge strings, which gave more flexibility when applying pressure to them.

The note then moves up one, two or three semitones, depending on how far the string is pushed. It was the first time I had ever heard such a magical sound. In 1965 it was pure innovation.

'Green Onions' was famously used to great effect in the 1973 George Lucas' film 'American Graffiti', when a youthful Harrison Ford challenges another young punk to a drag race through town. It was the perfect mood song for that gripping moment in the film.

I often look back when hearing that track again now. The bending of that single note on the guitar was so very simple, yet so effective, and so influential on future guitarists – why hadn't I thought of doing that! I suppose that's what sorts out the men from the boys. Being innovative is a gift – or does it depend on where you were born! It is a well-known fact that within a 30 mile radius of Guildford in Surrey, and in the space of 16 months between 1944 and 1945, three of the greatest ever rock guitarists were born – Eric Clapton, Jeff Beck and Jimmy Page. As far as I know, no famous guitarists were ever born in Romford, so I didn't stand a chance!

The building, which housed the Club Noreik, was originally built as cinema in 1911. It was called the Corner Picture Theatre and got its name from being situated on the corner of Seven Sisters Road and Tottenham High Road in North London. It ceased to be a working cinema in 1960 and then became a bingo hall before being converted into a music club hosting live music at the weekends. Between 1964 and 1966, the Noreik became one of the hottest Mod clubs in London and played host to many of the big name groups of the time. Inside, the original rows of cinema seats had been removed to make way for a dance floor and, for a real 'basement club' effect, the walls and ceiling had been painted matte black. Although the original cinema wall lights remained, the overall effect in the club was very dark and dingy. There were two bars, one situated at the back of the club on the ground floor, and the other upstairs in the old cinema circle area. Looking back now, it's quite amazing to think they only served soft drinks.

THE CORNER PICTURE THEATRE, ORIGINALLY A CINEMA BEFORE BECOMING A BINGO HALL AND THEN THE CLUB NOREIK

Facing the bar at the other end of the dance floor was the stage, which was quite small considering the overall size of the club. Although fairly high, at about four feet, the stage size was around 20 feet long and 15 feet deep. This small stage area only allowed for one lot of equipment to be set up at any one time. Most headlining acts only played one set, usually getting on the stage around 3am and playing for an hour or so, and then their gear was removed from the stage and they departed.

Having set up our gear and tuned our guitars, the empty drum and guitar cases had to be taken out and stored in the back of our van due to the cramped conditions on and off the stage. The headlining act, The Who, had just arrived outside and their helper (later to be known in the rock world as a roadie) had started to bring in their equipment, while members of the group wandered around the club checking things out. As I walked back into the club towards the stage, two members of the group came up to me and the taller of the two asked if they could use our gear as the stage was so small. This would save them having to set up their own equipment. As we had recently spent over £1,200 replacing our amplifiers, sound system and drum kit, I explained this to them, saying sorry, they would have to use their own gear. This refusal didn't appear to faze them too much, probably because they had their own guy who would be doing all the lifting anyway. With hindsight, I had made the right decision!

The smaller of the two guys who had been glancing around the club when I was explaining about our equipment, turned to me and asked me in a slightly rough London accent 'What's the crumpet like here then?' Obviously he thought I was an authority on the subject! I told him 'Pretty good normally.' He nodded 'Thanks mate' and they both turned and strode off. His name was Roger Daltrey and the taller one was Pete Townshend, both members of The Who, that evening's headlining act.

Before starting our first set, we used a small room at the side of the stage to change into our stage gear. It was still the thing for most pop groups in 1965 to wear identical clothing on stage. Interestingly, only 18 months earlier, The Rolling Stones had made their first TV appearance on the popular music show 'Thank Your Lucky Stars', promoting their first record 'Come On'. They all wore shirts and ties and identical jackets, trimmed with velvet collars. Apparently, they had never worn stage outfits in their early days of appearing in public, but their new manager, Andrew Loog Oldham, had insisted they dressed in identical outfits when appearing on the show. They went on to appear in less formal outfits, but equally identical, consisting of leather waistcoats, white shirts, black ties and black trousers, before finally abandoning wearing identical clothing altogether.

However astute Andrew Loog Oldham was in promoting his new group, even he had been influenced by the fashion of the time, brought about by his previous employer, NEMS Enterprises. This was Brian Epstein's extremely successful management company, who had insisted that all his groups should wear identical suits, shirts and ties on stage, the trend having been set by their top act, The Beatles.

But as more and more groups started to dress individually and casually on stage, fans were desperate to emulate their heroes and dress in similar outfits. The entrepreneur, John Stephen, who came from a clothing background, was quick to spot the new trend and started to extend the number of retail clothing outlets he had in Carnaby Street in London's West End, but very cunningly gave each boutique a different name. Other retailers, seeing the huge pulling power of this trendy street, opened further boutiques there and very soon it became the Mecca for modern clothing in London. From adopting trends, it went on to set trends. It was unique, even in central London, to find so many clothing shops situated in one street, all aimed at the young and fashionable of the day. Very soon, famous 60s' groups and celebrities were photographed shopping in Carnaby Street – the 'Swinging Sixties' was about to explode!

I had accepted our booking at the Noreik without knowing if it was just us and the DJ supplying the music on the night, as sometimes happened, or if we were supporting another group. A couple of days before our scheduled appearance at the club, I spotted an advertisement for the gig in the NME (New Musical Express) and read that we were supporting a group called The Who. As part of my weekly ritual on the train to work, I always scoured the NME's Hit Parade chart just to establish what songs were in the top 20 positions and if there were any new entries. Interestingly, a song called 'I Can't Explain' by The Who, their first-ever chart entry, had just crept in the lower section of the chart at number 26. This was the first time I had actually heard of a group called The Who and I never gave it another thought. A month later 'I Can't Explain' peaked at number eight!

When we had finished playing our hour-long set, the DJ started to play his music while we moved every last bit of our equipment down the wooden steps and stored it at the side of the stage. As we all stood at the bar having a drink, I watched enviously as the roadie assembled The Who's equipment on stage – would we ever reach those dizzy heights, when we could afford to pay somebody to lug our heavy gear from van to stage?

Each member of the group was now on stage making final adjustments to their particular instrument, working in the murky light provided by the two lights mounted on the wall behind the drummer. The amps were switched on, leads plugged in and the usual 'one, two, three testing' was aired a few times into the mikes to obtain the right voice balance. All the necessary adjustments were made as the lead guitar and bass tuned up and the drummer hit the odd cymbal and skins. In 1965, portable sound mixing desks, stage monitors and portable lighting rigs didn't exist. Six spotlights mounted on the ceiling just in front of the stage provided the only stage lighting on this particular night.

Still dressed in our stage gear, we stood at the bar and waited for the group to start. We had assumed the group wouldn't be starting just yet as they were still wearing the clothes they had arrived in and were casually sauntering around the stage and making last minute adjustments. Without warning, the group burst into life with their first number and simultaneously the stage was flooded with light. This took everyone by surprise and we were amazed by this dramatic start to their set. We all just watched silently until the end of the song. They had managed, in one fell swoop, to surprise and capture everyone's attention. It was like a small bomb had exploded! No announcements had been made to alert the crowd that they were about to begin and we were all stunned by the suddenness of being hit simultaneously with the high volume of sound and the intensity of the lights springing to life out of the darkness. Pure drama!

Even with this sudden assault on the senses, I can still remember inanely thinking to myself at the time 'My God – they haven't even bothered to change!' Wow, this group was loud and aggressive and when it came to the first guitar solo, the singer started swinging the microphone around and bouncing it off the drummer's cymbals! How could you abuse expensive sound equipment like that! I turned to the others and said 'That was a stroke of luck, not letting them use our gear!' The singer looked menacing for some unknown reason, but had a strong piercing voice and when not hurling a microphone around, held a tambourine, which he hit against his mike stand in time to the music. Occasionally the tambourine would be thrown into the air and caught.

They didn't have a rhythm guitarist or a keyboard player to help fill out their sound, which was pretty unusual, even in 1965. Their line-up just consisted of a drummer, bass and lead guitarist – the singer didn't play an instrument apart from using the tambourine. Once or twice, due to illness, we had to play without our rhythm guitarist and being the lead guitarist, I can tell you it made a hell of a difference to the overall sound. A year or so later, our rhythm guitarist left on a permanent basis and we decided not to replace him. Certain songs had to be dropped and I had to play louder and more aggressively, with more lead fill-ins to carpet over the 'holes' that appeared in a song when continuous chords weren't being played.

This lead guitarist with The Who was very different. He impressed me most with his ability to play chords at high volume and let the notes ring, while he 'windmilled' his arm in an arc. His lead solos were good, but certainly not outstanding. However, as with the other members of the group, he worked extremely hard to help complete their strong sound. It then dawned on me that whereas I simply copied lead guitar solos from the record, this guitarist made up his own solos and had developed his own style of playing.

The drummer was exceptional. He had added additional drums and cymbals to his drum kit and was quite manic in his approach to playing percussion. With his arms continually flailing around, he maintained a steady rhythm and besides using his bass drum, snare drum and hi-hat, he managed at the same time to play the additional drums and cymbals he had at his disposal, which created a loud rhythmic wall of sound.

The bass guitarist just stood there impassively, but was quite unconventional in his playing. He didn't just stick to the usual bass guitar riff in the required key, his fingers travelled all over the entire fretboard, creating a constant moving flow of notes.

The group were coming to the end of their set and during their last number, the most amazing and stunning thing happened. Firstly, I should point out that one of the most irritating things to happen when you are forced to stand close to the amplification on a small stage is feedback. This is a very loud high-pitched squealing sound and can affect both the microphone and the guitar, especially semi-acoustic electric guitars. This is caused through high volume control on the amplification. At the end of their final song, the lead guitarist turned his back on the audience and deliberately stood up close to his amplifier. Suddenly the high whistling feedback sound started and he proceeded to change the pitch by moving his guitar around. To my utter disbelief, he then thrust the head of his semi-acoustic electric Rickenbacker guitar into a speaker cabinet, tearing the fabric covering! Then the lights were extinguished and the show was over.

We were stunned! We stared silently at the stage, mesmerised. Slowly we started to come out of our trance-like state and then, one by one, began to comment on what we had just witnessed. Most of us were quite critical of our respective counterparts, who were now leaving the stage. I suspect that, like me, none of us really wanted to admit that they were very good and that we felt threatened. We were a very close bunch of friends and we wouldn't want to hurt one another's feelings. If I had said that I thought the drummer was fantastic, JG, our drummer, would have been hurt and if he had said that the guitarist was great, I most probably would have got the hump.

It wasn't jealously, I'm sure of that. It was just that this group was very different and unique and it had been difficult for us to accept what we had just seen. Without us realising it at the time, this group were pushing the boundaries. Rock music was evolving very quickly and if we weren't careful, we were going to get left behind. But at that moment in time, we were united on one thing, this group wouldn't make it – they were just too unconventional for their own good. The coming months, years and decades, were going to prove, on a spectacular scale, how very wrong we all were that night.

Later on, when transferring our equipment back onto the stage, I surreptitiously glanced at the Rickenbacker guitar leaning against an amp and there didn't appear to be any visual damage to the head of the guitar. It was then I saw the speaker cabinet with the gaping hole in the fabric. I took a closer look and discovered that it didn't actually contain a speaker – it was a completely empty cabinet! Presumably the fabric would be replaced in time for the next gig! OK, so the guitar and amplifier didn't sustain any damage, apart from the torn speaker fabric. Yet the naked aggression and anger of the act was very apparent, and quite chilling to watch at the time.

I learned a very important lesson that night, which I have applied to various events and situations throughout my personal and working life. Complacency is extremely dangerous. Never take anything for granted. Try and be individual and be bold enough to try new ideas even if, at the time, people laugh at you.

FOOTNOTE:

1. On Saturday 28 March 1964, nearly a year earlier to the day, The Rolling Stones played an early evening gig at The Wilton Hall in Bletchley, culminating with a late session at the Club Noreik in Tottenham, North London!

2. On the night we supported The Who, a new artist, Tom Jones, was riding high at number one in all the UK charts with the song 'It's Not Unusual'. We had supported Tom Jones and The Playboys at the Club Noreik only six months previously!

3. A book was published in 2002 called 'Anyway, Anyhow, Anywhere The Complete Chronicle of The Who 1958 – 1978'. The book gets its title from their second top ten hit and features the poster advertising The Who plus The Candles that I pulled off the wall outside the Club Noreik in the early hours of 13 March 1965. It has also been used in a collage of posters displayed on the inside covers of the book, back and front.

It was one of the proudest moments of my life when I saw that poster reproduced in full colour in this book. However, having already sold the poster to a rock memorabilia site on the Internet, I have often wondered how the poster made its way into the book.

4. Even more amazing that poster, decades later, was eventually made into a 21cm x 29cm tin sign and became available to buy worldwide via hundreds of poster sites on the Internet.

5. Club Noreik – It has always struck me as rather an unusual name, and over the years many people have asked me where the name originated. I had no idea! However, carrying out some research on the club on the Internet, I discovered the origins of the name. It was very simple – it was the name of the promoter's young son, Kieron, spelt backwards!

27

WE MEET THE WHO AGAIN – SUNDAY MAY 1965

A couple of months after we had supported The Who at the Club Noreik, we found ourselves playing a Sunday evening session at a highly popular pub called the Two Puddings, which was located on Stratford Broadway in East London.

The pub was run by Eddie and Shirley Johnson. Eddie served the drinks and also acted as a bouncer as well. Standing over 6 feet tall, no one but no one argued with Eddie. Shirley was in charge of food and sometimes pulled the odd pint.

THE TWO PUDDINGS

CALL ON SHIRLEY & EDDIE JOHNSON FOR THE BEST IN
FOOD & ENTERTAINMENT

THE TWO PUDDINGS.   Phone :-
27, BROADWAY STRATFORD, E.15.   MARyland 2604

To give you an idea of how hard Eddie was, one busy Saturday evening while we were playing, a drunk had come into the pub and stood with a number of people already waiting to be served at one end of the bar. The bar staff were pulling pints for other customers, when the drunk became agitated and started hurling abuse and swearing at the top of his voice, demanding to be served. Eddie called out 'Be with you in a minute mate' which only made the drunk more abusive. That was it! Eddie stormed down the bar, grabbed a half-pint bottle of lager off a shelf, bit the top off – yes, actually bit it off – and thrust the broken neck of the bottle to within an inch of the drunk's face. He turned his head, spat out the bottle top and bits of glass and yelled out 'You want a drink, then come and get it.' The drunk made a hasty exit. We were always very respectful to Eddie.

The pub was long and narrow and was entered via swing doors off the wide pavement of the Broadway. Near the entrance, on the right, was a fairly high, but very small stage, which visiting groups shared with an up-right piano. The high stage meant that groups had a great view of everything that took place during an evening. Opposite the stage, and only a few yards away on the right hand side, was a long bar which ran the full length of the premises. Apart from a small free area in front of the stage, customers stood and drank in the narrow area which ran parallel with the bar right to the back of the pub where a few tables and chairs were set out as a dining area.

After seeing The Who perform at the Club Noreik wearing their own casual clothes, we eventually came to a unanimous decision. No more wearing matching outfits and so the madras jackets were cast aside. This was one of our first appearances on stage just dressed in our 'street gear' and it would take me a while to get used to it.

Every Saturday, and the occasional Sunday, Eddie's brother, Ken Johnson, ran a dance in Stratford Town Hall, which was situated a few yards away from the pub. The town hall was a very large Victorian building, blackened by years of East London factories pumping out their grime. Weekly dances were held in the large banqueting hall and we ended up playing there on many a Saturday night. However, Sunday night 'specials' were reserved for the well-known groups of the time.

LIVE MUSIC INSIDE THE TWO PUDDINGS PUB

We had been playing regularly at the Two Puddings for well over two years and had built up a steady following, resulting in the pub always being packed out on a Saturday and Sunday evening by around 8.30pm.

We were well into the first of two one-hour sets one Sunday evening, when four young men entered the pub and passed close to the stage, dodging around people on their way to the bar. I recognised them, but couldn't quite place where I had seen them. Then it hit me. Of course, it was the group we had performed with eight weeks previously at the Club Noreik.

Unbeknown to us, The Who were playing a gig at the Stratford Town Hall that very evening! As they passed the stage, it was only Keith Moon who recognised and acknowledged us – the other three simply made their way to the bar. Keith came over and offered to buy us drinks and we ended up with five pints of lager. We chatted with him in between songs and he wanted to know how we were getting on and if we had plenty of work. He then suggested that, when we had our break, we should come and watch them play next door. He said he would inform security to expect us and then he went and joined the other group mem-

318

bers. They continued drinking and listened to our music for a while before leaving and nodded in acknowledgement as they passed the stage.

When we took our break, we walked round to the back of the Town Hall, into a courtyard and up a metal fire escape to double fire escape doors – a route we had taken on many a Saturday night when we played there. The bouncer who opened the doors was expecting us and we made our way through a door at the side of the stage, up some stairs and then stood in the wings watching The Who. Immediately it was noticeable how much more professional they had become since we had seen them perform two months ago. Although still dressing individually, the jeans and T-shirts had been replaced with more colourful Carnaby Street attire.

The band as a whole, apart from John Entwistle, had become much more active on stage. Pete Townshend was now even more aggressive, constantly moving around and windmilling his arm, thrusting the head of his guitar through the speaker fabric and producing big thunderous chords. He kept turning around and holding his guitar in front of the speakers creating squealing feedback, plus a new move I couldn't remember seeing before – he moved up to the microphone and slid the strings of the guitar backwards and forwards across the metal mike stand, creating a gigantic screeching sound.

It wasn't long after the Stratford Town Hall gig, that Pete Townshend's live act went up a notch. In addition to his usual on-stage aggressive acts, he started to physically abuse his guitar. Usually performed as the group finished playing their last number, he would unstrap his guitar, bounce it up and down on the floor, toss it into the air and throw it across the stage, sometimes even head-butting it! Increasingly, as a grand finale at more prestigious events, he would hold the head of the guitar and, with both hands, repeatedly smash the body of the guitar on the stage, until the guitar broke into many pieces. Pete Townshend called this period of instrument mutilation 'auto destructive art' and it gained the group a lot of publicity in the press.

Although Roger Daltrey was still swinging his microphone around and hitting it across Keith Moon's cymbals, he was now swinging it high above his head, somehow always managing to catch it on its way down.

John Entwistle had his usual impassive expression and remained relatively motionless, apart from his left hand, which was constantly racing up and down the fretboard.

Keith Moon – well, he was just as manic as before, leaning forward slightly with both arms outstretched as he hit every drum and cymbal as if his life depended on it. He was in the midst of a big drum roll when he looked across, saw us in the wings, smiled and nodded.

We reluctantly had to leave and get back to the Two Puddings to start our second set of the evening. Within a few days, The Who's second single 'Anyway, Anyhow, Anywhere' was released and became their second top ten hit. They had achieved lift off, while we continued to taxi along the runway!

FOOTNOTE:

1. Eddie Johnson, the 'big' man at the Two Puddings had two sons, Matt and Andrew. Matt went on to front a group called The The, a very successful post-punk band of the late 1970s and Andrew designed many of the The The's album covers. The The released a single called 'Mrs Mac' and the front cover of the sleeve shows a photograph taken outside the Two Puddings pub with Eddie holding hands with his two much younger sons.

2. A Rickenbacker guitar from this period belonging to Pete Townshend, and looking the worse for wear, turned up for sale at a Sotheby's 'Rock Memorabilia' auction. Although the neck was still attached to the body of the guitar, the machine head and the white scratch plate were missing. Any odd loose parts belonging to the guitar were included in the sale.

4 JUNE 1967 - SAVILLE THEATRE - LONDON

An unknown young black American guitarist suddenly burst onto the British music scene in 1966. His name was Jimi Hendrix and he became known as the 'wild man of rock'. As his career progressed, he started introducing feedback into his act and sliding his guitar strings across the mike stand – a compliment to Pete Townshend who had been doing just that a year before!

It's not recorded if Hendrix had smashed his guitar up on stage before his appearance at the Saville Theatre on 4 June 1967, but it had certainly undergone some rough treatment before then, even to the extent of being set on fire. I was in the audience the night Jimi Hendrix and The Experience played their final gig at the Saville Theatre in Shaftesbury Avenue, London. Near the end of the show, he announced that his work permit in the UK had expired and that he was forced to leave the UK temporarily. He then went on to say that in recognition of his success in the UK, he wanted to give something back to his British fans in the audience.

A few minutes into their next song, he suddenly turned away from the mike and walked up to the to the wall of speaker cabinets behind him. He then started to sway from side to side in front of the speakers, encouraging feedback. As the high-pitched squealing started, he slammed the head of his guitar time and time again into the speaker cabinets. He then strode over to the drummer's rostrum and wielding his guitar like an axe, proceeded to demolish his Fender Stratocaster guitar on the back leg of the rostrum in what was an act of sheer vandalism. It was as though he was trying to fell a tree and the noise was deafening. The leg finally gave way under the assault and the rostrum tilted backwards. The drummer, who was still frantically trying to play, slowly slid off the rostrum into a heap at the back of the stage.

Hendrix then walked to the front of the stage and raised what was left of his guitar above his head and brought it crashing down onto the stage floor. This act finally detached the body of the guitar from the neck and still holding the head of the guitar, he threw the neck into the audience, strings flailing everywhere. People in the stalls were immediately on their feet, arms reaching out ready to receive any sacrificial pieces. Hendrix then looked around, picked up some dismembered pieces of the guitar – the broken scratch plate, then the metal bridge – and threw them into the heaving crowd as well.

The body of the Fender Stratocaster had by now split into two near equal halves and his final act was to separate the pieces, raise them above his head and after a brief pause, these last remnants of his guitar ended up in the audience. Throughout most of this spectacle, the guitar had been plugged in and the noise was excruciating. Only near the end of this dramatic episode did the guitar lead become detached from the guitar, killing the sound. There was no encore and Hendrix and the other group members silently left the stage.

The lights in the theatre came on and the audience were eerily silent as they began filing out of the theatre and onto the street. This act of aggression was very reminiscent of a Who concert 12 months previously when Pete Townshend demolished his guitar on stage. As we left the Saville Theatre I can distinctly remember saying to John 'If only we hadn't paid extra for those circle seats, we might now be in possession of a piece of Hendrix's guitar.' However, the evening had been a very special event for me and viewed from the front seats of the circle, it had been magical. Rock luminaries were in attendance that night. To my right, in two theatre boxes, were members of The Beatles and The Rolling Stones together with their various girlfriends. And to my left, sitting immediately next to Pat, my wife, was Mike D'Abo, the lead singer of Manfred Mann, whom Pat fancied like mad at the time! No comment!

FOOTNOTE:

1. Both body sections of Hendrix's Fender Stratocaster eventually resurfaced at a Sotheby's Rock Memorabilia sale in 1991, fetching a multi-thousand pound price. Before his appearance at the theatre, Hendrix had

crudely painted a brightly coloured psychedelic pattern on the front of his Fender guitar. He had also painted in a scrawl, a poem he'd composed before the show.

2.   Much to everyone's surprise that evening, the first song Hendrix performed was a new Beatles' song called 'Sergeant Pepper's Lonely Hearts Club Band'. This song was taken from the album of the same name and had only just been released on the market two days beforehand. I've subsequently seen Paul McCartney talking on a TV programme and saying that hearing that song played by Jimi Hendrix only two days after its release was one of the highlights of his career.

3.   Feedback fascinated John Lennon and he was always searching for a 'new' sound to record. It was his idea to introduce feedback, in a controlled manner, at the beginning of the Beatles' song 'I Feel Fine' which was recorded in October 1964 and went to number one in December of that year. Now I wonder if that simple use of feedback by The Beatles in anyway influenced Pete Townshend. Townshend went on to use it in his guitar solo on the single 'Anyway, Anyhow, Anywhere', which was released in May 1965. However, before the release of this single, Townshend had already started using feedback quite actively at live performances and Jimi Hendrix went on to use it in his live shows in 1966. Now I wonder who influenced who?

28

WORKING FOR THE KRAY BROTHERS – ESMERALDA'S BARN
KNIGHTSBRIDGE, LONDON – MARCH 1965

Towards the end of 1960, the Westminster Bank sent me on a four-week training course, held in South Kensington. On day one, with a bunch of fellow trainees, we took our morning break in a local coffee bar, just over the road from the training school. While we waited for our frothy coffees to arrive, I got up and selected a few songs from the jukebox. It was while we sat there sipping our coffees and chatting away, I overheard a guy opposite say 'I love the guitar solo coming up on this Ricky Nelson record.' When the record finished, I leaned across the table and introduced myself to him. His name was John Jenkins and I discovered that he was also a lead guitarist in a group and that he lived just up the road from my brother in Billericay, which was about ten miles from where I lived in Romford.

Another discovery made that morning was that John and I both fancied the blond Swedish waitress who had served us earlier! She had beautiful slim legs encased in sexy black fishnet stockings. For the next four weeks we discussed guitars and music and sat in that coffee bar every day drooling over the waitress. That was the start of a lifelong friendship and we still have the odd guitar jam session some 50-odd years later. We still drool, but more from the effects of old age than the effects of beautiful women, although having said that…!

Some five years on from the training school, I was busy sorting and weighing up bags of silver coins at the till, before the bank opened its doors in East Ham's High Street, when the telephone rang. 'Call for Colin' somebody called out, so I swung off my chair and headed out to the back of the branch and into a small telephone cubicle. It was John Jenkins asking if we could help him out as they weren't able to make a booking that coming Sunday as their drummer had been taken ill. He wondered if we were free to fill in for him.

It was his lucky day. We were free on that date, 28 March, and I asked him more about the place. He told me it was a club called Esmeralda's Barn in Knightsbridge and that it was a bit of an odd place. He said it was a sort of club with a small bar and that there were only a handful of people there when they played a few weeks ago. However, the important bit was that they paid on the spot and that we would earn £20 for two one-hour sessions. That sounded good to me, and John then went on to confirm the starting time, the full address and the directions for getting there, before finally confirming that he would warn the club that we were filling in for his group.

On the day of the booking, we headed into Central London and following John's directions, we made our way down Park Lane, round the big roundabout at Hyde Park Corner and headed for Knightsbridge and ultimately Wilton Place. We pulled into a small cul-de-sac and were pleased to see that there was an empty parking bay available. The only light came from an old Victorian street light, close to where we were parked and as I climbed out of the van, it struck me how quiet it was. I looked around and on the left was a restaurant with the name emblazoned above the entrance, Joan's Kitchen. At first I thought it wasn't open, but on walking up to the glass windows and peering in, I could make out couples sitting inside, enjoying themselves eating and drinking. The only light inside came from flickering candles placed on each table. I looked at the menu by the window and at the top it stated Joan's Kitchen & Bistro. So this was one of the new trendy bistros that were springing up all over London. I made a mental note that, given the opportunity, I would take my new girlfriend Pat there very soon. Hopefully it would impress her and earn me some valuable brownie points!

JG's voice suddenly brought me back to reality. 'Here's the club.' Adjacent to the bistro was an imposing building. JG was standing in front of a large panelled door with a single lantern-type light hanging above it. As I approached, he pointed to a highly polished brass plaque on the wall etched with the name, Esmeralda's Barn. Martin leaned across and pressed the brass bell push. A few seconds passed in silence and I was just about to press the bell push again, when a buzzer sounded and the door opened slightly.

We climbed up the stairs, curious to see what this so-called club was like. At the top, I opened a door and entered a large dimly lit room, the only source of light coming from a small bar facing us and from a couple of low-wattage shaded wall lights. To our left were about half a dozen small tables and chairs and that basically was it. Not a customer in sight. The barman, who was busy polishing a glass, looked up and smiled. 'Hello, are you the band?' When I said we were, he told us to set up our equipment in a corner of the room, close to the entry door. I voiced my thanks and said we'd go and bring our gear in. We went back down the stairs and outside John was the first to comment. 'What a weird set up! How can that tiddly place make any money!' Martin turned to me and asked 'Did John Jenkins make any comments about the place?' 'No, not really' I replied. 'All he said was that it was a very quiet club, but they always paid in cash before you left, so that was the most important issue for me.'

With much huffing and puffing, we climbed the steep narrow staircase and set up our gear in the corner that the barman had indicated. Having tuned-up, we ordered some beers from the bar and I spoke to the barman. 'Is it always this quiet or is it because it's a Sunday?' 'No, not really' he said. 'This is a pretty average evening. People will start to appear later on.' 'Would you prefer it if we started a bit later when more people are here?' I offered. 'No, don't worry' was the reply. 'I would suggest you make a start now as it's coming up to eight o'clock.' It was certainly a first for us when we started our set in a completely empty room!

Being a quite a small place, we decided to play some of our quieter numbers first and save the more raunchy ones for later when the club filled up a bit. We must have been into our third or fourth song, when a door near the bar suddenly opened and a shaft of bright light spread into the room. A couple of older men wearing evening suits walked in and as we watched, they ordered drinks at the bar and then sat down. One of them lit up a cigar. We looked at one another, but just continued playing. We weren't used to seeing people in evening dress at our gigs and none of us could figure out what this place was about. A bit later on the door opened again and this time three men, again all much older than us and in evening suits, entered the room. They also went up to the bar, ordered drinks and sat down. Within a few minutes, the original two men got up, opened the door next to the bar and disappeared. Looking across at the other group members, I could see that, like me, they were also studying the comings and goings from that single door and were wondering what was going on.

The entry door to the club then opened yet again and about four men walked in, all wearing dark overcoats and one had a white silk scarf around his neck. They walked straight up to the door near the bar, opened it and disappeared up the stairs.

Eventually we finished our first set at 9.00 o'clock. By now there were half a dozen people sitting at the small bar and about five or six sitting at tables, all wearing evening suits. With the barman busy, we decided to go out of the club for some refreshments and found a pub just along the road. We sat there drinking our beers and discussing this strange club called Esmeralda's Barn. John reckoned it was a high-class brothel, which we agreed was a possibility. But the main topic of conversation was, how does the club make any money and were we going to get paid tonight? I assured them we would.

We ambled back to Wilton Place and pressed the doorbell. Within seconds the door opened and up we went. As we entered, we noticed that nothing much had changed. A few more people were now sitting at the bar and three of the tables were occupied. Feeling refreshed from our break, we switched on our amplifiers, checked our tunings and started playing. Still the pattern of people coming and going continued for the rest of our set and there were never more than about ten people maximum in the small club at any one time during our performance. Nobody at the bar or sitting at the tables paid us any attention or acknowledged any of our songs by applauding, which was strange. Our set finally came to an end and we all agreed that it had been a pretty boring evening. Everyone made me promise not to accept any more bookings at this place.

With our gear finally packed away, I told the others to get in the van while I collected our money. I was slightly concerned we wouldn't get paid, but didn't want to let on. I went back into the club and walked over to the bar and waited while the barman served two men with drinks. As I tried to catch the barman's eye, I happened to look across at the two men. The one facing me looked pretty menacing as he sat there in his tight-fitting navy blue dinner jacket, which emphasized his thickset body shape. The other one had his back to me. He looked considerably older, with thinning grey hair. As I stood there, the man facing me kept staring across at me with dark leaden eyes and, even as he spoke to the older man, he continued to look at me. I purposely didn't go for any long eye contact – he just looked too menacing. Finally the barman saw me and as he came over to me, he withdrew an envelope from his inside pocket and handed it to me saying, 'Thanks for the music, and also for helping us out at such short notice.' I replied that it had been no problem and that we were glad we could help out. The two men suddenly stopped talking and the older one spun round. They both gave me a cold stare. I nodded to them and headed for the door, trying to walk nonchalantly across the room, I could feel their eyes watching me and as I got near the door, I speeded up, yanked the door open and ran down the stairs. Before going out into the street, I quickly opened the envelope. Please let there be £20 inside I prayed! I didn't fancy going back and having it out with the barman, especially in front of those two men. Luck was on my side – four five-pound notes! That was the one and only time we ever played at that club and we never ever heard from them again – easy money, but a pretty boring place.

Fast forward by about 20 years and I am about to find out how wrong I was about Esmeralda's Barn being boring! I was in in a bookshop wondering what paperback to buy to take with me on holiday. Ten years of my now defunct banking career had been spent working in the East End of London and in our group days we had played in many East End pubs. Although I had heard of the Kray brothers and was aware that one of the brothers had coolly walked into the Blind Beggar pub in Bethnal Green and shot another gangster in the head – that was about it. So when I came face to face with a book entitled 'The Profession of Violence – The Rise and Fall of the Kray Twins', that was the end of my search and the book was purchased.

A few weeks later I was lying in the sun next to a large swimming pool in Italy, deeply engrossed in my new book. I was about to turn the page to start a new chapter, when two words leapt out at me in the last sentence – Esmeralda's Barn! I couldn't believe my eyes! I quickly read the next chapter, which was entitled 'Barn of Gold' and after more than 20 years, learned that Esmeralda's Barn in Knightsbridge had been a gaming club, part owned by the Kray brothers!

It had started life during the 1950s as an exclusive nightclub for the well heeled. Even royalty had been guests there. However, Esmeralda's Barn became a gaming club when the government of the day introduced the Gaming Act in 1960 and gaming clubs were allowed to open and operate, but solely as member-only clubs. At the same time, the Krays were looking for a way to expand their empire and move into the West End of London. They were offered part ownership of the club by another big player in the criminal world, as a way of paying off a debt and getting the twins off his back.

I put the book down. I was still in a bit of a daze from what I'd just read and lay there in the sun, reflecting back to that Sunday evening all those years ago. Apparently the club had had three Chemin de Fer tables, one Roulette table and a restaurant. All this activity took place in the floor above us and where we had performed was just a cooling off place for the wealthy punters to relax and unwind, before heading back upstairs to the gambling tables. That explained all the comings and goings through that door next to the bar!

That chapter in the book went on to describe how the Krays, both dressed in their Savile Row navy blue dinner jackets, would regularly arrive at the club before midnight and have a drink at the bar before retiring to the restaurant.

As I recalled the events of that evening, it suddenly hit me. The younger of the two men who had sat at the bar in the tight-fitting navy blue dinner jacket – was it one of the Krays? I'd read that Ronnie Kray was a homosexual. Crikey, was that Ronnie staring at me in the bar!

THE MUSIC BUSINESS IS CHANGING FAST - 1965

The music business in the early 1960s was slow to respond to change. At that time, it was virtually unheard of for young groups or singers to write and perform their own songs. If any up-and-coming youngsters were fortunate enough to be signed up to make a record, then Tin Pan Alley would supply a selection of songs for their consideration. Tin Pan Alley was the nickname for Denmark Street, a small street in Central London, which was the centre of the music publishing business in Britain.

George Martin, head of EMI's Parlophone Records, who had recently signed up The Beatles to his label, broke with tradition. Impressed by their repertoire of self-penned songs, he selected two of them as their first single. The A-side was 'Love Me Do' and the B-side 'P.S. I Love You'. Unknowingly, this was the catalyst for big changes ahead in Tin Pan Alley. Soon repercussions were felt throughout the music publishing business. As The Beatles' popularity grew, so did their power and influence in the music world. They, and other major groups, sought to have greater control over their own songs by forming their own music publishing companies.

Even in the Abbey Road recording studios, during the early era of The Beatles, old traditions continued to reign. Sound engineers wore white overalls and carried clipboards, defining their position within the hierarchy, whereas other studio employees, involved in less technical work, wore dark beige overalls. So it's no wonder that in the early days of The Beatles and the groups that followed in their wake, wearing suits and ties on stage was still quite acceptable as everything else involved with the music business was still quite archaic and old-fashioned.

But a change was slowly taking place and a new music ethos was beginning to gain momentum. Together music and fashion now played a key role. What group members wore on and off the stage influenced the fans who wanted to dress similarly. Entrepreneurs were quick to spot the demand and trendy boutiques soon opened up, especially in Carnaby Street in London, which became a Mecca for youngsters wanting to find that new fab outfit. If they were lucky, they would find themselves mingling there with famous 60s groups and celebrities who were being photographed and filmed shopping in Carnaby Street. The 'Swinging Sixties' had arrived!

A massive hit by the Kinks called 'Dedicated Follower of Fashion' immortalised this fashion period of 'Swinging London'. Written by Ray Davies, the lead singer in The Kinks, he refers to the shoppers of Carnaby Street as the 'Carnabetian army'. The words, 'one week he's in polka dots, the next week he is in stripes', refers to those dedicated followers of fashion. The song also makes reference to the nearby areas of Regent Street and Leicester Square, and 'round the boutiques of London Town'.

29

THE 'BROADS' IN NORFOLK – JULY 1965

Y ou would have thought that, seeing one another three or four times a week, year in year out, the last thing we'd want to do is go on holiday together. But no, we were like a close family. Even Martin, who in previous years had done his own thing holidaying with his girlfriend, now wanted to join us and Patrick said he wanted to as well. Dave was now a married man and had family commitments.

The big question was – where should we go? Over a number of weeks suggestions were made and rejected, until the consensus was, let's hire a boat and explore the Norfolk Broads for a fortnight. Eddie Caswell also expressed the desire to join us. Although not acting as our personal manager anymore, he was still a good friend and employed us regularly at his club. I booked a boat for a fortnight and early one Saturday morning the six of us crowded into Eddie's rather large and impressive American car, a Fairlane 500, and headed off to Oulton Broad in Norfolk to pick up our six-berth cabin cruiser.

It was a lovely sunny morning and we were in high spirits as we drove along the A12, cracking jokes and taking the pee out of one another. Whenever we came up against some old codger pootling along at 30 mph, Eddie would curse and then slowly pass the car with just inches to spare. The look of horror on the drivers' faces as we passed by, had us in stitches. Just outside Braintree, we hit a slow-moving traffic jam and for the next 15 minutes we crawled along in the summer sun, getting hotter and hotter, until Eddie had had enough and pulled over into a large layby. We all got out of the car to stretch our legs and watched the queue of traffic stop and start, slowly edging forward without making much headway. Suddenly we could hear frantic screaming and hanging out of a back window of a car travelling slowly on the inside lane, were three young girls. We'd been recognised! We all waved to them, which brought about even louder hysterical squeals and they continued screaming as the car slowly moved forward. That's show business for you! After about ten minutes, the traffic started to flow a lot faster and so we got back in the car and edged our way back into the line of traffic.

EDDIE'S FAIRLANE 500

Arriving at Oulton Broad, the hire company provided us with some basic instructions on how to operate the boat and then the keys were handed over. This boat would now become our home for the next two weeks. We had even splashed out and hired a small wooden dinghy, which we would tow behind us. Before leaving our mooring we drew straws to see who would share the two twin-bed bedrooms at the front and rear of the boat. Martin and I lost and so we ended up sleeping in the bunk beds located in the small dining area. Having unpacked our clothes, Eddie took the wheel and we cast off, heading for King's Lynn, our first port of call.

Martin had insisted on bringing along one of his large bass cabinets, which was securely tethered on the roof of the small wheelhouse. We chugged quietly along with open countryside all around while Martin busied himself setting up the record player and it wasn't long before we had music blaring away. As we meandered along at five mph, we passed fields where cattle and sheep were grazing quietly. I'm sure they hadn't heard such loud rock music before! There were speed limits on the Broads, which varied from three to six mph. For the first few days, we all took turns in steering the boat but slowly the novelty began to wear off and so we had to set-up a rota system, allocating an hour at a time behind the helm.

We cruised into King's Lynn, secured our boat to another boat already moored up against the harbour wall, and headed off into King's Lynn, looking for a steak house. Having eaten a delicious meal, we returned to our boat to find four Liverpudlians sitting on the deck of the boat next to us, drinking beers. We grabbed some beers and joined them, just sitting and chatting away, getting to know each other. After a while, Eddie, a keen gambler and a pretty ruthless player, suggested a game of Pontoon with our new friends. We ended up playing from ten o'clock at night until five o'clock in the morning. By the time we all got to bed, the Liverpudlians were £30 down. Eddie had made about £20, which was a good week's salary for a qualified person back in 1965. The rest of us just gathered up a few pounds each.

For the remainder of our first week, we cruised along the quiet water-ways of the Broads, introducing rock 'n' roll music to all and sundry. However, cruising along at a maximum speed of five to six mph meant we didn't really cover a lot of ground. We would sometimes moor the boat outside a riverbank pub in the evening, eat a meal and have a few beers, only to find the pub closed its doors at ten-thirty. So there we were, six young men stuck in the middle of nowhere, with nothing to do but gamble and drink. A couple of times we moored up and wandered into a small picturesque village, only to discover there wasn't a restaurant in sight. But you could always count on a village having at least a couple of decent pubs where we could eat and enjoy ourselves, but always the same old problem would occur. The pubs would shut at ten-thirty and within a few minutes of leaving the pub, the streetlights in the village went off and we would have to make our way back to the boat in total darkness. All that there was left for us to do was play another few games of Pontoon for a couple of hours.

One of the highlights of our first week came about when we made an unscheduled stop for lunch at Wroxham Broad. As we were passing a toyshop in the town centre, I spotted a plastic water pistol in the window. What a great idea it would be to have a water pistol fight on the boat to relieve our boredom! Everyone agreed and we walked out of the shop with a water pistol each. We got back to the boat after lunch and quickly filled up our newly acquired weapons – it was every man for himself! We spent the next couple of hours having a wonderful time darting around the boat like demented children, hiding and firing at one another.

We felt like we were kids again – and acted like it! At one stage I was up on deck when I spotted Patrick through a glass skylight hiding in the dining area below deck so, lifting up the skylight quietly, I managed to fire a good few shots of water over him before he fled, only to be confronted by someone else who was hiding in the next room. Suddenly it was five against one. Poor old Patrick! Eventually he locked himself in the little toilet but I managed to lean over the deck and by laying flat on my stomach, pulled open the small frosted glass porthole and emptied my water pistol all over him. He exited the loo straight into another barrage of shots. We couldn't stop laughing and ended up calling a truce. Patrick was drenched but none of us had escaped getting wet, so we changed into dry clothes and sailed forth. We'd had a marvellous couple of hours! It was all very childish I know, but we had thoroughly enjoyed ourselves and it had relieved some of the boredom for a while. Travelling all day along narrow smelly rivers at a snail's pace, with nothing to look at but row upon row of hedgerows, has been known to turn sane men quite mad. Well, that's my excuse for such behaviour!

By Thursday we'd all simply had enough of the peace and tranquillity of the Broads and to make matters worse, it had been raining heavily all morning. Eddie needed to get back to Chingford to run the Lorain Club the following evening and as John was only staying with us for a week, he was going back with Eddie the next morning. We agreed unanimously that we would head for the bright lights of Great Yarmouth, mooring up there for the rest of the holiday and enjoying the local entertainment. The following morning Eddie and John would head off to Oulton Broad to pick up the car and make their way home. It had finally stopped raining as we approached Great Yarmouth, but by now the water level had risen quite dramatically. Manoeuvring the boat was made increasingly difficult by the fast flowing water and the task of mooring the boat was handed over to Eddie. However, when we arrived, the large mooring area was packed with boats stacked three-deep up against the quay. We reached the end of the quay and had to make a quick turn, heading back up-river to avoid sailing under a metal bridge with a big sign saying NO BROAD BOATS ALLOWED BEYOND THIS POINT. We slowly made our way back, struggling against the strong current, searching for a space. Suddenly a boat pulled away from its moorings and Eddie quickly manoeuvred into the space and we tied up against the second boat. With the boat now firmly secured, we made our way over the two boats and climbed a metal ladder up onto the quay from where we headed into town to explore the area.

GT. YARMOUTH - HERE WE COME

We'd heard that Great Yarmouth was a busy and lively holiday resort, especially at this time of year, so we were all excited at the prospect of some interesting times ahead investigating the nightlife. In the 60s, Great Yarmouth was a typical English seaside town catering mainly for the working classes who took their annual holiday there during the summer months. It was a loud and colourful town, full of large bars, cafes, amusement arcades, bingo halls and amusement parks.

THE CANDLES ARRIVE IN GT. YARMOUTH –
'OK GIRLS, SETTLE DOWN'!

After stopping for a few beers, we then wandered into an amusement arcade. Walking up to the little coin booth inside, I asked for pennies, handed over two shillings and sixpence and in return received 30 pennies. I spent a good half-an-hour on one particular machine, convinced I could win some money. This machine consisted of a large glass cabinet containing shelves that continuously moved backwards and forwards. On the shelves were layers and layers of pennies deposited there by previous players, some pennies hanging tantalisingly halfway over the edge of the shelf. The object of the game was to roll a penny down a movable slide, aiming the coin towards the back wall. The penny would then drop down either onto the moving shelf or onto the layers of coins. With a bit of practice, you could aim the slide so that the penny dropped down and lay flat just as the shelf moved backwards. When it made its return journey, the coin would be pushed forward and, in turn, push the mound of pennies forward. With a bit of luck some pennies would fall over the edge and into the cup.

These machines were quite big and some had up to eight movable slides which could accommodate eight players at any one time. I always made for a machine that nobody was using and I'd start by aiming a coin slide and dropping a penny into it, then quickly move to the next coin slide, aim and drop the penny in and so on. I continued doing this around the machine as quickly as I could, until I'd used up my supply of pennies. I would then go to each of the metal cups and hopefully scoop up my winnings. It was all a matter of luck really, with a little bit of skill thrown in, but of course, as with any gambling machine, it's designed to make money not lose it, so over time you end up with nothing left in your pocket. That's the time to move on.

On our way back to the boat we were passing a café, when a red neon light in the window caught our eye 'Freshly Cooked Fish and Chips'. Tonight's meal decision made in an instant! As we huddled round a table at the back of the cafe enjoying our fish suppers, Eddie announced that he was enjoying our company so much he had changed his plans. When the Lorain Club closed on Friday evening, instead of going home and joining us a few days later, he would clear up at the club first and then drive through the night to Great Yarmouth to join us in the morning.

It had rained heavily all night and we awoke to find the water level had risen quite substantially. The pathway next to the quay had flooded and is clearly visible in the above photograph. When it was time to depart, Eddie took off his shoes and socks, rolled up his trousers and, with John on his back, waded through the water to dry land. We said our goodbyes and they went off to order a taxi to take them to Oulton Broad to pick up the car.

Although it had stopped raining, it was still very overcast and grey, and so we passed the time by cooking ourselves breakfast and then lazing around for the rest of the morning. Finally the clouds parted and the sun made an appearance encouraging us to head into town to investigate further. It was certainly a lively town. We wandered in and out of numerous amusement arcades and eventually found ourselves in an amusement park. When we came across the dodgem cars we just couldn't resist the temptation and climbing into individual cars, we raced around bumping into one another and everyone else relentlessly, all to the accompaniment of loud rock 'n' roll music.

By late afternoon we'd had enough, so we took a vote and all agreed to head back to the boat, grab some beers and food on the way and watch a film that had been advertised on our little portable TV. It was an old black and white British film made in 1957 called 'Hell Drivers' starring Stanley Baker and Herbert Lom, together with a cast of assorted up-and-coming British actors.

Next morning we sat around, unshaven and dishevelled, having a lazy breakfast, when suddenly the hatch slid back and there was Eddie grinning away at us. He came down the steps and joined us at the breakfast table, placing a small metal cashbox on the table. Outside it had started to rain quite heavily, so no point in getting ready just yet. We had yet more coffee and toast and chatted away amongst ourselves. Eddie fumbled in his pocket, withdrew a key and made a suggestion. 'How about we have a game of Pontoon? I've got lots of money in here from last night's takings at the club.' He opened the cashbox and piles of compressed banknotes of all denominations sprung out onto the small table. Eddie was showing off a bit, but we were certainly impressed as to how much money the club made for him. The dirty breakfast things were quickly piled up in the sink, the table cleared and out came a pack of cards.

I'm a cautious gambler, as I hate to lose money. I think the others felt the same way and so we all agreed that the maximum bet should be no more than one shilling (5p). Eddie thought that was a bit pathetic. It was all right for him with his cashbox of money – we just weren't quite so flush as him. We also knew that Eddie had regular weekly card games with friends, so he was a bit of a hardened and experienced gambler compared to the rest of us. The four of us started the game with some trepidation, whereas Eddie was full of confidence. After about half-an-hour of playing, I turned and looked out through the porthole. The rain outside had intensified – and so had the game inside!

Eddie seemed to be on a bit of a high, most probably having had a successful evening at the club last night. He was being pretty reckless with his money, never betting under a shilling. When occasionally he was dealt two aces, he would call out 'split' and both cards would be placed face down separately on the table. He would then buy two cards from the banker at a shilling each, and these cards were placed face down on each ace. We all waited in anticipation as Eddie made exaggerated movements looking at each pair of cards, knowing full well he was teasing us. If one of the bought cards was a king, he was obliged to turn the card face up, indicating that he had Pontoon, and that meant he had increased his stake on one card to two shillings. But he could still buy blind on the other ace, and if the second card turned out to be of a low denomination, he would buy blind again. With a lot of luck, he might even achieve a five-card trick. Providing the five cards didn't exceed 21, his stake would have increased to four shillings. From his initial shilling bet, he had now increased his bet to six shillings. This happened a few times during the game and would cost one of us dearly, depending on who was acting as the banker.

Unfortunately, as the game progressed, the gods of good fortune stopped looking over Eddie's shoulder and his luck started to run out. The cards he was being dealt by the banker just weren't in his favour at all. By mid-day, he'd started to lose some money and with us playing cautiously, we had all started to build up our reserves. Eddie hadn't slept the night before, so he needed a pick-me-up to keep awake and remain alert. He poured himself a whisky, then another, and another. By mid-afternoon we were all tired and hungry and we decided to call it a day. Certainly for the moment anyway.

A few beers were handed round the table as we ate. We were all a bit dazed from the tension of the game and it was good to relax for a bit. I just happened to mention to Eddie that we'd watched the film 'Hell Drivers' the previous night and that I had recognised Sean Connery as one of the actors who had played a minor role. By now he had become a famous actor, playing the role of James Bond in the Bond movies. Eddie said he'd seen the film some while ago and was sure that Sean Connery definitely was not in the film. I turned to the others for their opinion, but none of them were as convinced as I was that it was him. 'Well, I know it was him' I said. Now, with no support, I was feeling a bit isolated over the matter. Out of the blue Eddie suddenly said in a loud voice 'You're wrong – I bet you £10 he wasn't in the film', this reckless bet spurred on no doubt by his whisky intake. £10, my God that was a week's wages for me! I certainly couldn't afford to lose that amount of money! As much as I was convinced I was right, I was beginning to waver slightly and have second thoughts. Perhaps I had been mistaken and it wasn't Sean Connery after all. 'Come on then, £10. Put your money where your mouth is' said Eddie, taunting me. My pride got the better of me and without thinking about the consequences if I was wrong, I extended my hand and we shook on the bet. As soon as we had shaken hands, the reality of what I had just done hit me. I could now kick myself for being so stupid, and the others looked at me in disbelief.

The tension had got to me – I needed to stretch my legs and think about what I'd just done. I made some excuse about going to buy some cigarettes, left the boat and headed into town. Fortunately by now the rain had stopped and the sun was breaking through the clouds. I thought about what I had done and what a fool I'd been for getting drawn into a situation like that. If only I had a copy of yesterday's paper, that might list the film and the actors who appeared in the film. And if only Google had been around at the time! However, I seemed to remember that Sean Connery had only played a minor part, so he might not even be listed. I decided to try a newsagent to see if perhaps they still had a copy.

The first newsagent I came across didn't have any of yesterday's papers left. I glanced along the shelf on my way out and spotted a copy of the Radio Times. Of course! I was being a bit slow. That publication should have the film listed inside and the actors who appeared in it. I grabbed a copy of the magazine off the shelf but noticed that this was the latest issue, starting today, and wouldn't have last night's TV listings. I went back to the counter and asked if they had a copy of last week's Radio Times. The assistant disappeared through some curtains into a back room and appeared moments later with last week's copy in her hand. I thanked her profusely, paid and left the shop. Outside I quickly turned to last night's TV listings and there it was, on the BBC, starting at eight o'clock, 'Hell Drivers'. Even better, the actors were listed below – Stanley Baker, Herbert Lom, David McCallum, William Hartnell, and many more. I was reaching the last line when I spotted what I was looking for – Johnny Kates played by Sean Connery. 'Yes!' I exclaimed loudly as I punched the air.

Armed with my proof, I made my way back to the boat. I was elated and so relieved that I wasn't going to lose nearly a week's salary after all. However elation turned to a feeling of guilt as I realised I couldn't possibly take £10 off Eddie, a good friend. I was deep in thought as I approached the spot where our boat was moored. Suddenly a head appeared from the hatch. It was Martin. 'You've just missed some fun. The two boats next to us were heading back to the boatyard, so we had a hell of a time manoeuvring the boats around to let them out. Some guy from the boatyard office came over and told us what to do, thank goodness.' I clambered on board, went down below and found Eddie. I opened the Radio Times and pointed to the film and to the name Sean Connery at the bottom without saying a word, trying not to appear too pleased with myself. I mumbled 'Sorry about that.' He took it well, saying 'Oh well, you live and learn something every day' and with that he fumbled in his pocket and handed over two five pound notes. 'I can't take your money Eddie' I said. 'Take it' he insisted. 'You won it fair and square. You'll offend me if you don't take it.' So I did!

By mid-afternoon we were already bored again and didn't know what to do with ourselves. Eddie came up with the suggestion to have a party on board the boat that night. A great idea but who did we know in Great Yarmouth to invite to this party! Eddie said to leave it to him, and he was gone. An hour or so later he reappeared with large sheets of white cardboard and some wax crayons. He then proceeded to write out posters saying 'Girls Only – Party on board the Gleam of York moored at Quay B, Great Yarmouth – Tonight 8.00pm-11.00pm – Saturday 31 July'. JG was the first to say 'Do you really expect girls to turn up out of the blue to attend a party on a boat?' Mr 'Confident', Eddie Caswell, just smiled and said, 'Why not, it's a Saturday night, and we've got nothing to lose.' With that, having written out six posters, he stood up and said 'Anyone want to join me? We'll go and pin these posters up around town.' 'I will' said Martin, and they were gone. Half-an-hour later they were back. Eddie had bought beers and wine, a few packs of plastic cups and some pink tissue paper. He went round the boat, unscrewing the light fittings and covering the bulbs with pink tissue. 'This will create some atmosphere on the boat tonight and will soften the lights' he said.

Having changed into our best togs, we assembled on the quay just before eight o'clock. Eddie was going to act as DJ and had sorted out a pile of records ready to play on deck that night. His plan was dancing on the deck. Below deck would be reserved for more intimate moments! At eight o'clock on the nail, our DJ started to play some music. We waited, not knowing quite what to expect. Ten minutes dragged by – nothing. Suddenly a taxi pulled up at the quay and four giggling girls got out. 'Hello girls, are you here for the party? Yes? Great, come aboard' said Martin guiding them onto the deck at the front of the boat. 'Would you like a drink?' I heard him ask. Five minutes later, two more girls walked up to us and asked where the party was. I pointed to the boat just as another taxi pulled up and more girls piled out and made their own way in the direction of the music. 'Right lads' I said. 'Let's get on board and enjoy ourselves.'

By nine o'clock, there were about 15 girls jigging around in very cramped conditions on deck. That made it about two girls each. So far, so good. But it wasn't to last. Standing on the deck, we were studying the girls dancing and about to muscle in, when there were a few spots of rain and then the heavens opened up. The girls ran for cover but, for some inexplicable reason, not one of them took our advice to go down below deck! They jumped off the boat, screaming, laughing and giggling, and took shelter under an overhang on the quay. Within minutes, a bus heading into town arrived and all the girls got on and disappeared into the night. It was probably just as well it had rained and stopped the party, as I can't believe that we weren't reprimanded for playing the music so loud for an hour. Considering the harbour was packed with boats some, no doubt, with young families on board, it was amazing that we didn't receive one complaint.

Eddie hadn't mentioned it, but he must have been looking on enviously at the sleek speedboats we'd spotted darting around as we slowly toured the Broads during our first week. One morning, he got up really early and announced that he was off to hire a speedboat. And with that he was gone. 'I wonder what brought that on?' I said to Martin who was lying in the bunk bed below me.

By mid-day Eddie still hadn't returned. With the sun now shining, we were stretched out on the deck when I spotted in the distance a lovely sleek speedboat. I called out, 'Look at this wonderful boat coming downstream. Bet Eddie would like one like that.' We stood up to watch it pass, when an arm went up and a hand waved. We couldn't believe it – it was Eddie! It transpired that when we picked up our boat in Oulton Broad last week, he'd spotted a sign advertising speedboats for hire. When he left us this morning, he'd driven back to Oulton Broad and hired a speedboat, leaving his car there. He wanted to surprise us by arriving in this spectacular way. He had most certainly succeeded!

As we made our way across the two moored boats to gaze in awe at this beautiful speedboat, Eddie was grinning from ear to ear like a Cheshire cat. It could seat at least four people and was about ten feet long. The hull was white and the decking was varnished natural wood with extensive chrome fittings that sparkled away in the sun. At the rear of the boat, a large black outboard motor gurgled away. 'Watch this' Eddie said, and pulled the accelerator back. With that, the boat's nose rose out of the water and he was off. Suddenly he dropped the revs, turned the wheel and coasted back, but that was enough to impress us. However, he'd have to be careful as already he'd created quite a wake and all the boats were now bobbing madly around in the water.

For the rest of the afternoon, Eddie generously took us for rides and even let us take the boat out along the river on our own. The following morning, he was up again at the crack of dawn and cooked breakfast for us all. I could tell he was really excited at the prospect of playing around in the speedboat again. 'Anyone fancy getting in the boat and we'll take off under that bridge and explore the harbour area?' he called out. 'Brilliant idea' somebody yelled back and there was an immediate scramble to get dressed.

It was a bit of a tight squeeze to get us all in the boat but we made it and in the warmth of the mid-morning sun, we sailed under the bridge, ignoring the warning sign, and headed out into the large harbour area. We chugged along, amazed at the size of the freighters towering over us as we passed by. They were moored up on both sides of the harbour and some had large cranes swinging over their holds, either loading or offloading their cargo. Nobody took any notice of us or tried to warn us away. After about 15 minutes, we started to approach the end of the harbour and could clearly see the waves of the North Sea. We quickly turned the boat around and headed back. Ahead of us, a large boat had left its moorings and was heading out to sea, so Eddie kept as close to the side of the harbour as possible. As the boat passed us by, we were caught up in its wake and we bobbed around violently in the water for a while, hanging on tightly for dear life.

Towards the end of our last week, we all toasted Eddie for hiring the boat, which had really contributed to livening up what could have been a rather boring stay in Great Yarmouth. The next day was Friday and collectively we decided we'd spend the last day of our holiday in the centre of Great Yarmouth. However, that night there was a massive storm with thunder and lightning and the noise of the wind and rain hitting the deck kept me awake. Eventually the thunder and lightning abated, but the rain continued to pour down. We sat having breakfast, surveying the scene outside through the portholes as the wind and rain still lashed the boat – what an end to our holiday. It continued like this all day and to stave off the boredom factor, we started to play cards again. Eddie started on the whisky once more – he was obviously so peed off with the weather and not being able to use the speedboat. The rain was still falling heavily when Martin and JG ventured outside to bring back fish and chips for dinner.

Having filled ourselves, we stretched out and watched some TV, but even that was dull. Suddenly Eddie sprung to his feet saying 'I've had enough of this. I'm going for a ride in the boat.' As he started to pull on a waterproof jacket, we desperately tried to reason with him that it wasn't safe to be out in a boat in this weather, especially as it would be dark very soon. I pointed out that the boat didn't have any lights, so he couldn't use it on the river. That didn't deter him and he went over and rummaged in a cupboard, bringing out a battery driven lantern. 'See you' he said, slid back the hatch and was gone. None of us bothered to venture outside – we just thought once out there, he'd change his mind. That was the last we saw of Eddie for nearly two hours. We watched some more TV, but as time went on we started to get worried about him. We decided we'd give it another half-an-hour and if he hadn't turned up by then, we'd report him missing to the police.

Suddenly there were footsteps on the deck but before I could get to the hatch, it slid back and there was a very wet, cold and bedraggled Eddie. 'Where've you been for goodness sake?' I said. 'We were so worried about you.' He was a bit wobbly as he made his way down the steps, clutching what looked like a poster of some kind. His teeth were chattering so much he could hardly talk. Martin poured him a whisky, which he knocked back in one mouthful and that appeared to help. As he started to slowly warm up, he told us where he'd been.

'When I left, I headed under the bridge and into the harbour, and kept going until I could make out the harbour entrance ahead of me. As I got closer, I could hear the sea crashing outside the harbour and could even make out the white tops of the waves in the moonlight. I should have turned back there and then, but I'd had a few whiskies and felt confident I could handle the boat out there. A bad decision.' As we listened to him, we couldn't believe he could be so reckless. He continued, 'At first it didn't appear so rough as I ventured out of the harbour, but as I sailed out further, the waves got bigger and bigger and started to crash over me, so I turned the boat intending to head back into the harbour.'

'It was then that I spotted the pier at Great Yarmouth jutting out to sea, with all it's lights twinkling against the night sky. I knew you wouldn't believe my story and I wanted to give you some proof, so I headed to the pier to look for something to bring back to prove my story. At one stage I was on top of a large wave, and then the boat plunged down into a large trough. That was when I lost the lantern.' 'So where was the lantern at the time?' JG asked. 'Well, I'd slipped the lantern's carrying handle over the radio aerial on the boat when I left here, never thinking it could come off, but the boat dropped down so quickly into the trough, the lantern just flew off. I finally made it to the pier and with great difficulty, tied up the boat, clambered up the metal ladder to the top and hauled myself over. I spotted what I wanted – a poster board advertising What's On in Great Yarmouth, so I untied it and somehow managed to climb back down and into the boat, which was bobbing around madly in the water like a cork.' He proudly picked up the sodden advertising board from the Britannia Pier and showed it to us. How much whisky did you drink before you left?' asked Martin. Eddie picked up the bottle, checked the contents and said 'At least half a bottle.' 'You're mad' I said. 'You could easily have been drowned out there.' 'But I wasn't, was I' and you could tell he was pretty pleased with himself.

'What I hadn't bargained for was the return journey. I was now sailing into the wind and battling against the waves. It seemed to take forever and sometimes I didn't appear to be making any headway at all. That was when I started to panic a bit as so much water was coming into the boat and I'd no idea if I had enough petrol to make it back. Eventually I could just about make out the lights of the harbour entrance and slowly but surely I managed to steer the boat into the calmer waters. It was like entering another world – the wind suddenly died down and the water was relatively calm. So here I am – I made it back in one piece!' I think Eddie knew he'd had a narrow escape, and was lucky to be here. After about half-an-hour, he made his excuses and headed to bed.

We got up early the following morning, as we had to head back to Oulton Broad and return the boat. After a quick breakfast, we assembled on the deck and quietly made our way over the two boats moored against us, to study Eddie's boat. We looked down and there must have been a good ten inches of water sloshing around in the bottom. Eddie just stood there silently looking down at the boat, no doubt re-living last night's experience. He finally climbed into the boat and with the help of a saucepan, he started to ladle out the water. Although it had finally stopped raining, the River Bure was now badly swollen from all the rain that had fallen over the past few days and there was a strong current as the water rushed passed us heading into the harbour and out to sea.

Eddie had managed to ladle out most of the water from the boat. Surprisingly the engine started on the first pull and he tethered it up to another boat. We then stood there contemplating how we were going to release the two boats moored against us, make our exit and then moor up the two boats again to the quay. There was no sign of life from either of the boats, so we assumed they were still fast asleep and as we didn't know them, we felt we couldn't wake them up. Anyway, there were six of us, so we should be able to cope. Eddie knew the procedure we had to undertake to get us out of our mooring, so we listened carefully as he talked us through what we had to do. A few days earlier, everyone except me had helped two boats get away, so the others had some sort of idea what to do. Two of us would first untie the rope at the stern on the third boat and as the boat swung out into the river, hold the rope taut while standing on the second boat, which would prevent the boat from swinging out any further into the river. Another pair of us would do exactly the same with the second boat, but this time standing on the quay. We also had to tie the ropes at the front end of the second boat onto a capstan on the quay. Eddie would start the engine on our boat and untie the ropes at both ends, which allowed us to move out of our mooring position and into the river. We would then pull in the second boat and tie it to the quay, while the other two pulled in the third boat and tied that up to the other boat. It all sounded straightforward but putting it into practice was going to be difficult.

JG and Patrick released the third boat, which immediately swung round very quickly in the fast flowing river. As much as they tried, they just couldn't hold the boat back. In desperation they had to let the ropes go or be pulled into the water. Martin and I were now hanging on to the ropes of the second boat, but we experienced the same problem – the power of the water was just too strong for us. JG and Patrick quickly clambered across the boats and onto the quay, but even with four of us pulling on the ropes, we just couldn't prevent the second boat from swinging further round. We started to panic. What could we do! We turned to Eddie who ran onto the deck of our boat and released the single rope holding the other two boats, which twisted and turned in the current and then headed off down-river towards the metal bridge. We just stood there watching in amazement.

Eddie suddenly shouted 'Quick, untie our ropes and let's get out of here!' We did as he said and were all back on board as he slowly pulled out of our mooring position. Initially we were protected from the strong current by the surrounding boats, but as we edged out into the river, our bow came in contact with the fast flowing water and the boat was pushed back. Suddenly there was a loud crunching sound as wood splintered and my immediate thought was that we'd holed our own boat. I rushed to the rear of the boat and looking down, saw a mass of splintered wood swirling around in the water. It was our poor little dinghy that had been crushed against the wall of the quay. It was already half submerged, so I quickly untied the rope and it disappeared from view.

I turned and gave the thumbs-up to Eddie. All that remained of the dinghy were little chips of woods swirling around in the water as the pro-peller speed increased and Eddie battled with the river. I just couldn't believe what had just taken place. It was like a bad dream and everything had happened so quickly. Slowly but surely, with increased power, Eddie was able to nudge the boat further into the centre of the river and we started to head up-river. I looked downstream, just as the two boats were disappearing under the bridge, but still with no sign of life on board. Could they still be asleep, I wondered? I asked Eddie what he thought might happen to those two boats. I hoped they wouldn't drift out to sea. 'I doubt it' he said. 'The water was flowing very fast close to the bridge, but was slowing down as it opened out into the harbour, so the boats will probably drift around for a bit. Let's hope that if there's anyone on board, they wake up soon. Can you take over and pull the boat over to the bank' pointing to where he'd tethered his speedboat. Soon it was tied on the back of our boat and we headed off to Oulton Broad.

Fortunately, I had taken out an insurance against damage and loss on both boats when I booked the holiday, so we were covered under the terms of the policy for the loss of the dinghy. Thank goodness! After Eddie returned the speedboat, we loaded our cases into his car and headed home.

That holiday put me off for life ever returning to the Norfolk Broads for a boating holiday, but for Eddie, boating became a passion. Within six months of our holiday, he'd bought himself a powerful speedboat and trailer and we all had some fantastic times in it. In years to follow, he bought a large cabin cruiser and we sailed from his mooring in Kent across the Thames estuary along to Great Yarmouth. He brought the boat in close to Britannia Pier and amazingly we could make out the metal ladder he'd climbed on that stormy night all those years ago. We again said how reckless he'd been and how extremely lucky he had been to have survived the ordeal.

30

CLIMBING THE SOCIAL LADDER - 1965

In 1965, groups like The Beatles and The Rolling Stones, who came from ordinary working class backgrounds, were eroding the traditional social barriers in the UK. They were seen mixing with royalty and the upper classes. Suddenly it was fashionable and acceptable for debutantes and the like to be seen with rock stars. Music was the driving force and the common denominator.

Working with the various London entertainment agencies was paying dividends and it was amazing how our group was growing in stature and popularity. Slowly but surely we were breaking out of our East End boundaries and heading into central London and even further afield. The social barriers were coming down around us as well. One night we'd be playing in an East London pub, entertaining a crowd of working class drinkers who occasionally liked to beat the hell out of one another. The next evening could find us playing in a local youth club, entertaining teenagers, and then the following night rubbing shoulders with the 'well heeled' under crystal chandeliers.

It's hard to believe, looking back, that four years previously we were only performing in public once a fortnight at a local school youth club and transporting our meagre equipment in a wooden cart. In 1964, which had been our busiest year so far, we completed a total of 129 gigs. We were basically on a roll. The more we performed in public and practiced on a regular basis, the better we became musically. But then the demand grew for better equipment, especially as we were now performing in larger venues and it became imperative to use quality amplification. Plus, as we travelled further afield, a larger and more reliable van was required. As our fees increased and we earned more money, so it was being ploughed back into the group's coffers to finance our new demands. But finally we were now in a position to take on all-comers.

THE WALDORF HOTEL - SUNDAY - APRIL 1965

Our first major 'up market' appearance in Central London took us to the Waldorf Hotel in The Aldwych, right in the heart of London's theatre land. For us, it was our first experience of a five-star luxury hotel and we were all pretty excited at the prospect as we drove into London. We had been told by the agency that we had been booked to perform for an hour at a private function to be held in the hotel's ballroom. An orchestra had been hired to provide the main music for most of the evening, but we were booked to play just for an hour, no doubt providing the 'new' dance music for younger guests.

We pulled up outside the brightly lit entrance and leaning out of the driver's window, I explained to the uniformed doorman who we were. We had speculated amongst ourselves on the drive there, that taking our equipment through the lavish reception area would be an experience in itself. However, no grand entrance for us – we were politely directed to a side street entrance where we were met by a member of staff.

We were escorted along numerous corridors until we came to a series of folding glass doors, which led onto a raised area at the rear of the hotel's ballroom. As we approached the area, we could hear the orchestra in full swing. Our instructions were to assemble our equipment, including JG's drum kit, in readiness to be moved into the ballroom. As we unpacked our gear, I peered through the lace curtains and could see the orchestra playing away with couples twirling around on the dance floor. The women were dressed in glittering evening gowns and the men in evening suits. For a brief moment, I really felt I had been transported into an alien world. Guitars were taken out of their cases and tuned up, ready for the off. We were then shown into a storeroom, where we stacked the empty equipment cases and covers. We were informed that at the designated time of 9.00pm the doors would be folded back to allow us to move our equipment forward into the ballroom.

We waited nervously behind the doors. At exactly the allotted time, the doors were folded back and we quickly moved our gear forward a few feet. The doors closed behind us and we found ourselves next to the orchestra. They had finished playing and were leaving the rostrum one by one. I plugged in our main plug board and instantly little red lights blinked back at me. Guitars were then plugged in and the tuning checked. JG made final adjustments to his drums and John made sure the mikes were switched on and the volume controls turned up. We were about to start, when the orchestra leader shouted across, 'Are you ready boys?' As we nodded in agreement, he turned on his microphone and announced via the in-house Tannoy system 'Ladies and gentlemen, for the next hour you will be entertained by The Candles, and then we will return to close the evenings' events. Thank you.'

I thought to myself that this was a first, playing for people attired in full evening dress. Hopefully there would be some younger guests who want to dance to our music. John looked around to make sure everybody was ready and I played the opening arpeggio on my guitar. We had decided to start with something not too rocky and thought 'Bad To Me' would be just right. John sang the opening verse, 'If you ever leave me, I'll be sad and blue. Don't you ever leave me, I'm so in love with you', followed by my short guitar riff, and then the rest of the group came in. It was obviously a good opening song as immediately the dance floor filled up and although 'Bad To Me' wasn't a waltz, many of the guests were dancing along to it as though it was. While we performed and went through our tamer repertoire, I stood there admiring the opulence of the grand ballroom and the twinkling crystal chandeliers.

'Bad To Me' was a song written and recorded by The Beatles and I had read in one of the music weeklies that George Martin, their producer, had deemed it not commercial enough as a future single release for the Beatles. It was offered to Billy J. Kramer and The Dakotas, a group coincidentally also managed by Brian Epstein, the Beatles' manager. George Martin went on to record and produce the 'inferior' song 'Bad To Me' for Billy J. Kramer and The Dakotas and it went to number one in the British charts!

The evening progressed well and we watched in amusement at some of the older couples attempted to dance the Twist when we did a fast number. As the dancers went down on their haunches, there were plenty of large female bottoms straining to escape the constraints of a tight fig-ure-hugging evening dress. The hour passed quickly and when John announced our last number, the guests applauded spontaneously. The orchestra then took over again. The doors behind us were opened, we moved our gear back a few feet, the doors were closed, and that was it.

THE SAVOY HOTEL - DR. BARNARDO'S BALL - MAY 1965

A month later, early on Tuesday evening, 11 May 1965 to be precise, we found ourselves heading into London again, but this time we were travel-ling along the Embankment by the River Thames. We turned right into Savoy Place and pulled up at the back entrance to the Savoy Hotel in the Strand where Bryan Mason was waiting for us in his open top red Tri-umph TR4A sports car, looking very dapper dressed in his black evening suit.

Bryan was one of the promoters who ran The King Alfred dance on a Sunday evening. He had approached us a few weeks earlier and asked if we would be interested in playing at a charity ball in aid of the Dr Bar-nardo's Homes for Orphans at the Savoy Hotel. Being a charity affair, Bryan explained that we would have to offer our services for free, but the exposure at such a high profile event in Central London could be good for us, with the likelihood of being offered some paid bookings following our appearance. We had a discussion about this and decided that it wasn't every day we had an opportunity to perform at the world-famous Savoy Hotel, plus it was a charity affair with Bryan donating his services as well, so would be good PR for future appearances at the King Alfred. We jumped at the opportunity!

Bryan directed us to a narrow side street at the side of the hotel. Outside an open fire escape door, we unpacked our gear and carried it down a long passageway until we entered a small ballroom, via yet another fire escape door. We deposited our gear onto a two-foot high stage at the back of the ballroom but before we had a chance to set it up, Bryan insisted on dragging us to the ballroom entrance and we were really chuffed when he pointed to a large sign that stated 'Candles Room'. While we were setting up our equipment, Bryan came up to me and introduced Lady Jacqueline Rufus-Isaacs, chairman of the Young Committee of the Dr Barnardo's Ball Committee. She thanked me, and the other group members, for donating our services for free. Bryan told me later that Lady Jacqueline had only just arrived moments before by helicopter, landing at the Savoy's helipad – I say!

DR. BARNARDO'S BALL

SAVOY HOTEL

Tuesday 11th May 1965

So here we were, mingling with the 'elite' of society, and getting ready to rock 'n' roll with them.

THE PROGRAMME OF THE EVENING'S EVENTS

8pm – Reception in the Lincoln Room by the Viscount and Viscountess Bledisloe.

9pm – Dinner will be served in the

Lancaster Room, and dancing to Confrey Phillips and His Orchestra and 'Some Sloan Squares'.

12.00 midnight – Dancing will begin in the 'Candles Room', presented by Bryan K Mason, featuring the well-known group The Candles.

1am – Cabaret Time with the Great American Blues Pianist and Singer Memphis Slim, who will introduce his favourite British Artist, Long John Baldry.

We finished setting up our gear, carried out a sound test by playing a couple of songs, and then went to join our girlfriends who were sitting at a table near the stage. Sitting close by on an adjacent table were two young men and as they finished their drinks and stood up to leave, one of them turned to us and said, 'Great sound boys, enjoy your evening' and walked away. I recognised the pair – it was Allan Clarke and Graham Nash from The Hollies, one of the most successful British groups during the 60s, with over 30 chart entries. Graham Nash later joined the American group, Crosby, Stills and Nash, and went on to even greater success.

We were now ready and waiting on the stage for midnight to arrive. The numerous small lights recessed into the low ceiling had been dimmed and I stood there, quietly taking in the moment, admiring the magical effect of candles flickering on each table, which were arranged around the perimeter of the dance floor. On each table was an ice bucket filled with ice and a bottle of champagne plus six glasses. Young people were now drifting in from the Lancaster Room, probably having had enough of the music supplied by Confrey Phillips and his Orchestra for one night, and were now ready for an early morning session of good old rock 'n' roll.

It was midnight. John went up to his mike and spoke to the assembled guests. 'Good evening everybody. We are The Candles and we'd like to start off this morning with a little number called...' He moved back slightly and with his strong voice, immediately screamed 'A mashed potato yeah'! As we all came crashing in, with Dave's raunchy sax riff dominating the song, instantly everybody was up on the floor, dancing wildly. The dance floor was awash with writhing female bodies all dressed in a variety of evening and cocktail dresses, with the men in their evening suits. As the evening progressed, most jackets were discarded and then bow ties were finally removed – this was going to be a memorable night. I must say that if a lot of these females were debs (debutantes), or Sloane Rangers as they were sometimes called, they certainly knew how let their hair down, and their escorts, known as Hooray Henrys, weren't far behind either.

The air-conditioning in this small ballroom with its low ceiling was struggling to cope with the 200-plus sweaty, heaving bodies, situated as it was in the basement of the Savoy Hotel. As the evening progressed, it became increasingly hot and stuffy, which naturally encouraged more drinking. We tried to lower the pace a bit by playing the odd slow number, but the revellers weren't having any of it and within seconds of a slow song finishing, we would get requests for a fast number. With just under an hour left to play, every song we now performed was just good old rock 'n' roll. We loved it – and they loved it! But all good things must come to an end and John eventually announced the last number, a fast rocky blues number called 'Shame, Shame, Shame'. I loved playing this song live and the place just rocked.

When the final chord was played, a cheer went up and most people on the dance floor walked to the front of the stage and clapped in appreciation, and then started to chant in unison 'More, more, more'. It was now two o'clock in the morning – would the management allow us to play one more song? I spotted Bryan Mason standing at the back of the ballroom and managed to catch his attention. He gave us a rolling hand signal to play another song, and then a finger went up to indicate just the one. John spoke. 'OK folks, one final number, and thanks for being such a great audience. We've had many requests to play the song we started with so, without further ado.' As soon as we started, everybody in the room squeezed onto the dance floor, determined to enjoy the last song of the evening. Then it was all over. The lights came on and the dancers turned and faced us, clapping and cheering for a good minute. In an emotional voice, John responded 'Good night, and thank you once again for being such a wonderful audience.' We all nodded our appreciation and then just stood there and applauded the audience – what a memorable night!

It was now almost three o'clock in the morning as we headed back along the Embankment and through a deserted City of London. My head finally hit the pillow at around four o'clock and I lay there in total darkness mulling over our performance for a few seconds, with my ears still ringing from the high volume of the evening's performance. As I closed my eyes, I immediately fell into a deep sleep – I was exhausted, but very happy!

I reluctantly came out of a deep sleep with my alarm clocking ringing. It was seven thirty. I lay there, momentarily stunned. I'd only had three and a half hours sleep and I felt lousy. I could easily have drifted back to sleep and I had to muster up all my will power to move. I sat on the edge of the bed with my head in my hands. I felt confused, my head was in a whirl. Slowly but surely my brain started to slip into gear and I began to recall where we had played last night and what a good night we had had. But what day was it? Then it hit me. It was only Wednesday – another three days of work before the weekend! When were we playing again? I thought for a moment and then I remembered – the Two Puddings in Stratford on Sunday evening. I breathed a sigh of relief. Four days free of bookings with a long lie-in over the weekend. I slowly stood up, stretched, and staggered off to the bathroom wondering how many of last night's revellers were still in bed sleeping it off.

THAMES RIVERBOAT PRIVATE PARTY – JUNE 1965

After our successful appearance at the Savoy Hotel, we were booked by one of the guests, a London stockbroker, to play at a private party on board a Thames riverboat. It was a lovely warm spring evening when we arrived at the Embankment Pier on the Victoria Embankment in Central

London. As we unloaded our gear, we were instructed to set up on the top deck, where there would be sufficient room for us to perform and for the party guests to dance the night away. We were informed that our drinks were on the house and a steward came and took our order. Within minutes, a tray full of drinks arrived. I discovered from the steward that the boat would head down river to Hampton Court, before heading back up to the Embankment Pier. I had a feeling that this was going to be a good night.

While I was tuning my guitar, I looked down from high up on the top deck and could see numerous taxis arriving at the pier and offloading guests who then made their way up the gangplank. As they came on board, they were offered champagne. Some remained on deck, while others made their way below deck to a bar where a large buffet was laid out.

The host came up to us to make sure everything was OK and suggested that we began to play as soon as the boat cast off and started its journey. We were all set to go. We sat having our drinks and eventually heard the boat's engine starting to rev up. I watched as the crew untied the ropes and slowly the boat started to move away from the pier, a signal for us to make our start. However, as soon as we started playing, it was evident that a lot of our sound was simply dissipating into the night, so the volume knobs were turned up higher. Playing in the open air on the top deck of a moving boat was an exhilarating experience and we were well into our first song as we approached Westminster Bridge when something unforeseen happened which caught us all by surprise. As we sailed under the bridge, for a brief moment our music was trapped in a large cavernous area and with our amplification turned up higher, our music suddenly bounced back at us at a deafening pitch. The reaction by the dancers was to let out a big cheer and this reaction was to set a trend for the rest of the evening.

One of the early highlights for me came as we emerged from under Westminster Bridge to the wonderful sight of the Houses of Parliament lit up against the early evening sky.

As the voyage continued and the guests below deck had eaten and drunk their fill, they started to emerge onto the deck to get some fresh air and cool down, or just to let their hair down on the dance floor. As we sailed under the numerous bridges that connected north London with south London, it brought about that same sudden increased wall of sound and with more people up dancing, so the cheering got even louder. Plenty of booze was being drunk that evening and someone somewhere had the foresight to ensure the group was well looked after as every so often a tray of drinks would materialise, which kept us nicely lubricated.

The evening was coming to an end and we had already launched into our final number, when the boat stopped adjacent to the Royal Festival Hall waiting for a clear turning circle to take the boat back to the Embankment Pier opposite. As I stood there playing my guitar, I looked up at the imposing Royal Festival Hall, which loomed over us. Situated on the South Bank of the Thames, it was awash with lights and no doubt an event was taking place there that evening. Our boat was bobbing gently in the wash of other boats as they passed by and the top deck was now packed solid with dancers making a lot of noise and simply enjoying themselves.

Suddenly a crowd of people from inside the Festival Hall came running out onto the terrace, no doubt to find out what all the noise was about down below. I watched with amusement as more and more people were coming out onto the terrace and peering down to investigate the noise. I do hope we interrupted during an intermission and not during a classical recital! Perhaps it would have been more appropriate if we had been performing Chuck Berry's 'Roll Over Beethoven'!

The boat moved forward and started turning just as the last chord of our final song was played. It edged out into the centre of the river before making a tight turn, pulling up along side the Embankment Pier and the wooden gangplank. Wow, now that was a good gig!

31

A PRIVATE PARTY - BERKSHIRE - JULY 1965

A private party in Royal Berkshire! Now that's something! We'd already played at a private party cruising down the River Thames and now we were booked to do one on terra firma. I was just reading the contract from A.B. Entertainments, one of the West End agencies we were currently working with. We had been booked to play three sessions over three hours, with a proviso stating 'possible extension after midnight at agreed extra cost' handwritten by the client. Interesting. History was in the making here. We were to be paid £32 for the evening, the highest fee we had ever been paid since we started the group, and possibly being paid even more if we were required to play after midnight!

We had no idea what to expect as we set off for Little Orchards in Shurlock Row in a village called Waltham St Lawrence, somewhere in deepest Berkshire. We came off the M4 and found ourselves travelling along leafy country lanes and through picturesque villages. What a lovely part of the world I thought to myself as I pulled up at a crossroad. 'What's was the name of the road we're looking for?' I called out. Martin checked the contract. 'Shurlock Row.' I looked left and right, but no street signs in sight. Suddenly Martin pointed, 'There, at the beginning of the lane opposite, that looks like a street sign.' I drove over to the lane opposite and stopped the van. Yes, there was a street sign partially covered by the branch of a bush. Martin jumped out of the van to take a look and pushing back the branch, all was revealed – Shurlock Row.

'Thanks Mart' I shouted, and then turned and spoke to the four in the back who were obviously relying on us to get them to our booking. 'Don't worry boys, Martin and I will get you there'.' 'OK sarky' somebody replied. Martin was back in his seat and off we drove, keeping our eyes open for a house called Little Orchards. No house numbers were in sight, only house names, which were either attached to a gate or nailed on a post at the end of a drive. We stopped at the bottom of a number of drives, but still no Little Orchards.

As I drove slowly round a bend we had quite a surprise. In a field, in full swing, stood a large vintage steam-driven merry-go-round. 'This has to be the place' I said, 'Otherwise what's a merry-go-round doing in the middle of a field in the middle of the countryside making all this noise!' A large gate was open, so I drove the van slowly into the field. Someone approached us and I stopped and slid down the driver's window. 'Yes, can I help you?' he said. 'I hope so' I responded. 'We're the band that's been booked to appear a private party for a Mr Clive Scott-Hopkins.' 'Oh good, I was told to expect you' he replied. 'Just pull up over there' and pointed to a gate at the side of the field, which I could see led to a large white farmhouse.

I swung the van over and slowly headed towards the gate, passing the lovely old piece of fairground equipment on the way. Drawing level with the merry-go-round, I stopped the van for a moment so that we could all have a look at this amazing sight. Coloured light bulbs flashed on and off as large, gaudily painted wooden horses attached to vertical poles slowly galloped up and down to the music. I parked the van as instructed and as we got out, the man walked over to us and explained that the field had been opened up as a car park for the party guests. 'Follow me' he said, as he opened the gate, and we followed him along a path, which led up to the kitchen door at the back of the house. He knocked on the door. Seconds later it swung open and we were introduced to the gentleman standing in the doorway as 'the band'. This very charming man introduced himself as Clive Scott-Hopkins, the party host, and we all shook hands. 'Come with me' he said. 'I'll show you where you'll be playing this evening,' and we followed him into a very large garden.

We were taken completely by surprise to see two large white marquees erected in the garden. We'd never seen anything like this before! They were open at the sides and as we followed Mr Scott-Hopkins into the first marquee, he went up to a long bar that had been set up inside. Behind the bar were three male bartenders, all dressed in black with long white starched aprons, busy cleaning glasses. 'This is the band who will be providing the music for this evening and they are to given any drink or food of their choice. Is that understood?' he said. 'Yes sir' they replied in unison. We were overwhelmed with his generosity and thanked him profusely. He then led us into the attached second marquee and there at the back was a small raised wooden stage. 'Just bring your gear through and set up here' he said. He turned to a young guy who was setting up some equipment on a table next to the stage. 'This is our DJ for tonight. His name is Ian Samwell.' We all said hello and shook hands.

Although our band suits and madras jackets were a thing of the past, at more prestigious events we had each started to take along our own individual change of more flamboyant clothing to wear on stage. I explained that we would need to change our clothing, so we were led inside the house and into a large ground-floor bathroom. 'Change in here. Don't worry, my guests will be using the portable toilets in the garden, so everything will be safe.' We followed him back into the kitchen and as we left to get our gear, he pointed to a small garden close to the kitchen door. 'Please, be careful not to walk on this section of the garden as it's my wife's labour of love, her herb garden.' We gave him our reassurances and headed back to the van.

I'd set up my amplifier, made sure it was plugged in and went to get my guitar out of the case to tune-up – but no sign of it anywhere. 'Has anybody seen my guitar?' I called out. 'It's probably still in the van' Martin replied. I nodded, and made my way back to the van. Opening the two rear doors, I peered in and moved the empty drum cases and the amplifier covers – no sign of my guitar! I couldn't believe it! I then walked round to the side door – perhaps it was still on the rear seat but no, it wasn't there. Panic then started to set in. I looked around the outside of the van. Maybe it had been left in the grass or propped up against the side of the van, but nothing. I then climbed into the van and moved everything again, but to no avail. It definitely wasn't there, but where the hell was it! I ran back to the stage. 'Found it?' asked John. 'No, but it must be around here somewhere' I said. Now the situation was being taken seriously and everyone helped me look for my beloved Gibson guitar.

Surely I must have put the guitar in the back of the van when Martin and I set off! I suddenly had a brainwave. I would call home and check that the guitar wasn't there and if wasn't, then I would call Martin's parents, just in case I'd left the guitar outside their house. My stomach churned at the thought. I ran back to the house, knocked on the kitchen door and explained my dilemma to the host who led me into a hallway where there was a telephone. I quickly dialled my home number and my mother answered the phone. I explained the problem to her and she immediately responded by saying the guitar was sitting there in the hall. They were wondering when I'd discover that I'd left it behind.

I'd never ever forgotten my guitar before. Why now, with such an important booking ahead, and we were miles away in Berkshire. To make matters worse, we were under contract to appear there that night, so we might even get sued. My mind was racing ahead, trying to come up with a solution. I looked at my watch. We were due to start playing in just over an hour, so there was simply no time for me to jump in our van and head back to Romford. My mum broke the silence. 'We have Jim and Gwen with us for the evening.' Jim and Gwen were Martin's Mum and Dad. 'Your dad said that when you realise the guitar is missing and call us, he and Jim will bring the guitar to you.' I couldn't believe what I was hearing. 'Wow, that's fantastic news Mum. Can you put Dad on the phone?' I gave Dad full directions how to get to Little Orchards and the telephone number, just in case they had any problems finding us. 'Thanks Dad, I really do appreciate you and Jim putting yourselves out like this.' 'That's OK' he said. 'We're leaving now. See you soon.' My heart was pounding. With a bit of luck they should be here just in the nick of time.

I went back and explained the situation to the rest of the boys so now with time on our hands we decided to sample some of the free booze. We were all around 22 years old at the time, but still none of us were into heavy drinking. We only drank the occasional beer and my favourite tipple at the time was a vodka and lime, but I could make two of those last all evening. We went up to the bar, which had now been transformed by racks and racks of various wines and spirits. On tap was a full selection of ales. Along from the bar was a large table with over a dozen huge round cheeses of every variety and ceramic pots filled with French loaves. On the next table along sat large urns of cream and massive bowls of fresh strawberries. How lavish! I sat down but couldn't relax and kept checking my watch. My nervousness made me down a few extra vodka and limes.

It was now just under an hour since my dad and Jim had left, so I wandered off to go and meet them. As I walked into the temporary car park, lo and behold, I recognized my dad's car pulling into the field. Was I pleased to see them! I thanked them both profusely as I retrieved my guitar case off the back seat and apologised for having to rush off. Martin and I speculated later that they had probably jumped at the opportunity of getting out of the house and no doubt would spend time in a pub somewhere on the return journey, downing a few pints of beer.

When I walked onto the stage with my guitar in hand, a big cheer went up and I quickly tuned up. Ian Samwell, the DJ, put us at ease. 'Don't panic boys. People won't be arriving yet for about another half an hour. I'll cover for you and play a few extra records in the meantime.' We expressed our thanks. I was now feeling a lot more relaxed and suggested another round of drinks. More alcohol slipped down our throats. It's surprising, when drinks are free, how much more you consume!

Quite a lot of the guests had started to arrive and although the party appeared to be quite a casual affair, people were generally formally dressed.

Most of the men wore suits with ties, and the women cocktail dresses. It would be another decade or so before attending such an occasion in casual clothing would be perfectly acceptable. I did notice that a number of the men had badges pinned to their lapels and wondered what that was about.

Ian Samwell had worked his spell putting on the right records as already people were up and dancing. He signalled he was putting on the last record of his set, so we discussed amongst ourselves what number to start with. Looking at the guests milling around, a good many were probably in their 30s, but there was also quite a large contingent of older people. We decided on 'Fortune Teller', a fairly old rhythm and blues number recorded by a number of British groups, including The Rolling Stones, The Hollies and The Merseybeats.

As we made our final adjustments, Ian faded his last record and then spoke to the audience. 'Good evening ladies and gentlemen. My name is Ian Samwell and I'd like to introduce you to The Candles. I will be back later to play some more records for you.' John then announced 'Good evening everyone. We'd like to start with 'Fortune Teller', a number by the Rolling Stones' and I started the four-chord riff on my own. After repeating it twice, the rest of the band came in. This was one of the few numbers when John used a tambourine, which he banged against his leg to add additional rhythm to the song. It was a good choice, as even more people started dancing on the grass in front of the stage. After nearly three quarters of an hour, we were coming to the end of our first set and Ian had already positioned himself behind his twin turntables. As soon as the last song finished, Ian spoke to the ever-expanding number of guests. 'Thank you The Candles. They are taking a short break and will be performing again in just under an hour. I'm Ian Samwell and I'm your DJ for this evening. So let's kick-off with 'I'm Alive', the new release from The Hollies.'

We put down our instruments, wandered over to the bar and another round of free drinks turned up. As we tucked into some bread and cheese, a tall older gentleman, wearing an expensive-looking charcoal grey pin-striped suit and silk club tie, walked over to me and said in a very posh voice, 'I say, jolly good show.' 'Thank you very much' I replied. 'Do you do this sort of thing for a living?' he went on to ask. 'No' I responded. 'I work in a bank'. 'Oh, so do I. Whereabouts are you in the City then?' I suddenly felt out of my depth. He was obviously in another league. When I told him that I worked for the National Westminster Bank in East Ham High Street, he looked at me as though I was from another planet. To try and change the subject as quickly as I could, I asked him about the dark green badge on his lapel, which had the word 'Judge' printed in gold on it. This immediately brought him back to life. 'Oh, I'm one of the official judges for the Henley Regatta and have been attending the races all day.' With that, he made a feeble excuse about seeing somebody he wanted to talk to, and was gone.

Before heading back to the stage, we all had another round of drinks. I don't know about the others, but I was feeling pretty good. The guests by now were loosening up as the drink flowed – or was it me that had loosened up! We started our next set with the stomping song' Just A Little Bit', which brought more people to their feet and onto the dance area in front of the stage. We'd been playing for about 20 minutes or so and had lowered the tempo by launching into a slow rendition of 'Summertime', when something interesting happened. One couple were trying to waltz to the song and I could see them slowly swirling around until eventually they were very close to the stage. As they swung past, the woman very discreetly slipped something into John's hand. John managed to continue singing as though nothing had happened. When the song finished, both Martin and I moved across to John, who had casually turned round and was unfolding a piece of paper. 'What's it say John?' Martin asked. I half expected him to say a request for a song and was surprised when instead John replied 'All it says is Lady Penelope Dyson and a SLO (Sloane Square, London) telephone number.' 'Trust you' I said. What was it that singers had that guitarists, drummers, or saxophonists didn't have? Perhaps we don't get messages because our hands are occupied playing our instruments! Or maybe it could have something to do with the fact that he was quite good-looking – and the singer to boot!

Our second break became a bit of a haze for me as I downed yet another two vodkas. The way the others were downing their drinks too, they must be feeling just like me – or worse.

I cannot recall too much about our last set, apart and when it came to my guitar solo, my fretboard seemed to disappear into the clouds. What came next was also a bit of a blur. It was already midnight and we had played our last song, when a flustered host came onto the stage pleading with us to play for another hour. By this time we had had enough of performing and drinking, so I pointed out that we had completed our contract, forgetting that it stated we might be expected to play an additional set. The host was by now getting quite hysterical. 'I'll pay you an extra £20 for an extra hour' he said. Normally I wouldn't be quite so forward, but the vodka was talking on my behalf. 'Why don't you ask the DJ to play some more records?' I suggested. But as I turned to ask Ian, I spotted him sitting crossed-legged on a box of records, having packed up his equipment while we were playing.

'Please boys' said the host. 'I'm really desperate here' and he swung an arm out, gesturing to his guests. 'They are all enjoying themselves so much and want to continue dancing.' He then unfolded a copy of our contract, pointing out the additional clause stating 'with possible extension after midnight at agreed extra cost'. I turned to the others, but before I could say anything, Dave spoke out. 'Make it £30 and we'll play for another hour.' 'Agreed' said the host. He appeared totally unfazed having to pay out the extra money. He withdrew a wad of money from his pocket and handed over £32. 'That's for this evening's performance.' He then handed over an additional £30 saying 'And that's to perform for the additional hour. I really appreciate it' he said. I took the money and thanked him, and with that he left the stage. My God, we were being paid a total of £62 for an evening's performance! That was nearly the equivalent of £800 at today's spending power!

John then made an announcement to the guests. 'We have been

asked to play for another hour, so let's not waste any more time. I want to see you all up dancing.' I smiled to myself. Normally any announcements made by John were kept to a minimum, so he was certainly excelling himself tonight. Was it the drink talking – or was it for Lady Penelope's benefit I wondered?

I had sobered up a bit as we launched into 'Lucille', a fast rocking number, which had everybody up and dancing. We kept up this pace for a good half an hour before introducing a couple of slow songs which everybody, including us, needed just to get our breath back. John made his final announcement. 'And now we'd like to finish the evening with 'My Babe', which has been requested by Lady Penelope Dyson.' Crikey, John was pushing his luck. I looked round and everyone in the group had wry smiles on their faces. Then I noticed the party host standing at the side of the stage. He leaned across and I held my breath. Don't say he's going to mention Lady Penelope! 'When you've finished, I'd like to say a few words to my guests before they leave.' 'No problem' I replied, breathing a sigh of relief.

I started the intro riff and the band came crashing in. The remaining guests got up to dance, but as I looked out over the crowd of dancers, I couldn't see Lady Penelope anywhere. Perhaps she'd left already. As the song finally came to an end, the guests immediately started moving towards the front of the stage, clapping and chanting 'More, more, more.' I looked across at the host, who was standing at the side of the stage. 'OK if we do one more number?' 'Be my guest' he said smiling. John turned round to face us. 'Let's do 'Woolly Bully' – OK?' and we nodded. John turned to face the guests and with his usual strong voice, launched into the song 'One I love, and it goes like this' and we all came in on cue. As we finished, the guests clapped and then it went quiet when they saw the host walk up to the mike. 'Ladies and gentlemen, thank you for coming this evening. I do hope you all enjoyed yourselves.' As people started clapping and cheering, he put his hands up. 'And I'd like to thank The Candles and the DJ for providing the wonderful music this evening' and more clapping and cheering continued. 'Have a safe journey home' he said. And that was it – it was all over.

Feeling extremely tired by this time, we slowly started to pack up our gear. The empty cases were being retrieved from the van, when Ian Samwell wandered onto the stage and spoke to us. 'Any chance of a lift boys? I've been let down. Somebody else can pick me up but unfortunately they can only get to Reading Station.' 'No problem' said John. We all thought Reading Station was just up the road. Meanwhile, unbeknown to us, Dave had gone to the bar and scrounged a last round of drinks. He now appeared on stage with the drinks on a tray. 'Well done Dave' somebody called out and we sat around, mostly talking about the evening's events.

Drinks finished, and with the last of the gear stashed away in the van, we made our way back along the path to the host's house to change. As we approached the kitchen door, John, who had been larking around with JG, suddenly leapt onto JG's back and the two fell onto the garden. We started laughing, when it suddenly occurred to me it must be the famous herb garden.

'Crikey' I exclaimed, 'I think you've fallen into the herb garden. Quickly, get up before you're spotted.' We stood there in the dark as Patrick moved forward and flicked his lighter. In the dim light we could make out a flattened area where the two bodies had fallen onto the herbs. 'Oh my God' said John. 'I'd forgotten all about the bloody herb garden.' That last round of drinks had certainly loosened us up and we just couldn't help ourselves. We all burst out laughing. When the laughing had subsided I said 'Let's make a hasty exit out of here' and we all bundled into the house to quickly change.

We said our goodbyes and helped Ian Samwell carry his turntable deck and boxes of records to the van. We finally drove out of a very dark field at nearly two o'clock in the morning. We were a bit peeved to then discover that we had to head west on the M4 motorway and then drive into the centre of Reading to drop Ian Samwell off at the station. This was in completely the opposite direction to where we wanted to go. We finally dropped him off, together with his gear, outside a deserted Reading Station, where supposedly somebody was meeting him. We didn't hang around. We said goodbye and headed back to the motorway and home. Surely a DJ would have his own mode of transport and not rely on other people to ferry him around. Obviously pretty small time, I thought to myself.

It was Monday afternoon and I was back at work. 'Colin, telephone.' I turned my TILL CLOSED sign around and made for the telephone cubicle. Another booking I presumed as I picked up the telephone. 'A.B. Entertainments here. We've just received a very disappointing report from our DJ, Ian Samwell. He felt you had all drunk too much on Saturday evening and subsequently didn't play your best. Also, we understand that you were paid an additional £30 in cash to play for an extra hour, so that means you owe us in total nearly £10. We'd appreciate a cheque being sent to us immediately.' I was momentarily taken aback but determined to have my say. 'No problem, I'll make sure a cheque is in the post this evening. However, yes we had a few drinks, but I can assure you that this did not hamper our playing ability in any way. In fact, the guests loved us and we had to give an encore at the end. Also, we had to go out of our way at two o'clock in the morning to drop Ian Samwell off at Reading Station.' The reply was 'Well, we've worked with Ian for a long time and we believe what he has told us. We'll be in touch.'

I just knew that we wouldn't be hearing from A.B. Entertainments again, but I posted their commission cheque to them that evening as promised. I came out of the telephone cubicle thinking to myself, that ungrateful little weasel of a DJ! Yes we'd had a few extra drinks, but we weren't that drunk or unruly and we had gone down well with the guests. Then it crossed my mind. Had the host complained about the damage to his wife's herb garden? At our next rehearsal night, when I told the group about the telephone conversation I'd had with A.B. Entertainment, we all agreed that Ian Samwell was well out of order.

Sitting on the train a few weeks later on my way to work, I was deeply engrossed in the latest copy of the NME and studying the current music charts. As I turned the page, there staring at me, was a face I recognized but couldn't recall his name or where I had seen him before. I looked at the caption under the photograph and it stated Ian 'Sammy' Samwell – Singer, Songwriter, DJ. Immediately the penny dropped and I realised it was the DJ from the private party the other week. I put the paper down on my lap and turned to look out of the window, watching row upon row of terraced Victorian houses whizzing past. It had never occurred to me at the party that this man could be the same Ian Samwell who wrote Cliff Richard's first hit 'Move It' and played rhythm guitar on the record. That was the first song we learned to play. He had been the guitarist in Cliff Richard's first band The Drifters before they became The Shadows, and it was Ian Samwell who left to concentrate on a songwriting career. He went on to write other hits for Cliff, one being 'Dynamite', another number in our repertoire.

Researching Ian Samwell's background on the Internet some 45 years later, I discovered that about a year after the private party, he had co-written a song with two members of The Small Faces. It became their first major hit and was called 'Watcha Gonna Do About It', a song I loved and which we played in the group. He went on to even greater heights, producing one of my all-time favourite groups, the US group America. Their first album established them as a major international group in 1972 and a single taken from the album called 'A Horse With No Name' became an international hit around the world.

Many years later I was driving up to London on my way to work, a tedious daily journey that took around two to two and a half hours and, as usual, I was listening to the news on BBC Radio Four. During a political discussion concerning a current issue at the time, it was suddenly announced, 'And now we'd like to go over to Brussels to discuss this issue with Euro MP, Mr Clive Scott-Hopkins.' What a surprise to hear that name again after all those years! It was the nice man who had hosted that garden party in Berkshire! After listening to what he had to say, I sat there in my car, reminiscing about all that had happened that night over 20 years ago, while waiting for the traffic to move.

NOT JUST PUBS AND CLUBS

From the first chart murmurings of The Beatles in late 1962 and their subsequent explosion and influence on the British music scene in 1963, the 'Liverpool Sound' dominated the British music charts. The Beatles were the first but were soon followed by other groups from Liverpool. Then the London group, The Rolling Stones, entered the charts and popularised rhythm and blues music. More and more groups were coming out of the woodwork from around the country, many playing and recording old blues numbers and breaking into the charts. It was music, music, music everywhere. Young people also wanted to listen to live music and so professional and semi-professional groups were in big demand. Besides performing in the odd school youth club, we had progressed into performing in pubs, clubs, hotels, private parties, weddings, cinemas and even American airbases – it was endless!

ALCONBURY - UNITED STATES AIR BASE - SEPTEMBER 1965

We had already performed at the Lakenheath United States Air Base in Suffolk a year earlier and been made most welcome on that occasion, so when a booking was confirmed at Alconbury Air Base, I was quite excited to think that once again we would be performing in front of Americans, the originators of rock 'n' roll music. We had been booked to play in the privates' mess at lunchtime, followed by an evening session in the officers' mess.

We set off early on a Sunday morning heading towards Cambridge and then branched off onto the A14. After about half an hour we spotted a sign for Little Stukeley, a small village close to the entrance of the large US airbase. This base was originally called RAF Alconbury and was used by Bomber Command during the early part of the Second World War. It was after America was attacked at Pearl Harbour and had entered the Second World War, that RAF Alconbury became a US base from where they flew their bombers. It has remained a US base ever since.

On the approach road to Little Stukeley, we started to spot a few American left-hand drive cars. These huge brightly coloured giants with their large tail wings and big chrome grill and bumpers fascinated me. I was in my element, just looking at them being driven around by men wearing fatigues and also sporting crew cuts. This was a popular pre-rock 'n' roll hairstyle of the America male. The hair at the back and sides was cut very close to the head and the hair on top cropped evenly, so that it stood up. Just past the village, we found ourselves driving along the perimeter road to the base.

The first things I spotted through the wire fencing were the tarmacked runways and then large hangars with fighter jets parked inside and outside. US personnel were everywhere and we spotted rows and rows of small bungalows with big American cars parked in the driveways. Ahead was the entrance and as we drove up to a small office window, a red and white barrier pole barred our entry. I was sitting in the passenger's seat so I slid down the window and told the guy in the office who we were and why we were there. He just looked at me without showing any emotion and then ran his eyes along the van. He then referred to a clipboard, running his finger down the list of today's visitors. His finger suddenly stopped and he picked up a phone and spoke with a deep Southern States drawl. 'Sergeant Kalowski, I have The Candles here. Where shall I send them? OK sir, will do.' He looked up at me and pointed a finger. 'See that building over there, that's the privates' mess. Drive over there and Sergeant Kalowski will meet you.' I said my thanks and off we drove.

We pulled up outside the building and there to meet us was this short stocky man in fatigues with a crew cut. I couldn't get over how men on the base were all starting to look the same! 'Hello you guys, I'm Sergeant Kalowski. Welcome to the base,' and we shook hands. 'Follow me' he said and we walked into a large bar with a big dining area/snack bar. Various US college pennants were pinned on the walls and also on the wall hung a framed coloured photograph of President Lyndon B. Johnson. 'Set up on the stage over there' said the Sergeant, pointing to a low stage in the corner, 'and make a start at one o'clock. You only need to play here for an hour, but this evening it'll be a two-hour spot in the officers' mess, starting at eight o'clock. Any questions?' 'How do we get to the officers' mess from here' I asked. 'Don't worry about a thing. When you've finished playing, grab some lunch, and you can play some pool over there.' He nodded to a couple of pool tables in the corner. 'Just relax and make yourselves at home and I'll come for you at six-thirty to take you to the officers' mess. See you later.' With that, he turned and was gone.

With our gear set up and ten minutes to spare, I went up to the bar to get a Coke. The barman selected a glass, scooped in some ice cubes, and then grabbed what looked a bit like a small shower-head attached to a single tube from a cradle. He pressed a button and instantly Coca-Cola gushed into the glass. I was amazed. This was a new one on me! I paid the man and went back to where the others were sitting. 'You won't believe how this Coke was served.' After I explained the method, all of them made a beeline for the bar. None of us had ever seen anything like this in all our travels and for me it would be about 10 to 15 years before I ever saw one again, in a London bar. Also, in most pubs in 1965, if you asked for say a gin and tonic with ice and lemon, you'd receive a bemused look from the bartender. However, it was possible that in an up-market pub, a small slice of lemon would be retrieved from a jar of preserved lemon pieces with a cocktail stick – but no ice! It would be another good few years before it became the norm to hear a barman ask 'with ice and lemon?' But here, a G&T was served automatically with ice and lemon and, with the press of a button, tonic poured into the glass.

We played our one-hour set but didn't get any real appreciation or response from anyone in the bar, which we found a bit strange. However, we just assumed that this was how things worked in American bars. While we were playing, I glanced at the menu on the wall. I was getting hungry, as I expect the rest were. It was hard to decide what to have. The list seemed endless and there was so much to choose from! Some of the food listed was quite alien to me – Braised Fresh Brisket, French Fries,

Dogs, Sundaes, Shakes, Soda Pop and Pecan Pie. Listed under 'Today's Special' was chalked up T-bone steak and French fries. I'd heard of T-Bone Walker, an old blues guitarist, but I'd never ever heard of a T-bone steak!

After we had finished playing, we sat at a table and discussed what we wanted to eat, but I'd already made up my mind. I was going for the T-bone steak simply because I was curious to see what it was like. Any form of steak in 1965 was a sheer luxury for an average family in Britain, but here the prices were incredibly cheap, no doubt especially for the US military. Eventually a waiter came over to us and took our order. Ten minutes later, this huge lump of steak was put down in front of me. In a side dish was a mound of very small potato chips and another had a small mixed salad. I sat looking at my meal. I'd never seen a steak so large – or chips so small. The salad, thankfully, looked like a salad. Boy, I was hungry and the first mouthful was pure heaven. I quickly got stuck in, but I wasn't used to eating so much and I caved in, having eaten over half of the steak. I pushed my plate forward and the hungry gannets around me soon devoured what was left.

We then packed our gear into the van ready to take it to the officers' mess, and for the rest of the afternoon just played records on the jukebox, enjoyed a few games of pool and generally relaxed. We all got a kick out of going up to the bar and ordering a Coca-Cola or a soda pop or even a gin and tonic, just to watch a button being pressed and drink coming out of a long tube. Sergeant Kalowski, being a military man, turned up at exactly six-thirty. I thought he might salute us but no, he simply said 'OK guys, follow me.' Outside he jumped into a jeep, while we piled into our van, and we followed him along the edge of a runway, passing a few planes and vehicles on the way, until he pulled up outside a single story building.

The exterior didn't look much but once inside, it was a whole different kettle of fish to the privates' mess. The décor was much more up-market with a fitted carpet running around the edge of a large room. Along one wall was a long bar, panelled in dark wood. There were lots of tables and chairs scattered around the edge of the wooden dance floor and each table had a white tablecloth and a small table lamp. Although I had enjoyed the ambience of the privates' mess, which was so like the bars portrayed in American movies, the officers' mess was more luxurious and had a nightclub feel about it.

We started playing to a small audience, but within half an hour there was an influx of young ladies into the room. Within minutes, officers came flooding into the bar and started chatting and dancing with them. It was only when we took our first break and I was chatting to a couple of these girls, that I established they were from Harold Hill near Romford! I was fascinated to learn that the US airbase had its own bus stop in Harold Hill and that the girls were ferried back and forwards to the base every Sunday. Why Harold Hill of all places when the airbase was about 70 miles away! A question I should have asked Sergeant Kalowski, but I never got round to it.

After the lights had been dimmed, there was a lot of close dancing and smooching taking place on the dance floor. To capture the mood, we started our second set with 'Blue Moon', a nice slow romantic song. It was obviously well received because just as we were just about to launch into another number, a barman came up to the stage and asked us what we'd like to drink, courtesy of one of the officers. We gave him our order, and when the drinks arrived, John thanked the officer over the PA system. After about 20 minutes, with our glasses now empty, I suggested we play 'Blue Moon' again thinking you never know, we might just get another round of drinks. Sure enough, we had finished the song and were halfway through another, when the barman came up to the stage again, this time carrying a tray with a repeat of our first order. John thanked the officer once more and we raised our glasses in the direction of the tables. We had no idea which officer was responsible for such generosity. Near the end of our set, an officer approached the stage and asked if we could play 'Blue Moon' just one more time before we finished. As we played the song, I looked onto the dance floor and the officer who requested it was making out pretty well with one of the girls from Harold Hill. Sure enough, five minutes later, just as we were finishing the song, another tray of drinks arrived, but this time we raised our glasses knowing the officer who was responsible. Let's hope that 'Blue Moon' did it for them!

It was after midnight before we set off on our return journey. Dave, who was driving, suddenly noticed that we were low on petrol and needed to look out for a 24-hour petrol station. Petrol stations that remained open for 24 hours during the mid-sixties were fairly plentiful on main A roads in Britain and in inner city areas, but we were off the beaten track in the wilds of Cambridgeshire. Dave was confident that we had sufficient petrol to get us onto the A14, which in those days was a two-lane B road, and that we would find a petrol station open. Three of us were in the back of the van trying to get some shut-eye, while the passenger stayed awake beside the driver.

However, by now none of us could relax in the back knowing we were nearly out of petrol and we kept asking Dave for an up-date on the petrol level. 'The needle is just touching the red level, so we have about a gallon of fuel left.' With no street lighting, it was pitch black outside and all five of us were now anxiously peering into the darkness looking for the welcoming lights of a petrol station. After about ten minutes, Dave announced 'I've been on this road before and I'm sure there's a petrol station about a mile ahead on the next roundabout.' We felt better hearing that news and, with our headlights on main beam, we could just about make out a roundabout ahead of us. Dave was right, there was a petrol station there, but it was bloody well closed! We were so dismayed. 'I can see us spending the night in the van' stated John glumly. 'What's the needle saying now Dave?' asked Martin. 'It's just touching empty and I reckon we now have about a quarter of a gallon of petrol left.' We continued along the road in total silence as we contemplated the worse case scenario, waiting for the engine to splutter to a halt.

As we were making our way up a long gradient in the road, John pointed ahead and shouted out 'The sky's lit up above those trees ahead!' We reached the brow of the hill and there, on the right with lights blazing away, was a petrol station. Without exception all five of us cheered in unison. What a sense of relief, we'd actually made it by the skin of our teeth.

HELLO MR TAXMAN - 1965

It came out of the blue – no warning! There, lying on the coconut mat by the front door of my parents' bungalow was a plain manila window envelope addressed to The Manager, The Candles. Without realising it at the time, this envelope and the letter contained within would have repercussions for all of us, and threatened the very core and existence of the group.

Since we first started getting paid for playing music, nearly every penny we earned was ploughed back into the group. Of course, as the bookings increased, so did our fees, and so did our annual turnover. However, on occasions we paid ourselves a little bonus, but never very much, and then only if we could afford to. Or we'd stop off somewhere and the group funds picked up the odd restaurant bill. From the very beginning, we had personally financed the purchase of our own guitars, amplifiers, mikes and drum kit from the money we earned in our day jobs. I was in charge of the group finances from day one. Our initial major group expense came when we bought our first van and had to pay the annual tax and insurance, which was paid for with group money. We all loved playing in the group and we didn't do it for the money. We did it because we enjoyed it. As we grew as a band, our expenses grew with us. Petrol and maintenance costs on the various vans we bought, were always paid for by the group. We saved up for everything, even when we had ordered our band suits from Burtons, and the final bill was paid for out of money from the group's earnings. So the group was self-financing until the day came when we decided collectively that in order to progress to greater heights, we desperately needed to invest in new, top-of-the-range equipment.

From day one, the guitars used in the group were individually purchased and the money we earned in our day jobs governed the quality and make of the guitar. It had been a slow progression. As we earned more, so guitars were exchanged for better models, until finally we all owned the best guitars money could buy. However, what was now hindering our progress was our overall sound. We needed to project the sounds we created through the best amplification and vocal sound system money could buy. JG also needed a new drum kit and again, that needed to be top of the range. We ended up buying the identical Ludwig drum kit that Ringo Starr of The Beatles used. If it was good enough for him, then it was good enough for our mate JG. We made a number of visits up to London to test and try out the various amplifiers that were currently available on the market, until we eventually settled for two big Gibson Mercury amplifiers. John already knew he wanted a Selmer vocal system and Shure mikes, having heard a number of professional and semi-professional groups using them.

Eventually, in February 1965, we marched into Hodges and Johnson, our local music shop in Romford, to do the dirty deed. It was a small shop that sold sheet music but also had on display a few pianos, together with some cheap guitars and amplifiers, but definitely did not hold stock of the quality gear we required. The salesman that morning must have thought he'd died and gone to heaven! The nearest equivalent for him would have been a win on the football pools! In the past the group had always financed any purchases by paying cash, but in this instance we all agreed that saving up for this new gear would simply take too long – we needed it now. Every single piece of equipment we required had to be specially ordered in for us and came to a total outlay of just over £1,200. With the assistance of a friendly hire purchase company, the total outlay was shared over four separate hire purchase agreements and four sets of parents kindly agreed to act as guarantors. A few weeks later I received a call from the music shop – our equipment was ready for collection.

Dave, our sax player, did not want to get involved in buying any new equipment as he had recently wed his girlfriend of many years. By coincidence, it was my mother who officiated at Dave and Gill's wedding and wrote out their marriage certificate, as she was then a registrar working at the local offices for the Registration of Births and Deaths. Gill was now pregnant and because of his new commitments, Dave was now desperate to earn and retain any additional money to survive in his new life. Plus Patrick, his close friend, had approached his own parents about signing an HP agreement but his father simply refused on principle. He just did not believe in borrowing money. So, problem solved. The original four members agreed to pay both Dave and Patrick a weekly salary based upon what was earned by the group each week, after general expenses had been deducted.

The group had now made some serious financial commitments, but what nobody foresaw in the great scheme of things, was the taxman coming along and demanding his share of our money! I took the letter along to the local tax office in Stratford, close to where I worked which, coincidentally, was where the tax letter had originated. I was shown into a cubicle and sat at a desk waiting for a tax representative to join me. He arrived carrying a folder, sat down and I explained that I had received a letter from the Inland Revenue, but was mystified as to what it was all about. He looked at my letter, opened the folder and then, having realised he'd need a tax return form to give me, he quickly left the desk, inadvertently leaving the folder open. I glanced at the folder and there, sitting on the top of some papers and staring me in the face, was a handwritten letter. Attached to the top corner of the letter was a newspaper advertisement. I instantly recognised it as an advertisement for one of our appearances at the Lorain Club in Chingford. Next minute the guy returned and handed me the tax return form. It all happened so quickly that unfortunately I didn't have time to read the letter or, more importantly, the signature at the bottom.

Someone had deliberately shopped us to the tax authorities! Was it a clerk in the Stratford office who, when he saw the advertisement in the paper, wondered if we were paying tax on the money we earned – a modern day bounty hunter! Or was it a member of another group or a promoter who, for whatever reason, simply wanted to damage us. The source of this letter was never revealed, and probably just as well for all concerned. However, the consequences were very significant for us. We now had to employ an accountant to prepare accounts going back four years and I had to trawl through the group's diaries and enter every fee we'd ever received from every booking. I had never kept any receipts, so the petrol costs and any other expenditures had to be estimated. Meetings were held with the accountants, who also wanted their pound of flesh, and I had to present any paperwork relevant to our case, such as insurance policies and HP agreements. Within a few months of signing up with the hire purchase company and agreeing to pay Dave and Patrick a weekly salary, we now had to pay accountant's fees and eventually unpaid taxes. We certainly had a big financial dilemma ahead of us.

Our finances had now become very complicated to administer. Dave and Patrick were responsible for paying back their share of any tax due and to make a contribution towards the accountant's fees. All this had to be calculated and deducted from their weekly salaries. All we had ever wanted to do was to play music and have some fun along the way. Now, we couldn't afford to be fussy about where we played or turn down any bookings. In fact I had to tout around for more work to help get us out of this mess. Despite all this pressure, I still attempted to be fair with Dave and Patrick and paid them some money whenever we had any spare cash.

Within a year, and now with an additional mouth to feed and only one salary coming in, Dave was feeling the pinch and every so often demanded more money, which unfortunately we didn't have. With tensions rising, I suggested to Martin, John and JG that we should meet to discuss the situation. After much deliberation, it was decided I would inform Dave we couldn't afford him any more, not a job I relished I have to say. The dirty deed was done after a booking at the Crystal Palace Hotel on 6 June 1966. On the drive home the atmosphere was extremely tense. Nobody spoke. Having dropped Dave off in Chadwell Heath, we made our way to Dagenham and, pulling up outside Patrick's house, he collected his guitar from the back of the van. Before slamming the door shut, he yelled out 'I quit!' Another bombshell had been dropped. Things were now going from bad to worse and it was time to call an emergency summit meeting.

It was decision time. Where do we go from here? Our next booking was in four days' time, at Harrowfields Youth Centre. At rehearsals one Tuesday, all four remaining band members sat down and discussed the options open to us. There weren't many. We were in debt, and to pay off this debt we had to continue performing. Alternatively, we could simply disband the group, sell our new equipment, and pay off any outstanding income tax between us. What, no group! Not an option! Do we attempt to carry on with just the four of us or do we start looking around for replacements? But that would involve paying them money. With plenty of bookings ahead, we had decided to find out what we sounded like without the other two members of the band and then come to a final decision.

As we started to run through our current repertoire, what a surprise we had. We sounded good even though we were missing a rhythm guitar and a saxophone. It was a much cleaner sound. Without really being fully aware of it, after five years of performing as musicians, we had all improved considerably. That, coupled with playing through our new gear, was the cherry on top of the cake. We discovered that we didn't have to drop as many sax-based songs from our playlist as we thought we would and in some cases, simply replaced a sax solo with a guitar solo. I also had to change my style of lead guitar, playing to compensate for not having a rhythm guitar but again, in most cases, the songs still sounded good. All in all, we only had to drop about ten songs, and so it was an easy decision. The Candles' flame would still continue to burn – and brightly.

Appearing at Harrowfields would be our first important test and we passed it with flying colours. We went down extremely well and to be honest, I don't think anyone in the audience even noticed that two group members were missing.

Financially speaking, we were now in a slightly healthier position by not having to pay Dave and Patrick a weekly salary. In addition, once the new equipment was paid off, it would then belong to the four of us. All very nice and simple. But we still had a long slog ahead of us to repay the debts we had already accumulated, plus the accountant's fees and income tax were still outstanding.

32

MARTIN BIDS US FAREWELL

OUR NEW BASS GUITARIST – RAY STEVENSON (TOP)

A lot had been thrown at us as a group recently. We had had the departure of Dave and Patrick from the group and we still hadn't fully recovered from the shock of the taxman demanding money. However, the next shock was a full body blow when, without any advance warning, Martin suddenly announced on the way back from a booking in January 1966, that he was leaving the group. We thought at first he must be joking with us, but no, he was deadly serious. Martin had been together with Jean, his long-term girlfriend, since our schooldays, and of late Jean had become unhappy at seeing less and less of Martin as the group's workload increased. Following an argument, she said she couldn't take it anymore and gave him an ultimatum telling him it was either her or the group. Over the past few weeks, Martin had been going through a lot of soul searching but in the end, love conquered all, and he made the big decision to quit the group. We were all devastated. It had come as a big surprise to me especially as Martin was a close friend of mine. We had started the group together and I thought he would have confided in me concerning Jean's ultimatum.

Having dropped this unexpected bombshell, Martin went on to redeem himself slightly by announcing that he'd found a replacement bass guitarist for us. His name was Ray Stevenson and he was coming to our next rehearsal evening on Tuesday to meet and audition for us. To give him credit, Martin had certainly done the honourable thing and had made every effort to ensure that the transition went as smoothly as possible. We wondered what Ray would be like. Would he fit in? Was he a good bass guitarist? Martin assured us he'd seen him play recently and that he was good. With a bit of luck, we wouldn't have to cancel any bookings, which was crucial to our financial recovery.

At the next rehearsal, Martin introduced us to Ray and although a couple of years younger than us, he had a similar sense of humour and fitted in almost immediately. That evening, we ran through our playlist of songs and Martin was on hand to help Ray where necessary. However, he was a competent player and picked things up very quickly. By the time we finished that evening, our new bass guitarist was up and running, and we were ready for our first engagement together. It had always been a pain, having to drive to Dagenham in the past to pick up Dave and Patrick, and everything had been easy for a while with the four original members of the group all living in the Romford area. Unfortunately, Ray lived in Barking and that meant we now had to drive even further out of our way before we could set off for a booking.

Before Ray left that first evening, I felt I had to broach the financial problems we had, pointing out that for some while now we hadn't been taking any money out of the group for ourselves. I offered to pay him whenever we had some spare cash and overall he was very supportive about our problem. He just responded by saying 'Thanks, but don't worry about it.' We discovered later that Martin had already advised him of our financial situation, so he knew he wouldn't be paid on a regular basis, especially at the beginning. I suspected that he was so excited to be playing on a regular basis in a well-known local group, that the money was incidental. But in time that would become a major issue.

We soon discovered that Ray could also sing and was a staunch fan of The Beach Boys. With his enthusiasm for their music, he started to encourage us to learn some of their songs. I have to say that I was reluctant to try at first because I just couldn't sing in tune, a problem both Martin and I had encountered in the past. This had restricted us in the songs we chose to play. However, I soon discovered that with Ray's encouragement, for some strange reason I could actually sing harmony parts. Besides introducing a couple of Beach Boys' songs into our repertoire, now with our new ability to harmonise together, our horizons had broadened and we started to learn songs that in the past we just wouldn't have considered. Our range of songs became more eclectic and helped along by my newly found singing confidence it injected new life into the group. The days of having a saxophone and a rhythm guitarist were fast fading from memory as we unwittingly started to develop a new sound on stage.

COOKS FERRY INN – MARCH 1966

By this time, we had amicably parted company with our manager, Eddie Caswell, but we still remained good friends. He had closed his office in Stratford and the Kavern Club in Forest Gate, as both were draining his finances. But fortunately for Eddie, he still had his cash cow, the Lorain Club in Chingford. In addition, the Ed Williams Sound System, his mobile disc jockey business, was providing plenty of work and one Sunday at the Cooks Ferry Inn in Edmonton, North London, we found ourselves sharing the same stage with Eddie. Ray had been with us for a month or so and it was the first time Eddie had heard us perform with our new line-up.

Eddie was playing the last record of his set and we had just mounted the small open stage ready to perform. He announced that we were about to start, nodded to us, and headed for a small bar, which was in a large alcove just to the left of the stage. Our opening number was 'Hideaway', a new song for us and a recent hit for another very successful British group, Dave Dee, Dozy, Beaky, Mick and Tich. We'd only recently learned it and had only played it once before in public. It was a mid-paced pop song, which required continuous harmonising from Ray and I, against John's lead vocals. The lights had been lowered in the hall, but still shone brightly in the small bar. Looking down from the stage into this bar, I could see Eddie had ordered a pint and it was just being pulled. I turned and called out, 'Is everybody ready?' They nodded, and we started with the opening riff. I knew we played this song well and it sounded very close to the original recording. My suspicions were confirmed when I glanced across to see if there was any response from Eddie as I respected his judgement.

He had his back to us and as he raised the pint of beer to take his first gulp, his arm suddenly froze when he heard us all singing and playing. His arm remained frozen for a few seconds while he continued to listen to us. He then very slowly turned around and stared at us in disbelief. Spotting me looking at him, he raised his glass. With his other hand he gave the thumbs-up sign and grinned. Only then did he take his first sip of beer. I knew he was impressed and I was well chuffed.

Ray had dovetailed into the group perfectly and we continued to expand our repertoire of songs. It was very interesting to see how a new member could inject a new lease of life into the band and broaden our horizons musically. I didn't intentionally take advantage of Ray but, as the money flowed in, it immediately flowed out again to pay the mounting bills. It was a very frustrating time and on occasions I did hand some money over to Ray who was very appreciative. We all thought he was happy with the situation, and he probably was, but unfortunately his father didn't agree.

We had pulled up outside Ray's parents' house on our way to a booking and gave our customary hoot. The door opened and Ray stood there looking very sheepish. As he beckoned us into the house, I slid down the window and shouted out, 'What's up Ray?' He yelled back, 'My dad wants to have a word with you all.' This was totally unexpected. I couldn't believe his dad just wanted to be introduced to us and was suspicious that something was else was afoot. We followed Ray into the house where we were introduced to his dad. He didn't even ask us to sit down, but just launched into a tirade. 'I'm not happy with Ray not earning regular money from the group. I know you've paid him some money already and he tells me you have a lot of debts, but I'm sorry, your debts aren't Ray's problem.' We stood there silent for a brief moment, and I sensed everyone was waiting for my response.

I pointed out respectfully that we'd been upfront with Ray from day one and had explained our financial position to him. I went on to say that Ray had been quite happy to accept our offer of only receiving some money when we could afford it and explained that it was just a temporary situation while we had paid off the back taxes to the Inland Revenue. 'And when will that be?' he interrupted. I told him I couldn't give him a timeline until we heard back from our accountants, but it shouldn't be that long. However, he wasn't having any of it, and poor old Ray looked devastated. I'm sure he would have been quite happy to continue as we had originally arranged.

His father then dropped the bombshell. 'If you can't start to pay my son on a regular basis what he is due, then I've instructed him to honour the bookings you have this week, including the weekend, but then after that he leaves the band.' I looked across at Ray, but his eyes dropped to the floor, so I spoke to directly to his father. 'I'm sure you can appreciate that I can't stand here and make an instant decision. I'd like to talk things through with the other members of the group first, to see what we can do about the situation.' I paused for a moment, and then continued.

'We really like having Ray in the group and wouldn't want to lose him. We do appreciate your concern and I can assure you we are definitely not trying to rip Ray off – honestly.' The others muttered their agreement. I then had to quickly point out, as politely as I could, that we were going to be late for our booking this evening if we didn't get a move on. I promised we would discuss the situation and, if necessary, talk to our accountants and then let Ray know the outcome.

That appeared to placate Ray's father, so we said our goodbyes and headed off to the booking. Ray was naturally quite subdued during the journey and we all took it in turns to chat with him and to assure him we wanted him to stay in the group. Gradually feeling more at ease, Ray went on to explain that his father ruled the roost at home and assured us he only had his son's welfare at heart. He went on to say that he had argued with his father beforehand, but he was adamant that he must be paid on a regular basis. I could tell that Ray was very upset about the whole affair, but at the end of the day he had to abide by what his father said. I didn't say it to Ray directly, but his father was right of course. We should be paying him on a regular basis. Nevertheless, we daren't default on the crippling monthly repayments to the HP company and run the risk of having our gear confiscated. Plus, we didn't want to fall foul of the accountant and the Inland Revenue by not paying them. However, all this had nothing to do with Ray and he shouldn't be penalised over it. So now we had another major problem on our hands.

During the period when Ray was a member of the group, we still continued to park our van next to Martin's driveway even though he was no longer in the band. On many occasions, as I was getting into the van on my way to pick everyone up, Martin would come over and we'd have a chat. Or returning late at night to park the van, his bedroom window would swing open and he'd ask how we had got on that night. I would always reply with lots of enthusiasm. 'We really went down well tonight at the Cooks Ferry Inn. Lots of cheering and clapping.' Poor old Martin, I knew he was missing the group who were also his good buddies, but he wouldn't confess to it. I also knew that deep down, although it had worked out well with Ray, without my old mate in the group it would never be quite the same again.

After dropping Ray off that evening, the three of us discussed the problem during the remainder of our journey home, but we just couldn't come up with an answer and decided to sleep on it. Lately, Martin had started to open his bedroom window on nearly every occasion when I parked the van after a booking. I knew he was now really missing the group, but neither of us really talked about it. As I drove home from JG's I pondered over the issue of Ray and hoped Martin would hang out of his bedroom window tonight. It would certainly be a very opportune moment for us all, if I told Martin about the problem we had with Ray – he might just say he wanted back in the group.

I had just reversed the van into its usual position, parked, and was climbing out of the cab, when the bedroom window swung open and Martin shouted down to me, 'So, how did it go this evening?' There was no point in beating around the bush and I immediately told him about the confrontation we had had with Ray's dad, his ultimatum and the dilemma we now faced. I held my breath. Without hesitation Martin responded 'Any chance I could come back into the group then?' I had to make doubly sure he wasn't being too hasty and that he really meant it, so I said, 'We'd love to have you back. You know that. But are you really sure you want to? And anyway, what about Jean?'

There was no hesitation from him. 'Of course I want to come back. I've been so miserable since I left and I've made Jean's life a misery too' he said. 'So I know she wouldn't mind if I re-joined the group.' 'Well that's fantastic! Welcome back! Just one thing, what about a bass guitar?' 'Don't worry about that, I'll get hold of one' he beamed out of the window. 'I always thought you were a bit hasty selling your lovely Epiphone as soon as you left' I said. 'Don't even go there' was his only response. So that was that. Problem solved. We were back on track.

We decided to let Ray play the final two bookings before Martin came back and we paid him £30 for his troubles. We were basically sorry to see him go as he'd been good for the group and had fitted in well. He genuinely didn't want to leave. But it would have been a financial strain on the band if he'd remained and anyway, it was great having our old bass guitarist back with us again. We dropped Ray off after the last booking, said our goodbyes and wished him good luck. That was the last time any of us ever saw or heard from Ray Stevenson again.

33

MR BASS MAN RETURNS

During the short period Ray had been with the group, he had given me the confidence to sing and harmonise, and subsequently a number of new songs had entered our repertoire. It had given the group a new lease of life. So with this new confidence within the group, Martin returned and after a couple of intensive evenings of rehearsals, he was singing Ray's vocal parts. It certainly felt good to have Martin back in the fold and a booking at the Eagle Pub in Tottenham in April 1966 was his first appearance since re-joining the group.

THE EAGLE PUBLIC HOUSE – TOTTENHAM – NORTH LONDON

We had never played at the Eagle public house before and when I received a message to phone a Mr Ramsey at a Tottenham telephone number, I wondered if it was anywhere near the Club Noreik in Seven Sisters Road, just on the corner with Tottenham High Road. It turned out the Eagle was situated in Chestnut Road, immediately behind the Tottenham Police Station in the High Road, about a mile away. We ended up with bookings for a Friday and Saturday evening in March.

As I turned the van into Chestnut Road that Friday evening, you couldn't miss the pub. There, on the right, was this large Georgian-style building with the name 'Eagle' highlighted in gold over the entrance door. I pulled up outside the pub and volunteered to go in and find out where to park and unload our gear. We didn't want to take a chance parking outside for too long as it was a busy road and the police station was just around the corner. I ran up the steps and into a large brightly lit saloon bar, where a handful of people stood talking and drinking. I caught the barman's attention. 'I'm with the group and we're booked to play here tonight. Is it OK to park outside while we unload our equipment?' 'I wouldn't chance your luck with the cops so close. If you drive up the alleyway at the side of the pub and park outside the double fire exit doors at the end of the building on the left, I'll let you in' came his friendly response.

I drove the van up the alleyway and could just make out the open fire escape doors at the end where the barman was waiting for us. 'Once you've unloaded, you can leave your van here for the evening. It'll be quite safe' he said as I got out of the van. I followed him inside where he flicked a few light switches and a dozen or so wall lights sprung into life and lit up in what must have originally been a ballroom. 'What time do you want us to start' I asked. '8.30, and if you play for an hour, take a half hour break and then play for another hour, that will take you through to closing time.' With that he left us and headed back to the bar.

Apart from a small dance area in front of the stage, the remaining space was filled with tables and chairs. This led into a large saloon bar at the front of the pub. I stood there looking around, thinking that this must have been quite a grand place in its day, but now the décor looked very tired. The flock wallpaper was torn in places, the ornate gold-painted cornice below the ceiling had faded into a dark matte colour and the ceiling was a dingy yellow caused by years of cigarette smoke. 'What an exciting looking place' was John's sarcastic comment as he and the rest of the group walked in. 'Oh well,' I said. 'Lets make the most of it. You never know, if it fills up later on, it might turn out to be quite lively.'

We started dead on 8.30 and by 9 o'clock the place was starting to fill up nicely. People were strolling in from the saloon bar with trays of beers and other assorted drinks and claiming their individual tables for the evening's entertainment. By the time we came to our break, every table in the hall was occupied and people had to stand around the perimeter with drinks in their hands.

As we were sitting on the edge of the stage, having a quiet drink during our break, the publican, Mr Ramsey, came up to us and introduced himself. 'Hope you boys are enjoying yourselves. From the comments I'm receiving in the saloon bar, the customers really like you.' He then continued to say, 'One thing I must ask you however. When you get to your last number, please make sure you finish dead on 10.30. And don't attempt any encores. Trying to get this lot out isn't an easy task' and he turned his head and nodded at the crowd behind him. He continued, 'As you probably know, the police station is just the other side of the fire exit over there and we certainly don't want any complaints from them about not closing on time, otherwise it's….' and he drew his forefinger across his throat. I assured him we would stop playing at exactly 10.30 and as he started to leave, he said 'See you tomorrow night then at the same time. If you want to leave your gear here overnight, don't worry. I can assure you it will be perfectly safe. We draw the folding doors across and seal off the hall from the saloon bar during the lunchtime sessions.' After he had gone, we discussed his offer and agreed, as the hall was sealed off to take a chance and leave our gear here overnight, except for our guitars. This meant we could head off earlier than usual and be home for a reasonably early night.

We were just a few minutes into our second set and people were already up dancing in front of the stage. More and more people joined them until it was packed solid. An evening of steady drinking had started to have its effect and so, with the audience nicely loosened up, we upped the tempo a notch or two. During the last 20 minutes of our final set, the hall was really rocking. When we finished our last number of the evening, a big cheer rang out and the lights were turned up.

We decided to wait for the hall to empty before setting off home, as we didn't want to make it too obvious that we were leaving our gear behind. We sat on the stage finishing our drinks and watched as the bar staff started clearing the empty glasses and encouraging people to finish their drinks. A short thick-set bald man in his forties, with his shirt sleeves rolled up revealing large bulging biceps, was walking round the tables shouting 'Come along please, ladies and gentlemen, drink up.' We later discovered his name was Arthur and that he was the resident bouncer. His presence alone, walking amongst the tables, had the desired effect and people quickly finished their drinks and left. With our guitars packed away into their cases, we opened the fire exit doors, said our goodbyes and headed for home.

We must have made quite an impression with the punters because I received another telephone call from Mr Ramsey the following week, with more regular weekend bookings going into the diary. In fact, we ended up playing on a fairly regular basis at the Eagle over the next five months, which resulted in a noticeable increase in the weekend attendance at the pub.

During our tenure at the pub, there is one incident that really sticks out in my mind. Towards the end of April, on a lovely mild evening, we arrived to find the fire exit doors already open to help ventilate the interior. We entered carrying pieces of equipment and waved to the bar staff down in the saloon bar. After setting up and having a quick sound test, we kicked off our first hour's set. As per usual, people slowly started to arrive from the saloon bar with their drinks and then made their way to a table for the evening.

It was interesting that as we played, I could hear the police dogs barking through the open fire exit doors. The dogs were kennelled at the back of the police station, so they were very close to the pub. A nudge from John brought my attention to four women who stood close to the open fire doors and who, every so often, glanced across at us and smiled. They were in the late 20s, so a few years older than us, which made a change from the usual young dolly birds we tended to attract. By the time we reached our break, all four of us were eyeing up these women. However, it was noticeable to us now that they knew the four guys who sat at a table in the middle of the hall. They were certainly paying more attention to them than us. We didn't want to upset any of the local lads, so we sat on the edge of the stage with our drinks, occasionally glancing across at the women and were rewarded now and again with the odd smile.

Being a Friday, and with us playing again the following evening, we didn't have to pack up our equipment. By now, we had become a bit complacent and didn't even bother to hang around for the punters to leave before setting off. There was a round of applause after the final number and Martin and I quickly packed up our guitars and we all headed for the open fire exit. The women moved aside and smiled as we passed. We said our goodbyes and climbed into the van with JG driving and Martin next to him. As the engine was started, one of the women came up to the van and Martin wound his window down. 'Any chance of a lift to Walthamstow'?' 'No problem' came Martin's reply, and the four women climbed into the back of the van. John and I moved and sat on the floor so that the four ladies could squeeze onto the bench seat – and we were off.

We exchanged small talk for the next ten minutes or so, then one of them asked, 'Can you drop us outside the Walthamstow Assembly Hall?' This was an old venue where we had played many times and we knew it well. Within minutes, JG had pulled the van into a layby, and I jumped out and helped the four ladies, one by one, to exit the van. 'See you tomorrow night then?' I asked 'Possibly. Thanks for the lift.' 'Bye' came the response from one of them, and they were gone.

When we arrived the next evening, although still as warm as the previous night, the fire exit doors were closed. Apparently the pub had received a complaint from the police station that the noise from our playing had disturbed the police dogs. They had become restless, so the doors had to remain closed and we made our entrance through the saloon bar. As we entered the bar, Arthur, the bouncer, greeted us. 'Hello boys. Did you give some women a lift home last night?' 'Yes,' replied Martin. 'Why, what's the problem?' Arthur grinned. 'You're in big trouble tonight – their husbands are after you lot.' I quickly responded, 'But nothing happened. We just dropped them off in Walthamstow.' Arthur stopped smiling. 'Try telling them that when you see them' he said. We walked quietly through the bar and into the hall. John broke the silence. 'Bloody hell, we didn't do anything for God's sake.' Rather subdued and nervous, we started playing our first set, each of us anxiously surveying the hall trying to locate any menacing looking characters that might be the angry husbands. I certainly couldn't see any sign of the four women, but I could see the four men who the night before, had gained their attention.

We then noticed four rather large guys standing by the fire exit doors. As I glanced over in their direction, one of the men stared back at me. In between numbers, I turned to the others and in a quiet voice said 'Oh shit, I think we're in trouble tonight.' Heads nodded in agreement as we went into our next song. After a couple of numbers, and deciding what number to continue with, John sneaked a look across at these four men. 'Crikey, that hard-looking one with the short hair has rolled up his sleeves and his arms are covered in tattoos.' As discreetly as I could, I looked across just as another one started to roll up his sleeves. 'It might be because it's very hot in the hall tonight' I tried to convince John. 'Or they're getting ready for action,' came JG's response. We started the next song and I was beginning to wish we didn't have to take a break. Perhaps if we continued playing, these thugs would leave us alone. But I needed a pee badly, so we played the last number of our first set. I rested my guitar against the amp, Martin joined me and we made our way to the toilets just off the saloon bar.

I glanced back a couple of times but the men hadn't moved and just stood there staring into the crowd. As we made our way back, weaving our way in between the tables, there was Arthur in front of us. 'Don't look so serious. I was only joking about those guys coming here tonight to get you' he said. 'But I am expecting trouble. I've been informed that they're after some men who took their wives out last week.' Martin and I looked at one another with relief and I turned to Arthur and said, 'Thanks a lot, but that wasn't funny.' Arthur smiled and sauntered off.

We couldn't wait to pass on the good news as we stepped onto the stage and the sense of relief was palpable after I explained that Arthur had only been joking with us. We loosened up quite a bit as we started our second set! However, I couldn't help but glance across every so often, just to keep an eye on the men. The four by the fire exit doors were now staring at the four men seated at the table who seemed to be deliberately ignoring them. Or perhaps that was just a ploy. Surely they knew they were being watched.

Suddenly, the guy with the short hair and tattoos started to walk quickly towards the table and the other three followed. As he reached the table, one of the other men jumped up. Instantly, an arm was around a neck and a head pulled down and as they stumbled forward, a table was pushed aside and people around them jumped up from their chairs to avoid getting hurt. They wrestled onto the dance floor area in front of the stage and within seconds were exchanging punches. Without warning, they rolled onto the stage itself and John had to quickly manoeuvre himself and his mike to avoid a collision.

Tattoo man was on now on top and holding the other man by his hair, he repeatedly started to bang his head on our Vortexion amp, which was used for our vocal mikes. There I am, playing away, looking down at these two men only inches away bashing lumps out of one another. My main concern was for the amplifier, but I didn't want to interfere. I just loved the shape of my nose! The amplifier sat on the floor and was a tough bit of heavy gear, about 14 inches long by 8 inches in width and 7 inches high, with the valves set within a metal casing and two metal carrying handles at either end. So, not a particularly soft landing for a head!

Suddenly Arthur was there, legs astride, yelling out to us 'Keep playing!' and with that he grabbed the shoulders of tattoo man and still clinging together, the two men were hurled onto the dance floor. Quickly tattoo man got to his feet, moved towards the nearest table and grabbed an empty pint mug. In one movement, the glass was lifted up, brought down on the table, smashed and as the other man closed in, the remains of the broken mug was brought up and shoved against his ear. As the man quickly put his hand over his ear, blood started to seep through his fingers. He took his hand away and looked the blood. It was then I could see that his ear was hanging at a funny angle. By now Arthur was behind the man who had the broken glass in his hand. He picked up a solid oak chair, raised it above his head and brought it down onto the man's skull. Even with us playing, I could hear a loud thud. The man just crumpled and lay motionless on the floor.

Having seen so many bar room brawls in Western films, I half expected the chair simply to shatter into little pieces, but no, the chair remained unmarked and intact. People all around were screaming and shouting and began running into the saloon bar. Arthur, with the help of some bar staff, came between the men who were now shouting at one another, and prevented further trouble erupting. With the situation now calmer, Arthur led the bleeding man through the now open fire doors. Presumably one of the bar staff must have called an ambulance as we could hear a distant siren approaching. We had continued playing throughout all this commotion, but now the song had finished and it was eerily quiet in the hall, apart from one or two people who were standing around discussing the fight, the majority of people having fled the hall. We just stood there, shaken by the events that had just taken place. Witnessing such raw violence is pretty frightening and we were shocked. We still had ten minutes left to play, but with hardly anyone around, we decided to call it a day. Interestingly, with the pub situated behind the police station, no police arrived, or perhaps they hadn't been called. I suspect the publican wanted to keep the police out of it if possible, to avoid any fallout with the law and the brewery. As we packed away our gear, I couldn't help but glance at the blood and broken glass on the floor, and reflect on how close we had been to the violence. Fortunately we didn't witness any further violent trouble like that ever again.

WHAT A DISASTER - ASSEMBLY HALL - WOODFORD - AUGUST 1966

We arrived at the Assembly Hall in Woodford to find that we were on first, with Tony Rivers and The Castaways following us. This local group had been around for a number of years and had recorded a few singles, but none had been hits. Tony Rivers eventually left The Castaways to go solo and ended up doing a lot of session work for other artists. Notably for a number of years, he sang backing vocals on many of Cliff Richard's hits and accompanied him on tours as part of Cliff's backing band.

Since re-joining the group, Martin's on-stage gear hadn't been very exciting, and whereas Ray had been very active on stage, Martin hardly moved at all. On this particular night, John had handed Martin a pair of his multi-coloured striped trousers and in the dressing room we encouraged him to move around a bit more on stage. Our performance started well, but we had to laugh behind Martin's back as he kept moving to the front of this large stage and thrusting his hips out in a rather suggestive manner, made even funnier with him wearing the multi-coloured striped trousers, which really wasn't Martin at all. Watching us from the wings was Tony Rivers and The Castaways. We were halfway through our set, when disaster struck – my high E string snapped. The others tried to carry on with the next number with just the bass and drums as backing, but it sounded bad. In the meantime, I had hastily retrieved my guitar case and was rummaging through a pile of spare strings, but no 1st string. All this time, the other group just stood in the wings watching, and obviously found the whole situation immensely funny. Not one of their guitarists bothered to help out by offering me a spare string. I had no choice but to put on a B string and tune it up to E, which was a bit risky and, with increased tension, the string could snap at any time.

So far so good. We managed a few more numbers and everything was going well, when suddenly JG's snare drum skin split! In all our years of playing, this was the first time ever a drum skin had split and of course, the group in the wings thought this was side-splittingly funny. JG didn't have a spare and, true to their colours, their drummer offered no assistance. We couldn't possibly perform without a drummer, so the audience had to wait while JG turned his drum over and made adjustments, but the crisp sound of his snare drum was lost. We soldiered on and as we went into the next song, a string on Martin's borrowed bass guitar snapped! I couldn't believe all this was happening to us! Of course, he didn't have a spare string either. I shouldn't have looked, but I couldn't help it. In the wings, Tony Rivers and The Castaways were killing themselves with laughter. We only had a couple more songs to go, so Martin managed to get by with just three strings. It was such a bad night all round and the worst we'd ever experienced for breakages in one single evening. There was certainly no camaraderie extended by this group and so, needless to say, we didn't enter into any conversation with Tony Rivers or his band as we removed our gear from the stage. Deep down I was so pleased that not one of their single releases had ever made the charts! Despite all the mishaps that had occurred, it was great to have Martin back on board and hopefully the evening's events were just a one-off blip and wouldn't be repeated again.

WE BUY OUR FINAL VAN – AUGUST 1966

Getting to and from Woodford had been a bit problematic. Our poor old Austin van had served us so well, especially considering it had never had a proper service while in our hands. We had at least changed the oil and filter a few times, renewed sparks plugs when necessary and also replaced the tyres. To save money, we'd even toiled away putting on a new exhaust pipe, which was a real pain. However, we were booked to play at the Eagle pub in Tottenham for two nights and it was becoming a struggle to start the van from cold. The gearbox was giving us some problems as well and with quite a bit of rust on the bodywork, it probably wouldn't make it through the next MOT test, which was due shortly. The old van had certainly seen better days and it would certainly be cheaper to buy another van than fork out to get it fully roadworthy again.

The problem was, I'd only just recently paid back a lot of outstanding income tax plus settled up with the accountants and money was currently in short supply. So much so, that I didn't have enough money in the kitty to renew the van's insurance and road tax which had expired the previous week. Earning some money from the two performances at the Eagle this coming weekend was crucial. Without an insurance certificate, we couldn't apply for a road tax disc. Fortunately, although the van was in a poor state of repair, our MOT certificate was still valid. We had plenty of advance bookings in the diary, so it wouldn't be long before we would be flush again, but the reliability of the van was a worry. For the first time ever, we simply had to take a gamble and use the van this coming weekend without road tax or insurance.

On both nights I struggled to start the van before and after our performance at the Eagle in Tottenham. When we came to leave the pub on the Saturday evening, I just couldn't get the engine to fire up and the battery was slowly losing its power. Luckily, with some additional help from late-night revellers who came to our assistance, the van was bump started back into life. I was extremely nervous driving home in case the van stalled at any of the numerous traffic lights and I couldn't re-start the engine. We certainly wouldn't want to leave our van at the side of the road, unattended overnight and full of expensive equipment. Somehow we managed to limp our way back to Romford but as we turned into John's road to drop him off, I noticed in the side mirror that a police car was following us. 'Oh shit' I called out. 'There's only a police car behind us' and just as I said that, the blue lights came on, signalling me to stop.

I drew to a halt, but left the engine running just in case and slid down the window as the two policemen approached the van. I heard one of them say in a stern voice, 'Please turn the engine off.' I did what I was told as I certainly didn't want to upset them. The police hadn't stopped us in years and we'd never driven without current tax and insurance before. Of all the bloody rotten luck, to get pulled over now!

The first question I was asked was where were we going and what did we have in the back of the van. I explained we were a group and were heading home after playing at a pub in Tottenham. With that, he and his partner switched on their torches and proceeded to walk round to the back of the van, open the back door and inspect the contents. Then the side door was opened and the torches were shone inside, not only revealing the gear but also John and JG sitting on the bench seat. Making light of the situation, John suddenly blurted out, 'Just as well we didn't have any girls in the back with us.' Both policemen chuckled and made a crack about how lucky we were, playing in a group, and how groups were so popular with the girls these days. John responded saying, 'Why do you think we have curtains in the van? We like a bit of privacy' and they both laughed. Good old John, trying to divert their attention, I thought to myself. Perhaps they'll forget to ask to see documentation and not inspect the road tax on the windscreen.

I watched in the side mirror as one policeman returned to his car and then I held my breath as the other policeman made his way round to the front of the van and up to my open window and said, 'OK then boys, be on your way. I'm sure you must all be tired. I'll watch out for you on TV.' We all thanked him, and with that he made his way back to join his partner. 'I don't believe it' I said, 'They didn't spot the out-of-date tax disc on the windscreen!' I turned the ignition key and said a silent prayer, but the engine was still warm and thankfully after a couple of turns it slowly sprung into life. We said our goodbyes to John who headed off home and now I just couldn't wait to drop JG off, park the van and get it off the road.

We knew we had about a year left before we were going to call it a day with the group, so we definitely needed a replacement van, but it had to be cheap and reliable. Martin made some enquiries at the engineering company where he was working and, lo and behold, they had an old Ford Thames van that had been sitting in their yard unused for months. It didn't have any side windows, but that wasn't so important now. It was about six years old and it drove well, so we bought it for £120. Within a few days, our old van was towed away to a breaker's yard and we pocketed £15. Our replacement van was duly taxed and insured and we were back on the road again – legitimately.

THE CHISLEHURST CAVES - KENT - DECEMBER 1966

Chislehurst Caves, located in Chislehurst, Kent, were actually entirely all man-made and early records show that around the year 1250, mining was taking place on the site. However, in the 1800s, mining production increased dramatically due to the high demand for chalk, which was used in the manufacture of bricks and mortar. Vast quantities of bricks, manufactured in the Kent area, were needed in the building expansion of suburban London during the industrial revolution.

Flintstone was also mined there around the same time, to fire tinderboxes and flintlock guns. The tinderbox soon disappeared when the common matchstick came into being in the early mid 18th century and, with the invention of the percussion cap soon following, the flintlock gun became obsolete.

When mining finally halted, a labyrinth of around 22 miles of tunnels had been created and in 1900 they were opened to the public as a tourist attraction. During the First World War, the caves were used as an ammunition depot and then in the Second World War, at the start of the bombing of London, the caves became an official air raid shelter. The tunnels soon became a mini underground city, housing some 15,000 people, with its own electricity supply, a hospital and a chapel.

In the 1960s, an aspiring promoter rented the caves as a venue for live rock bands. This music venue rapidly became very popular and played host to such rock luminaries as Jimi Hendrix, The Rolling Stones, David Bowie and Pink Floyd.

Around this time, Martin had inherited a vintage, British-built 1935 Lanchester car and although he was itching to drive his new acquisition, he was still officially a learner driver. As required by the law and being a fully-fledged licence holder, I agreed to accompany him and we drove to the gig in Chislehurst in the Lanchester with John and JG taking the van.

It was a bitterly cold day and by six o'clock that evening a heavy frost had covered the Lanchester. Martin started the engine and we set about clearing the windscreen and the side windows of ice. He attached his 'L' plates while I put our guitar cases on the back seat. In 1963 this car was 28 years old. It certainly looked ancient and I was soon to find out that it didn't have all the mod cons of a modern car.

No sooner had we set off when our breath starting misting up the inside of the windscreen and I quickly searched along the dashboard for a demister switch. Before I could ask, Martin said 'There isn't one, use this' and handed me a duster.

It was still as cold inside the car as when we first set off on our journey, so I asked 'Is there a heater in the car? 'Of course' he replied, and pointed to a copper pipe that ran along under the dashboard, a few inches above our knees. I felt the copper pipe. 'It's freezing' I said. With his eyes still firmly on the road, he fumbled under the dashboard with his right hand. 'Sorry, that should make a difference' he said. 'I've turned the tap on,' and sure enough, as I clutched the copper pipe with both hands, I could feel it getting warmer and warmer. 'So, how does this work then?' 'It's hot water from the car's radiator, which now I've turned the tap on, is allowing hot water to flow through the copper pipe' came his reply. 'Isn't there a fan somewhere, which will circulate the warm air?' I asked. Without hesitation Martin said 'Don't be silly – this car was built in 1935.'

Half an hour later, we were approaching the Blackwall Tunnel and although it wasn't freezing inside the car, it was still pretty cold. The car was badly insulated and jets of ice-cold air entered from every nook and cranny. My feet were now numb from the cold. 'How're you doing Martin?' I asked. 'Fine' came the response. 'I'm glad I put my fur-lined gloves on, but my feet are damn cold.' After another 30 minutes or so, we passed a sign saying 'Welcome to Kent'. Not long now I thought and looked at the map on my lap as I tried to establish by the light of the passing street lamps, exactly where we were. As I looked up, I saw a sign directing us to Chislehurst and from then on we followed the signs for Chislehurst Caves. Within a few minutes, we pulled up in a small car park, close to the caves' entrance. Apart from one other car, it was empty, so we'd beaten the van. I certainly didn't fancy venturing outside, so we sat huddled up in the darkness, when thankfully the van entered the car park. The headlights picked us out and the van swung over and stopped beside us. We all got out into the freezing air. I walked over to John and said, 'Martin's car was like a fridge inside. I'm so damn cold and I bet you were all nice and warm in the van.' He grinned at me and replied 'It was like an oven.' I didn't bother replying to that comment.

We wandered over to the entrance door and into the ticket office area where there was a distinctly damp mouldy smell, obviously emanating from the caves. The promoter welcomed us and pointed to a trolley we could use for transporting our equipment. He then handed over a small map of the caves and marked with an X the alcove off the main walkway where we would be playing. The different alcoves were all numbered and a few had a wooden stage erected plus lights and a plug socket. We were booked to start playing at 8.15pm for 45 minutes, then a 15-minute break, continuing again, plus another break, and finishing at 11 o'clock. 'Are there any other groups playing tonight?' I asked the promoter. 'Yes. In total there are three bands including yourselves. If you have any problems, come back to me.' He went on to say 'But please keep to those performance and break times as it means that at any given time during the evening, two groups will be playing while you take your break.' 'No problem' I replied.

We managed to load about half of our equipment onto the trolley, locked the van and headed back to the caves' entrance. Although nobody said anything, I think we were all a bit excited and curious at the prospect of playing deep down in the famous Chislehurst Caves. We stopped for a moment in the reception area and I unfolded the map. We all huddled round to study our route. It all looked pretty straightforward. We went through some double doors and left the brightly lit and warm ticket office for the gloomy, dank environment of the caves. It was poorly lit and the once-white chalk ceilings and walls were now dirty and grubby. I could just make out crude wooden signs on the walls directing visitors to various paths, but tonight those paths weren't lit up. It immediately crossed my mind how convenient this would be if we happened to meet some nice young girls tonight!

Pushing the trolley along the main cobbled pathway wasn't easy and was made even more difficult by the lack of light. There were only very low wattage light bulbs that were strung up along the walls of the caves about every ten feet or so. Without warning, the trolley ground to a juddering halt and mike stands, cymbals and leads crashed to the ground. 'What the f…' was my immediate reaction and I hauled the trolley back, revealing a large protruding stone. After loading up again, we continued on our journey, with John and JG now ahead of us scouring the pathway for more large stones, while Martin and I pushed the trolley. As we turned a bend, we could hear the familiar sounds of a group tuning up somewhere in the distance. Within a few minutes, we trundled past a brightly lit alcove, with a narrow stage at the back, where a group were setting up their gear.

It wasn't long before there was silence again, apart from the racket the trolley made. After passing by a number of darkened alcoves we could hear another band going through the motions of tuning up, with the obligatory 'one, two, three testing' as mikes were switched on. We went round another bend, passed a few more unlit alcoves and finally reached our allotted alcove A36. We stopped the trolley and peered into the darkness.

With our plastic cigarette lighters held high, we entered the alcove searching for a light switch. 'I can see some electrical cable up there' said JG pointing towards the ceiling, and he followed it along to where the stage had been erected. He climbed up onto the stage and called out, 'I've found a plug', and the next second, the alcove was suddenly filled with light. We all cheered. Pushing the trolley up to the stage, we started to unload the gear. 'JG and I will go back for the remainder of the gear' said Martin.

We plugged in our power board, flicked the switches and the little red neon lights on our amplifiers blinked into life. So far, so good, I thought as I looked around. The alcove was no more than about 30 feet long by 15 feet wide and the curved ceiling was at least ten feet high. The small stage was about two feet high and five feet in depth, which would just about give JG sufficient room in which to set up his drums. 'I wonder where Martin and JG are?' I called out to John. 'We're due to start playing in 20 minutes and JG hasn't even set up his drum kit yet.' I jumped off the stage and made my way out into the dimly lit main shaft. I could just about make out some music playing in the distance, but couldn't quite make out what the actual song was. I learnt later from the promoter, that the caves unique soundproofing came from the highly porous structure of chalk, which meant as many as five different bands could play simultaneously in different alcoves, without the sound overlapping. I stopped for a moment and looked around, absorbing the strange experience of being underground in these rather creepy, damp smelling ancient caves.

I was starting to wonder where Martin and JG were when I heard the sound of a trolley bouncing over the stones. Next minute, out of the shadows, appeared two grinning faces and a laden trolley. 'You won't believe it' said Martin. 'A wheel came off the first trolley, but fortunately we were close to the ticket office and the promoter got us another one.' As they had managed to get all the rest of our equipment on the trolley, another journey was thankfully not necessary. I asked them if they could see many people arriving. 'The first alcove is filling up and there are a quite a few people milling around the second one' said Martin. My reply to this was 'Well, I just hope people know we're down here, because I doubt they'll hear us.'

Within ten minutes we were all set up and ready to go, but not one person had appeared. John suggested we made a start anyway, so we launched into 'Watcha Gonna Do About It', but it sounded strangely flat. Obviously the soft chalk walls and ceiling were absorbing the sound and subsequently there was no echo. After a while we got used to it and we were into our fourth song, when two couples appeared and stood outside the alcove watching and listening. Then more people arrived and slowly they all began to venture into the alcove, carrying their cans of soft drinks. Within another ten minutes or so, the alcove was filling up nicely. Some couples were trying to dance in the confined space, but most just stood around watching us. As we approached nine o'clock, the alcove was now overflowing with people.

We all knew that as soon as we stopped for a break, the crowd would drift away, so it was tempting to continue playing over our allotted time, but that wouldn't be fair to the other two groups. As we finished the last song of the set, John made an announcement. 'Thank you folks, we're taking a short break now and we'll be back in 15 minutes.' People slowly shuffled out of the alcove and within five minutes we were completely on our own. What a strange place I thought to myself. We had no idea how many people were in the caves in total and just hoped we would have an audience again after our break. Perhaps the other groups were going through the same experience.

We had just started on the third number in our second set, with an audience of only six people, when suddenly the power went off and instantly it was pitch black, especially where we were located at the back of the alcove. Thankfully, the lighting outside in the main cave area wasn't affected by the power cut, so we were able to head for the dimly lit archway. We stood outside the alcove and watched as the six members of our audience sauntered off. After a few minutes standing around, we came to the conclusion that probably the promoter had no idea our power supply had been cut so I decided to go and report it. John said he'd come with me, so off we went, leaving the others standing in the murky darkness.

We walked quickly up the main passageway and eventually passed an alcove where a group was playing to quite a large audience. The alcove was at least three-quarters full. As we continued on our journey, the music quickly receded behind us. We passed quite a few people, some making their way towards the surface, and some heading down into the caves. As we turned a corner we could hear music again. We passed yet another alcove, which was pretty packed out. We realised that there were quite a lot of people in these caves but as they were so huge, it didn't seem crowded.

Within another five minutes or so, we pushed open the double doors and strode into the ticket office to confront the promoter. We explained that the power had gone in our alcove and that we were in total darkness. He immediately picked up the telephone on his desk and pressed a button. 'Sid, I need you now. It's an emergency. There's no power in A36.' In next to no time, Sid appeared dressed in navy blue overalls and carrying a toolbox. 'Go with Sid lads. He'll get the power back on for you' said the promoter and we made our way back to our alcove.

Sid switched on a torch and made his way onto the stage. He unlocked the door of a metal box suspended on the back wall, fiddled around with a few inches of fuse wire and soon we had power again. We thanked Sid as he made his departure and with guitars slung over the shoulders once again, we sprung back into life. A few people drifted in and out of the alcove and by the time we came to finish our second set, it was pretty well packed, but as soon as we stopped playing, everyone was gone. We sat on the stage smoking and discussing what we thought of the place and of the evening itself. The conclusion was unanimous – the Chislehurst Caves was a soulless place with terrible acoustics and although it wasn't as cold as outside, it was still a bit chilly, the atmosphere was damp and the air was stale.

'Come on, let's get it over with' John called out, and we reluctantly got to our feet, checked the tuning of our guitars and in an empty alcove, we started our last set. Although it wasn't long before people started to drift in again, our hearts weren't in it. We couldn't wait to finish, pack up and head off home, but I doubt anyone in the small audience detected that. When John finally announced, 'We'd now like to finish the evening with an Undertakers' song called 'Mashed Potato'. OK boys!' we started with a new lease of life knowing that the end was in sight. When we'd finished, the remaining 40 or so people in the alcove clapped, and were gone.

We didn't hang around that night. The trolley was quickly loaded up and we made the two arduous journeys through the caves to the van and I went and collected our fee for the night from the promoter. Martin and I said our farewells to the others, who headed back in a nice warm van, while we set off in a refrigerated 1935 Lanchester. Not one of our best gigs, but it was different, and in its own way quite memorable for many reasons!

The Lanchester sat outside Martin's house under a tarpaulin cover, but was hardly ever used again. After passing his driving test, Martin had the use of his father's new car, which had all the mod cons, and I suspect the novelty of driving a vintage car had worn very thin. In the end, the car was rusting badly and coupled with mechanical problems and not being able to obtain spares, this splendid old vintage car was finally towed to a breaker's yard.

34

THE BLACKHEATH RUGBY CLUB – SEPTEMBER 1966 – JUNE 1967

As I dashed out of the house, I grabbed an envelope addressed to The Candles that had been lying on the front doormat. Travelling to work had now changed for me. No more trains – I now drove to work in my navy blue Ford Anglia. What hadn't changed were the late nights and the lack of sleep, which was still proving a major problem. Yet again, I was late leaving home.

Sitting in a long queue heading up to traffic lights on the A12, I picked up the envelope from the passenger seat and opened it. Inside was a contract from A.B. Entertainments and in between the stop and start of the traffic I read that we were booked to appear at the Blackheath Football Club, Rectory Field on September 24.

We were all in the van that evening, heading for the Blackwell Tunnel and ultimately, Blackheath. It always fascinated me, when exiting the tunnel on the Kent side, the bullet marks that were apparent on both sides of the red brick wall, where German bombers strafed the tunnel during the Second World War. Once through the industrial area of Greenwich, we came into Blackheath, so called because buried on the heath itself, were many of the dead from the Great Plague of London in 1665, also known as the Black Death.

Eventually we pulled up opposite two detached houses with double wrought iron gates. These opened onto a driveway and a sign informed us that this was Rectory Field, the home of the Blackheath Rugby Club.

This was a bit confusing as we were booked to play at the Blackheath Football Club. We started down the driveway and there on our left was a rugby pitch and on our right a sports pavilion. We drove into the car park and close to the main entrance.

As we all got out of the van, a guy walked towards us gripping two green plastic watering cans. 'Are you the group?' he asked. 'Yes' I said, 'Providing this is the Blackheath Football Club.' 'Yes it is' he replied. 'Actually it's a rugby club, but historically it's known as Blackheath Football Club. Welcome. This is for you' and he put the watering cans down in front of us. We must have looked slightly bemused as he went on to say 'Don't look so worried, boys. They're full of mild bitter, courtesy of the club. Please help yourself to glasses. They're on the bar counter inside. By the way, my name is Peter.' We all shook hands and thanked him for the beer. 'I think we've struck gold' said Martin, peering into the watering cans and he went on to inform us that each watering can held two gallons, which equated to 16 pints of beer. We were starting to like this booking more and more!

Following our new friend into the clubhouse, he apologised for the fact that there was no stage but said we could set up against the wall across from the wooden-floored dancing area. As he started to walk away, he turned and said, 'By the way, I nearly forgot. When the watering cans are empty, just take them up to the bar for refills. They know all about the arrangement.' We couldn't believe our luck! 'Well, we've certainly cracked it this time. I wonder what other delights are in store for us tonight' I said, and everyone grinned.

As we unloaded the van and set up our gear, I turned to John and JG, 'I don't know about you but I think this mild bitter is more up Martin's street,' and we agreed to hand over one of the watering cans for his own personal consumption. When I presented the watering can to him, the look on his face was one of sheer delight. My drinking habits hadn't really changed that much, nor had John's or JG's, but we had all moved away from drinking spirits. If we went to a pub, we would order half pints of larger and lime and perhaps down two or three rounds in an evening. Martin, however, would order pints to our halves, so he was the more experienced beer drinker.

Knowing our drinking habits, we were surprised when Martin came back from the bar carrying four pint glasses. 'Sorry boys, there weren't any half pint glasses on the counter and I didn't want to embarrass myself asking for them in front of these beer swilling rugby players.' We didn't protest as I suppose he had a point. We all filled up our glasses and I watched in amazement as Martin downed half of his glass in one fell swoop. I just don't know how he manages to pour so much liquid down his throat in one go. As I was tuning up my guitar, I noticed some big burly men, one by one coming out of the changing room with wet hair, all instinctively heading to the bar to join their fellow team mates who were already there. I then found out that the first team had just won a game, which had finished an hour before we arrived. Hence the loud laughter and banter coming from the bar area – they were celebrating an important win. I had a feeling that this was going to be a good night. Looking at our contract, I remembered that we were being paid £20 for this evening's work, but no mention of the continuous supply of beer. What a bonus!

We started our first set at 8'clock to a half-filled dance area. By comparison, the bar area was seething with these rather large men who, judging by the noise they made, were now really enjoying themselves. They were obviously also really enjoying our music too as the response we received after finishing every song was pretty amazing. However, I'm sure the heavy drinking possibly helped as well. In between a song, I turned to John and said 'Not many women around. Surely these guys have got girlfriends and wives.' He agreed with me that it was a bit odd. We couldn't imagine them dancing with one another all evening!

We had just taken our first break and records were being played, when the main door opened and in walked about 15 women. We were told later that it was common practice, after a game, for the men to meet around the bar while the club's mini bus did the rounds picking up the various wives and girlfriends. The same then happened again about half an hour later. The door opened and around the same number of women strolled into the clubhouse. It was filling up nicely and the dance floor was packed. The atmosphere, although quite raucous, was very good hearted, spurred on no doubt by the club's earlier victory.

During our next break, and with our watering cans now empty, Martin was assigned to get them filled up. Within a couple of minutes he was back with a big grin across his face and our glasses were filled yet again. It wasn't a very strong beer, thank goodness, but it had started to flow through the body and every so often, one by one, we kept disappearing to the loo.

It was during one of our breaks, while we were sitting at a table next to our equipment, that I spotted four rather attractive girls sitting across the dance floor from us. Every so often I glanced across and instantly got a lingering eye contact from one of them. I turned and said to John 'Have you noticed those girls over there?' 'Yes, I'd been getting the odd smile from one of them while we were playing' replied John. Martin and JG overheard what we were saying and immediately swung round in their chairs to have a look. The girls spotted us all looking at them and started giggling. 'I fancy the blonde one with the red top' said Martin. 'I thought you might' came my reply. I knew Martin so well – blondes were always his first choice, and although there was another blonde amongst them, he was always attracted to the pretty, pretty type.

However, John's next remark immediately quashed any move in their direction. 'They've probably got boyfriends or even husbands here tonight. Could be any of those monsters over at the bar.' We glanced across at the bar, just as another joke had been told, and a big roar of laughter rang out. 'You're right' I said, 'I wouldn't want to tangle with any of those blokes – just look at the size of them!' But we couldn't stop stealing the odd glance across, and they were obviously enjoying this attention from the band as we still kept getting the same eye contact back. But we thought it best to keep them at arm's length, as any one of the huge rugby players at the bar could be a husband or boyfriend.

It was time to start our last set and by now nearly everyone, male and female, were pretty well tanked up. We went straight into 'Shame, Shame, Shame', a song always guaranteed to get everybody up and rocking. We played a couple of requests, when John unexpectedly announced, 'Sorry folks. I've been drinking too much beer and I need to go to the loo.' A big cheer went up from the crowd, who laughed even more when we all followed John into the gents. 'I'm so glad you said that' said JG. 'I was desperate.' Martin and I nodded in agreement. When we came out of the loo and marched in a line back to our equipment, another cheer went up from the crowd. What a good-humoured lot they were. This then became the norm – after about every third song, the four of us trooped off to the loo accompanied by a big cheer.

John announced our final song and after we had finished, a big cheer went up. Peter, the guy who had greeted us when we first arrived, rushed up to us. 'Everyone's having such a great time. Any chance you could play a bit longer?' he pleaded. We looked at one another. By now we all felt good on the beer and were enjoying ourselves. Also, we had all been quite taken aback with their generosity of the free beer, so we agreed without hesitation, but not before another visit to the loo and the usual cheering. For nearly half an hour we played our best numbers, finishing on a final request for 'Shame, Shame, Shame' once again. As the last chord was played, the crowd erupted and some came over to us, shook our hands and thanked us. What a great night!

We started to pack up our gear and Peter came over to us with a diary in his hand. 'Thanks for playing that extra half an hour. Very much appreciated. Any chance we could book you direct in advance, rather than through the agency? We'll pay you the same, that way you won't have to pay the 15% commission.' Everyone turned to me for a decision. It would be a bit against the rules, but we knew we intended to finish with the group the next summer, 1967, as some of us were getting married. Plus we hadn't received that much work via the agency recently. 'No problem,' I replied. 'When would you like us to appear again?' Peter opened his diary and asked if we could make 26 November. I said that was fine and we agreed to the same time schedule and fee of £20.

As we all shook hands and returned to the job of packing up the gear and loading it into the van, I spotted the two watering cans sitting on the floor, so I decided to return them to the bar. Our can was empty, but when I picked up Martin's, it was at least half full. I couldn't believe he hadn't finished it, so when he came to collect his bass guitar, I said to him 'Unlike you not to finish your beer.' He looked at me through bleary eyes and said 'I've drunk so much, I just couldn't face another drop.' I watched as he made his way out of the clubhouse. He was walking in a perfectly straight line. I couldn't believe it after all that drink. With the van loaded, we all made our last visit to the loo before setting off.

We were making our way back to the van when I realised I didn't feel so good and my head was spinning. John said his was too. 'Dread to think how many pints of beer we've drunk tonight.' 'Well' said JG, 'Martin went up to the bar twice to refill the watering cans, so in total, between the three of us, we must have finished three full cans, which is 24 pints. That means we've drunk about eight pints each.' That would explain my spinning head! I had never drunk eight pints straight off like that in my life before. Martin, in the meantime, had stopped to talk to somebody, so I said the others, 'And how many pints do you think Martin drank then?' Thinking about it, we came to the conclusion that, allowing for the half can that he had left, Martin must have drunk around 20 pints!

When we climbed into the van, John sat in the front passenger seat and JG and I stretched out on the bench seat in the back. We waited to see Martin's reaction when he realised he was the driver. Next minute Martin climbed behind the wheel and started the engine. John turned to him and asked 'Are you fit enough to drive home?' Martin looked at him and said, 'Yes, no problem. I'm just a bit tired, that's all,' and nothing more was said. As it was just the original four members again, we didn't have to make the usual detour via Dagenham, so our journey home was a lot quicker, apart from a number of pee stops.

This was the 1960s and in 1962 it became an offence by law for any person to drive, attempt to drive, or be in charge of a motor vehicle, if their 'ability to drive properly was for the time being impaired'. It wasn't until 1967 that a legal drink drive limit of 80mg of alcohol per 100ml of blood was introduced. However, there was no foolproof way of calculating whether you were over the limit or not. If, for example, you drank two pints of beer, would you still be within the legal limit? So much depended on your weight, when you last ate, your age, your metabolism and your sex. Younger people tend to process alcohol in their system more slowly and if you are a male, then the alcohol in the body gets processed faster than in women.

On our drive over to Blackheath eight weeks later, we promised ourselves to take the beer drinking steadier this time as we had come to realise the excessive amount we had consumed on our previous visit. Well, three of us did anyway! Martin's response was, 'I'll see how it goes.' He continued, 'Anyway, I drove back last time, so one of you three can drive back tonight.' Although he didn't show it at the time, perhaps he did have some after-effects from drinking around 20 pints that evening! Even now, I find it hard to believe he drank that amount and still drove home. 'It'll be interesting to see if meeting us with two watering cans of beer last time was a one-off' I said. 'Well, we'll see in just a moment' replied Martin as we drove through the gates and parked outside the clubhouse.

We climbed out of the van and I went round to the back and opened the doors. Before we had a chance to take out some equipment, there was a cheery 'Hello boys. Nice to see you again. Here's your sustenance for the evening' and there was Peter, once again walking towards us with two heavy-looking watering cans, filled to the brim with bitter. We shook hands, said a few pleasantries, and started to unload the van.

We set up our gear in the usual spot, then sat down and started on our first drink of the evening. Slowly the clubhouse was filling up and it was time to make a start. We stubbed out our last cigarettes and made our way over to our gear. Martin and I checked our guitar tuning while JG made some final adjustments to his drums. John checked individually that we were ready. 'So, what shall we start with?' he asked. 'I wouldn't mind giving 'Sorrow' a try' I suggested, even though we had only rehearsed it recently. We all agreed it was a good idea.

In 1964 we supported our first major group from Liverpool called The Merseybeats, who had a string of hits before disbanding in early 1966. Two members reformed and called themselves The Merseys and had a top ten hit with 'Sorrow', later recorded by David Bowie.

'Sorrow' was one of the new songs we'd rehearsed since Martin had returned to the fold and I harmonised along with John's vocals on this number. My singing confidence was growing, but I still couldn't understand why I could sing in tune when harmonising, but I couldn't sing in tune if I attempted to sing a song solo!

We started our next set and I could tell that we had all slowed down on the amount of beer we were drinking, as the glasses on top of the amps remained half full for quite sometime.

Finishing our last number, John thanked everyone, when suddenly a rather drunk club member pleaded with us for just one more song and insisted it had to be 'Shame, Shame, Shame'. As it was my favourite song, and fast becoming our signature tune at the club, we agreed to play this last number. People rushed to find a space on the dance floor and just stood there, patiently waiting for us to begin. I started my guitar intro and then, when the bass and drums came in, the floor simply erupted into a mass of heaving bodies. It was glorious mayhem. But all good things must come to an end and as I played the final chord and JG crashed down on his cymbals, it signalled the end of the song and the lights came on. What a shame our next appearance at the club wasn't until January. We continued performing at the club regularly until our final appearance there on the 24 June 1967.

It was with mixed emotions that we arrived at the clubhouse to play for the very last time. This was our eighth performance at the club and we had by now become part of the close-knit rugby community and were on first-name terms with many of the members. From day one, being greeted with open arms and two watering cans of bitter, we knew we had hit on something special. We were never quizzed or criticised over our lack of rugby knowledge – we simply provided the music for everyone to enjoy. It was a chance for them to let their hair down on the dance floor, especially for some after playing a brutal game of rugby. I had informed Peter some time ago that we were calling it a day in June and that this would be our last appearance at the club. But whether he had remembered or not, we'd decided beforehand to announce, close to the end of our performance, that this was our last appearance at the club.

Equipped with our usual liquid sustenance, we were going to whip up a storm and make this a memorable evening, both for the audience and for us. Playing in a group and making music had become an integral part of our lives over the past eight years. It was difficult for me, and I'm sure also for the other members of the group, to fully comprehend that this would be one our last performances, ever!

During our first set, people were still arriving at the club and many would give us a cheery wave as they passed us by on their way to the bar. However, we knew from past experience, that our second set would be a much more raucous affair as everyone would have been drinking for quite a while by then. We were determined to make it special for them.

While we took our break, we were inundated with requests for individual favourite songs to be played and the most requested was my favourite as well, 'Shame, Shame, Shame'. We were just about to make a start, when Peter walked over to us and said he wanted to make an announcement. He walked up to the microphone and suddenly there was a hush, even from the bar, as Peter spoke. 'Some of you already know, but for those who don't, our favourite group'… and with that he turned and gestured to us. A big cheer rang out. He raised his hand for quiet and continued …'our favourite group is playing at the club for the last time tonight and they are quitting the music scene altogether next month as some of them are getting married soon. I for one will be sorry to see them go, and I'm sure you'll all agree with me when I say we have enjoyed their music immensely. So let's give them a special Blackheath Rugby Club farewell' and the packed audience clapped and cheered loudly. Peter wandered off, and then John spoke briefly. 'Thank you all so much.

We've loved playing here and we'll miss you all.' As the audience acknowledged us once again, I started with the intro to 'Shame, Shame, Shame', and as the rest of the group came in, the crowd turned into a mass of heaving bodies. We made sure we fulfilled all the requests and after performing two encores at the end, that was it. It was all over. People clapped us and slowly left the floor. As we packed up our equipment, a lot of the club members came up to us and shook our hands. It was all quite emotional and I was beginning to question in my mind if we had made the right decision to call it a day.

While attending a party not long after our final evening at the club, I bumped into an old friend and knowing that he was a big rugby buff, I brought up the subject of the Blackheath Rugby Club. He was very impressed that we had played there. Apparently the club was the first fully independent rugby club in the world not to have restricted membership and the early games were played on the heath itself, until they moved to Rectory Field in 1883. Some of the official rules of rugby that apply today throughout the world can be attributed to this club, especially the time-honoured tradition of always greeting visiting musicians on arrival with two large receptacles full of local ale! Well, well, who would have thought it!

35

THE MITRE PUB - EAST GREENWICH - MARCH - JULY 1967

By early 1967 we had finally caught up with paying off our back taxes and accountant's fees. Sadly, we had started to talk about when we would pack up the group as in September both Martin and I were getting married, with John and JG the following year.

The four of us were still having a lot of fun playing together in The Candles. After nearly eight years of performing together, we were like a family of brothers, having spent most of our youth playing and creating music. We'd all given it our best shot and come close to making it big a few times. But enough was enough, and we all accepted the group's demise. We were still busy with plenty of bookings, appearing at our favourite haunts like the Blackheath Rugby Club, the King Alfred and the Two Puddings. But now, with the end in sight, we started talking about bowing out by playing at some of our really old haunts around Romford where we started out, such as the youth clubs at Harrowfields, Quarles and Pettits Lane schools. Even though we wouldn't be paid very much, it would be just for old times' sake.

In early March, I received a call from a pub in East Greenwich called the Mitre, and arranged to appear there at the end of that month. None of us had heard of this pub before and when I asked for directions, the landlord explained it was on the left-hand side of the road, a few hundred yards after coming out of the Blackwall Tunnel heading towards Green- wich. It was strange that we hadn't noticed it as we'd passed through this area on so many occasions on our way to play in south London. The pub was set in the heart of an industrial area, close to the River Thames, and towering behind it was a massive gasometer. During the day, the Mitre would be busy serving a large local workforce, but it would be relatively empty at night, apart from serving a few locals that lived nearby in a small estate of grimy Victorian two-up two-down houses.

The Blackwall Tunnel had always fascinate me and I discovered that it was opened in 1897 and was a single bore tunnel that connected Poplar in the East End of London, with Greenwich in south London. The tunnel itself was lined with white ceramic tiles and had several sharp bends along its route, which was hazardous to say the least when faced with a large lorry coming from the opposite direction. I often wondered when driving through the tunnel, why it had to have bends in it, why it hadn't been built in a straight line. Naively, I had always assumed it was something to do with the strong water currents of the River Thames. However, the explanation was far more interesting than that. When the tunnel was first opened in Victorian times, the vehicles using it were all horse driven and the bends were there to prevent the horses from bolting once they saw daylight ahead.

It was all eyes left, looking for the Mitre pub, when I drove our van out of the tunnel that Thursday evening. And there it was, on a bend, set back from the road but facing the busy A102. Conveniently, it had its own little slip road and that allowed us to pull up and park right outside the entrance door.

From the outside it looked quite big, but a large integral garage took up a lot of the ground floor space and the first floor was used to accommodate the landlord, his family and staff. In we went and made ourselves known. The bar wasn't particularly big although it was quite long and the walls were all oak panelled. Hanging under small wall lights. were old black and white framed photographs depicting the local area in bygone days.

We set up our gear first, then ordered some beers and sat down at a table close to a jukebox and played a few records. At 8.30 we wandered on to the stage and started playing to an audience of two – or five if you included the bar staff. By the end of the evening there were no more than a dozen or so people there and it had been quite a depressing experience playing to just a handful of people. However, the landlord was obviously impressed with us and wanted to book us again. He went on to tell us that he was running a series of advertisements in a local Greenwich newspaper advertising live music at the Mitre on a Thursday, Friday and Saturday evening. He booked us for the following Thursday and Saturday, and also months ahead, so this venue was to become our second home for quite a while until the 21 July, when we were to perform for the last time.

We had learned earlier from the landlord that a punter who lived in Stratford had recommended us to him, having seen us perform on many occasions at the Two Puddings pub. We also found out that the licensing laws at that time were different in the Stratford area, a few miles from the northern end of the tunnel, where pubs pulled their last pint at 10.30 in the evening, whereas in Greenwich the licensing laws stipulated that the last pint was pulled at 11 o'clock.

We stopped playing at 10.30 and as we finished our drinks, we started packing up our gear, when suddenly four guys burst into the pub. They rushed straight up the bar and ordered four pints of beer and immediately started knocking them back. I recognised a couple of them from playing at the Two Puddings pub in Stratford, and when they spotted us, one of them came over and introduced himself. It turned out that he was the guy who'd recommended us to the landlord, so we thanked him. He told us they'd ordered their last round of beers when the bell was rung for final orders at the Two Puddings at 10.30pm. Drinking them quickly, they jumped in their car and drove from Stratford, through the Blackwall Tunnel, to the Mitre Pub, a distance of about four miles, just so they could carry on drinking! At 11 o'clock the bell was rung for last orders and we watched as they quickly went up to the bar and ordered another four pints of beer.

I particularly remember one evening in the bar at the Mitre, when we were having a swift half pint each before going on stage. We were sitting close to the jukebox and I decided to put on a record. Scanning the list of records, I spotted 'Hey Joe' by Jimi Hendrix, a song I knew quite well. This was Hendrix's first record release in the UK and I'd read that his guitar playing was exceptional. Although I liked 'Hey Joe', as a song it did nothing to promote his so-called guitar expertise, so out of curiosity I dropped a coin into the slot and selected 'Stone Free', the B-side. The record started just as I sat down. It had a great feel to it and I loved his singing. However, when it came to the guitar solo, I froze. It was phenomenal! I was so impressed, I had to put the record on again and this time we all sat there listening to it. I realised then that rock 'n' roll was entering a new phase and was pleased in a way that the group was finishing soon. I just wouldn't have been able to keep up with this exceptional and inventive quality of guitar playing.

We performed at the Mitre 25 times in the space of just four months, and slowly but surely the pub had started to fill up with more and more people attending the live music nights. The advertising had started to pay dividends and apparently the landlord was receiving positive feedback from the punters – they loved us! There was one glitch however. The pub was situated in an industrial area of Greenwich and wasn't accessible by regular public transport in the evening and so he came up with a brilliant idea. He laid on a mini-bus service that would make regular trips from the centre of Greenwich to the pub, and advertised the fact that the mini-bus would also take the punters back to Greenwich as well.

Another very clever move by the landlord was to have the mini-bus pick-up point close to a nurses' hostel, next door to the main Greenwich Hospital. This meant more young females came to the pub, which in turn attracted more young males. We couldn't believe our eyes when we arrived one Friday evening a couple of weeks later to see a queue of people snaking around the corner of the pub, waiting for the doors to open. The bar had a limited capacity, so people had arrived early in order not to be turned away as entry was on a first come, first serve basis.

Now the Mitre had become a dream of a venue. The atmosphere was electric and the regulars knew our repertoire and started to request particular numbers. A big bonus for us was being booked to play on a Friday and Saturday evening, as it meant we could leave our gear set up on the stage when we left on a Friday, walk out with our guitars, get into the van, and be home within an hour.

Without any prior warning from the landlord, we arrived one Friday evening to find that the stage had been rebuilt and heightened by a good couple of feet. Built in front of the new stage was a lower narrow stage and on the ceiling, pointing down to the lower stage, was an ultra-violet strip light. I think the penny had dropped long before the landlord started to explain to us that he was introducing go-go dancers to add a bit of spice to the live music evenings. Before we started playing that evening, we were introduced to them.

We hadn't experienced anything like this before but they were really lovely girls with great bodies. The landlord briefly explained they would perform their routine for about 15 minutes during the middle of our first hour's set, and the same during our second set. One of the dancers asked if we could reserve some of our faster numbers for each of their sessions and it was agreed that, nearer the time of their performance, the girls would assemble close to the side of the stage. A signal from the landlord would indicate that things were about to commence. He would then lower the lights in the bar and we would start with one of our fast songs.

A few innuendos were being bantered about on stage as we got ready to start, most of them being directed at poor old John as he was going to have to sing while they gyrated around in front of him. We started with a couple of slow numbers and then moved up a notch and played a few mid-tempo songs. The anticipation was killing us. We kept glancing across at the landlord and at last he indicated from the bar, just one more song. The two dancers suddenly appeared at the side of the stage, dressed in what looked like short black negligees, and smiled up at us. We finished the song, the lights were lowered in the bar and the ultra-violet light flickered on. As the girls mounted the lower stage, I turned and smiled at the rest of the group and three sets of teeth smiled back, illuminated by the ultra-violet light above.

We had agreed to start with 'Lucille', so I started my solo guitar riff, Martin followed with his bass riff, and then JG came crashing in. The two dancers pranced across the small stage and took up positions directly facing John, with their backs to the audience. Simultaneously, as John started singing, they started dancing, thrusting their hips towards him, their hands held high above their heads. What made this so hilarious was that the ultra-violet light picked up anything white, which meant that their black negligees had now melted away, and all that could be seen were two silhouetted bodies in the dark, with two pairs of highly illuminated white bras and panties leaping around in front of us. They then spread out across the stage and Martin and I were getting the thrusting hips, inches away from our loins. Just as I started my guitar solo, they both leapt into the air and turned and faced the audience and continued throwing their bodies around. I glanced across at John, just as he turned around to face us, and I could tell from his glowing white teeth, that he was laughing nervously as they continued gyrating around in front of us on the narrow stage. This was certainly distracting stuff and something we hadn't experienced before. I knew Martin was being turned on by it all as he had ramped up the volume on his bass guitar. The most difficult part for us was trying to keep a straight face throughout their performance, pretending that we were used to such things.

Unfortunately, after a few weeks the go-go dancers suddenly disappeared. Nothing was ever said by the landlord, but we heard from some regulars that they hadn't gone down particularly well, and so presumably he had told them not to return. However, from then on it meant that we played to the audience perched up high on the stage, from where we could view all the comings and goings.

With the music nights at the Mitre still packing them in, the landlord wasn't taking any chances with new groups and had booked us well ahead. In fact, our last night at the Mitre on 20 July, was our penultimate live performance. That night was soon upon us, but we didn't make any public announcements that this was going to be our last appearance there. I don't think the reality of it all had really sunk in – for us it was just another night at the Mitre. Later that night, we shook hands with the landlord and his bar staff, and headed off home.

SIBYLLA'S NIGHTCLUB - SWALLOW STREET - LONDON - APRIL 1967

I hadn't seen or heard from Eddie Caswell for quite a while, so it was a pleasant surprise when he called me at home. I could tell he was quite excited, which wasn't like the normal relaxed Eddie. He explained how, through a contact, he had arranged for us to play at one of London's new and trendy nightspots, Sibylla's. I didn't want to sound ungrateful, but I had to admit that I hadn't heard of this club before, plus they wanted us to do a free audition. We had been playing as a group for a long while now with a good reputation and I felt we were past doing free auditions. Besides, we intended calling it a day sometime in the summer. However, we weren't announcing that fact yet, just in case it affected any future bookings, so I let Eddie continue as I didn't want to offend him.

When he said it was it was on 1 April, I checked in my diary and was secretly pleased to tell him that we'd been booked to play at the Two Pudding Pub in Stratford on that Saturday evening. That didn't deter him at all as apparently we didn't need to start playing at the club until one o'clock in the morning. Plus, as he pointed out, by playing in Stratford, we would already be halfway to the West End. I asked him what the score was with this club and he went on to explain the background. It was in Swallow Street, a small side road off Regent Street, and had opened its doors in June of the previous year. He left this little teaser to the end, when he said it was owned by a consortium of people, including George Harrison of The Beatles, the Australian DJ Alan Freeman, and many other well-known personalities. I was impressed to say the least and felt in a bit of a tight corner as Eddie had already promised we'd play there on that evening. He said that we only needed to play for one hour and would be paid £15 in expenses. If they liked us, then they would pay us a lot more to come back. He went on to say that the club was frequented by members of the music fraternity, from musicians to managers and record executives. It would obviously be a great opportunity for us to play there and who knows what it could lead to! With those thoughts running through my mind, I agreed we'd do it.

Having finished playing at the Two Puddings, we quickly packed up the van and headed off to central London and Sibylla's nightclub. As I drove the van into Swallow Street, there was Eddie waiting outside the entrance to the club in his Ford Fairlane. We spoke briefly before he disappeared down the steps and into the club, only to emerge a minute or so later. 'Get your gear in as quick as you can. I'll give you a hand, but you'll have to bring your drum cases etc. back up and store them in the van as there isn't much room down there.'

We quickly transported our equipment down the stairs, cleared the cases away and busied ourselves setting up our gear. Eddie said he'd be back later. It was not a particularly large club and the main restaurant area, with its dozen or so tables covered in white starched tablecloths, was dimly lit, giving its occupants a degree of privacy. In the centre of the dining area was a small stage enclosed by smoked glass panels and the main source of lighting in the club came from a well-lit bar. It wasn't particularly busy at just before one o'clock in the morning, but through the smoked glass we could see that there were a few couples dining in the restaurant.

John went up the bar and ordered himself a beer. He came back in total shock at the cost, which was £1, the equivalent of nearly £13 in today's money! The price of a bottle of beer in a pub at the time was only

8p! We later discovered that all drinks served at the bar cost £1, irrespective of what you ordered.

It was all a bit strange really. Nobody had approached us or spoken to us since we had arrived. So we just started our one-hour set on time and because of the quiet and discreet ambience of the club, we began with a couple of our softer songs. When we livened it up a bit with 'Sorrow', a few couples got up to dance on the small wooden dance floor in front of the stage. Halfway through our set, Martin nodded his head in the direction of a couple sitting at a table close to the smoked glass panel where he was standing. I couldn't make out who it was, so Martin whispered to John, and John turned to me, saying 'It's Sandie Shaw with some guy.' She was a very popular young female singer at the time and had had a number of records in the charts, always performing in her bare feet. That prompted me to have a quick look around to see if I recognised anybody else out there, but sadly no. We played a couple of faster songs, and a few more couples drifted onto the floor. When we came to play our last number of the evening at two o'clock, there were 20 or so people on the dance floor.

As we were packing up our gear, Eddie arrived and insisted on buying us a round of drinks. We made ourselves at home and lounged around in the luxurious leather chairs watching everything that was going on. I saw a few people arrive and a few people leave, but didn't spot any more famous faces. Sandie Shaw still sat there, eating, drinking and chatting away to her companion. As far as I could see, she was the only pop celebrity there. I asked Eddie who was going to pay us and he immediately handed over £15. Now wasn't the time to ask him where he'd been for the past hour and a half, and how come it was him who was paying us the money and not the club. I never did get around to asking Eddie these questions, and I never had any feedback from him concerning our appearance at Sibylla's that night.

36

OUR FINAL PERFORMANCE - GOOD NIGHT AND THANK YOU

HABERDASHERS' ASKE'S SCHOOL - 21 JULY 1967

With the summer holidays fast approaching, we decided that playing at this Grammar School in Pepys Road, New Cross, South London for an end of term dance, would be our last ever performance.

Being a very special Friday evening for us, we each took along our respective fiancées to witness our final performance. Deep down, I suspect they were all quite relieved that we had finally decided to call it a day. The eight of us squeezed into the old Thames van and headed for New Cross. As we made our way out of the Blackwall Tunnel, I did point out, yet again, the bullet holes in the wall, which brought about a few groans from the back of the van. Then we passed the Mitre pub, where only the night before we had said our final goodbyes.

Following the directions I had been given, we easily found Pepys Road and the Haberdashers' Aske's Grammar School. It was a large imposing Victorian building and as we drove under the arched entrance, we could see the date1875 chiselled into the stone. We were directed to a door that led directly onto a very spacious stage, which overlooked an equally spacious assembly hall. Looking around, I assumed this cavernous stage was currently being used for theatrical productions, as in the wings were many floor-standing spotlights. Up in the ceiling, I could see even more large spotlights.

We were unusually quiet as we went about the routine task of setting up the gear – plugging in amplifiers, setting up the drums, attaching mikes to stands and plugging them in, tuning up our guitars, and removing cases into the wings. It was a very surreal moment for me as I stopped for a moment and gazed around the stage, watching my close mates busying themselves with the equipment, knowing we would never be doing this again after tonight. I felt quite sad. It was too late now but had we made the right decision to disband the group? To make it a night to remember, we had all agreed earlier that we really wanted to make the evening special and different, so each of us was taking a bottle of wine on stage to celebrate the occasion. We'd never drunk alcohol on stage before, except for Blackheath Rugby Club, and I'm sure the teachers in attendance would not approve, even though we were appearing in front of older school kids. What could be the worse case scenario? This was our very last performance as The Candles and we wanted to go out with a bang.

We had set up our gear well back from the front of the stage and it was probably being in this position, combined with the extremely bright spotlights, that prevented us from seeing any further than a few feet in front us. We knew our fiancées were sitting somewhere out there in the dark hall, and we could hear kids dancing around, but I felt a bit isolated from the audience because of this. However, we knew there must people out there as every so often a young face would appear at the front of the stage to peer at us at close quarters. It didn't really matter to us anyway, as we were having a great time on stage, laughing and goofing around as the alcohol began to flow through our veins.

Starting our second set, we had all agreed beforehand to just play the songs we individually enjoyed performing and so it all became a bit self-indulgent, but I doubt the audience even realised. By now, we were basically playing for ourselves anyway and enjoying every second of it, with no regard for anyone else. We could have probably carried on playing to our hearts' content, as one by one we'd remember another favourite song we'd forgotten about and wanted to play. Suddenly a teacher's head appeared at the foot of the stage, announcing it was time to wrap it up. I turned and spoke to the others. 'Could we finish on 'Shame, Shame, Shame'? Please, even though we've played it earlier.' No one objected and John announced that this was going to be our final song of the evening – and forever! And so I launched into my guitar intro to this fast 12-bar blues song for the last time. John indicated I should do another guitar solo in order to extend the length of the song, so that we could all treasure this final moment. Then it was all over. I glanced across in time to see Martin swing round and thrust his bass guitar head through his bass speaker cabinet, just as the curtains closed to clapping and cheering.

We all stood there for a moment, swaying a bit from the effects of the wine, then fell about laughing when we spotted Martin's bass guitar cabinet with a gaping hole in the fabric. During the drive home, all our partners agreed that it had been one of our best performances ever, which was gratifying to know. It was probably just as well it was our last performance as we might have been tempted to drink bottles of wine at every booking in order to play as well as we did that night!

Our accountants calculated any final taxes due and we settled up with them. A few weeks later, we drove up to London and wheeled in our two Gibson amplifiers, our Selmer speaker system and microphones, and JG's Ludwig drums, to a clearinghouse for group equipment. Compared to what we'd originally paid for it all, we only received a pittance back. But it had been used regularly over the past 18 months, shunted from van to stage and back again and had withstood the rigours of the road. It had certainly proved worthwhile investing in the best gear money could buy as it had served us well and not once let us down, apart from a drum skin splitting a year before. Martin went on to sell our Ford Thames van to a colleague at work.

With all the money now in the bank, I closed our account and divided up the total into four equal amounts. I then went on to sell my beautiful blond Gibson 330 a year later and this exciting chapter in all our lives was finally closed. All I had left to show for eight years of playing and managing the group was a mound of contracts, diaries, photographs, posters, letters, etc., which I've kept ever since. Oh, and some wonderful memories!

CHEERS!

IT'S ALL OVER NOW

BAND OF BROTHERS

THAT'S IT FOLKS – GOOD NIGHT AND THANK YOU

37

LIFE AFTER THE GROUP – MY BANKING DAYS ARE NUMBERED – 1968

The group had disbanded in July1967 and I was now married and living in Blackheath, chosen because I particularly liked the look of the area after driving through it many times to perform at the Blackheath R.F.C. I was still working as a relief cashier for the bank when in 1968, I was sent to the Canning Town branch to help out. It so happened that the bank was only a matter of yards away from the Bridge House pub, and I was to discover that the pub had their bank account there.

I walked into the small banking hall around mid-morning to find it packed with customers, so I waited patiently to get a member of staff's attention. I was aware of music being played and as I looked around, I noticed there was a transistor radio on top of a filing cabinet. When the DJ announced the next record, I recognised his voice – the radio was tuned in to Radio Caroline. This was a pirate radio ship that was anchored three miles off the Essex coast just outside British territorial waters, and broadcast rock music 24 hours a day. I just couldn't believe it! Playing music in a bank was totally unheard of then – and still is today, 50 years later. While I stood there trying to get somebody's atten-tion, I started to check out the various members of staff and noticed a young clerk with long auburn hair sitting at a Boroughs machine, typing data onto customers' statements – this was still pre-computer days. Another surprise, not the actual length of his hair, but more the fact that he was working in a bank with such long hair! I started to think that I would like working here!

I ended up working for three weeks at this branch and thoroughly enjoyed the people I worked with, the relaxed atmosphere, the music, and the many laughs we had, something I hadn't experienced in the bank before. However, my mind was made up. I didn't like working in a bank anymore – it just wasn't for me. But it would be nice to while away my time at this branch until I could find another job. I approached the manager to see if I could apply for a permanent posting and luck was on my side. It just so happened he'd already applied to Head Office for an additional member of staff! After making a few telephone calls, I was transferred to the Canning Town branch a month later and I spent two of my happiest years in the bank working at this branch – until I finally escaped.

I discovered my new bank friends would quite often pop into a local pub for a quick pint before heading home and within days of joining the branch I was invited to join them. The bank was sandwiched between two pubs, the Bridge House and the Royal Oak, but they only ever went to the Royal Oak, which was slightly nearer and more convenient. However, I did ask them why they didn't drink at the Bridge House and a simple response came back 'too rough'. Interestingly, the Royal Oak was famous in the area for having a full-size boxing ring on the first floor, where boxing training took place. The publican, Morry Vickers, was a daily bank customer.

One evening, having finished work, four of us went into the Royal Oak pub to have a drink before heading off home. The pub had only just opened, so we were the only people sitting at the bar, when I recognised my father's voice. I looked across and he was talking to Morry Vickers, but before I could make myself known, he'd disappeared upstairs to the gym. My father was the boxing correspondent for the Romford Recorder, writing under the name of 'The Ringman'. Speaking with my father later, I discovered he was at the Royal Oak to interview a young up-and-coming boxer called Joe Bugner, who went on to become British Commonwealth and European heavyweight champion.

I was never going to be managerial material in the banking world. Although I had been told that my history of involvement in the Mods and Rockers battle in 1962 wouldn't go against me, I didn't believe them. This incident must have remained on my records and therefore hindered any possible future promotion. However, while I searched for a more suitable job, over the next two years I had many happy days working in Canning Town. I enjoyed dealing with the locals. Many were real rough diamonds, down to earth people with no airs or graces that you could openly joke with. During that time, in keeping with the fashion and also to keep two of my colleagues company, I let my hair grow and even grew a beard. 'Far out man!'

Another year had passed since the group had disbanded and although life as a married man was extremely agreeable, without performing in the group had left a large void. It had occupied so much of my life and now without it, had exposed how unhappy I actually was working in the bank, and how unbearable I found it. Our apartment in Blackheath had been purchased with a bank mortgage at a special fixed rate for bank employees of 2.5%. My dilemma now was to find a new job with a sufficient increase in my annual salary to cover the increased cost of moving my mortgage from the bank to an outside building society, when the mortgage rate in 1968 was around 7%.

The following story is testament to my increasing frustration at the age of 25 of being unable to find a suitable job that I would enjoy at the right salary. Well, that's the only feasible explanation I can give for my actions! On 23 September 1969, dustmen around the country went on an unofficial strike for more pay and on 9 October 1969 they returned to work, having won their fight to receive a pay increase. Within days of the strike beginning, garbage started piling up on every street corner throughout London, and Canning Town was no exception. The weather was mild, so it wasn't long before the waste started to decompose – and smell. Blue bottle flies increased in number, and in size, as they gorged themselves to their hearts' content on the decaying matter and they were becoming a real nuisance in homes and places of business. I was now first cashier at the Canning Town branch, but that didn't stop me and a few colleagues taking up the challenge to see how many of these monster flies we could individually kill within 5 days. I chatted up a local customer who had a trophy shop and he very kindly donated a small plastic and silver cup, engraved with Fly Swatter of the Year – 1969.

Before commencement of activities on Monday morning Jim, our stationery clerk, was given an order for four of the bank's standard 14-inch wooden rulers plus a large box of thick rubber bands. There were no rules as such and it was basically every man for himself. I stretched a large rubber band along the length of the ruler and this was kept in a drawer, ready for action. The local blue bottles must have got wind of our intentions as only one was spotted during the entire day, which flew off before anybody could get it. The following day I was busy working at the till when a cheer went up behind me. A fly had been killed on the wall and a notch was cut in the ruler. Within minutes another cheer went up – another fly had been annihilated, and another ruler was notched.

By Thursday lunchtime I was lagging behind with only three notches, the highest number of notches being five. The manager and sub-manager were out of the bank, spending their usual two-hour lunch session at the seamen's hostel down the road. I was just serving a young lady from the local hairdressing salon, when suddenly a large fly landed on the tall security glass separating us both. I quickly looked over my shoulder. All heads were down working, so nobody had spotted it. It was just sitting there, not moving, teasing me, and I simply didn't have a choice. 'Excuse me for a moment' I said. Very slowly I retrieved my loaded ruler from the drawer, took aim – splat! 'Yes! Four!' I called out triumphantly. I went back to serving my customer but there was a horrified look on the girl's face as directly in front of her eyes, but fortunately on the opposite side of the glass, yellow goo was slowly sliding down. I apologised profusely and with a duster wiped away the remains of the fly. I then went on to briefly explain the game and as I handed across her change, I did get a wry smile from her as she departed. Not exactly the normal behaviour of a bank cashier!

Our last day, and the top score of notches had now risen to six. Just before the bank opened its doors, I spotted a fly walking across a filing cabinet. 'Got it' I called out and I put another notch on my ruler. I was now in second place. Lunchtime arrived and someone else scored a hit, but I was still in second position. As usual, the manager and sub-manager made their way out of the branch and as it was Friday, they always had an extended lunch at the seamen's hostel. From the start, we had agreed that the challenge would finish at four o'clock on Friday, so the pressure was now on. I took a quick look across at the small trophy sitting on top of a filing cabinet. It was a busy lunchtime for us two cashiers, with queues at each till. I was feverishly counting through a bundle of one hundred pound notes, when there came a yell from behind me 'There's one!' I turned around to see what all the noise was about and immediately spotted three rulers pointing up the ceiling. Suddenly, a volley of rubber bands headed for the unsuspecting fly. They all missed their target and the fly continued walking nonchalantly across the ceiling, totally unperturbed, and made its way above the top of the security glass and into the banking hall.

This could possibly be my last opportunity to down a fly before four o'clock and tie for first place. I apologised to my customer, took out my loaded ruler, hurriedly closed my till, opened the door into the banking hall, and climbed up onto the counter. About ten customers just stood there in astonishment as I ran along the counter, heading for that strutting fly. I raised my ruler, took aim, slowly pushed the rubber band up, and it was off. The poor fly never knew what hit it. My sixth kill! As I proudly walked back along the till, customers started clapping so, just before jumping down, I bowed to them. This could only have happened in the Canning Town branch of the NatWest Bank!

The large clock in the banking hall said 3.55pm, and still no more kills. Suddenly I heard a voice ring out behind me. 'Yes! Got it!' and I turned around to see one of my colleagues standing there, punching the air, and pointing to a squashed fly on the wall. The manager and sub-manager had, by now, returned from their extended lunch and they both looked up and smiled. I doubt they were quite fully aware of what had taken place over the past five days. Later, over a couple of beers in the Royal Oak, the winner received his trophy. As I drove home, I had time to think about my behaviour. I was 27 years old and should have known better, but I was bored and the past week's activities showed how desperately I needed to get out of the bank.

I did discover during my time at the branch, that from the manager down to the five male staff members, most of us had all been a bit naughty or troublesome at some time or other during our banking careers. The manager had defaulted at a previous branch by giving out personal loans to visiting seamen from Tilbury Docks, who were never to be seen again. The sub-manager had a drinking problem and, of course, there was me!

When I worked at the Stratford branch, I'd complained bitterly to the manager because he kept calling me 'old chap' and the chief clerk always referred to me as 'old boy'. I told them to please call me either Colin or Mr Stoddart, but they took exception to my demand and telephoned Head Office. The following day I was summoned to Head Office in central London, where I was accused of being insolent.

Bank managers were obliged to complete an annual detailed assessment of every member of staff, covering their aptitude in the workplace, punctuality, dealing with customers and lastly, appearance. Generally, I received the odd A, but mostly B, for my branch work. However, now with my long hair and a beard, my manager had only given me a minus D, the absolute bottom of the scale. My assessment had been submitted to the staff department at Lothbury and a few weeks had passed when I was summoned into the manager's office one morning and informed that Head Office wanted to see me the following day at 11.00pm. I guessed my long hair and beard would be the main topic of discussion.

Around this period the bank introduced a very controversial scheme, encouraging university graduates to apply for a managerial post in the bank when they left university. If accepted, they would be expected to work at branch level for six months, gaining experience across the board working as a cashier, a general clerk, a securities clerk and a chief clerk. After six months they would be assessed, and providing they passed, a managerial position would be offered to them. Of course, this scheme did not go down well with the current bank staff around the country as many young bank clerks were studying to complete the Institute of Bankers examinations and were committed to making a career in banking, To suddenly find out that a university graduate would most probably jump the queue ahead of them by many years, seemed totally out of order and could discourage people from making a career in the bank if taking the conventional route.

I had recently cut out an advertisement from the Daily Telegraph, just in case the bank ever confronted me concerning my long hair and beard. It read something like 'University graduates required for managerial positions in the NatWest banking group. Get your scissors out, not to cut your hair, but to cut this advertisement out, and apply for a job at the NatWest bank'. I felt this might be a very useful bit of ammunition to take along with me for my interview.

I was ten minutes early for my appointment and sat quietly in the waiting room. At precisely 11.00am, I was escorted into a room, offered a seat, and found myself facing a middle-aged gentleman with regulation short back and sides haircut. For the next 15 minutes, he went through each section of my manager's report and I was doing pretty well, getting one A but mostly B and B minuses, for various jobs I'd undertaken over the past year. However, I braced myself for what I knew was coming – for appearance I had been given D minus, the worst possible mark.

I sat there quietly, being lectured to by this boring gentleman, who pointed out that my appearance would most definitely affect any possible chance of future promotion. He then fell right into my little trap by suggesting I should have my hair cut. I started off by stating 'With all due respect, please have a look at this recent advertisement.' I waited while he read it before launching into my argument. 'In this recent advertisement, the bank is openly encouraging university graduates to apply for work in the bank, but not to cut their hair. So why the double standards?' My ambush worked perfectly. After a lot of stammering and clearing of the throat, he blurted out that the students would be expected to cut their hair if they were offered a full-time job. I couldn't resist responding 'Then the bank is being very deceitful.' Mission accomplished. Within five minutes, I pushed open the double glass doors and made my way down the steps. I knew I had just put the final nail in my banking coffin, but I was pleased. I'd stood my ground and I made up my mind there and then, that I must make a concerted effort to push ahead in my search for a new job.

Interestingly, no females were allowed to work at this branch as Head Office had decreed that Canning Town was too rough an area. If the truth be told, the Canning Town branch of the NatWest bank was really just a borstal for offending bank clerks. In the sixties, banks had a very sound reputation and the only time you'd ever be sacked was for stealing money, so they had to put the odd reprobates somewhere!

Two months later, my search was rewarded when I spotted an advert-isement in the Daily Telegraph. A non-profit making organisation in central London was seeking a person with banking experience to work in their accounts department. I applied for the position and after several interviews, I was offered the job which I accepted. I waved goodbye to the bank forever. After serving 11 years, I was FREEeeeeeeee!

THE WHO POSTER IS SOLD - 1999

By nature, I've always been a keen collector and when I was really young, I collected sets of cigarette cards and also cards that came with packets of Typhoo tea. I then started collecting matchbox tops and processed cheese labels. I would cut out newspaper cuttings of my favourite footballers and stick them in a scrap album. Basically nothing was ever thrown away – I was a natural hoarder. This preoccupation of mine spilled over into the group and from day one of it being formed, I collected every poster and kept every contract, letter, newspaper article and photograph. I also assiduously kept a diary of all our bookings. The group was my passion and I just loved seeing our name in print.

Every week during the sixties, three national music papers were delivered to my home and I read them avidly during my train journeys to work. I wanted to know who had entered the charts that week, who was number one and which was the best selling album. I was obsessed with the whole music scene and loved reading about an unknown Liverpool group called The Beatles who had entered the charts with their first record release 'Love Me Do'. 'Beatlemania' was on the rise and only months later their follow-up single 'Please Please Me' went to the top of the hit parade. I would look through the charts and see that other Liverpool groups were having hit records, followed by groups from all over the country. It was as if music was completely taking over and, to coin a much-used phrase, it was a 'Fab' time!

This for me was so gratifying as only a few years previously, American acts had dominated the British charts and had done so since rock 'n' roll had burst onto the British music scene in the late fifties. Now the tables were turning and I can distinctly remember opening a musical paper to study the American charts and witnessing the impossible – in 1965 The Beatles occupied the top five positions in the American charts! No artist or act had ever achieved this feat before, and it hasn't been matched since. Over the coming months The Beatles conquered America and spearheaded by their popularity, the 'British Invasion' as it was called, soon followed as more and more British groups toured the States and invaded the charts. It was certainly a magical time for British popular music.

25 years later, I retrieved about 800 of these assorted weekly music papers from my parents' loft where they had been carefully stored since the sixties. I'd read that they had become very collectible and so they were eventually sold, a necessary move at the time in order to keep the family finances on track!

Rock and pop memorabilia in general had become very collectible, and my reasoning to sell The Who poster in 1999 was driven primarily by the need to prop up the family coffers once again. The Who had by now become 'old hat' in the music business, but when their song 'Who Are You' was chosen as the theme music for the TV series 'CSI', they were back in business again, even more so when other Who songs were used as the intro music for subsequent 'CSI' series. With the popularity of The Who riding high, it was a good time to test the water, and to sell the poster.

This poster had been rolled up with other group posters and stored in the basement of our house for ten years. Yes, I was immensely proud of them, but they weren't achieving very much hidden from view. They had all been photographed a few years previously, so at least I had a permanent record of them. Plus it was much easier showing people photographs of the posters than resurrecting them from the basement.

After a lot of soul searching, I came to the conclusion that the benefits of selling some of the posters now outweighed keeping them hidden in a basement for who knows how long. The Who poster was my least favourite because the date of the original gig had been changed and we had been booked to appear at the last minute. Subsequently, the promoter had the date 'Sat, Mar. 13' and our name 'The Candles' printed in red on separate paper and stuck over the original date and support group, who presumably couldn't appear on that particular night. For me, the poster didn't look totally

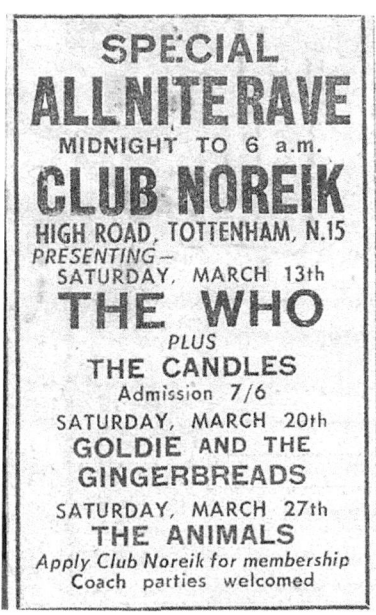

authentic, although of course it was, but fortunately the gig was advertised in the back of the NME music paper stating that The Who plus The Candles were appearing at the Club Noreik on the 13 March 1965.

Things were always a bit tight moneywise with two teenage boys around. Our eldest son, Daniel, had obtained good A Level passes and we wanted to reward him for working so hard. We had learned that a few of his friends' parents were paying for their kids to go on a holiday together to Spain in recognition of their respective exam passes. Daniel was desperate to join them, so the money from the sale of the music papers was used to fund this holiday.

Now, four years on, our youngest son, Thomas, also needed recognition for his hard work in obtaining good A Level results, but money again was the problem. My parents had always gone out of their way to ensure that my brother and I were treated equally, and I was determined to do the same for my two sons. Daniel, by now, had finished his three-year stint at Manchester University and had taken off with friends to travel the world backpacking. Paying for all this university education had seriously depleted the family finances somewhat but we wanted to do for Thomas what we had done for Daniel and the only way to raise additional cash was to sell some of the group posters I had collected over the years.

The Who poster, together with some other posters when we supported groups like The Merseybeats and Jimmy Powell and The Five Dimensions, whose harmonica player, Rod Stewart, had only just left the group weeks before we played with them, were finally sold to an online rock memorabilia company and the proceeds banked. Thomas was now in his first year at University in Bristol and during a telephone conversation with him, he said he had always wanted to go to New York. I suggested a long weekend there and much to my surprise, he jumped at the idea. I was rather flattered and surprised that he wanted to go there with his old dad!

NEW YORK - JUNE 1999

As the plane banked over to the right, I could clearly see JFK Airport stretching out below, and I smiled to myself. Who would have believed that the paper poster I had removed from a wall outside the Club Noreik early on a cold Sunday morning 34 years ago, would now be paying for a long weekend break in New York with my youngest son, Thomas!

Daniel has always berated me for selling The Who poster as he had always admired them as a group, more so after the poster had been sold! He even went to see them perform live a number of years ago, at a one-off concert in London. He called me at home on his mobile phone when The Who started to play the opening chords to 'I Can't Explain', and I was able to listen to the entire song. All a bit spooky really. My son goes to see a group perform that, over 30 years ago had played in London and were supported by a group called The Candles, the lead guitarist of which was his father! At that gig all those years ago, 'I Can't Explain', The Who's first hit, had just entered the charts, and they played it that night. It seems unbelievable that 30-odd years later, I was to hear the same song being performed live by the same group, and all via a small hand-held mobile phone held by my son!

Thomas remains quite indifferent on the subject, probably because he's never shown a lot of interest in The Who, although I do know he thoroughly enjoyed his first visit to New York!

To this day, I have no idea if The Who poster was retained or sold on by the rock memorabilia company, but a few years later in 2002, I was in a bookshop browsing through a new publication entitled 'The Complete Chronicle of the Who – Anyway Anyhow Anywhere'. This book listed every Who gig in date order, up to the present time. Having not been mentioned as the support group in an earlier book entitled 'The Who Concert File', I was intrigued to see if we had been mentioned by name as the support group in this new book. Flicking through the pages, I finally reached the date 13 March 1965 – and there it was in full colour, my old poster!

The poster popped up again when it was included in a book published in 2010 called 'The Art of British Rock – 50 years of Rock Posters, Flyers and Handbills'. The original poster hadn't been used. Instead it was a reproduction that was freely available to purchase from a major online auction site. But I'm not complaining. There we were again – The Who plus The Candles. The flame still continued to burn brightly!

A few years ago, while sitting at my computer, I made an even more startling discovery. I had been surfing the Internet for over an hour, searching for nothing in particular, when I decided I'd had enough but would have just one more browse. Sitting there, wondering what to enter in the search engine, I noticed the framed poster hanging on the wall in front of me – Jerry Lee Lewis plus The Candles appearing at the Club Noreik. So I entered The Who plus The Candles at Club Noreik and lo and behold, a whole list of sites appeared on the screen. One in particular caught my eye, which stated 'Club Noreik – The Who – Tin Sign'. I clicked on this site and found myself staring once more at my old poster, complete with all the torn edges, which had now been reproduced in full colour, but reduced in size, and was available to buy as an 11 inch x 8 inch tin sign!

I was stunned. I just couldn't believe it and I couldn't wait to tell the other group members. I continued to scour the numerous websites, all advertising the sale of the tin sign. There was page after page, but after about 40 pages, I simply gave up. What I'd stumbled upon showed that the tin sign was available to buy from various online sites worldwide! How amazing was that! Amongst all the sites for the tin sign, one in particular caught my eye. It was the Iraq Museum International in Baghdad, which had recently hosted an international poster exhibition and among the exhibits was the original poster for The Who plus The Candles.

On reflection, reluctant as I had been to do it, if I hadn't sold the poster when I did, it wouldn't have appeared in one of the definitive books published about The Who's concerts or been included in the book on British poster art or reproduced as a tin sign and sold throughout the world. Naturally, I bought the tin sign and so did the other members of the group, and both of my sons have one hanging in their respective kitchens. How many people worldwide have this tin sign hanging in their homes and wonder who The Candles were!

My predictions were certainly completely wrong back then when we played with The Who that very first time and I thought they wouldn't come to much! They are probably bigger now than they were back in 1999, when I sold the poster! An album of new songs was finally released in 2006, and immediately entered into both the British and American charts. The Who are still performing to this day and in 2015 undertook a 50th Anniversary European and USA Tour, 50 years on from our little gig with them in North London. There have been a few ups and downs on their journey, but they have weathered the storms, carving out an illustrious career. Tragedy struck the group with the death of Keith Moon in 1978, when he died of an overdose of sedatives, prescribed by his doctor to alleviate alcohol withdrawal symptoms.

However, The Who continued performing live with Kenney Jones, the drummer with The Small Faces and The Faces. They finally disbanded in 1983 but reformed in 1985 to perform at the world's biggest televised benefit rock show 'Live Aid', with all the profits going to The Relief of Famine in Africa, still using Kenney Jones as their drummer. The concerts were held jointly at Wembley Stadium in London and the JFK Stadium in Philadelphia, USA, and were watched by an estimated 1.9 billion people in 150 countries.

In 1990 The Who were inducted into the Rock and Roll Hall of Fame in Cleveland, USA. Inductees were only given consideration for this accolade 25 years after the release of their first record and the criteria for receiving this honour were based upon the artist's influence and significant contributions to the development and perpetuation of rock and roll.

In 1994 Zak Starkey, son of Ringo Starr of The Beatles, joined The

Who as their new drummer. Interestingly Keith Moon and Ringo Starr had been close friends and Moon was godfather to Starkey and went on to buy him his first professional drum kit. Ringo Starr's first drum kit was given to him by his father and was purchased at Pioneer, a musical instrument shop in North Street, Romford, my home town, while visiting relatives in the area. Pioneer was five minutes' walk from my parents' house and was where I bought a number of my early guitars.

The Who have continued performing and touring on and off since the Live Aid Concert in 1985, but experienced yet another tragedy when John Entwistle died at the Hard Rock Hotel in Las Vegas in 2002 from a heart attack induced by cocaine. This was just prior to the start of an American tour, but The Who hired a bass guitarist and completed the tour.

Another major accolade was when they performed live during the half-time slot at the American Super Bowl, National Football League final on 7 February 2010. It was broadcast to over 150 million television viewers in 230 countries worldwide. I saw their 15-minute performance on YouTube and it was stunning – an inspiration for all aging rockers!

Still they wouldn't lie down! When Britain hosted the 2012 Olympic Games, The Who was the final act to appear at the closing ceremony held in the Olympic Stadium in Stratford, London. What an honour! And what a fantastic performance! Strange to think that the stadium was less than a mile away from where the Two Puddings pub used to be, and where Keith Moon had bought us a round of drinks. Then during our break, by invitation we went next door to the Stratford Town Hall and stood in the wings watching them play 47 years previously!

38

MY LIVE STORY - THE WHO PLUS THE CANDLES

45 YEARS LATER - 25 NOVEMBER 2010

S itting in the sunshine on our terrace in southern Spain 45 years after that memorable night in 1965, my recollection of the entire experience was soon to be revived once again. If the truth be told, it had never ever entirely gone away and had been told to many willing, and unwilling, listeners over the years. I was just reading a British newspaper when a headline, entitled My Live Story, caught my attention. Reading the article, I discovered that Channel 4 television, in conjunction with

American Express, were running an online competition in the search to find the UK's most memorable live music moments.

As it so happened, having retired to Spain with my wife in 2006, I had, out of pleasurable boredom, decided to write the story about my life during the 60s, including The Candles supporting The Who. I had been encouraged to do so by my sons and so with nothing better to do in life, I sat at my computer and started to relate my memories. Now, a year on from my endeavours, I was interested to learn more about this competition, which I thought sounded just the ticket for me. I opened up Channel 4's My Live Story website and discovered that there were quite a lot of entries already, the majority being of stories written by young people and their exciting experiences at music events. Many had either submitted an accompanying video or at least photographs of their experience. That was going to cause a slight problem as no photographs existed of The Candles taken on 25 March 1965. Once again, I was going to rely on that bloody poster. I was counting on the fact that many young people had heard of The Who, albeit from the TV series 'CSI', and seeing the name would be intrigued to read my story. This competition was clearly aimed at a younger generation, but why? I then discovered the answer. This was a promotion by American Express to make people aware that they offered its cardholders exclusive priority tickets to many music and cultural events, with access to some of the best and most exclusive seats. Now it was all beginning to make sense.

What was the incentive for me to enter such a competition? Out of the thousands of stories submitted, 120 entries would be shortlisted by a selected panel of judges. The stories would then be whittled down to just 21 finalists who would then be invited to a Gala Evening to be held at the famous Abbey Road Studios in London, somewhere I have always wanted to visit. On that night, a short film called 'Epic' would be premiered featuring the 21 stories. The company of the famous movie director, Ridley Scott, would undertake to make this film. Also during that Gala Evening, a final winner would be selected from the 21 finalists and they would be sent, together with their partner of choice, on a VIP trip to Los Angeles. But for me, just being at the Abbey Road Studios would be enough!

The biggest problem was going to be condensing my original story of around 5,000 words down to the maximum limit of 200 words imposed by the competition rules. This wasn't going to be easy, but eventually the job was done, and I entered my story onto the website. The judges' decision would be influenced by the number of hits each story received from people visiting the website over the weeks ahead. I was now relying heavily on my photograph of The Who poster, which illustrated my story. The number of hits for each story was shown beneath the titles, so it was interesting to see which stories were attracting the most visitors. Although I was a bit of a late starter with my entry, the story began to attract quite a lot of visitors, and within a few weeks it had gained many hits. By the time the final choice was made by the judges, my story was up there with the top 30! After about a week, I received an email from the promoters informing me that I was one of the 21 finalists! I was on my way to Abbey Road Studios – the most famous recording studio in the world!

It was a bitterly cold evening in November as I sat, nervous and excited, in the back of a taxi with my two invited guests – my wife Pat and my old mate and bass guitarist from The Candles, Martin Palmer. An incident on the Underground that night of all nights, meant we had to ditch the tube train and jump in a taxi, which finally dropped us right outside the studios in Abbey Road. Being a finalist, I had first to be photographed upon arrival outside the entrance to the studios. We then we made our way up those familiar steps where so many famous groups and artistes had trod, and on into the foyer. We were directed to Studio 2, passing along corridors covered with photographs of many of the stars that had recorded there over the years. As we entered Studio 2, which had been elaborately decorated for the evening, we could see young girls floating around offering guests glasses of champagne and canapés. We moved further into the studio, blending in with the mass of people milling around. Looking around, apart from perhaps one or two people, we were, without doubt, the oldest people there, and I was beginning to think that perhaps my story had been selected merely to represent the obligatory 'older' person.

I was in awe as I stood there sipping my drink, surveying the scene around me. The studio had been completely transformed for this evening's gala event. It had a long glittering bar, moving lights, music and, with so many people there, it was more like a buzzing nightclub. I had, in the past, viewed the many photographs taken inside the studio of some of my favourite groups, so I knew what it looked like during a normal working day. But the one photograph that stood out for me was the shot of The Beatles huddled together playing away in a distant corner of the studio. Compared to the small studios where we recorded some of our music, Studio 2 was the size of a small ballroom. However, there were still one or two telltale signs that this was normally a working recording studio. Hanging on hooks around the walls were reels and reels of cables, and there in the corner was the flight of steps that led up the control room and the window from where George Martin, the producer, would have looked down surveying his many recording artists. Close to the steps was a large grand piano, covered with a heavy-duty protective cover and guarded by security. The guard told me it was the grand piano George Martin and Paul McCartney had used so many times on those Beatles' recordings.

Later on we were ushered into the gigantic, cathedral-like Studio 1 for some live music. This particular studio is the world's largest purpose-built recording studio and can comfortably accommodate a 110-piece orchestra. The interior had been decorated for the event with large photographs of famous artistes who had recorded at the Abbey Road Studios over the years, ranging from Glen Miller, Shirley Bassey, Cliff Richard and The Shadows to Pink Floyd, Queen, Oasis, Radiohead and, I nearly forgot, The Beatles! Hung beneath these photographs, which were suspended from the ceiling at regular intervals around the studio, were the 21 finalists' stories that had been printed onto large boards. As you would expect, the best story, mine, hung beneath the photograph of The Beatles, but unfortunately, the judges didn't agree with me!

MARTIN (LEFT) WITH ME IN STUDIO 2 DRINKS IN HAND. BEHIND US ARE THE STAIRS LEADING UP TO THE CONTROL ROOM AND IN THE BOTTOM LEFT OF THE PHOTOGRAPH, THE FAMOUS GRAND PIANO CAN JUST BE SEEN PROTECTED BY A SECURITY GUARD.

We then watched the short film entitled 'Epic', which was very loosely based on the 21 stories, and The Who poster made a brief appearance once again. After the film, the overall winner of the competition was announced and it was a young man who had proposed to his girlfriend on the stage in front of crowds at a concert held at Wembley Arena. They would be given a camcorder each and had to film themselves during their three-day VIP visit to Los Angeles, for future showing on TV. American Express, quite understandably, were targeting young people with this promotion so, let's face it, giving camcorders to two old pensioners to film themselves in LA would not have made good television viewing! However, I am so glad I entered this competition and found myself among the 21 finalists. Just being at the Abbey Road Studios that evening was reward enough for me!

THE END

About the Author

Colin Ferguson Stoddart (1943 - still alive and kicking) was born in Romford, a market town in Essex, to an English mother and a Scottish father. Educated at St Edward's Church of England school, he left in 1960 to work for a national high street banking organisation for the next 11 arduous years.

During this dark period in his working life he found solace in being the lead guitarist of a popular rock group who performed together for 8 blissful years. Finally succumbing to married life, Colin found himself still working in the bank and 'depression' setting in.

His life was changed by a call from the group's vocalist who had emigrated to South Africa to work in the clothing industry. Arriving in Cape Town in 1973, Colin finally found his true vocation working in the fashion tie business. Five years later he returned to the UK and continued working in the tie business, eventually becoming sales director for a tie company based in Bond Street in central London.

But changes were ahead as the popular trend in America for 'dress down days' in the work place started to take hold in the UK, and the ubiquitous tie slowly became obsolete, Colin decided to jump the sinking ship and took early retirement. In 2006, leaving behind their 2 adult sons in London, he and his wife headed for the sun of southern Spain where they remain to this day enjoying 'La Vida Loca'.

Printed in Great Britain
by Amazon

14839780R00264